Substance Use
and Abuse

Substance Use and Abuse

Exploring Alcohol and Drug Issues

Sylvia I. Mignon,
Marjorie Marcoux Faiia,
Peter L. Myers, and
Earl Rubington

LYNNE
RIENNER
PUBLISHERS

Published in the United States of America in 2009 by
Lynne Rienner Publishers, Inc.
1800 30th Street, Boulder, Colorado 80301
www.rienner.com

and in the United Kingdom by
Lynne Rienner Publishers, Inc.
3 Henrietta Street, Covent Garden, London WC2E 8LU

Library of Congress Cataloging-in-Publication Data
Substance use and abuse : exploring alcohol and drug issues / by Sylvia I.
Mignon . . . [et al.].
   p. cm.
  Includes bibliographical references and index.
  ISBN 978-1-58826-620-0 (hardcover : alk. paper)
  ISBN 978-1-58826-645-3 (pbk. : alk. paper)
  1. Substance abuse. 2. Alcoholism. 3. Drug abuse. 4. Substance
abuse—Prevention. I. Mignon, Sylvia I.
  HV4998.S84 2009
  362.29—dc22

                          2008048405

British Cataloguing in Publication Data
A Cataloguing in Publication record for this book
is available from the British Library.

Printed and bound in the United States of America

 The paper used in this publication meets the requirements
of the American National Standard for Permanence of
Paper for Printed Library Materials Z39.48-1992.

5   4   3   2   1

For Tall Oak, Anna, Cameron, and Aunt Cissy
—S.I.M.

For Auntie May, my family, and my students
—M.M.F.

For Susie, Mom, Molly, Emma, and Zane
—P.L.M.

For Sara and Alex
—E.R.

Contents

Part 2   Diverse Populations:
Patterns of Substance Use and Abuse

4   Children and Adolescents   69

5   Women and Substance Abuse   87

6   Race and Ethnicity   107

Preface

In this new text, we examine the role of alcohol and drugs in society and consider the consequences of their abuse for the individual, the family, and the population. Our approach emphasizes the practical, as well as the theoretical. In addition to our academic positions, several of us are also clinicians, and therefore the text is informed by our practical experience with substance-abusing individuals. Additionally, because public policy plays such a critical role in determining how substance abusers are perceived and the treatment they receive, we grapple with the policy issues surrounding alcohol and drug use over time and among diverse populations.

We open the book by focusing on the concept that social and cultural factors influence substance use within society. The physical effects of drugs and alcohol, and the medical consequences of their abuse, are important to understand, but we make equally clear that understanding how people think, feel, and act with regard to these substances is key to understanding behavior. In this light, we consider how society responds to substance use and abuse, paying special attention to the debate over the legalization of currently illicit drugs. These issues are all addressed in Part 1.

The five chapters in Part 2 redress the lack of attention that historically has been given to the patterns of alcohol and drug use among particular segments of the population—women; children; the elderly; and racial, ethnic, and sexual minorities. These chapters demonstrate how prejudice and discrimination can further complicate substance abuse problems. Overall, this section reveals the necessity of tailoring prevention, diagnosis, and treatment efforts to meet the needs of very diverse users.

In Part 3, we discuss in detail, and across a broad spectrum, the repercussions of substance abuse. We tackle in Part 4 the process of diagnosing abuse, methods of intervention, and the various treatment and self-help options available to substance abusers. We conclude by appraising the public policies affecting treatment in the United States and call for new strategies that will reduce the debilitating effects of substance abuse.

We hope that this book will stimulate broad thinking about the core issues at stake in the realm of substance use and abuse. To further that goal, we have developed a set of discussion questions highlighting the themes of the text; these begin on p. 301.

1 Introduction: Substances and Society

It seems that every day another news report details how some-
one famous has struggled with substance use and abuse. In 2007 and 2008,
seemingly every supermarket tabloid and magazine featured weekly headlines about the substance abuse depredations of Britney Spears and Lind-
say Lohan. Drew Barrymore was in rehabilitation—rehab—twice by the
time she was thirteen, and in 1996 she admitted she had a coke (cocaine)
problem. Robin Williams admitted to keeping a bottle of vodka in his
fridge that he drank from throughout the day. The death of Anna Nicole
Smith in 2007 was ruled an accidental overdose from prescription medications; this is eerily similar to the death of her idol, Marilyn Monroe.
Smith's son Daniel had died only months earlier from a heart attack
brought on by prescription antidepressant medications and methadone. In
2008 actor Heath Ledger died of an overdose of six different prescription
medications.

Some celebrities have behaved in such bizarre ways while under the
influence that the drama surrounding their substance abuse is compelling.
Mel Gibson was stopped for drunk driving and shouted anti-Semitic slurs
at the arresting officer. Britney Spears shaved her head, lost custody of her
children, and entered rehab several times. Spears's highly publicized substance abuse drew the attention of pop psychologist Dr. Phil (McGraw),
who attempted an intervention that initially he planned to air on television.
A 2008 television show, *Celebrity Rehab with Dr. Drew,* showcased the
trysts, trials, and tribulations of celebrities.

Well-known religious and political figures have also been in the news
offering apologies for bad behavior related to substance abuse. The Rev-
erend Ted Haggard entered rehab after accusations that he snorted meth

(methamphetamine) and had sex with a male prostitute. Mark Foley, a Florida congressman, resigned and entered rehab for alcoholism after sending sexually explicit e-mails to congressional pages. Patrick Kennedy, a Rhode Island congressman, entered rehab after he drove his car into a cement wall and claimed to have no memory of the incident.

Of course, it is not only celebrities and notables who struggle with the use and abuse of alcohol and drugs. Estimates from national data from 2007 found almost 20 million Americans (8 percent of the population) used illicit drugs within the past month (Substance Abuse and Mental Health Services Administration [hereafter, SAMHSA], 2008). Heavy use of alcohol was reported by 17 million (6.9 percent). Current national estimates are that 22.3 million people (9 percent) in the United States have substance abuse or substance dependence problems (SAMHSA, 2008). However, only approximately 10 percent of those in need of specialized substance abuse treatment receive it.

Substance use and abuse create significant societal problems with enormous personal, family, social, and health costs. On an individual level, substance abuse can create ravaged lives for the addicted and a rippling of negative consequences for family members, some of which can be lifelong. At a societal level, substance abuse is strongly associated with medical problems, crime, poor work performance, and absenteeism. The major institutions of health care, business and industry, and criminal justice bear much of the burden of responding to those with substance abuse problems. In reality, the costs of substance abuse permeate every facet of American society.

In turn, social context plays a significant role in how we understand drug use and drug policy. Social institutions such as religion, medicine, law, and education each have the authority to define appropriate and inappropriate use of alcohol and drugs. The role of cultural perceptions and classification are seen in the fact that tobacco products, delivering the highly addictive substance nicotine, were overlooked for their abuse potential until the 1980s. Although Surgeon General Luther Terry warned of the health hazards of smoking in 1964, it was not until 1997 that the Liggett Group became the first tobacco company to acknowledge smoking is hazardous to health.

Similarly, alcohol—the most used and abused drug in the United States—is not defined as a drug, but rather is perceived as a social beverage. Though it is not listed as a controlled substance, it clearly has considerable abuse potential, and some drinkers become physically dependent on it. Alcohol is the drug most implicated in personal, social, and economic damage. Examples of personal damage include deaths from cirrhosis of the liver and other alcohol-related illnesses, from impaired operation of automobiles and boats, from aggravated assaults, rapes, homicide, and suicide. Social costs include domestic violence and divorce. Economic damages include lost hours at work, industrial accidents, poor work performance, health costs, and expenses incurred by the entire system of criminal justice.

Additionally, the social and cultural standing of substances drives law enforcement efforts. As we shall see, the major growth in the criminal justice system over the past three decades can be attributed to societal concern—described by some commentators as "moral panic"—about substance abuse. In the 1980s and 1990s, public opinion polls regularly recorded that Americans considered drugs to be the most severe social problem, and supported legal sanctions. On the other hand, champions of drug decriminalization claim that drug laws are an unwarranted effort to police decisions by individuals to alter their own consciousness.

Social forces may also factor into the prosecution of substance use and abuse. Alcohol use is one of many instances of the selective enforcement of substance control laws. While the proportion of alcoholics may be distributed throughout the social classes, alcoholics from the lower classes are more socially visible and therefore more likely to come to the attention of the police. This generalization about visibility holds for all varieties of substance use. It is further known that alcohol is more readily available in poor, black neighborhoods (Jones-Webb et al., 2008).

Drugs and alcohol permeate the social fabric of the United States. However, before we can truly investigate their role in society today, we must set the stage with a brief history of the use and abuse of major drugs such as narcotics, marijuana, hallucinogens, and cocaine as well as societal responses, including drug control policies.

Development of Narcotic Use

During the eighteenth century, some Americans used laudanum, a mixture of alcohol and opium, while others consumed opium in solid or liquid form. While not illegal, opiate use and addiction grew in the nineteenth century. Use typically took place in homes, making it hard to estimate the number of users. The fledgling medical profession adopted morphine, soon after it was derived from opium in 1809. Physicians soon came to see morphine as a cure-all and prescribed it for almost every ailment (Terry and Pellens, 1928). The arrival of the hypodermic needle in 1849 increased the use of morphine by physicians and laypeople alike. The last half of the nineteenth century became "a dope fiend's paradise" (Brecher et al., 1972).

Grocery stores and pharmacies sold patent medicines, all containing a variety of opiates, and Sears Roebuck sold opiates through mail order. Physicians prescribed morphine, sometimes giving their patients hypodermics; pharmacists dispensed narcotics without prescriptions. Half the addict population was medically addicted through overmedication by physicians, with more addicted women than men. The typical addict was white, rural, female, lower-middle-class and middle-aged, although the poor and minority populations were also afflicted.

In 1875 a number of western states, fearful of the effect of Chinese opium dens on their youth, outlawed either attendance at opium-smoking dens or smoking opium. By the mid-1880s a dozen states had passed a variety of antinarcotics legislation, much of it fueled by anti-immigrant prejudice (Musto, 1987). Many influential groups became concerned about the increase in the number of addicts, the importation of opium and other drugs, and the manufacture and sale of over-the-counter products that contained opiates. They helped to achieve passage of the Pure Food and Drug Act of 1906, which required labeling contents of all over-the-counter products containing opiates. Reformers recognized the states' inability to enforce their drug laws and pressed for a federal response. National drug control finally became law with the passage of the Harrison Narcotic Control Act of 1914.

Passage of the 1914 act, originally designed as a tax act, marked the first step in the evolution of our punitive national drug control policy (White, 1998). Treasury enforcement agents interpreted physicians' numerous refills of prescriptions as illegal, rather than as appropriate treatment. Their interpretation of the act drove physicians out of practice, criminalized drug addicts, and fostered a black market supplying drugs at inflated prices (Musto, 1987).

The Harrison Act foretold the victory of the "hard on drugs" constituency over the "soft on drugs" approach. Punishment prevailed over treatment, and law prevailed over medicine. Treasury agents interpreted gradual withdrawal or maintenance doses by physicians as illegal narcotic sales rather than legitimate medical treatment (Lindesmith, 1965). Some 25,000 physicians were arrested and 3,000 jailed. With drug addiction considered a crime rather than a disease, addicts, deprived of legitimate access, sought another source of supply. A black market developed to fulfill the demand at inflated prices. The drug of choice had become heroin.

In 1901 the German firm Bayer began marketing heroin legally after its derivation from morphine in 1898. It soon became the new wonder drug, a cure-all especially for morphinism and alcoholism. Early on, however, officials soon recognized the addictive power of heroin—ten times the strength of morphine—and it became outlawed. The setting of use and the characteristics of the heroin-using population changed after the Harrison Act. Low-income youths, white, black, and Hispanic, in inner-city neighborhoods became the most visible users. "Crime in the streets" became a politician's mantra, with harsh mandated prison terms standard policy. The Boggs Act of 1950 mandated the death penalty for those selling narcotics to anybody under the age of eighteen.

The peak of heroin use occurred in the late 1960s, with a reported 750,000 heroin addicts in the United States. As of this writing, approximately 3.7 million Americans 12 and older have tried heroin at least once in their lifetimes. In 2007, people who had tried heroin for the first time within a one-year period numbered 106,000, an increase over the 91,000 people who first tried heroin in 2006 (SAMHSA, 2007a, 2008). The average age of first use was 20.7 in 2006 and 21.8 in 2007. Approximately 227,000 heroin users were diagnosed with heroin abuse or dependence in 2004, 323,000 in 2006, and 335,000 in 2007 (SAMHSA, 2005b, 2007a, 2008).

Development of Marijuana Use

Planters grew the marijuana plant hemp during the early years in America, and physicians found some medical uses for marijuana. The drug became notorious when newspapers reported crime waves in New Orleans in 1926. According to police, the rise in crime was attributable to smoking marijuana, a habit acquired from Mexican immigrants. Police, much like many physicians, thought marijuana gave smokers the courage to commit criminal acts. They mistakenly attributed the characteristics of cocaine, a stimulant, to marijuana, a drug more likely to induce passivity and detachment rather than aggressive action. Louisiana made possession or sale of marijuana punishable by six months in jail or a $500 fine. In 1929, Colorado passed similar laws after an influx of Mexican laborers migrated to work in the sugar-beet fields (Brecher et al., 1972).

Anxiety and concern about the use of marijuana spread mainly through the efforts of Harry Anslinger. Though a Prohibition enforcement agent, Anslinger had actually argued that reports of widespread use of marijuana had been exaggerated by the press. However, as the new head of the Federal Bureau of Narcotics, he waged a powerful campaign in all the media against marijuana, the "killer weed" (Becker, 1963; Bonnie and Whitebread, 1974). The documentary *Reefer Madness* illustrated the life of debauchery and crime for which marijuana users were destined (Faupel,

Horowitz, and Weaver, 2004). Anslinger lobbied Congress to endorse a punitive policy to curtail the marijuana menace. Impressed by Anslinger's argument, Congress passed the Marijuana Tax Act of 1937, which placed a tax on marijuana of $100 per ounce. The act effectively outlawed marijuana. Anslinger's antidrug policy consisted of mandatory harsh penalties with increasing severity for repeaters. By 1937, forty-six states passed laws whose penalties equaled the severity of those imposed for cocaine, heroin, and morphine violations.

Meanwhile, marijuana had begun its cultural climb through the American social structure. Sailors, prostitutes, and criminals took to smoking marijuana. Jazz musicians also adopted marijuana use and, when they later moved to Chicago and New York, contributed to its spread. In time, the "beat generation" of the 1950s took up marijuana smoking, to be followed by the hippies of the 1960s (Polsky, 1969). It soon spread to the college students of that generation and antimarijuana hysteria gripped middle-class America.

Before Anslinger's campaign there had been low use of marijuana and high social tolerance. After Anslinger left office, tolerance lessened while use increased. Arrests mounted, legal penalties grew harsher, and antimarijuana propaganda stoked growing fears that smoking "reefer" would only be followed by "madness," rape, and murder. California's arrests for possession or sale of marijuana swelled to 50,127 by 1968. President Richard Nixon's commission's special report on marijuana law enforcement revealed that college students had replaced low-status smokers as the prime violators (Shafer Commission Report, 1972). However, some middle-class judicial personnel were unwilling to find students guilty and sentence them to jail. Children of governors, senators, and others in the public eye rarely received even short prison terms (Brecher et al., 1972).

While the high arrest–low conviction ratio frustrated blue-collar police, the white-collar elite triggered a movement for decriminalization. A dozen states lowered the penalties, with a few reducing possession of a small amount of marijuana to the status of a traffic offense. And as personal knowledge as well as accurate information about marijuana's characteristic effects spread, its mythic description as both a stimulant and a narcotic lost credibility.

As we have seen, attitudes toward drugs such as marijuana vary with the generations and the times. A total of 96.8 million people have tried marijuana at least once in their lifetimes as of this writing. Some 25.5 million used it at least once in 2004, and this number dropped to 2.1 million in 2006, remaining the same in 2007 (SAMHSA, 2007a, 2008). In self-reports of marijuana users, 4.2 million acknowledged marijuana abuse or dependence in 2006 with a slight reduction to 3.9 million users in 2007 (SAMHSA, 2007a, 2008). Unlike most users of illicit drugs, only 40 percent of users had to buy marijuana and more than half got the drug for free or shared someone else's marijuana. Some states have decriminalized marijuana, although in 2006 there were over 700,000 marijuana arrests, most of them for possession.

While those who support decriminalization often say it is less harmful than alcohol, marijuana use is not without some long-term effects. These can include loss of motivation, known as amotivational syndrome (see Box 1.1), and a lower sperm count for men (Drug Enforcement Administration [hereafter, DEA], 2005; Grinspoon and Bakalar, 1997).

Development of Hallucinogen Use

In 1943 Albert Hofmann, a chemist at Sandoz Laboratories in Basel, Switzerland, took the first recorded LSD (lysergic acid diethylamide-25) "trip." Hofmann had discovered LSD when studying the medicinal use of

---

Box 1.1   Kurt Smokes Marijuana

Kurt, a man in his midtwenties, contacted the Employee Assistance Program offered through the popular restaurant he worked for in New Bedford, Massachusetts. Meeting with a social worker in a private office, he explained that he needed some help in moving forward with his life. He had dropped out of college several years before and was working as a waiter. While the money wasn't bad, Kurt told the social worker that he felt he was not living up to his potential and that he seemed to lack motivation. He discussed his family background and his early success in school. In asking Kurt about his use of substances, the social worker learned that Kurt consumed heavy amounts of marijuana on a daily basis and had done so for several years. The social worker suggested there might be some relationship between his heavy pot-smoking and feeling he was not able to accomplish much in his life. Kurt responded that he had never considered his daily marijuana smoking could be a problem. Kurt agreed to another appointment with the social worker, but failed to show up. The social worker called Kurt and wrote him a letter, trying to engage him in therapy, but received no response. The social worker later reflected that Kurt did not want to stop smoking marijuana or examine the relationship between marijuana use and his behavior. Could Kurt be an example of amotivational behavior?

fungus on grains, including wheat. He described his first trip as "wonderful visions. What I was thinking appeared in colors and pictures" (Associated Press, 2008, 21).

Hofmann hoped LSD would be used to treat mental illness. By 1965 some 30,000 to 40,000 patients had been treated with LSD in the United States and Europe, reportedly with no adverse effects (Brecher et al., 1972). When Hofmann died at the age of 102 in 2008, his obituary recounted his view: "I produced the substance as a medicine. It's not my fault if people abused it" (Associated Press, 2008, 21).

Timothy Leary, a Harvard University faculty member, is perhaps the best-known academic to research the effects of LSD and other hallucinogens. See Box 1.2 for a description of Leary's activities.

Box 1.2   Timothy Leary (1920–1996)

Timothy Leary became famous for coining the popular catchphrase of the 1960s: "Turn on, tune in, drop out." A psychologist and writer, Leary was also a campaigner for the use of psychedelic drugs.

Leary was born in Springfield, Massachusetts, and attended the College of the Holy Cross in Worcester, Massachusetts, and also West Point. He dropped out of both but went on to earn a bachelor's degree in psychology from the University of Alabama in 1943. In 1950 he earned a Ph.D. in psychology from the University of California at Berkeley. Leary spent years as an assistant professor at Berkeley and as a director of research for the Kaiser Foundation in Oakland, California, before becoming a lecturer in psychology at Harvard University, where he remained during 1959–1963.

On vacation in Mexico in 1960, Leary used psilocybin mushrooms for the first time. This captured his interest and led him to conduct research into the hallucinogenic properties of psilocybin and, later, the effects of LSD on graduate students. Leary and his colleague Dr. Richard Alpert, who later became known as Ram Dass, believed that with the appropriate guidance and supervision, LSD could benefit users by giving them mystical and spiritual experiences that had the potential to be life transforming in positive ways. Volunteers for his experiments included graduate students and the author Jack Kerouac. Leary hoped this work would improve treatments for alcoholism and help prison inmates become rehabilitated. However, parents of Harvard students complained, and other colleagues found the work of Leary and Alpert more than disquieting. Both were fired by Harvard. They continued their work at a mansion known as Millbrook in New York and were raided later by the Federal Bureau of Investigation (FBI).

continues

Box 1.2   (continued)

In 1965 Leary's daughter was caught with marijuana while traveling from Mexico into the United States. Accepting responsibility, Leary received a thirty-seven-year prison sentence under the Marijuana Tax Act! The case was appealed on the basis that self-incrimination was required in order to comply with the Marijuana Tax Act. Leary won the case in the US Supreme Court, and in 1969 his conviction was overturned and the Marijuana Tax Act was found unconstitutional. Leary was, however, convicted of charges of drug possession and spent several years in prison. In 1970 the Weather Underground Organization, a group opposed to the government establishment, was paid to break Leary out of prison; they smuggled Leary and his wife into Algiers. Refuge had been planned in Algiers with Black Panther Eldridge Cleaver; however, this did not work out, and Leary and his wife went to Switzerland. Caught there, Leary was brought back to the United States in 1974 and received a reduced prison sentence for cooperating with the FBI investigation of the Weather Underground.

During his life Leary published many books. After a diagnosis of inoperable prostate cancer, he went on to write *Design for Death,* about new ways to think about end-of-life experiences, before his own death in 1996.

Source: Timothy Leary (2004). Retrieved on March 10, 2008, from http://www.mywiseowl.com/articles/Timothy_Leary.

After the discovery of LSD in 1943, a history of significant legal controls and drug subcultures developed. Social conditions changed after 1965, and the Food and Drug Administration (FDA) tightened regulations (Brecher et al., 1972). This was in part a response to the effects of Thalidomide, a drug given to pregnant women to prevent miscarriage that caused an epidemic of deformed babies.

In 2005, 22.4 million Americans reported lifetime use of LSD and 1.1 million reported past year use, the same figures applying to 2006 (SAMHSA, 2007a). For another hallucinogenic, PCP (phencyclidine), lifetime users totaled 6.5 million with 164,000 with past year use (SAMHSA, 2005b). In 2007, 1.1 million people used hallucinogenics within a one-year period (SAMHSA, 2008). The history of their fluctuating use in the United States is quite instructive. PCP, known as "angel dust," became notorious for its apparent increased use among adolescents. It drew considerable media and research attention over ten years ago but since then has received little media coverage and has a pattern of declining use. After considerable use in the treatment of mental patients and alcoholics, the government ended the medical use of LSD in the mid-1960s. Recreational use led to a small number of "bad trips," which were heavily publicized. Illegal labs dispensed LSD of dubious purity and potency. Emergency room visits increased mainly owing to inexperienced users, unstable individuals, and contaminated drugs (Becker, 1967). The conditions of "good" trips included a serene situation of use, experienced guides, and reliable expectations about the drug experience.

By the early 2000s, an estimated 11.8 million had tried ecstasy (MDMA) at least once. Ecstasy is a "designer" drug—that is, a synthetically engineered drug similar to an existing illegal substance but differing enough in its molecular structure to initially avoid being classed as an illicit substance. Those who tried ecstasy for the first time in 2002 numbered 1.2 million; this number dropped to 607,000 in 2004, rose to 860,000 in 2006, and then dropped to 781,000 in 2007 (SAMHSA, 2007a, 2008). In 2004, hallucinogenic users numbering 371,000 were declared abusers or dependent, the number falling very slightly to 368,000 in 2007 (SAMHSA, 2005b, 2008). Compared with teenagers, college students, and young adults, middle-aged professionals are more likely to be controlled ecstasy users. Psychological effects of ecstasy such as confusion, depression, sleep problems, drug craving, and severe anxiety can occur during use as well as days or weeks after use.

MDMA-related arrests, 1,974 in 2001, had decreased to 764 by 2005. The Ecstasy Anti-Proliferation Act of 2000 increased sentences for trafficking by 300 percent. The criminal sanction for trafficking in 800 pills has risen from fifteen months to five years in prison, while the sanction for trafficking 8,000 pills has increased from forty-one months to ten years (Drug Abuse Warning Network, 2005). Paradoxically, as estimated use of ecstasy decreased in the early 2000s, federal seizures of dosage units climbed from 1.92 million dosage units in 2004 to more than 5 million in 2005.

Development of Cocaine Use

The Harrison Act of 1914 banned importation and nonmedical use of cocaine. It imposed the same criminal penalties for cocaine use as for opium, morphine, and heroin use. Requiring strict accounting and prescriptions for cocaine, the act classed cocaine, a stimulant, with heroin and morphine, both narcotics. *Narcotics* became the generic term for all drugs in common parlance. Cocaine attained widespread use during two periods of US history, not because it was a narcotic but because it was a stimulant.

The first cocaine epidemic ran from 1884 to 1930. An ingredient both in coca wines and in Coca-Cola, it was marketed freely, extolled in print by celebrities, and used by movie stars and professional athletes. Thomas A. Edison and Sarah Bernhardt, a famous French actress, both used and praised the virtues of cocaine. Sigmund Freud, the father of psychoanalysis, used cocaine and claimed it was not addictive; he wrote a book describing its use and its effects, and said it was most helpful in treating a variety of ailments. However, heavy cocaine use took its toll. Heavy users became restless, disoriented, and anxious. The tide turned against cocaine, and Coca-Cola was forced in 1903 to switch from cocaine to caffeine in its recipe. More important, southerners believed cocaine triggered blacks' violence against whites. White fear of blacks only increased with newspaper exaggerations of the frequency of cocaine-induced crimes of violence (Musto, 1987).

By the time the Harrison Narcotic Control Act was passed in 1914, forty-six states had already passed laws attempting to control cocaine, evidence that it was considered the nation's number-one drug problem (Musto, 1987). However, between 1930 and 1960, cocaine use had dwindled considerably.

Drug epidemics run in cycles: prevalence rises and falls, only to rise again as a new cycle gets under way (Hamid, 1992). Generational amnesia as well as supply, demand, and drug prices all play a role in fluctuations in illicit drug consumption. During the marijuana explosion of the 1960s, cocaine reappeared on the drug scene. However, the cocaine explosion did not occur until the 1980s. Generating a good deal of "moral panic" and hysterical news coverage, it declined markedly by the 1990s. In 1985 there were 5.7 million current users, and by 1995 the number of current users had shrunk to 1.5 million. The year 2001 saw a rise among a new generation of users in the absence of great publicity (Office of National Drug Control Policy, 2007), reflecting the fact that coverage in the various media can cycle as well and not always parallel consumption—press attention decreasing while consumption is climbing and vice versa.

In 2002 there were 2.0 million current users of cocaine, 1.5 million of whom were judged to be either cocaine abusers or cocaine dependents (National Institute on Drug Abuse, 2006). In 2006, 1.7 million people were estimated to be cocaine abusers or cocaine dependent (SAMHSA, 2007a). In 2006, Americans trying cocaine for the first time within the past year numbered 977,000, up from 875,000 in 2005, with an increase to 906,000 in first-time users in 2007 (SAMHSA, 2007a, 2008). A total of 33.7 million Americans twelve years or older reported in 2005 they had tried cocaine at least once in their lifetimes. The highest rate of current users was in the eighteen- to twenty-five-year-old age group. Men are more often current users than women. At the peak of the cocaine explosion in the late 1980s, there were almost 6 million current users of cocaine. From 2006 to 2008 current use seemed to have stabilized around 2 million users. Figures show in 2004 that 256,491 persons received treatment for cocaine abuse; in 2006 the comparable figure was 928,000; however, the number receiving treatment dropped to 809,000 in 2007 (SAMHSA, 2005b, 2007a, 2008). Statistics reflect some stabilization of cocaine use and indicate that treatment has made inroads in the established punitive response to illicit drug use, yet access to treatment remains a huge issue.

Crack cocaine became popular in the mid-1980s. Costing considerably less than powder cocaine, crack produced the desired effect as quickly and as effectively. Users obtain a rock or a brick of crack, heat it, and then smoke it in a pipe. By the time crack use had peaked, some events typical of the arrival of a new drug had already occurred. The media exaggerated its character, consequences, and extent of use. Politicians called for and got more mandatory sentences and heavier penalties. Jails soon became overcrowded, and fears of a violent crime wave mounted. A flourishing street market afforded economic opportunity to inexperienced, ambitious individual youths as well as organized gangs in neighborhoods of high unemployment. And the media claimed that a small platoon of compulsive users was actually an army of users addicted to crack, a newer and more dangerous drug than all the others (Reinarman and Levine, 1997).

The controversy over longer sentences for crack cocaine over powder cocaine continues as inner-city blacks and the poor disproportionately use crack. In the federal system, 0.18 ounce (5 grams) of crack cocaine and 18 ounces (500 grams) of powder cocaine each bring a mandatory five-year prison sentence. In 2007 the US Sentencing Commission acknowledged the disparity in sentencing and recommended lowering sentence ranges (Associated Press, 2007). This includes reducing sentences of those previously convicted. Cocaine sentencing disparities are discussed in more detail in Chapter 11.

According to the 2005 National Survey on Drug Use and Health, 7.9 million people aged twelve or older had tried crack cocaine at least once in their lifetimes (SAMHSA, 2006c). And 1.4 million reported past-year crack cocaine use. These are all increases over the 2004 National Survey on Drug Use and Health that reported 7.8 million lifetime users, 1.3 million past-year users, and 467,000 current users. While the increase indicates the initiation of a new generation of users, it still falls considerably short of the mid-1980s peak.

Development of Amphetamine Use

During the 1960s there were 14.6 million people who had used amphetamines. The 2005 National Survey of Drug Use and Health reported an estimated 10.4 million lifetime users and 1.3 million who used in the last year (SAMHSA, 2006c). The year 2006 saw considerable media coverage of methamphetamine use. Methamphetamine use reportedly has been concentrated in the Midwest—particularly in Arkansas, Missouri, and Ohio—in California, and in Hawaii (Garrity et al., 2007). Some experts cautioned about assumptions of a methamphetamine "plague" (Garrity et al., 2007). Once again, media attention to a new drug does not necessarily mean another explosion of use. The 1990s also saw a good deal of attention paid to "ice" (street term for methamphetamine) that did not culminate in high rates of use (Lauderback and Waldorf, 1993). However, the 2006 National Survey on Drug Use and Health reported that estimates of methamphetamine use are 15 to 25 percent higher than prior published reports (SAMHSA, 2007a). An important finding of the 2007 survey was that 157,000 were initiated into methamphetamine within the past year, a substantial drop from the 259,000 initiated into methamphetamine use in 2006 (SAMHSA, 2008).

From 1994 to 2004, treatments for methamphetamine abuse increased from 33,443 to 129,079 (SAMHSA, 2005a, 2005b). The Drug Enforcement Administration (DEA) reported a total of 5,393 metamphetamine-related arrests in 2004. Most arrests have been for trafficking. On the assumption that treatments outnumber arrests, the social response to methamphetamine abuse would appear to be more therapeutic than punitive in contrast with responses to traditional narcotics.

President Nixon declared the first "war on drugs" and established the DEA, the federal agency in charge of the nation's drug policy and its enforcement. Congress passed the Controlled Substances Act and established the National Institute of Drug Abuse (NIDA) in 1970. By the 1970s the DEA had become the major bureaucracy coordinating the operation of a host of national agencies dealing with drugs. This marked the dominance of the punitive over the public health approach to drug control. Passage of the Controlled Substances Act in 1970 classified drugs that had some or no medical use, as well as their potential for abuse. In the early 2000s the DEA's budget still was four times that of NIDA and the country continued to adhere to a "hard on drugs" policy.

While in the past it was more common to abuse one substance, most substance abusers and addicts, at this writing, use multiple substances (see Box 1.3). However, all users tend to have a drug of choice.

Box 1.3   Dan's Entrée into Substance Abuse

Dan, age twenty-one, was serving seven years in prison for armed robbery. Here is what Dan had to say about the development of his substance use:

> I started smoking pot when I was about 15, something like that. I started taking acid and from acid, ecstasy to drugs like that. Then, all of a sudden someone introduced me to heroin and I was takin' that now and again and then crack came along and that was it. It all went haywire . . . it's addictive . . . you get a rush, you blow the smoke out, but it's only for a couple of seconds, then it's gone . . . then you feel stressed out and paranoid. . . . It was crack and heroin 24-7 (24 hours a day, 7 days a week). I'd wake up in the mornings and when I was smokin' crack and needing heroin, takin' heroin to sort of take the bad one away, level your head a bit. (Cope, 2006, 288)

Drug Classification and Scheduling

Classification of drugs is complicated and confusing. It is perhaps easiest to understand by examining a threefold classification of drugs. First, controlled substances are defined from the point of view of drug control, especially by the federal DEA. While the federal government approves the scheduling (categorizing) of drugs, it is not without controversy. For example, the classification of marijuana as a Schedule I drug with a high potential for abuse and no medical use calls the scheduling of drugs into question.

Second, drugs can be classified by pharmaceutical companies and those that develop them, as well as by those who prescribe and dispense them, such as physicians and pharmacists. These classifications include stimulants and depressants, discussed in Chapter 3. Third, there is the classification of effects by users. Street terms give some indication—"Special K" for ketamine and ecstasy for MDMA, both dissociative drugs. These names address the significance of the subjective experience of drug use. That is, effects vary for a variety of reasons, including history of use, tolerance, purity and potency of the drugs, the circumstances under which drugs are used, and whether multiple drugs are used. The first classification, the federal scheduling of drugs, is discussed in this section. The second and third classifications are discussed in Chapter 3.

The 1970 United States Controlled Substances Act regulates the availability of drugs as part of the Comprehensive Drug Abuse Prevention and Control Act of 1970. Five schedules, or categories, of controlled substances were developed and are reviewed and updated on an annual basis (DEA, 2008). Tobacco and alcohol are not included in the scheduling of drugs, an interesting point, since both are the most widely abused drugs and cause the most significant medical problems.

As indicated, drug scheduling, through state and federal efforts to categorize drugs, is a mechanism to assist in determining legal sanctions for illicit sales and possession of drugs. The severity of sentences for drug violations is related to both the schedule of the drug and the amount of the illicit drug. Drug scheduling is therefore an important part of the US government's effort to control and combat drug abuse. *Schedule I* drugs have no currently accepted medical use in the United States and are drugs deemed to have high potential for abuse. Examples include heroin, LSD, mescaline, ecstasy, and gamma hydroxybutyrate (GHB). Marijuana—the most popular and frequently used of the illicit drugs—is also classified as a Schedule I drug. Controversy continues to swirl around the appropriate use of marijuana in the treatment of cancer and other health problems. The DEA insists that it remain a Schedule I controlled substance, and the Supreme Court ruled in 2005 that no exception could be made for the medical use of marijuana. Consequently, the eleven states that permit such use of marijuana are in conflict with federal law. (See Chapter 14 for a full discussion of medical marijuana.)

Schedule II drugs have a currently accepted medical use, although they have a high potential for abuse and severe psychological or physical dependence. These drugs include cocaine (accepted use is as a topical anesthetic), morphine, phencyclidine (PCP), opioid agonists, methadone, short-acting barbiturates, and amphetamines, including methamphetamine. Ritalin, prescribed for the treatment of attention deficit hyperactivity disorder (ADHD) in children, is a Schedule II drug. OxyContin, the powerful pain reliever, well-known for its abuse potential, is also a Schedule II drug.

Schedule III drugs have currently accepted medical use and low to moderate risk of physical dependence but high risk of psychological dependence. This classification includes anabolic steroids (used by some athletes), ketamine (a veterinary anesthetic, which is also a club drug—often used in clubs), marinol (derived from marijuana for pain control), and buprenorphine (a relatively new drug used in the treatment of addiction).

Schedule IV drugs have relatively low potential for abuse and have a currently accepted medical use. These include benzodiazepines such as Xanax, Librium, Valium, and others prescribed for anxiety and as a sleep aid. Also here are the long-acting barbiturates such as phenobarbitol.

Schedule V drugs have an even lower potential for abuse and have medically accepted uses. Sometimes Schedule V drugs are available without prescription. Examples include cough suppressants with codeine and preparations to treat diarrhea that may include opium (DEA, 2008).

We begin to see that the social environment and characteristics of drug users affect the reaction of society. In turn, this has an impact on the possible sanctions for substance abuse and addiction.

The Drug Legalization Debate

Considerable federal and state financial resources are spent enforcing drug policies, typically divided into enforcement, prevention, and treatment efforts. Drug-related arrests have been up considerably since the early 1990s, as have been drug-related incarcerations. Support for drug laws has been strong because many people feel they serve a protective function, especially for children. Yet the consequences are enormous, with urban minority communities bearing the brunt of law enforcement efforts and high incarceration rates (Boyum and Kleiman, 2003).

Enforcing drug laws has always placed enforcement agents at risk of employing questionable methods of interrogations, entrapping drug violators, and paying informants with drugs. Drug-war reformers have questioned disparities in penalties for powder versus crack cocaine, in arrests of minorities, and in the preponderance of arrests for marijuana relative to such drugs as cocaine, heroin, or synthetic opiates. Advancement in the policing ranks, going from beat cop to detective, can depend on production of arrests. Such production depends greatly on obtaining information in ways the law forbids and police culture finds acceptable (Conlon, 2004).

Some use the terms *legalization* and *decriminalization* interchangeably; however, there is a distinction (Bretteville-Jensen, 2006). Decriminalization can be seen as a compromise or "halfway step" between drug prohibition and drug legalization (Faupel et al., 2004). Decriminalization removes criminal sanctions although there may still be civil sanctions such as fines. Some who favor decriminalization want to decriminalize marijuana and leave sanctions intact for selling and distributing drugs such as cocaine and heroin. Others who support legalization recommend treating drugs the same way as alcohol—regulating the sale and consumption. Another interpretation of legalization is letting market forces decide the price of drugs.

Those who support decriminalizing or legalizing all drugs as well as those who support harsh drug laws ask the question: "Do drugs, or drug laws, cause crime?" (Boyum and Kleiman, 2003, 21). The answer appears to be "yes" to both. Intoxication and addiction can certainly increase crime due to the pharmacological effects and the economics of buying and selling. It is well-known that drug laws contribute to crime by creating black markets (Bretteville-Jensen, 2006). With legalization, prices fall and this can reduce crime; however, it is likely the number of drug users will increase, at least in the short term. The concern is that a great proportion of the population becomes at risk if currently illegal drugs become available (Inciardi, 1996). Research reflects the majority of economists support drug legalization and overall public support for legalization has grown over the last ten years (Thornton, 2007). See Chapter 11 for a detailed examination of the relationships among alcohol, drugs, and crime.

While drug policies cannot ensure a drug-free society, there are certainly opportunities to create a safer society (Boyum and Kleiman, 2003). As we will explore in this text, policy changes may include raising alcohol taxes, redirecting criminal justice resources to severe drug-related violence, and expanding the availability of voluntary and compulsory substance abuse prevention and treatment programs, especially those in the criminal justice sphere (Inciardi, 1996). The politics of science is at work as well. Needle exchange programs have shown their effectiveness in reducing the spread of HIV/AIDS (human immunodeficiency virus/acquired immunodeficiency syndrome), yet the public and politicians remain critical of them (Sherman, 2006). The future of US drug policy is discussed in the final chapter.

Conclusion

What is old and what is new about early twenty-first-century illicit drug use and social responses? The punitive response—mandatory sentences and harsh penalties—persists. Prisons continue to be crowded with nonviolent drug violators. A small number of highly visible drug users are more likely to be arrested than the large number of people who use drugs. Physicians are more likely to treat the less visible users and more likely to medically addict them through overprescribing. Enforcement agents are much more likely to arrest blacks and Hispanics for marijuana possession in urban areas where there are higher concentrations of minorities. And agents continue to pay close attention to the number of drug prescriptions physicians write, just as they did after passage of the Harrison Act in 1914.

Smuggling drugs will continue as a lucrative economic pursuit. New drugs will come on the market, and enterprising experimenters will find addictive uses for many of the new and some of the older pharmaceuticals. While the drug policy establishment of the early 2000s is not likely to fade away, treatment will continue to show steady incremental increases if financial resources are available. Not surprisingly, the drug prohibition versus decriminalization and legalization debate will go on.

PART 1

Alcohol, Drugs, and Society: An Overview

2 Alcohol and Alcoholism

Discussions of substance use and abuse need to pay attention to the definition and the enforcement of substance use rules, whether they are based in law, custom, or morality. Consequently, this chapter examines alcohol use and prevailing definitions of *alcoholism*. It reviews the demography of drinking, the epidemiology of drinking problems, and the changes in drinking patterns over the life course of drinkers. The chapter argues that the definition and enforcement of alcohol rules figure largely in the social conditions under which drinking problems occur and change during different stages of the drinkers' life span.

Characteristic Effects of Alcohol

Classified as a depressant, alcohol acts on the central nervous system. On any given drinking occasion, people feel relaxed after one or two drinks. As their intake increases, they feel less and less inhibited. Early signs of intoxication are slurred speech, lack of coordination, and poor information-processing. When the blood alcohol level (BAL) reaches 0.08, drinkers are deemed legally intoxicated in all fifty states. Even one episode of extremely heavy drinking can have consequences—alcohol poisoning can result in death. Heavy drinking over the life span produces a vast number of chronic effects with damages both physical and psychological.

The principal component of alcoholic beverages is ethyl alcohol, or ethanol. There are a variety of other alcohols, but no other is safe for humans to drink. During Prohibition (1920–1933), over 10,000 died from drinking bootleg whiskey that had been distilled from methyl alcohol or methanol.

The prominent alcoholic beverages consumed today are beer, wine, and spirits. A 12-ounce bottle of beer usually contains 0.04 absolute alcohol; the average bottle of wine contains 0.14 absolute alcohol, and fortified wines such as champagne and sherry contain 0.20 absolute alcohol. The average bottle of distilled spirits (gin, tequila, vodka, whiskey) contains either 0.40 or 0.50 absolute alcohol. For most purposes when calculating consumption, the rule of equivalence applies. That is, one drink—whether a glass of beer, a glass of wine, a shot, or a mixed drink—equals approximately 1 ounce of absolute alcohol. Thus, the recommended dosage of moderate intake is two drinks at one sitting for men, one for women (since women absorb alcohol into the bloodstream more quickly than men).

As with all drugs, the larger the dose, the greater the effect. The first drink affects the cerebrum; subsequent drinks, the cerebellum; and finally the spinal cord (Rivers, 1994). With a BAL, or blood alcohol content (BAC), of 0.02, drinkers feel relaxed and less inhibited. At 0.10 (usually five drinks, depending on size), the drinkers are unsteady on their feet, slur their speech, and show poor motor coordination. The blood or breath alcohol concentration is "the weight of ethanol, measured in grams, in 100 milliliters of blood, or 210 liters of breath" (Wisconsin Department of Transportation, 2006). At 0.10, one-tenth of 1 percent of the drinker's blood contains alcohol.

Alcohol is officially classified as a depressant, but the first effects of drinking alcohol are those of a stimulant—the drinker feels good. At later stages in the drinking episode, alcohol has become a depressant. Now the drinker has become anxious and depressed, typically when the BAL is on the decline (Jung, 2001; Pandina, 1982). After ten drinks the BAL is 0.20 and the person has already been legally intoxicated for some time. After twenty drinks the drinker has become stuporous, and lacks all judgment or coordination (Hamilton, 2007). At a BAL of 0.40 and above, the drinker is either in a coma or has already died of alcohol poisoning. As discussed in Chapter 3, alcohol and other drugs can be used in combination, causing even more serious difficulties.

Numerous conditions affect the absorption of alcohol and thus the BAL. A few of them are the contents of the stomach, the rate of drinking, whether the blood alcohol level is rising or falling, body weight, and the years of experience in drinking. All of the above relate to the acute effects of drinking. Chronic effects are those that follow years of excessive drinking and can include considerable physical damage to almost every organ of the body (Cargiulo, 2007; Rivers, 1994). Unlike most other psychoactive drugs, chronic heavy drinking produces considerable physical and psychological damage, as discussed later in this chapter.

©iStockphoto.com/donald_gruener

Effective in 2005, all states have made 0.08 the legal limit in the effort to reduce drunk driving accidents (Hamilton, 2007). Due to the efforts of Mothers Against Drunk Driving (MADD), states were under pressure from the federal government with the threat of withdrawal of federal highway funds if they failed to lower the limit from 0.10. In 2005, 39 percent of all traffic-related deaths (16,885 people) were related to alcohol consumption and nearly 1.4 million drivers were arrested for driving under the influence of alcohol or narcotics (Centers for Disease Control, 2006a).

History and Definitions of Alcoholism

Historically, definitions of *alcoholism* have contained instructions on what to do about the excessive drinker. Magnus Huss coined the term *alcoholism* in 1840. Prior to that time, heavy drinkers were more often referred to as habitual or common drunkards. During the colonial period, a time of considerable alcohol consumption by the general population, most drinking was controlled by both religious and legal regulations. Drunkenness was considered a crime as well as a sin. In earliest colonial days the drunkard was regarded as a sinner, a moral degenerate who needed prayer and salvation. After three arrests, the person was excommunicated. Any person charged with being a common drunkard was sentenced to two years in jail. Most of the persons arrested for public drunkenness were either indentured servants or common laborers. In addition to imprisonment, drunkards could be whipped or placed in the stocks. In the first instance of selective enforcement, however, gentlemen could not be put to the lash (Lender and Martin, 1982).

Benjamin Rush, one of the signers of the Declaration of Independence, wrote essays on drunkenness as a disease in the late 1700s. He described the symptoms of chronic drunkenness as "wasting away," "jaundice," and "mental dysfunction." Shortly after the establishment of independence from the mother country, physicians claimed that drunkenness was some kind of mental or nervous condition. In the 1880s the approach to substance abuse defined those addicted to "intemperate" use of alcohol and narcotics as "dypsomaniacs." While some were imprisoned, others were sent to the insane asylum (Lender and Martin, 1982; White, 1998).

Until the twentieth century, religion contested with the law as the principal social sanction against drunkenness. Medicine ranked a poor third. For the first third of the twentieth century, the jail and the mental hospital were the principal detoxification sites for chronic drunkenness offenders.

Three social movements shaped alcohol control in the United States: temperance, anti-alcohol, and the alcoholism movement of the 1970s. Up to the Civil War (1861–1865), the temperance movement sought moderation in drinking. After the Civil War the temperance movement became an anti-alcohol movement, reaching its ultimate goal with the passage of the Eighteenth Amendment. From 1920 to 1933, Prohibition outlawed the production and distribution of alcoholic beverages across state lines. After the repeal of Prohibition, the alcoholism movement came into being when members of Alcoholics Anonymous (AA) joined with the Yale (now Rutgers) Center of Alcohol Studies and the National Council on Alcoholism. It sought to change the social definition of the alcoholic from sinner, criminal, or moral weakling to that of a sick person (White, 1998).

More than 100 alcohol sanitariums had closed in the unfulfilled belief that Prohibition would eliminate public drunkenness. Confinement in mental hospitals or jails became the principal response to chronic public drunkenness offenders (Nimmer, 1971). The end of Prohibition returned liquor control to the states only to find that alcoholism had become a major social problem. The rise of Alcoholics Anonymous sparked the change (Alcoholics Anonymous, 1939).

Alcoholics Anonymous in the late 1930s had already developed a set of beliefs about both the causes of alcoholism and what to do about it (Al-

coholics Anonymous, 1939). AA claimed that alcoholics could never become social drinkers. "Allergic" to alcohol, they were constitutionally unable to control their drinking. If they continued to drink, there was only
one outcome—the inevitable progression of increased drinking followed
by a cumulating downward spiral of physical, psychological, social, and
economic problems. The only way to avoid insanity, suicide, or an early
death was to stop drinking and become a lifetime abstainer.

By the 1950s a major question concerned both clinicians and researchers. Why had some drinkers become alcoholics while others did not?
E. M. Jellinek's analysis of questionnaires completed by a sample of AA
members became an important moment for clinicians, the emerging social
movement to define alcoholics as sick people rather than criminals (Jellinek,
1952). Jellinek described symptoms that occurred in a sequence of four
phases: prealcoholic symptomatic, prodromal, crucial, and chronic. The key
symptom marking entry into the crucial stage was the "loss of control."
When the drinker started to drink and could not stop until becoming acutely
intoxicated, physically sick, or unconscious, the drinker had "crossed over
the line" marking the distinction between social drinker and alcoholic. Loss
of control signaled the beginnings of alcohol addiction. Jellinek maintained
that only addictive alcoholics could be said to have the disease of alcoholism. His chart of fifty-two symptoms became both a useful clinical as
well as educational tool. It helped clinicians to diagnose their patients as alcoholics, and it helped people concerned about their own drinking to decide
whether they were alcoholics (see Box 2.1).

Jellinek's classification of phases, each characterized by its own specific sequence of symptoms, begged to be put to the scientific test. The
idea of an inevitable progression had already come into question. A study
comparing AA members with a sample of hospitalized alcoholics revealed
that not all of Jellinek's symptoms were found and that many symptoms
that were found occurred in a different sequence (Trice and Wahl, 1958).
A psychiatrist reported that twelve patients he had treated for alcoholism
were, years later, able to return to controlled drinking (Davics, 1962). A
number of experimental studies in hospitals treating alcoholics established
that some chronic alcoholics could regulate their intake and could stop
drinking if they wanted.

Critics noted that Jellinek's study was based on a biased sample, draw-
ing on only AA members who chose to complete the questionnaire. The
questionnaire failed to meet the rigorous standards of survey methodology,
and there was concern that respondents' memory of when specific past
events occurred might not be accurate. Also, AA members might be re-
interpreting their drinking experiences in light of what they had come to

Box 2.1   E. M. Jellinek's Phases of Alcohol Addiction

- The *Prealcoholic Symptomatic Phase* is characterized by increased physical tolerance and relief drinking, that is, drinking to feel better physically (Jellinek, 1952).
- The *Prodromal Phase* is characterized by alcoholic palimpsests (blackouts—after drinking, a drinker cannot remember what he or she did while drinking), a preoccupation with alcohol, sneaking drinks, gulping drinks, and guilt feelings about drinking behavior.
- The *Crucial Phase* is characterized by loss of control over drinking, including morning drinking, some periods of abstinence, changing the pattern of drinking, and grandiose or aggressive behavior. The drinker in this phase loses outside interests and friends as behavior becomes alcohol centered. There is self-pity, self-neglect including poor nutrition, decreased sex drive, and perhaps a first hospitalization.
- The *Chronic Phase* is characterized by prolonged drinking episodes known as "benders," loss of alcohol tolerance, hand tremors, impaired thinking including alcoholic psychoses, drinking with persons previously seen as below one's social status, and drinking other products such as rubbing alcohol when beverage alcohol is not available. Drinking takes on an obsessive character, and there is marked deterioration in the drinker's ethics.

believe about themselves as a result of their affiliation with AA (Clark, 1991).

In 1956 the American Medical Association declared alcoholism a disease; however, that did not mean that physicians had an interest in or willingness to treat alcoholics (Mignon, 1995, 1996). By the 1960s most treatment personnel accepted the disease concept of alcoholism, including that alcoholism was a progressive and terminal disease. Several important legal cases in the 1960s challenged the appropriateness of locking up the alcoholic who was in need of treatment. In the case of *Easter v. District of Columbia,* Dewitt Easter, a chronic alcoholic of some thirty years, had been convicted seventy times of public drunkenness (Royce and Scratchley, 1996; White, 1998). The American Civil Liberties Union (ACLU) appealed his conviction on the grounds that the disease of alcoholism caused his public drunkenness. A US Court of Appeals reversed his conviction in 1966. In the case of *Driver v. Hinnant,* Joe Driver had 203 convictions for public drunkenness. While the US District Court upheld Driver's conviction, it was reversed by the US Court of Appeals in 1966 on the grounds that punishing a sick person violated the Eighth Amendment's prohibition of "cruel and unusual punishment."

In the case of *Powell v. Texas,* Leroy Powell was arrested in 1966 on charges of public drunkenness. He appealed his conviction and $20 fine until the case finally reached the US Supreme Court. The grounds for the appeal were that as a chronic alcoholic he had no control over his drinking and therefore his behavior should not be considered voluntary criminal conduct. In 1968 the Supreme Court upheld Powell's conviction by a five-to-four vote with disagreement over issues of evidence and whether this was an issue for states to resolve. The Court expressed concern that hospitals may become "drunk tanks," since there were no other appropriate alternatives. A majority of the Court judges, however, accepted the disease concept and that public intoxication is involuntary behavior (White, 1998). These important cases gave support to removing alcoholics from the criminal justice system and provided the impetus for treatment for alcoholism.

During the late 1960s and 1970s a social movement, the alcoholism movement, emerged to broaden and deepen the conception of alcoholism—to define it as a disease rather than a sin or a crime. The success of AA in sobering up many late-stage alcoholics helped shape the dominant conception of alcoholism and its course. First came heavy drinking, and then addiction, physical and psychological damage, shame and disgrace, and loss of self-respect. If the unfortunate alcoholic continued drinking, the only outcomes were suicide, insanity, or an early death. The only appropriate course of action for alcoholism was total abstinence.

The movement achieved its major goal when passage of the Comprehensive Alcoholism Prevention and Treatment Act, known as the Hughes Act, established the National Institute on Alcohol Abuse and Alcoholism (NIAAA) in 1970. See Box 2.2 for provisions of the act.

The Uniform Alcoholism and Intoxication Treatment Act of 1971 quickly followed and decriminalized public intoxication by setting up state and federally funded detoxification programs. Police could then pick up alcoholics sleeping or passed out on the streets and transport them to detox centers rather than to the police lockup to sleep it off. This act emphasized the importance of formulating comprehensive treatment plans, starting with detoxification. It also encouraged community outreach and education about alcoholism (White, 1998).

As we have seen, the roots of the disease concept were grown from the beginning of AA in 1935 and further developed by Jellinek. It has been the subject of considerable debate through the years—whether alcoholism is a disease because of its specific properties or whether it has been designated

**Box 2.2   The Comprehensive Alcoholism Prevention and
             Treatment Act of 1970**

Harold Hughes, three-term governor of Iowa, was elected to the US Senate
in 1968. He openly acknowledged that he was a recovered alcoholic. Hughes
became the chair of the US Senate's Subcommittee on Alcoholism and Narcotics. Initially, public hearings did not reveal much interest in federal support for the treatment of alcoholism. However, Bill W., cofounder of AA,
testified before the subcommittee to enlist interest, as did Mercedes
McCambridge, an Academy Award–winning actress. The involvement of
these public figures brought increased attention to the plight of alcoholics.
The Hughes Act was signed into law by President Richard Nixon on December 31, 1970. This legislation created the National Institute on Alcohol
Abuse and Alcoholism and began the modern era of substance abuse treatment. These efforts solidified the disease concept of alcoholism, separated
the field from the mental health field, and provided political momentum to
expand treatment services (White, 1998).

a disease for other reasons. The most critical point in arguing in favor of
the disease concept is that it removes the stigma of being an alcoholic or
addict. That is, treatment can be provided without the stigma of moral
weakness. Thus, the disease concept can free alcoholics and addicts from
guilt over their drinking or drugging (or both) behaviors. This makes it
much more likely that alcoholics and addicts will seek help. The disease
concept of alcoholism also helped to stimulate research on alcohol and
drug problems. Another major consideration is that the disease concept
places treatment within the medical establishment and provides health insurance to cover that treatment.

Stanton Peele (1989) has been the most vocal in trying to counter support for the disease concept. Peele's opposition stems from his reasoning
that this concept might discourage alcoholics from trying to stop drinking
if they thought it was hopeless. That is, the idea of total abstinence may be
overwhelming to some drinkers. Taking this line of reasoning further, the
disease concept might actually provoke an increase in deviant behavior if
people were to become convinced they are not responsible for their behavior. While these remain interesting ideas, they came to be considered out-
of-date by the early 2000s. The 1970s and 1980s saw an increase in polysubstance abuse, and the treatment system never reconciled whether
addiction to other drugs such as heroin should be considered disease. For a
few years, substance abuse counselors spoke of the "disease of addiction";

however, this conceptualization fell out of favor. At this writing, the vast majority of substance abusers are using multiple drugs and debates over the disease concept seem to have lost their steam.

Both researchers and clinicians began to make distinctions between alcohol dependence and alcohol abuse. Abuse included the battery of negative social consequences such as problems with family, employer, or the legal system. Dependence included such attributes as physical tolerance, craving, and withdrawal symptoms. In time, the American Psychiatric Association adopted this classification of alcoholic disorders in its *Diagnostic and Statistical Manual of Mental Disorders,* known as the DSM (American Psychiatric Association, 1994). The DSM listed items similar to Jellinek's in its classification of alcohol dependence. Reflecting the rise of polysubstance abuse, the DSM-IV-TR (2000) of the early 2000s uses the categories of substance abuse and dependence, discussed in Chapter 12.

The "drinking problems approach" has had considerable influence on alcohol research and clinical practice. This approach has both broadened and deepened the conception of alcohol problems. In the first decades after Prohibition repeal in 1933, clinicians and researchers focused on alcoholism, its definition, causes, and treatment. The decades after the first national drinking survey changed how clinicians and researchers viewed drinking. Alcoholism became only one of the problems of drinking alcohol. Clinicians and researchers no longer subscribed to the all-or-none conception of alcoholism as presented by Alcoholics Anonymous. According to AA's ideology, an excessive drinker was either an alcoholic or not. And once a person had crossed over the line, the outcome of continued drinking was never in doubt. The "problems approach" argues that alcohol abuse and alcoholism are both matters of degree; that at each of the several stages of the human life cycle, drinking could start, increase, decrease, or stop; and that a variety of problems could attend these changes. The result was a shift from the binary model (you are either an alcoholic or you are not) to viewing alcoholism as having multiple causes, expressions, and outcomes (Rivers, 1994). At this writing, there is agreement that there are different developmental courses for alcoholism (Jacob et al., 2005).

Alcohol Consumption in the United States

Slightly more than half of Americans aged twelve and older are current drinkers in the United States, according to the *Results from the 2007 National Survey on Drug Use and Health: National Findings* (SAMHSA, 2008). Annual national alcohol surveys usually report the per capita absolute alcohol consumption in gallons. Thus, in 2002 the total gallons consumed came to 2.22 per capita. The total was distributed among the three beverages as follows: beer, 1.22; wine, 0.34; and spirits, 0.67. Over the years, significant fluctuations have occurred in rates of alcohol consumption as well as the beverage of choice. In 1810, apparent per capita absolute alcohol consumption reached its highest point in the nation's history, 7.10 gallons. At that time, the young United States was considered to be "a nation of drunkards," since most people drank whiskey (Lender and Martin, 1982). By 1898, beer had supplanted distilled spirits as the beverage of choice. Beer peaked at 1.39 gallons in 1981. In 2003, beer went down 0.17 gallon while spirits decreased by 0.35. Experts generally attribute the decline, especially in spirits, to the conservatism of the late 1980s to the early 2000s, including increased concern about health and alcohol problems, especially drunk driving.

Overall, a total of 34 percent of those in the United States were abstainers in 2002, representing 29 percent of men and 38 percent of women (World Health Organization, 2004). Regional variations in drinking, counting the population twelve years and older, reveal stability and change. In the Northeast 56.0 percent of the population are drinkers, defined as those who have had at least one drink in the past thirty days (SAMHSA, 2008). The Midwest, with 54.6 percent current drinkers, is just shy of the Northeast's percentage. The West is in third place with 50.8, while the South brings up the rear with 46.8 percent of the population who are current drinkers.

Consumption of alcohol typically decreases with age. The largest proportion of drinkers are found in the 18–39 age range, the next lowest in the 40–59 age range, and the lowest in the 60-and-over age range. Similarly, the quantity and frequency of alcohol consumption also decrease with age. Drinking status (abstainer, former, or current) and drinking level of the population 18 and older vary by gender. In 2004, lifetime abstainers numbered 24.6 million and 14.6 million were former drinkers (National Institute on Alcohol Abuse and Alcoholism, 2006). While 17.8 million lifetime abstainers were men, 30.7 million were women. The 2007 National Survey on Drug Use and Health found that, overall, 126.8 million (51.1 percent of the population) were current drinkers (SAMHSA, 2008).

Gender differences in drinking hold throughout the life cycle. Women are much more likely to be abstainers, slightly more apt to be light drinkers, and much less likely to be heavier drinkers than men. These differences remain the same regardless of what age range researchers examine. After age fifty, both the quantity and frequency of drinking decline for both men and women. Women who have alcohol problems are more likely to keep it hidden and not receive treatment, as discussed in Chapter 5.

Alcohol consumption began to peak in the early 1980s and then began a gradual decline by the 1990s. The declines are perceptible in all age ranges. In many instances, some older drinkers gradually decrease the quantity of consumption while slightly increasing the frequency. Surveys of alcohol consumption have commented on two changes, increasing numbers of abstainers and stable estimates of the number of alcohol dependents and alcohol abusers (Clark and Hilton, 1991). National surveys give most of their attention to the health consequences of excessive drinking. Thus, it is quite easy to overlook the preponderance of controlled drinking in the United States.

Since the 1990s, binge drinking among college students has caused considerable concern (Wechsler et al., 1994). Binge drinking presumably interferes with student developmental tasks such as gaining autonomy, planning a career, making friends, and getting good grades. However, most students are light or moderate drinkers, and drinking has little bearing on their development. At present, there seem to be four possible outcomes for persistent binge drinkers in college. An unknown percentage simply drops out of college in any of the undergraduate years. Another segment graduates and continues heavy drinking. The largest segment graduates or "matures out" of binge drinking, usually through the adoption of adult roles such as a new career, marriage, and raising a family (Schulenberg and Maggs, 2002). Still another group reduces drinking by the midtwenties, termed developmentally limited alcoholism by Zucker (1994). Binge drinking among college students is the subject of Chapter 9.

Another major turning point in the life course occurs when people marry. Engaged couples reduce the amounts they drink during the engagement period. Reduction toward the national moderate drinking norm typically continues after marriage. Spousal consensus on drinking strengthens the marital bond, while conflict weakens it. Couples living with a partner are more or less in agreement on light or moderate intake, less so on heavier drinking. People who have never married, have divorced or separated, or have been widowed usually report themselves as heavier drinkers. Since surveys do not study changes over time, heavy drinking can either be cause or effect. Men and women who have married are practically identical as light drinkers—men, 41.5 percent; women, 45.6 percent—and are even closer in heavy drinking, with men, 3.5 percent; and women, 3.2 percent (National Institute on Alcohol Abuse and Alcoholism [hereafter, NIAAA], 2006). Of those never married, 7.8 percent of the men are heavy drinkers, whereas 5.6 percent of the women are heavy drinkers. While 8.6 percent of divorced or separated men are heavy drinkers, 4.3 percent of divorced or separated women are heavy drinkers. Wives or husbands or both may give up drinking after parenthood (Dawson et al., 2006).

Rates of drinking vary with education, employment, income, and occupation. College-educated, full-time, well-paid employees working as managers or professionals are more often current drinkers than abstainers. By contrast, full-time, low-income employees with a high school education or less working in semiskilled or unskilled occupations are more often abstainers. They also have a higher proportion of heavy drinkers (SAMHSA, 2008). Taken together, education, employment, income, and occupation are proxy measures of social class. At the higher reaches of class structure, people drink frequently, consuming small amounts on each occasion. By contrast, at the poorer levels of the class structure, people consume large amounts infrequently; a typical example is the drinking episode that follows payday.

Drinking patterns also vary with race and ethnicity. More whites drink than African Americans. White males are more apt to be heavy drinkers than African American males. But low-income African American men constitute a higher proportion of all African American drinkers. Hispanic men are as likely to be drinkers as non-Hispanic men. Hispanic women, however, are much more likely to be abstainers. Both Hispanic men and women are somewhat less likely to be heavy drinkers than their non-Hispanic counterparts (SAMHSA, 2007a).

Among Asian Americans, men, not women, are the predominant drinkers. They are least likely to be either abstainers or heavy drinkers. Native Americans have a high proportion of abstainers, an even higher proportion of heavy drinkers, and a smaller proportion of moderate drinkers. Native American women are much more likely to be heavy drinkers when compared with women of all other ethnic categories. Drinking patterns and alcohol problems among racial and ethnic groups are examined in detail in Chapter 6.

The Epidemiology of Drinking Problems

Epidemiology studies the distribution of morbidity and mortality in the general population and segments of the population at risk. This section examines the distribution of drinking problems in the population of drinkers and the social conditions under which changes in drinking patterns are likely to take place. During the life course, people experience a number of changes in status, roles, and self-conceptions. They must deal with adjustments required as they move through the stages of childhood, adolescence, college, workplace, courtship and marriage, raising a family, managing a career, middle age, and old age. In addition to the standard and expected transitions, there are a host of unexpected collective events that make for changes—among these, war, natural disasters, economic depression, and unemployment. Further, the personal trials and tribulations of death, disease, divorce, and accidents often confront people with challenges. All of these standard, collective, and individual events can influence people to start, increase, decrease, stop, or stabilize their drinking. This portion of the chapter summarizes changes that may take place in drinking problems during any of these status changes.

Status changes, like alcoholism, are always biopsychosocial processes (Zucker and Gomberg, 1986). As processes of socialization, they require persons to learn new ways, incorporate old ways, forget old ways, and sometimes relearn them. These changes impose varying degrees of stress and evoke various coping styles, some of which may increase or decrease drinking problems. It is important to remember that socialization is a process that takes place throughout the life span.

An old saying has it that "alcoholism runs in families," and at this writing, there is ample scientific evidence of this. Many laypeople have heard this expression or have personal knowledge of alcoholism in families. Researchers have consistently found that having an alcoholic parent significantly increases the risk for developing alcoholism.

In the 1980s, Robert Cloninger and his colleagues (1986, 1987) focused on adoption studies and developed two types of alcoholism based on the drinking of the biological parents. Type 1, known as milieu-limited, refers to alcoholism developed after the age of twenty-five and is more associated with environmental factors. Type 2, male-limited alcoholism develops earlier and is thought to be inherited and more associated with criminal behavior.

Most researchers as of this writing agree that alcoholism has both genetic and environmental components. Increasing evidence points to a genetic relationship (Edenberg and Foroud, 2006). Lower levels of response to alcohol at an early age tend to predict that someone is at risk of alcohol problems. One study found that lower-level response described almost 40 percent of sons of alcoholics and could predict alcohol problems ten years later (Schuckit et al., 1996). Students can be at much greater risk of becoming problem drinkers if they were raised in an alcoholic family, started drinking at an earlier age, and reported feeling drunk after their first drinking experience (Warner, White, and Johnson, 2007). Another study supported the environmental perspective by tracking the social development of students at ages 10, 14, 15, and 16. Of 16-year-olds exposed to an excess of antisocial group influences, 8 percent had engaged in heavy episodic drinking during the past month, 32 percent drank in order to get drunk, and 33 percent had experienced problems caused by drinking (Lonczak et al., 2001).

Adolescence is a major life transition, replete with a number of biopsychosocial stresses. Studies all agree that early starts by young males in smoking, drinking, other substances, and sexual activity put them at greater risk of becoming multiproblem adults (Knight, Wechsler, and Seibring, 2002). Inconsistent definition and enforcement of drinking rules, indifference to adolescent drinking, and tolerance of drinking all increase the chances of adolescent drinking problems (Windle, 1996). Chapter 4 discusses the substance use and abuse patterns of children and adolescents. See Box 2.3 for a discussion of one girl's experience.

Researchers of marital relations and alcohol problems agree on the benign effects of drinking on marriage (Leonard and Rothbard, 1999). Divorced, separated, or never married individuals have three or four times more heavy drinkers when compared with married couples. Generally, both spouses reduce their consumption after marriage, while a sizable number actually begin a reduction in drinking during their engagement period (Homish and Leonard, 2007). Women are more apt to adopt their husband's drinking style rather than the other way around. Conflicts that develop in the course of a marriage may be the effect as well as the cause of drinking. When conflicts emerge, dissolution of the marriage may be the outcome. Also, when the husband is a heavy drinker, the wife is at greater risk of being abused (Dawson et al., 2007).

The resolution of alcohol problems in marriages varies in accordance with the spouse who has the problem. Women as "closet drinkers" are better able to conceal their problem. Once discovered, however, these women's problems mean their marriage may soon be dissolved. By contrast, the husband's problem becomes visible much sooner, yet the marriage, with all of its subsequent difficulties, can persist for years afterward. This difference in tolerance of alcoholic spouses is another example of selective definition and enforcement of drinking rules. The fact that women stay with alcoholic husbands longer than men stay with alcoholic wives can be related to cultural gender roles in which women are more likely to be financially dependent on a spouse.

Occupations vary in the extent to which they permit or allow drinking before coming to work, coming to work with a hangover, drinking on the job, or drinking after work (Frone, 2006). These variations depend on the amount of stress workers experience and the occupation's drinking culture. Other things being equal, the greater the stress, the more permissive the drinking culture. One compilation found the highest percentage of heavy drinkers in the following five occupational groupings: service; farming, fishery, and

Box 2.3   A Young Girl and Alcohol

At age twenty-four, Koren Zailckas had already written a memoir (Zailckas, 2005). She had her first drink at age fourteen and her first blackout at age sixteen, when she was rushed to the hospital for treatment of alcohol poisoning. Zailckas had appeared the all-American girl—bright, attractive, a strong student, a good writer, dancer, and skier. It was easy for everyone to think she had the world on a string. Zailckas's father recalled: "After the incident when we took her to the emergency room, we thought we were keeping a diligent vigil. Hindsight is 20/20, but even now we feel we provided a great deal of supervision. Obviously we missed whatever indications were there" (Mehegan, 2005, E6).

The binge drinking continued at Syracuse University. Zailckas experienced more blackouts, vomiting, and meaningless sexual escapades (Fisher, 2005). Her father said: "In college there was no hint of a problem. She was always on the dean's list. We were in contact with her by phone, talking about her day and weekend. When we went to visit her, we would go out to dinner and we would have a glass of wine, but she would abstain" (Mehegan, 2005, E6). While she managed to graduate with honors in 2002, Zailckas continued her excessive drinking and reached the point in 2003 of deciding to stop completely. While acknowledging a drinking problem, Zailckas denies that she is an alcoholic. She wrote about her drinking experiences as a way to process what was happening to her, and the result was a highly touted book.

Zailckas's parents did not know the extent of their daughter's problems with alcohol until they read her book themselves. Her mother said: "I read it in one sitting, on Labor Day weekend and I just grieved. It's a cautionary tale, not only for girls but parents. We never would have thought she had an alcohol problem; we were observant and involved. I was a full-time volunteer and mother, and stayed home with my children" (Mehegan, 2005, E6). Her father said: "The book had a profound effect on me. It took me a while to get over it. Now I am very proud of her and love her deeply" (Mehegan, 2005, E6).

Zailckas's advice for parents? "I would tell them to realize at what age these pressures start. Eleven or twelve is not too early to sit down with them and say 'the pressure is going to be building. People you know will be drinking.' Tell them it's not a good idea to take that first drink. It's important for parents to realize what they are up against" (Mehegan, 2005, E6).

forestry; transportation and material moving; handlers and helpers; and protective service (SAMHSA, 2005b). All of these occupations are known for sharing a heavy drinking culture. And the highest number of heavy drinkers in all five groupings was in the eighteen-to-twenty-four age range.

A study comparing occupational drinking norms in a Japanese and a US firm found that both the definition and enforcement of drinking norms in the US firm were highly inconsistent (Ames, Grube, and Moore, 2000). Other studies have found that women working in male-dominated occupations are more likely to become heavy drinkers (Cho, 2004). Women working in law firms and businesses where social drinking occurs during and after business hours are at risk of harassment and drunken driving (Shore and Pieri, 1992). Several studies have explored high rates of police and military drinking (Bray, Fairbank, and Marsden, 1999; Obst, Davey, and Sheehan, 2001). In the early 2000s, according to a *New York Times* report on soldiers' drinking in Iraq, "a Pentagon health study . . . found that the rate of binge drinking in the Army shot up by 30 per cent from 2002 to 2005" (von Zielbauer, 2007). Because of the strong environmental support for heavy drinking in some occupations, heavy drinking is more likely to persist over time. As a result, this drinking pattern is more likely to lead to what Zucker calls developmentally cumulative alcoholism (Zucker, 1994; Rivers, 1994).

Late-life problem drinkers are expected to increase as the US population ages. Estimates are that between 5 and 16 percent of the elderly are heavy or problem drinkers (Williams, Ballard, and Alessi, 2005). Late-onset drinkers, with fewer health problems, more social support, and more effective coping responses, manage better than early-onset drinkers. Reducing alcohol consumption or abstaining was much easier for them (Brennan and Moos, 1996). A ten-year follow-up of 184 untreated elderly problem drinkers found 30 percent in remission, that is, displaying no evidence of problem drinking. Those who had improved were women, late-onset drinkers, and those having fewer and less severe drinking problems as well as friends who disapproved of drinking (Schutte et al., 2001). Because the elderly have to deal with disengagement, isolation, loneliness, and depression, social support from friends increases the chances of reducing alcohol consumption. See Chapter 8 for a discussion of the substance abuse problems of the elderly.

Since there are a variety of drinking patterns among racial and ethnic groups, there are also variations in the distribution of alcohol problems among these groups. American Indians, perhaps the most extreme example, have the highest rate of abstainers and of heavy drinkers. Indian women have the highest rates in both categories. High rates of death from cirrhosis, violence, and suicide prevail. African Americans similarly have fairly high rates of abstainers as well as heavy drinkers. African American males tend to develop alcohol problems in their thirties. Like the women, they exhibit the same late start, rapid progression, and early entry into treatment (Johnson et al., 2005). Hispanic women have the highest rate of abstainers, while Hispanic males tend to experience severe alcohol problems in their forties. The rank order of binge drinking, from most to least, is as follows: American Indians and Alaskan Natives, whites, Hispanics, blacks, and then Asians (SAMHSA, 2008). The alcohol problems of racial and ethnic groups are discussed in Chapter 6.

Medical Consequences of Drinking and Alcoholism

There are a wide variety of short-term and long-term problems associated with alcohol and alcoholism, more than exist for drug abusers and addicts. The cluster of horrible feelings experienced by the person who has ingested large amounts of alcohol the night before is the familiar hangover (see Box 2.4). A hangover typically comprises headache, fatigue, sensitivity to sound and light, nausea, and irritability. The reasons for hangover include the loss of fluid due to the diuretic effect of alcohol, a disruption of the normal sleep cycle, and the suppression of rapid eye movement (REM) sleep. When ethyl alcohol is drunk in moderation, the body can in timely fashion eliminate the breakdown product acetaldehyde; however, when huge amounts are ingested, the liver cannot keep pace, and this toxic chemical can build up.

Box 2.4   Lucky Jim's Hangover

Kingsley Amis (1953, 64), in his classic work about academic life, offers one of the best descriptions in literature of the effects of a hangover:

> Dixon was alive again. Consciousness was upon him before he could get out of the way; not for him the slow, gracious wandering from the halls of sleep, but a summary, forcible ejection. He lay sprawled, too wicked to move, spewed up like a broken spider crab on the tarry shingle of the morning. The light did him harm, but not as much as looking at things did; he resolved, having done it once, never to move his eyeballs again. A dusty thudding in his head made the scene before him beat like a pulse. His mouth had been used as a latrine by some small creature of the night, and then as its mausoleum. During the night, too, he'd somehow been on a cross-country run and then been expertly beaten up by secret police. He felt bad.

If the person moves from social drinking to problem drinking, there is likely an increase in *tolerance*. This means that over time it may take more alcohol to bring a person to a level of intoxication previously reached at lower amounts. A drinker may experience *blackouts*, wherein, after a period of heavy drinking, the drinker cannot remember where she or he was or what she or he did. This is not to be confused with passing out or losing consciousness, since the drinker remains conscious. After physical dependence has developed, an alcoholic can develop *reverse tolerance,* meaning that a small amount of alcohol can quickly make the drinker intoxicated. This is related to a decrease in healthy liver functioning.

When physical dependence develops, an abstinence or acute withdrawal syndrome will occur if the person stops drinking. Sufferers are irritable and agitated, their hands shake, they are anxious and hypersensitive to stimuli, and they cannot sleep. A drink of alcohol will stop these symptoms; this accounts for some social service agencies in the 1970s keeping alcohol in the office—to allow the person showing signs of withdrawal to drink while being transported to a detoxification program. Without a drink, a person can suffer alcohol seizures or, in extreme cases, delirium tremens, known as DTs. The symptoms of DTs include fever, severe sweating, confusion, hallucination, and convulsions. It is difficult to recognize symptoms of DTs because they can be similar to withdrawal from other drugs. Of those who experience DTs, 5 to 15 percent die as a result. Medical management of DTs is complex, and few physicians have the expertise to treat these patients (DeBellis et al., 2005).

Drinking alcohol increases the risk of injury due to reduced judgment, coordination and balance (falls), and slower reaction time implicated in car accidents. One does not need to have alcoholism in order to suffer extreme risks, however. As previously noted, a single episode of consuming a large amount of alcohol can result in alcohol poisoning and even death. This is discussed in Chapter 9 on college drinking.

Alcohol, especially red wine, has been touted in recent years as a protective factor for some heart disease, specifically coronary artery disease (World Health Organization, 2004). But these same beneficial effects are available in grape juice, a safer alternative if one is seeking health benefits.

Alcoholism is associated with heart disease, high blood pressure, stroke, gastrointestinal problems, cancer, pancreatitis, and other problems. It is especially associated with cancers of the mouth, esophagus, larynx, stomach, colon, liver, and rectum (Cargiulo, 2007). For women, there is increased risk of breast and ovarian cancers. The severe problems associated with fetal alcohol spectrum disorders are discussed in Chapter 5.

Heavy drinking is associated with heart muscle wasting, or alcoholic cardiomyopathy, causing heart rhythm abnormalities and congestive heart failure. Alcoholics can suffer from anemia, which means there are not enough red blood cells to transport oxygen. Thus, blood tests are one important way to help diagnose alcoholism.

Liver disease is highly associated with alcoholism, although it remains unclear how much alcohol one must consume to develop liver disease. The liver manufactures essential chemicals or the precursors of essential chemicals; it breaks down wastes, fats, and poisons; it stores vitamins; and it helps regulate blood sugar levels. Acute fatty liver can be a sign of heavy drinking. When alcohol is present, it "distracts" the liver from the tasks of breaking down fatty acids, a normal metabolic function. Fatty deposits build up in the cells of the liver, leading to liver enlargement. Fatty liver can be reversed with abstinence. It can be easily diagnosed by blood tests or physical examination, and since it is a warning sign of alcohol abuse, should be addressed by medical professionals. Heavy drinkers can experience bouts of alcoholic hepatitis, inflammation of the liver cells from their bath of alcohol. Cirrhosis of the liver, the most serious of the liver ailments, can be a terminal illness. Although cirrhosis has other causes, alcoholism is the leading cause (World Health Organization, 2004).

Alcoholism is responsible for more neurological disorders than any other causes, including other drugs or toxins in the environment (Lehman, Pilich, and Andrews, 1993). Neurological impairments include peripheral neuropathy, where extremities may be tingly or lose feeling. Some patients report the inability to feel their feet. With abstinence these effects may decrease (Bartsch et al., 2007).

Over time, cognitive functions of alcoholics may decrease, as alcoholism is also associated with brain damage. It remains unclear whether the amount of cognitive deficit is correlated with the amount of alcohol consumed over time (Jung, 2001). Abstinence from alcohol is associated with some brain recovery (Bartsch et al., 2007). While alcoholic dementia falls along a continuum, other factors may be involved, among them the development of other illnesses such as Alzheimer's disease (Moriyama et al., 2006).

Wernicke-Korsakoff syndrome is a degenerative brain disorder linked specifically with alcoholism and caused by poor nutrition (Moriyama et al., 2006). Patients are confused and disoriented, and many have short-term memory loss. A major cause is thiamine (a B vitamin) deficiency associated with alcoholism. Evidence suggests that insensitivity to thiamine early in life can cause brain abnormalities, putting a person at greater risk of alcoholism (Manzardo and Penick, 2006). Since few physicians have knowledge of Wernicke-Korsakoff syndrome, it is likely that it is much more common than previously thought and that some elderly patients are misdiagnosed.

In the mid-twentieth century, some clinicians and researchers described *primary versus secondary alcoholism*. This is the chicken-and-egg game, with professionals trying to sort out whether the alcoholism came first and then caused mental health problems (primary) or if alcoholism developed later as a response to mental health problems (secondary). In the early 2000s, we speak of *dual diagnosis* or *co-occurring disorders*. Depression is the major psychiatric problem most closely associated with alcoholism. Alcoholism and depression are closely intertwined: depression may encourage the drinker to seek relief with alcohol; conversely, alcoholism can lead to depression. For some patients it can be difficult to determine which came first. Other mental health problems that may co-occur with alcoholism include panic disorders, schizophrenia, phobias, and increased risk of suicide (Cargiulo, 2007). There are higher rates of cognitive impairment when patients have both schizophrenia and alcoholism (Manning et al., 2007). Chapter 3 offers more discussion of dual diagnoses.

Problem drinkers have always tried to stop on their own, and some have succeeded. An early study reported that a father, aghast when a daughter recoiled at seeing him drunk, decided to quit and succeeded (Tuchfield, 1981). Another study of forty spontaneous remissions found that low contact with fellow users, less severe dependence, and refusal to accept self-definition as a sick person incapable of self-control triggered their natural recovery without treatment (Granfield and Cloud, 1996). Some eighty-three older and married problem drinkers who quit drinking on their own were members of a supportive social network that drank less, were less frequently intoxicated, and were less frequent drug users (Bischof et al., 2003). Studies of successful spontaneous remission find low contact with using friends and high contact with a nonusing support group are necessary social conditions.

Contemporary Trends in Alcohol Use, Abuse, and Addiction

Today there exists a vast alcohol treatment establishment, both public and private, offering a variety of treatments such as inpatient and outpatient, group and individual counseling, halfway houses, and relapse prevention. If most seek the traditional goal of abstinence, others seek a return to moderate drinking. Despite the popular acceptance of alcoholics as people who need treatment rather than confinement in jail, the vast majority of the estimated 18.6 million Americans with alcohol problems do not receive treatment (SAMHSA, 2008).

A number of drugs have become available for the treatment of alcohol problems and alcoholism. Antabuse (disulfirum) has been used for over fifty years as a form of aversion therapy for chronic alcoholics who are early in recovery (Jackim, 2003). The pill is available only with a physician's prescription, and the patient or client ingests it daily. Drinking while taking antabuse results in nausea, vomiting, facial flushing, dizziness, and headache among other symptoms. Unlike newer drugs that focus on a decrease in craving, antabuse works by reminding patients of the adverse physical effects. Since it takes four to five days for antabuse to be cleared from the body, the hope is that antabuse clients will change their minds and recommit to abstinence.

Naltrexone has been approved since 1994 for the reduction in cravings experienced by some alcoholics. Originally developed to treat heroin addiction, naltrexone has been found to reduce the positive sensations associated with drinking and increase the negative feelings such as fatigue. Thus, it is possible for those who do relapse to avoid returning to previous levels of heavy drinking (NIAAA, 2000a). Those with liver disorders should not take naltrexone.

Recent trends in treatment include Food and Drug Administration approval of the Alkermes alcoholism drug, Vivitrol, in April 2006 (Heuser, 2006). Vivitrol is naltrexone in the form of an injection administered once a month in a physician's office (Martinotti et al., 2007; Peterson, 2007). The Food and Drug Administration approved Acamprosate, another drug to reduce cravings, in 2004; however it has been widely available by prescription in France since 1989 (NIAAA, 2000a). It has no potential for abuse and can be taken by clients with liver disorders. Research in the early 2000s shows that oxcarbazepine may be more effective in preventing relapse than naltrexone (Martinotti et al., 2007). Having shown treatment effectiveness, Hazelden, one of the best-known treatment centers in the United States, is now using medications for alcoholic patients (Peterson, 2007). While these medications can be helpful to those in recovery, they should be used in conjunction with other forms of treatment. See Chapter 13 for more on the use of medications for the treatment of alcoholism and drug addiction.

Conclusion

There is ample evidence that drinking patterns can and do change, particularly during the years of developmental transitions. The case for the inevitable progression of increasingly severe symptoms has been weakened, while the drinking-problems argument has been strengthened. The evidence tends to support the proposition that the ages of eighteen to twenty-nine are the years in which a variety of drinking patterns come and go.

At all of the turning points when drinking increases, three features seem to be present. Drinking has proved to be personally rewarding, there is an excess of definitions favorable to heavy drinking, and there is a weakening of social controls. The most abundant evidence supporting this explanation stems from the extensive research on college drinking. It has also been demonstrated in surveys of noncollege youth as well as in ethnographic case studies of occupational drinking (Knight et al., 2002). Similarly, when drinking is believed to be unrewarding and social controls are in force, college students are protected from the risks of binge or heavy episodic drinking (Jessor et al., 2006).

Conceptions of alcohol problems have changed over time. Some may define alcoholics as those deserving of punishment for their bad behavior, while others define them as sick people in need of treatment. A wide variety of physical problems may develop as a result of excessive alcohol consumption, and it is clear that alcoholism can lead to severe disease.

The general conclusion is that heavy episodic drinking can be prevented by increasing contact with abstaining and light-drinking social networks and decreasing contact with heavy-using friends. Prevention of substance abuse is addressed in Chapter 14.

The individual, family, and societal consequences of alcohol abuse and alcoholism are enormous. Though a major social problem, as we will see, alcohol abuse and dependence remain underdiagnosed and undertreated.

3 Drugs and Drug Addiction

In this chapter we review how drugs are categorized and named, how they interact, patterns of drug use, the process of addiction, and how culture and expectation shape the experience of drug use. Psychopharmacology is a huge area; even physicians have to routinely consult the latest edition of the 3,000-page *Physicians' Desk Reference,* and that is only for the prescription drugs!

Drug Categories

Drug classification can be complex and confusing. The scheduling of drugs, as described in Chapter 1, addresses their potential for harm, according to the federal government, and is related to drug control policies. In this chapter we examine drug categories established by those who manufacture, prescribe, or dispense drugs. This chapter also considers the subjective experience of drug use and the effects on drug users.

Mental processes are complex interactions of chemical messengers (neurotransmitters) between brain cells (neurons) and electrical impulses within brain cells. Psychoactive chemicals throw a wrench into the neural network that is our brain. In addictions science, we classify drugs in terms of their effect on the body and mind, not whether they are legal, illegal, or under- or over-the-counter. After all, nerve cells do not care whether their activities are modified by a chemical prescribed by a physician, bought on the street or in a convenience store, or taken from a plant grown in your backyard. Categorizing drugs according to effect crosscuts and overlays legal and moral categories such as federal drug scheduling, "prescription medicine," "illegal" or "illicit" drug, and "over-the-counter medication."

Stimulants

Stimulants are similar to, or make available, chemical messengers (neurotransmitters) involved in amplifying nervous system activity. Low doses can cause wakefulness, increased energy, and greater focus. Higher doses can cause euphoria, anxiety, panic attacks, and overstimulation. Chronic use of powerful stimulants can result in belligerence, paranoia, and even hallucinations, resembling a manic episode or worse. For example, new, foreign-trained physicians at a hospital in Brooklyn in 1987 handed out paranoid schizophrenia diagnoses like hotcakes to crack cocaine users.

Cocaine, the most powerful stimulant, is derived from the leaves of the coca plant. Snorted powder cocaine is absorbed into the bloodstream through the nasal tissues. Injected cocaine enters directly into the bloodstream. When smoked, inhaled cocaine vapor enters the bloodstream directly from the lungs. Users achieve the desired effect more quickly and more intensively by either smoking or injection. Snorting produces a high in 3 minutes and lasts for a half an hour with a rush. Injection produces a high in 12 to 15 seconds that lasts for 15 to 20 minutes. Smoking produces a high in 6 seconds that lasts for 5 to 10 minutes. The rush lasts 2 minutes followed by an "afterglow" of 20 minutes. Cocaine is a Schedule II drug, meaning it has a high abuse potential and, at this writing, an accepted medical use with severe restrictions. Its use may lead to psychological or physical dependence.

Cocaine has always enjoyed its reputation as the "champagne of drugs" and has the greatest appeal for users who believe that cocaine intoxication produces the most pleasure. Its lofty reputation, high price, scarcity, and outlawed status restricted its use. In 2007, 0.04 ounce (1 gram) of powder cocaine sold for about $100, whereas a rock of crack cocaine cost only about $10 (Office of National Drug Control Policy, 2007).

The rush associated with use impels the user to want to use the drug over and over again. Because of the immediacy and intensity of the effect, compulsive users indulge in binges. Cocaine enthusiasts in the 1920s and again in the 1980s claimed that cocaine was not addictive. That claim is controversial; most treatment professionals do agree that cocaine use can become an addiction.

Withdrawal from cocaine is a painful "crash" resembling major depression, with major cravings to resume use. Crack cocaine addiction can be worse: even seasoned addicts were horrified by female crack addicts living in "crack houses" and exchanging all forms of sex for bits of "the rock" (Ratner, 1993). See Box 3.1 for a description of coca use in South America.

The major stimulants include caffeine, amphetamines, and herbal stimulants such as *Ephedra sinensis* (ma huang, containing ephedrine). Amphetamines also have an appetite-suppressing effect and are associated with abuse by dieters, a co-occurring disorder with anorexia nervosa, until recently found almost exclusively among young US and European women.

Methamphetamine, a highly addictive central-nervous-system stimulant, can be injected, snorted, smoked, or taken orally. Much like cocaine in its acute effects, it generates a sense of well-being and considerable physical activity, lessens appetite, and delays fatigue. Unlike cocaine, however, it is a long-acting drug. The sense of well-being from methamphetamine can last anywhere from twenty minutes to twelve hours. Physicians, limited in medical use of methamphetamine, make use of it only when they treat attention deficit disorder, narcolepsy, and obesity.

Methamphetamine is classified as a Schedule II stimulant under the Controlled Substances Act. Since it has a high potential for abuse, it is available only through a prescription that cannot be refilled. Some people make it in small illegal laboratories, however. Ease of synthesis guarantees large profits. Chronic effects of methamphetamine include addiction, psychotic behavior, and brain damage. Withdrawal symptoms include depression, anxiety, fatigue, paranoia, aggression, and intense craving for the drug. Chronic methamphetamine use can induce violent behavior, anxiety, confusion, and insomnia. The brain damage it causes is similar to that caused by Alzheimer's disease, stroke, and epilepsy.

Box 3.1   Another View of Coca Use

In *The Hold Life Has: Coca and Cultural Identity in an Andean Community,* by Catherine Allen (1988), coca chewing, an essential ingredient of all ritual activity in the community studied by the author, makes one a "real person" and affirms attitudes and values of indigenous Andean culture (Allen, 22). Other factors may play a part: anthropologists have also emphasized the beneficial effects of coca leaf chewing at high elevations, the alleviation of fatigue, and economic networking (Hanna, 1974). At the July 2001 inauguration of President Alejandro Toledo of Peru, the first Native American elevated to that office, coca leaves were among the offerings burned by priests in a celebration of cultural affirmation. It is ironic that when the active ingredient of this relatively benign plant species is extracted and refined into a smokable form, it becomes a drug—crack cocaine—that was the scourge of the US inner city in the 1990s.

Amphetamine-like drugs have the seemingly paradoxical utility of helping to calm and focus individuals with severe attention deficit hyperactivity disorder (ADHD). Methylphenidate (marketed as Ritalin and Concerta) and dextroamphetamine (marketed as Adderal) stimulate "sleepy" areas of the brain involved in focusing. Such drugs are at risk for diversion and abuse; in 48 percent of all emergency room visits involving methylphenidate, the patient did not have a prescription, 38 percent of visits involved medically sanctioned use, and 10 percent accidental ingestion (SAMHSA, 2006a). Considerable controversy exists as to whether ADHD drugs are overprescribed based on overdiagnosis of ADHD and very aggressive marketing by pharmaceutical companies (Goldstein, 2006). Interestingly, prescription rates for many psychiatric medications vary enormously by region.

Depressants

Depressants include beverage alcohol, sedatives, and narcotic-analgesics (opioids). This very broad and variegated class of substances includes all those that damp down processes in the brain and body.

Beverage alcohol (ethanol, ethyl alcohol) is the subject of Chapter 2. Since alcohol initially has stimulating effects, many drinkers are unaware that officially alcohol is classified as a depressant.

Opioids, also known as narcotics or narcotic-analgesics, have the properties of killing pain and providing a dreamlike "high." Tar from the bud of the opium poppy is the source of raw opium, which contains morphine and codeine. Heroin is synthesized from morphine. Users can inject, smoke, or inhale heroin, a powerful and addictive drug derived from morphine. Injection produces a rush in seven or eight seconds. After the initial euphoria, users experience flushing of the skin and a dry mouth. Alternately, users feel warm and drowsy. Regular heroin use produces tolerance, the need to increase the dosage in order to achieve the "high." Over time, regular heavier doses produce physical dependence. A few hours after the last injection, users may experience withdrawal symptoms (craving, restlessness, muscle and bone pain, and vomiting). Due to the fact that it has high abuse potential and no medical use, heroin is listed as a Schedule I controlled substance.

Oxycodone (OxyContin) and hydrocodone (Vicodin) are mentioned later in the section on epidemiology, in reference to a major drug scourge during this decade. Finally, one opioid, methadone HCL, is actually the predominant treatment for opioid addiction, as "opioid substitution therapy" or methadone maintenance, discussed at length in Chapter 13.

©iStockphoto.com/Sean_Warren

Sedative-hypnotics (*hypnotic* means "sleep inducing") are often prescribed to reduce anxiety and for the treatment of sleep disorders. Barbiturates carry a high risk of overdose, especially when synergistically combined with alcohol. Barbiturates are not likely to be prescribed today due to their addictive nature. Barbiturate-like sedatives include methaqualone (Quaalude) and glutethemide (Doriden). In the 1970s Quaaludes were thought to enhance sexuality. The very popular benzodiazepines, such as diazepam (Valium), are prescribed for sleep and anxiety. Despite their relatively mild effects, they are in fact highly addictive. Additionally, the popular class of supposedly nonaddictive hypnotics prescribed for sleep include eszopiclone (Lunesta), zaleplon (Sonata), and zolpidem tartrate (Ambien). Temporary amnesia has been reported as a side effect of these drugs. In addition, Ambien users have reported odd side effects such as sleepwalking, sleep-driving, or sleepwalking combined with uncontrolled eating of whatever they find in the kitchen, including raw eggs and flour (Downs, 2006).

Many nonpsychiatric medications have a sleep-inducing effect. Antihistamines such as dyphenhydramine (the active ingredient in Benadryl) and chlorpheniramine (Chlortrimeton) and many other over-the-counter (OTC) preparations, as well as the antinausea drug dimenhydrinate (Dramamine), have a depressant and sleep-inducing effect. As a sleep aid, they can be a safe substitute for addicting, prescription drugs but cause a great deal of drowsiness the next day. Their popularity has been in decline since the advent of nondrowsy antihistamines such as Allegra and Claritin.

Many people report that cyclobenzaprine (Flexeril), a muscle relaxant, puts them into a drugged sleep, unwanted during the daytime.

Marijuana

The leaves and stems of the plant *Cannabis sativa* can be classified as a sedative when used at lower doses, and as a mild hallucinogen at higher doses. The active ingredient in marijuana, THC, when extracted and concentrated, is in fact a powerful hallucinogen. Marijuana users have altered perceptions of time and slow reaction time while driving, for example. Research has demonstrated how marijuana impairs reaction time, perception of driving situations, and eye-hand coordination in driver simulation systems (Mathias, 1996).

Users smoke marijuana in cigarettes or in a pipe, sometimes in a blunt (a hollowed-out cigar filled with marijuana), or occasionally brew it in tea or mix it with food. The federal government claims marijuana slows down memory, clouds perception, and interferes with coordination, thinking, and problem solving (Office of National Drug Control Policy, 2006). Users say that after using marijuana, they feel good, mellow, and pleasant; enjoy listening to music; become detached, humorous, and nonaggressive; and have an appetite for food, known as the "munchies" (Drug Enforcement Administration, 2005).

Marijuana use is hard to study objectively because it is so ideologically loaded. Opponents demonize it, and some proponents support medical and recreational use. A major study by the Institute of Medicine found that marijuana was beneficial in stimulating appetite in those with chronic wasting from HIV/AIDS, in ameliorating intractable pain, in controlling nausea and vomiting associated with chemotherapy, and for reducing eye pressure in glaucoma sufferers (Joy et al., 1999). The institute cautioned, however, that smokable cannabis caused respiratory disease, and expressed preference for a nonsmokable version such as the THC patch, Marinol. They further recognized that the patch is not a rapid-onset method of drug administration, which is vastly preferred by medical marijuana users, and conceded that until such a system was developed, allowing patients to smoke marijuana on a short-term basis might be acceptable. The use of medical marijuana continues to be a highly politicized and controversial topic and is discussed in Chapter 14.

Hallucinogens

Hallucinogens, including LSD, mescaline, peyote, and THC, distort information processing in the brain, causing changes in users' perceptions of reality. LSD, PCP, and ecstasy (MDMA) are major examples. Lesser-known hallucinogens include DMT, mescaline, and psilocybin. LSD and ecstasy are Schedule I substances, classified as high abuse potential, no accepted medical use, and no safe use under medical supervision. After taking LSD, users experience effects within thirty to ninety minutes. The drug experience, called a trip, can last as long as twelve hours, and users may experience seeing sounds and hearing colors (synesthesia).

In the 1960s, hallucinogen use was popular among the counterculture hippies, who believed that it put one in touch with "cosmic consciousness," but the use of these substances goes back thousands of years in tribal cultures, as described in Box 3.2.

Box 3.2   Shamanism and Hallucinogens

In small-scale, traditional, and tribal cultures, shamans are part-time specialists who have access to supernatural realms that they may manipulate for the purpose of curing, divination and clairvoyance, or communication with spirits. Generally, a shaman gains access to the supernatural during an altered state of consciousness or trance. The trance state may be induced via fasting, dancing, drumming, sensory deprivation, or the ceremonial use of hallucinogenic drugs. Often during the trance, the shaman experiences encounters with spirits and other supernatural beings.

We have numerous hints that shamanism was widespread through prehistoric times. Ethnologists first examined shamanism among native Siberian peoples such as the Koryak, Yakut, Ostyak, Samoyed, and Tungus (the language from which the word *shaman* is derived). Siberian shamans used the hallucinogenic mushroom *Amanita muscaria,* or fly agaric.

The other cultural area in which shamanism survived into modern times was among the Native American peoples, for example, those of the upper Amazon rain forest. Of these, one of the best known is the Jivaro of the Ecuadorian Amazon. According to anthropologist Michael Harner, the normal waking life, for the Jivaro, is simply a "lie" or "illusion," while the true forces that determine daily events are supernatural and can be seen and manipulated only with the aid of hallucinogenic drugs. "A reality view of this kind creates a particularly strong demand for specialists who can cross over in the supernatural world at will to deal with the forces that influence and even determine the events of the waking life" (Harner 1973, 16).

Jivaro shamans take a drink containing four hallucinogenic alkaloids prepared from two local species of vine, called *ayahuasca* by several ethnic groups. Harner himself drank this brew and said he met bird-headed and dragonlike creatures that claimed to be the gods of this world.

continues

Box 3.2 (continued)

The psilocybin mushroom and the peyote cactus are used in shamanic and other ceremonial activities by Native American groups. In addition, a religion based on peyote use spread among various North American Indian tribes in the late nineteenth and early twentieth centuries, among northern Mexican and Plains Indian tribes (La Barre, 1938; Stewart, 1987). Peyote religion, which had prophetic and millennial aspects for the oppressed, reservation-confined tribes, combined Native and Christian elements, as did several other revolutionary religious movements that flourished among colonized indigenous peoples (Lanternari, 1963).

Finally, Harner, the preeminent anthropologist involved in the study of shamanism and hallucinogens, moved away from academia and set up shop as a trainer of shamanistic technique with his Foundation for Shamanic Studies, which sells drums and tapes online. Harner has come under tremendous criticism from native practitioners and anthropologists for appropriating, decontextualizing, simplifying, and commodifying indigenous culture in order to pander to New Age faddism for fame and profit (Castile, 1996; Johnson, 1995).

Dissociative and Designer Drugs

Acute intoxication with dissociative drugs such as PCP (angel dust, phencyclidine) and "Special K" (ketamine)—both veterinary anesthetics—produce symptoms that appear to mimic psychiatric disturbances. PCP use in particular is unpredictable, and users may experience visual hallucinations, rage, euphoria, altered perceptions of time and space, paranoia, belligerence, and assaultive behavior (Grinspoon and Bakalar, 1990; National Institute on Drug Abuse [hereafter, NIDA], 2006).

Police officers have commented that subjects apprehended under the influence of PCP sometimes seem to have unusually great strength. All of these symptoms may linger for days, weeks, or months, coupled with depression and social withdrawal. Chronic PCP users have been reported to develop a permanent schizophrenic-like disorder, which may simply represent individuals who were in the process of developing schizophrenia, or organic brain damage due to the sustained use of the drug. Animal studies have suggested the validity of the latter hypothesis (Jentsch et al., 1997).

Ketamine users report a temporary dissociative, out-of-body experience, which they call the k-hole. It became a popular designer drug of abuse in the 1990s. At low doses it causes a dreamlike state, but at high doses can cause memory loss, respiratory distress, and heart problems. Ketamine is also a popular drug among injection drug users (Lankenau and Clatts, 2004). See Chapter 4 for discussion of ketamine use by adolescents.

The term *designer drugs* is confusing, since so many drugs of all types are artificially synthesized. Most often the term is applied to ecstasy, popular in particular youth club scenes called "raves." Ecstasy has properties of both a stimulant and mild hallucinogen. Users report a heightened sense of well-being, of empathy and closeness to others, and sensuality. Ecstasy is a synthetic, psychoactive drug chemically similar to the stimulant methamphetamine and the hallucinogen mescaline. It became popular in the late 1980s and early 1990s among teens and young adults at dance clubs and raves. A long-acting drug, it produces acute effects, including warm feelings toward other people (drug marketers originally intended to name the drug Empathy). Lack of knowledge of the drug's effects or overdoses from a combination of substances led to numerous visits to emergency departments and several tragic deaths, which focused attention on ecstasy. MDMA was declared a Schedule I drug in 1998.

Drawbacks of ecstasy use include muscle tension and involuntary teeth-clenching, as well as increased heart rate, blood pressure, and body temperature, which, in the context of an all-night "rave," can lead to severe dehydration and physical collapse. Upon discontinuance, users report confusion, depression, anxiety, and sleep problems. The term *herbal ecstasy* is misleading, since it refers to tablets containing various stimulants such as caffeine and the herbal form of ephedrine, ma huang, which are found on the counter at convenience stores and gas stations. See Chapter 4 for discussion of ecstasy use by adolescents.

Inhalants

Inhalants are those substances brought into the body through the nose. This category refers to a route of administration for vapors emanating from volatile liquids or concentrated in canisters and sprays. According to the Substance Abuse and Mental Health Administration, almost 600,000 teens initiated inhalant abuse during a recent one-year period (SAMHSA, 2006b). In 2007, of people aged 12 years or older, 775,000 used inhalants for the first time within the past year (SAMHSA, 2008). The average age of first use was 15.7 years in 2006 and 17.1 in 2007. Inhalants include airplane glue, toluene, shoe polish, gasoline and lighter fluid, correction fluids, paint solvents, and amyl nitrate canisters ("poppers" or "whippets"). In third world countries, inhaling of gasoline fumes is endemic in areas where children are hungry, cold, or abused.

Psychiatric Medications

Psychiatric medications—other than those in the stimulant and sedative classes above—that are unlikely to be abused include antidepressants, mood stabilizers, and antipsychotic medications.

Antidepressants, such as those marketed under the brands Prozac, Effexor, Celexa, Cymbalta, and Lexapro, adjust the cycling of neurotransmitters in the brain. An antidepressant will not cause a "high" in a nondepressed individual, but will ameliorate severe depression after a number of days or weeks. It is usually recommended that antidepressants be used in conjunction with psychotherapy. While a proven lifesaver for people who are crippled by biologically based depression, prescription use has skyrocketed to the point that some critics feel it is overprescribed for every vagary of the human condition.

Mood stabilizers, such as lithium carbonate, are prescribed for bipolar disorder (previously known as manic-depression). For as yet unknown reasons, antiseizure medications such as Tegretol and Depakote also help stabilize the swings of mood that characterize this illness. In the latest "diagnosis du jour," some physicians even treat depression with these antiseizure drugs, on the theory that their patients are suffering from a newly conceived, bipolar II in which the manic phase is infrequent or scarcely apparent.

Antipsychotic medications, such as Risperidal, Abilify, and Zyprexa, are used primarily to control delusions, hallucinations, and bizarre behavior characterized by schizophrenia, a developmental brain disease. These newer medications have less of the dulling, tranquilizing effects of older medications such as Thorazine, Haldol, and Prolixin, which can also cause bizarre muscular symptoms known as tardive dyskinesia.

Drug Interactions

One-third to one-half of drug fatalities and emergency room visits are caused not by the effects of a single drug alone but by the innumerable combinations of drugs that people may ingest, out of recklessness, ignorance, or by accident. It is hard to keep track of all of these permutations, but we will survey the most common. The effects of drugs on drugs, or drugs taken together (drug interactions), may be additive, antagonistic, or synergistic.

Additive. If an individual takes two similar drugs together, the effect may be similar to the simple addition of two integers, as in 3 + 3 = 6. An example would be someone consuming two Valiums and two Libriums, both members of the benzodiazepine class of sedatives. Box 3.3 describes a combination of depressants that serves as a heroin substitute.

Antagonistic. Combinations of drugs with opposite effects provide a balance and avoid unpleasant side effects. In the 1950s and 1960s, there was the famous barbiturate-amphetamine combination, or "goofball." On the West Coast, illicit secobarbital ("red devils") contained a built-in 2.5 percent amphetamine to offset the hypnotic (sleep-inducing) effect of the barbiturate secobarbital. These combinations enabled the user to achieve a high without passing out. A drug often prescribed for migraine headaches is Fiorinal (Sandoz Pharmaceuticals). This legal goofball contains the barbiturate butalbital (50 mg); a big dose of aspirin (325 mg), which has no mind-altering effect; and 40 milligrams of caffeine. Fiorinal with codeine is also available.

In the realm of over-the-counter medications, many cold and allergy preparations contain two or more psychoactive substances: decongestants that have a stimulant effect, and antihistamines that have a depressant,

---

Box 3.3   "Hits"—a Drug Combo

Glutethemide was marketed by CIBA-Geigy and Rorer as Doriden in 125-milligram tablets. Opiate (heroin) addicts discovered that Doriden, nicknamed "cibas" owing to the company imprint on the capsule, could be mixed with codeine-containing cough syrups, to provide a serviceable substitute for heroin in times of scarcity, during the 1960s. This was called "syrup and cibas," or "pancakes and syrup." As codeine was removed from cough syrups, users moved on to matched sets of glutethemide tablets and tablets of drugs containing codeine (Tylenol #4). This was dubbed "hits" on the East Coast and "loads" in Philadelphia, and as "sets," "set-ups," "cibas and codeine," and "C & C" on the West Coast. There are dozens of pharmaceutical preparations with some amount of codeine added—thus, the nickname "doors and fours" (Doriden and Tylenol #4).

After Rorer discontinued Doriden in 1990, an existing market for smuggled glutethemide, originating in Mexican labs, was greatly expanded. The use of "hits" has varied inversely with the availability and price of heroin. In the 1980s the most frequent arrests for drugs in Newark, New Jersey, involved hits. By the early 1990s, with a new, plentiful supply of heroin, as well as more potent versions such as "p-dope," hits went into a sharp decline, although it is anticipated that similar drug "cocktails" will resurface during the next heroin shortage.

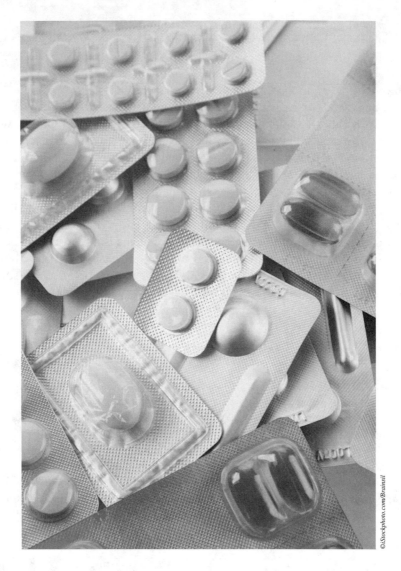

©iStockphoto.com/Brainsil

drowsy effect. On a much more intense scale, addicts combine heroin and cocaine, a powerful depressant and stimulant, in a practice known as "speedballing." Psychoactive drugs can also have antagonistic effects on other medications, such as anticoagulants or heart medications, which can pose unforeseen tragic results.

Synergistic, or multiplying, effects. As opposed to the "addition" analogy above, synergistic, or multiplying, effects are produced by certain drugs that have the effect of potentiating or making more effective the activity of another, when taken in combination. For example, if one consumed three barbiturate pills together with three alcoholic drinks, the effect would be multiplicative, that is, $3 \times 3 = 9$. Many drug overdoses and fatalities occur in this way.

Making Sense of Drug Names: From Pharmacy to Street

Like drug classifications, the naming of drugs can be complex and confusing. Drugs are named in four ways: chemical names, generic names, trade names, and nicknames, or "street" names.

1. *Chemical names* are often long and complicated. The chemical name for aspirin is monoacetic acid-ester of salicylic acid, and the name for the active ingredient in marijuana is Delta-9-tetrahydrocannabinol, or THC.

2. *Generic name*s are given to those drugs not protected by trademark registration and are commonly referred to by a short name. Examples are the pain-killing, antifever drugs aspirin and acetaminophen; the widely prescribed sedative diazepam; and the heroin substitute methadone.

3. *Trade names* are those given to drugs sold under brand or proprietary names. Bufferin is one of the trade names for aspirin, and Tylenol is a brand of acetaminophen. The sedative and muscle relaxant diazepam is marketed as Valium. The first of the class of antidepressants known as "selective serotonin re-uptake inhibitors" (SSRI) is the drug less known by its generic name of fluoxetine hydrochloride than by its famous trade name Prozac. In the early 2000s, fluoxetine began being marketed under the brand Sarafem for premenstrual dysphoric disorder, commonly known as premenstrual syndrome (PMS); not all patients are aware they are simply taking Prozac.

Some physicians prescribe under trade names (Valium, Librium), and others simply indicate the generic drug name (diazepam, chlordiazepoxide). Generic, no-frill forms of the drug are usually cheaper. While on the subject of trade names, it is interesting to note how the pharmaceutical firms come up with these names. Heroin actually started out as a trade name for diacetylmorphine. It was marketed by Bayer Pharmaceuticals in 1898 as a "heroic," nonaddictive substitute for morphine, which was causing tremendous addiction problems. It was banned as a medicine in 1924, but the trade name became our common name for the drug. An Orwellian twist in naming is seen in the name for Valium: "I am brave" in Latin. And

Librium, a similar sedative, is derived also from Latin: "I am free." Names of the popular SSRI antidepressants contain subtle messages—the "Pro" in Prozac, the "Well" in Wellbutrin, the "Pax" (Latin root for peace) in Paxil, the hint at "effective" in Effexor, and the woman's name Sara coupled with the "fem" in Sarafem.

4. *Nicknames or street names,* sometimes multiple ones, exist for each illegal drug or illegally used pharmaceutical. The chemical lysergic acid diethylamide-25, which has the generic name of LSD, is known on the street as "acid" (it even has illegal brand names). Phencyclidine, or PCP, has the street name angel dust. Secobarbital (trade name Seconal) is known as either reds or red devils. The opiate drug hydrocodone bitartrate, together with some acetaminophen, is marketed as Vicodin, and known as "Vikes" on the street. The opiate oxycodones, marketed as OxyContin, are known as "Oxys." OxyContin, which became very widespread in rural areas at the turn of the century, was also dubbed "hillbilly heroin" by the media. See Box 3.4 for generic and trade names of abused prescription medications.

Epidemiology of Drugs

Epidemiology is the study of incidence and prevalence of a pathological syndrome, whether physical or behavioral. We can study the incidence of schizophrenia, diabetes, or drug use. In the case of substance use, there are many instances of drug use that follow a pattern of early incubation within a fairly small subpopulation followed by rapid expansion to broader population categories. A plateau phase occurs when just about anyone who might use the substance has taken it up, and then a decline follows as negative effects become known or the drug loses its original charisma.

Sometimes another phase ensues when the next generation has forgotten about detriments of the drug and popularity grows once more. A good example is marijuana: in the late 1950s, use was predominantly within the small middle- and lower-middle-class beatnik counterculture. With the advent of the hippie counterculture in the 1960s, usage expanded exponentially. In the early 1970s, usage spread into the blue-collar population, while many of the 1960s hippie teen cohorts continued their use as young adults. Pot gained steadily in popularity in every year until 1979 and then went into a steady, year-by-year decline until 1990. Since then it has made a gradual comeback among youths aged eighteen to twenty-five but never to the "pothead" heights of the mid- to late 1970s. In this latest surge, marijuana use, especially among the hip-hop, African American youth cohort, has been associated with the practice of hollowing out a cigar (Phillies

**Box 3.4   Generic and Trade Names of Commonly
Abused Prescription Drugs**

Opioids (narcotic-analgesics, can be appropriately prescribed for pain)

Morphine	MS Contin, Oramorph, Roxanol
Codeine	Tylenol with codeine # 1, 2, 3, 4
Meperidine	Demerol
Hydromorphone	Dilaudid
Fentanyl	Sublimaze
Sufentanyl	Sufenta
Oxycodone HCL	OxyContin Percocet, Oxycocet, Percodan, Oxycodan
Hydrocodone	Vicodin, Dolagesic, Hycomed, Hydrocet, Lorcet, Lortab
Methadone HCL	dispensed as generic

Benzodiazepines (BZDs, minor tranquilizers and sedatives)

Alprozolam	Xanax
Lorazepam	Ativan
Triazolam	Halcion
Chlordiazepoxide	Librium
Clorazepate	Tranxene
Flurazepam	Dalmane
Clonazepam	Klonopin
Flunitrazepam	Rohypnol ("roofies")

Barbiturates (dangerous, older sedatives)

Pentobarbital	Nembutal
Secobarbital	Seconal
Amobarbital	Amytal
Phenobarbital	Luminal

Barbiturate-like sedatives (for anxiety and sleeplessness)

Methaqualone	Quaalude
Glutethemide	Doriden

Stimulants (drugs that elevate alertness)

Methylphenidate	Ritalin
Amphetamine	Adderall, Desoxyn

Blunt) and filling it with marijuana, producing the so-called blunt (Golub, Johnson, and Dunlap, 2005).

It is interesting to note that in every decade there are a much smaller number of marijuana users over the age of thirty. In other words, millions of teen and young adult users quit on their own (few pot smokers get into formal treatment). Accounts by former chronic heavy users cite feeling "out of it," depressed, and "burnt out," obviously unwanted states, and which interfere with career and interpersonal needs and goals, providing motivation to change.

Contemporary Trends in Drug Epidemiology

Drug abuse is now a worldwide problem. At this writing, approximately 28 percent of the adult (15–64) population in the world uses tobacco, more than all those who use illicit drugs combined (United Nations Office on Drugs and Crime, 2006). Cannabis (marijuana) is the most widely used drug, at 4 percent—representing some 162 million people—and is on the rise. Amphetamines are used by approximately 25 million people, with a sharp decline since 2000. Opiate abusers are estimated to be 16 million (0.4 percent), of whom 11 million are heroin abusers. There are approximately 13 million cocaine users (0.3 percent) with almost half of the global cocaine market found in the United States. There are also 10 million ecstasy users, with legal seizures of ecstasy exploding in the past few years (United Nations Office on Drugs and Crime, 2006).

Crack cocaine was considered to be the scourge of the inner cities shortly after its emergence in the mid-1980s. However, by the early 1990s, usage started to taper off considerably as it acquired a deservedly negative reputation. As fewer young people "picked up the pipe," by 2006 a majority of users were thirty-five years old or older in most epidemiological catchment areas surveyed (NIDA, 2006). Crack was, in the early 2000s, often listed as a "secondary drug" of choice, not as a primary addiction as it was in the late 1980s.

Heroin usage picked up from the late 1990s on, replacing crack, but became fairly stable overall in the early 2000s, declining in some areas and increasing in others. However, a new problem has emerged, the use of fentanyl, a synthetic opiate many times more powerful than morphine, for "revving up" heroin. In Chicago from mid-2005 to mid-2006, there were 102 fentanyl-related deaths, only 40 of which were "fentanyl alone" (NIDA, 2006, 9). Trends are very regional: in New Jersey, few deaths are reported for urban Newark; most fatalities are centered in the southern city of Camden. Nicknames of heroin and fentanyl mixtures include "drop dead," "lethal injection," "incredible hulk," and "the bomb."

Prescription opioid abuse, primarily of oxycodone (OxyContin) and hydrocodone (Vicodin), was a rural epidemic growing from the late 1990s into the mid-2000s, but seems to have halted its expansion in many metropolitan areas in 2005–2006. Methadone outside of opioid substitution therapy has been a growing problem since 2000. As physicians have increased the routine prescription of methadone for pain, it has become more available for theft and diversion. As discussed in Chapter 1, methamphetamine ("ice," smokable amphetamine) usage continues its spread in rural and urban areas. In several regions of Texas, it replaced crack as a drug of choice.

Caffeine use has grown exponentially in terms of caffeine-linked places and products. In large urban areas, Starbucks coffeehouses are as ubiquitous as fire hydrants, and hypercaffeinated drinks are the rage, sometimes in tandem with alcohol. Adolescents and young adults are habitually chugging Red Bull, an energy drink, and similar products to combat fatigue. This creates a form of chronic anxiety condition, with an exaggerated perception of stress (Mason, 2006). "Clubbers" keep going through the night— and stave off the tendency to fall asleep from binge drinking—by consuming these so-called energy drinks.

Set, Setting, and Expectation: What We Expect to Be True

Psychopharmacology alone does not explain the subjective experience of drug use. It was observed that barbiturates, a class of sedative drugs, had different subjective results in different settings. In the 1950s, barbiturates had the reputation as a giver of "Dutch courage" in a gang-fighting setting. The disinhibitory effect, together with the sedation of anxiety, actually facilitated the initiation of combat—thus, the street names "gorilla pills" and "gangster pills." In contrast, Donald Wesson and David E. Smith state that in the setting of a rock concert, 200 milligrams of secobarbital can produce a "disinhibitory euphoria" (1977, 35).

For twenty years starting in 1965, the sedative methaqualone (trade name Quaalude) was aggressively marketed as a safe and nonaddictive alternative to barbiturates. Physicians bought into this image for some time, until the drug caught on in the street and supplies were stolen or diverted. On the street, it was believed that Quaaludes were an aphrodisiac, and it was called the "love drug" or "heroin for lovers," with the street names of "disco biscuits" and "Ludes" (Abel, 1985). Myth, expectation, disinhibition, and sedation of interpersonal anxieties help to fulfill this prophecy.

Use to Abuse to Addiction

Risk factors for substance abuse exist at every system level: neurochemical and genetic, developmental, family and peer group, community, and sociocultural. These serve to propel individuals from experimental use to abuse. The mix of risk factors varies by individual. For example, one heavy drinker might be Irish Catholic and also suffer from depression, while another belongs to a binge-drinking fraternity and is having academic difficulties owing to undiagnosed learning disabilities. There are also special life-span risk factors for substance abuse. For example, adolescence is marked by heavy peer influence, risk taking, and conflicts about developmental tasks, as discussed in the next chapter. Middle age often involves disappointments, loss of roles, empty nest syndrome, and chronic ailments. The elderly face retirement, loss of spouse and others, increased social isolation, and significant health problems, as discussed in Chapter 8. See Box 3.5 for a discussion of risk factors associated with substance abuse.

Box 3.5   A Sampling of Risk Factors for Abuse and Addiction

At the genetic and neurochemical level:
   Feeling less intoxicated and needing to use more to become "high";
   Easy development of tolerance in liver and brain, so that addictive level
      is reached;
   Low stimulus barrier, feeling stressed and bombarded by stimuli;
   Stimulus augmentation leading to "awfulizing" stressors;
   Any psychiatric syndrome causing pain, dysfunction, low self-esteem,
      and marginalization, including depression and ADHD.

At the developmental and personality factor level:
   Unresolved conflicts generating anxiety, tension, and guilt;
   Unprocessed grief and rage;
   Experience of trauma.

At the sociocultural level:
   Easy availability of psychoactive substances;
   Peer norms favoring the use of psychoactive substances or exaggerated
      misperception of peer norms favoring use;
   Migration associated with social and familial disorganization and other
      acculturative stressors;
   Media representation of substance use as "cool," sexy, mature, fun.

Source: Adapted from Table 2.1, Risk factors for addiction, in Hanson, G. R., Venturelli, P. J., and Fleckenstein, A. E. (2006), *Drugs and society* (9th ed.), Sudbury, MA: Jones and Bartlett. This chart was developed by Peter Myers for the fifth edition of *Drugs and Society*.

Protective factors insulate individuals against the probabilities of developing a substance abuse problem. These include resilience, strong bonds with parents and friends who disapprove of substance use, and church affiliation.

Once a mix of risk (abuse-promoting) factors has propelled an individual to incorporate psychoactive chemical use into a pattern of adaptation to his or her difficulties, the following vicious cycles start to take hold:

1. Brain cell tolerance and increased liver metabolism efficiency make it necessary to consume increasing amounts of an intoxicant for it to have its desired effect.

2. Impairment of memory, judgment, problem solving, and other higher cortical functions results, leading to adverse social consequences causing pain, depression, helplessness, hopelessness, and lowered self-esteem.

3. Individuals construct an account of their loss of control and painful situation and seek to deny, minimize, or explain away the unpleasant realities. Members of the individual's family, peer group, and workplace environment also shy away from confronting the growing problem, and even "rescue" the abuser from negative consequences in the short run, which "enables" the progression of the addictive syndrome. Enabling and codependency are discussed in detail in Chapter 10.

4. What sociologists call primary deviance—in this case use of illicit drugs—leads to consequences. Substance abusers are labeled, stigmatized, segregated, and sanctioned, and set on a moral career wherein they accept the label, and commit further, "secondary" deviance. They adopt the deviant identity as a "master status." Thus, drug-using individuals will gravitate toward people and groups where substance use is normative, reinforced, and expected.

Note that each of these items leads to more chemical use, which in turn reinforces these vicious cycles. Thus, abuse progresses to the point that psychological and physiological dependence develops, and there is a loss of control over usage; in other words, the person has become addicted. Addicts cannot engage in moderate use, and if they abstain, they will experience physiological abstinence syndromes, which we commonly call withdrawal (see Box 3.6), and psychological craving to resume the comforting, reality-numbing addictive behavior. They cannot imagine stopping and are embedded in a lifestyle and culture of addiction they have adopted as their own. In Chapter 13 we discuss how, at any point in the progression of abuse into addiction, individuals also have motives to heal, recover, and live normal lives.

Box 3.6   Abstinence-Withdrawal Syndromes

Benzodiazepines   insomnia, agitation, headache, muscle twitching, seizures

Barbiturates   irritability, insomnia, nightmares (REM rebound), agitation

Opiates, Opioids   similar to an intestinal "flu": vomiting, diarrhea, cramps, chills, aching bones and muscles, muscle spasms, yawning, insomnia, craving

Cocaine   severe depression, craving, inability to experience pleasure, fatigue

Source: Beeder and Millman, 1997.

Drug addiction brings with it a host of unwanted and potentially very serious unintended consequences. Those who use injectable drugs and share needles place themselves at high risk for HIV/AIDs and hepatits C. Both are transmitted when blood from an infected person enters the body of a person not infected.

Over 1 million people in the United States had been diagnosed with HIV/AIDS by the end of 2003, with 38,000 new cases diagnosed in 2005 (Centers for Disease Control [hereafter, CDC, 2007). Men who have sex with men (MSM) accounted for 67 percent of new cases in 2005. Heterosexual contact accounted for 80 percent of HIV/AIDS in women. Of the new cases of HIV/AIDS transmitted by injection drug use and diagnosed in 2005, 13 percent were men and 19 percent were women (CDC, 2007).

Like HIV, hepatitis C can be spread through sharing of dirty needles and through needlesticks, or by an infected woman to her baby at birth, though most infections occur because of illegal injection drug use. Hepatitis C infection damages the liver. It is estimated that 4.1 million people in the United States (1.6 percent) have hepatitis C, with 3.2 million having chronic infection (CDC, 2005). The number of new infections each year has been greatly reduced since the 1980s, down from 240,000 to approximately 26,000 in 2004. Individuals can be infected with both HIV and hepatitis C, and co-infection seems to be on the rise (Cheng et al., 2007).

Another negative consequence of addiction is the need to obtain illegal drugs to support an addiction. This can push users toward committing crimes to meet the monetary demands of the addiction, further discussed in Chapter 11.

Dual Diagnosis, Co-morbidity, and Concurrent Disorders

Often an individual who has a substance abuse problem will abuse both alcohol and other drugs and may have a coexisting mental health problem or physical illness. It can be difficult to determine which came first, the substance abuse as a response to mental illness or vice versa. It is also possible to have two separate disorders, with neither one causing the other. It is crucial to identify the two or more problems because each has to be treated. Clients with both substance abuse and mental health problems have been referred to as having *dual diagnosis*. Twenty-first-century professionals are more likely to refer to *co-morbidity* or *co-occurring disorders*. Bipolar, anxiety, depressive, panic, obsessive-compulsive, and personality disorders as well as schizophrenia all coexist with substance abuse far more often than most people realize. The alcohol and drug abuse may be due to underlying untreated psychiatric problems. Antisocial personality disorder, borderline personality disorder, and paranoid personality disorder are correlated with serious alcohol problems.

It may be that people who suffer from mental illnesses use alcohol and drugs to cope with their illness and to relieve their symptoms (Compton et al., 2000). Using alcohol and drugs may make them feel happier, more cheerful, or less anxious. This may be more accurate with adult populations than with adolescents, whose early alcohol and drug abuse might cause a psychiatric disorder. Abuse of alcohol and drugs may lead to fits of rage, depression, and suicide attempts. Even when substance abuse is not the result or cause of a psychiatric disorder, these mental health problems can exacerbate substance abuse. The high-risk hypothesis and the susceptibility hypothesis each suggest how substance abusers may be prone to other disorders. Alcoholics and drug addicts are often in high-risk situations. Buying and dealing drugs put them in dangerous places with dangerous people. Alcoholics and drug addicts are easier targets for sexual abuse, rape, physical assaults, and serious accidents. The substance abuser is more vulnerable to post–traumatic stress disorder (PTSD) after experiencing these life events. PTSD is a common co-morbid disorder with substance abuse. Those who grew up in alcoholic homes where physical and emotional abuse occurred are also at risk of PTSD.

The American Medical Association estimates that nearly 40 percent of alcohol abusers and over 50 percent of drug abusers have a serious mental illness. The 2007 National Survey on Drug Use and Health estimated that 5.6 million adults aged eighteen or older have both serious psychological distress and substance use disorders (SAMHSA, 2008). Those with major depression were far more likely to have used an illicit drug within the past year than those without depression (27.4 versus 12.8 percent). It is some-times necessary for an individual to go through complete withdrawal from the substance in order to determine if the symptoms are due to a serious psychiatric condition or are the result of substance abuse. In the late 1960s and early 1970s, many young people were admitted to mental hospitals ex-periencing hallucinations and delusions that were actually brought on by drug use. Detoxification from the alcohol or drugs can take days or weeks depending on the substance abused.

Detoxification of the body may be life-threatening in some cases and should be accomplished with medical help. With prescribed medication in-stead of "cold turkey" withdrawal, the individual is in less danger and the withdrawal is less painful. Good nutrition, exercise, participation in indi-vidual and group treatments, medications, and other treatment options are combined to treat those with dual diagnosis. Integrated treatment enhances access to care by ensuring that substance abuse and mental health services are provided within one setting, combining these services to thus improve care of clients with dual disorders (Drake, O'Neal, and Wallach, 2008). While there is emerging consensus in the treatment field that patients with co-occurring disorders need combined mental health and substance abuse treatment, the effectiveness of integrated treatment has yet to be estab-lished (Tiet and Mausbach, 2007). Overall, there are low rates of treatment for those with dual disorders, and even lower rates among those who may receive mental health care but not the substance abuse treatment they also need (Harris and Edlund, 2005). In 2006, of all those deemed in need of treatment for dual diagnosis, only 10.4 percent received treatment for both mental health problems and specialty substance abuse treatment (SAMHSA, 2008). A recent review of treatments for dual-diagnosis pa-tients does not show any one clear or preferable treatment approach (Mar-tino, 2007). These findings reflect that treatment of co-occurring disorders is a new area of research where further development of treatment models and strategies is needed (McGovern et al., 2006; Sacks, Chandler, and Gonzales, 2008).

Use of Prescription Drugs

The National Institute of Drug Abuse (NIDA) reports that the prescription drugs most often abused are opioids, depressants, and stimulants. Non-medical use of prescription drugs has become a serious public health prob-lem. Prescription drug misuse ranks behind marijuana and ahead of co-caine, heroin, methamphetamine, and other drugs. Dealing with this misuse challenges authorities to balance prevention, education, and enforcement with safeguarding legitimate access to controlled substances. Even appropriate use of prescription drugs can be problematic, especially for those with mental health problems. In May 2007 the Food and Drug Administration ordered pharmaceutical companies to add warnings on antidepressant medications stating that youths and adults up to age twenty-five may be at increased risk for suicide (Carey, 2007).

Approximately 48.7 million US citizens have made nonmedical use of prescription drugs at least once in their lifetimes. More important, approximately 6.4 million reported past-month nonmedical use of prescription drugs (SAMHSA, 2005b). In 2006, 2.6 million people aged 12 or older used prescription drugs nonmedically for the first time within a one-year period (SAMHSA, 2007a). While men are twice as likely to use marijuana than are women, their current use percentage of illicit drugs is 10.2, compared with women's 6.1. However, the genders are equal when it comes to the nonmedical use of prescription drugs. The young adult age group (18–25) ranks highest in the nonmedical use of pain relievers (SAMHSA, 2005b). In 2004 there were an estimated 581,403 emergency department visits for nonmedical use of prescription drugs. And in 2005 there were a total of 1,849,548 treatment admissions for all types of drugs. A total of 3.7 percent (67,887) of admissions were for nonmedical use of prescription drugs (SAMHSA, 2006a).

It is well-known that pharmaceutical companies are the largest profit-makers in the world. Whether drugs are developed to assist patients in getting well or whether the profit motive has become more important is the subject of debate. A 2008 study in the *New England Journal of Medicine* found clinical trials reporting low effectiveness of antidepressants are not likely to be published (Turner et al., 2008). Ninety-four percent of studies showing positive effects of antidepressants were published, compared with only 14 percent of studies with disappointing or uncertain results.

Conclusion

A scientific understanding of drugs and their effects needs to remove the moral and political lenses through which substances are viewed, and return to the specific effects that they have on the body and mind. Thousands of substances act to stimulate or depress the central nervous system or cause disruption of information or awareness; they are known by their chemical names, proprietary or trade names, and street names. Users use them alone or in conjunction with other psychoactive substances, which can add to, subtract from, or potentiate drug effects. For each drug, prevalence of use rises and falls dramatically over the decades, as we have seen with crack cocaine and marijuana. A wide range of risk factors combine to create drug abuse syndromes; several vicious cycles cause abuse to progress into addiction, including tolerance, dependence, and loss of control. Finally, cultures and subcultures impose expectations on users that color their perception of drug effects and intoxicated behaviors.

PART 2

Diverse Populations: Patterns of Substance Use and Abuse

4 Children and Adolescents

There are as many different faces of the alcohol and drug user as there are different drinking and drug-using contexts. Social class standing, race, gender, and age each affect the picture of substance use and abuse. The theme of diversity within the world of alcohol and drug use will be discussed in the next several chapters of this text. This chapter introduces the concept of "diverse populations" and examines the substance use and abuse of children and adolescents. We will focus on those substances more closely associated with the youth culture: alcohol, marijuana, inhalants, steroids, and designer or club drugs.

In the 1970s the National Institute on Alcohol Abuse and Alcoholism (NIAAA) in Rockville, Maryland, designated "special populations" as a research priority. The category has since grown and expanded to include many different populations, such as Native Americans, the elderly, and women. In the twenty-first century, we study "diverse populations" rather than "special populations."

It is not easy to think about children and teenagers as users of alcohol and drugs, yet there are substance users and abusers within these age groups. Adolescent alcohol and drug use has been identified as a serious social problem for many years. For example, news reports in the early 2000s have focused on "robo-tripping" (drinking Robitussin cough syrup) by children and teens. Middle-school children abuse cold medicines, and many stores have taken medications like Robitussin, Nyquil, Sudafed, and Coricidin (nicknamed "chiclets" because of their appearance) off the open shelves and placed them in the pharmacy area.

Historical Recognition

Children and adolescents have used alcohol and drugs for centuries, and in many cultures around the world, substance use is part of rituals and traditions. In colonial America, ale was a food substance that everyone of every age drank. This was clearly before drinking or drug use was considered a problem. In the United States the definition of childhood drinking or other drug use as problematic can be traced back to Prohibition. The films *Reefer Madness* (1936) and Elmer Clifton's *Assassin of Youth* (1937) were produced around the hysteria associated with the passage of the 1937 Marijuana Tax Act. The representation of teenage alcohol and drug use as a serious social problem is evident in many other films, such as *High School Confidential* (1958), that were popular at the time (Starks, 1982). These films were intended to frighten parents and warn of the dangers of drug use by kids.

The temperance movement was successful at using selective prohibition (minimum drinking age) as a strategy toward total prohibition, achieved in 1920. When Prohibition was repealed by the Twenty-first Amendment in 1933, the temperance movement still had some power to influence lawmakers, and a compromise was made that returned selective prohibition (minimum drinking age) to the table. The rationale was that adults could drink responsibly but children could not (Males, 1996). At this time, each state determined drinking ages. Many states used twenty-one as an age of majority for purchasing alcohol, but in some states it was as low as eighteen. During the Vietnam War when the slogans cried out, "Old enough to die for your country but not old enough to drink," nearly all states lowered the drinking age to eighteen.

Mothers Against Drunk Driving (MADD), led by Candace Lightner in the early 1980s, emerged as a leader in a new social movement that was aimed at raising the minimum drinking age. Several studies in the 1970s and 1980s focused on the serious problems of teenage drinking and driving. This social movement was as successful as the earlier temperance movement in achieving national legislation. The National Minimum Drinking Age Act was passed in 1984. States that did not comply with this act would lose a portion of federal funding for highways. At this writing, the national minimum drinking age is twenty-one, and it is illegal for anyone under that age to purchase or consume alcohol.

Description of Substance Abuse of Children and Adolescents

In 2006, of youth from the ages of twelve to seventeen, 32.9 percent drank alcohol within the past year, 17 percent smoked cigarettes, and 13.2 percent smoked marijuana (SAMHSA, 2007a). An important concern is children's easy access to alcohol and drugs. Research on preteen drinking noted that children and teens are very resourceful when it comes to accessing alcohol and drugs. Sometimes they get adults to purchase alcohol for them. At other times, shoplifting is done to acquire alcohol, especially for obtaining beer from grocery stores. Occasionally, teens are able to acquire false identification, and some teens know retailers who will not check identification. Often getting booze is as simple as raiding a parent's liquor cabinet (Faiia, 1991; SAMHSA, 2008). There have been examples of teens calling up for "take-out" orders that include alcohol as well as food, on the premise that it may be less obvious if a delivery of food accompanies the alcohol order. Many children and teens also raid the home medicine cabinet in order to get prescription drugs. See Box 4.1 for a discussion of how teens use the Internet to acquire alcohol and drugs.

Use of alcohol, cigarettes, inhalants, and other drugs by children and adolescents causes concern for parents, teachers, and peers. Preteens and teens are starting to use harmful and illegal substances at younger ages, and this affects many areas of their life. Family relationships, overall health, physical growth, emotional development, and school performance may all be negatively affected by alcohol and drug use. While most children and teens will try experimenting with alcohol and drugs, many will never develop a serious problem. For some, however, the experimentation may lead to more extensive use and eventually cause problems. Some children may be heavy users of spirits such as whiskey, vodka, and gin and require hospitalization for alcohol poisoning (Weinberg and Wyatt, 2006), even after just one episode of heavy drinking. For teenagers who abuse alcohol or drugs, there may be encounters with the law. Possession of an illegal substance or driving under the influence can bring a teen into the juvenile or criminal justice system. If the use of alcohol and drugs develops into dependence and addiction, this can lead to serious harm and the potential for lifelong problems. At this writing, it is known that the earlier the age the child begins substance use, the more likely alcohol and drug problems are to develop.

The Monitoring the Future surveys examine the alcohol and drug use of US students in the eighth, tenth, and twelfth grades. This survey is sponsored by the National Institute of Drug Abuse (NIDA) and conducted by the University of Michigan. The year 2007 marked the 33rd national survey and revealed that overall illicit drug use is declining among adolescents (Johnston et al., 2007). Rates of drug use at that time were 13 percent of eighth graders, 28 percent of tenth graders, and 36 percent of twelfth graders. Both the Monitoring the Future survey and the National Survey on Drug Use and Health reflect decreases in the use of ecstasy and

Box 4.1   Teens, the Internet, and Drugs

Many teenagers work and have their own credit cards. Most young people have access to computers at home, at school, and at the public library. The combination of these realities results in teenagers being able to make purchases over the Internet and to have those purchases charged to their credit cards and delivered anywhere they choose. There is a growing market on the Internet for prescription drugs, and illegal pharmacy websites are providing opportunities for the consumers to bypass specific state and federal laws that regulate the sale of narcotics and other prescriptions. Many dangers are inherent in this practice. Individuals may not be aware of certain drug interactions, and, when they are not in a relationship with a doctor or pharmacist, their ignorance may be fatal. Also there are no real safeguards against tainted products being purchased, and there is no need of proof of a legal prescription to access the drugs. One study found that teenagers easily access prescription drugs on the Internet—94 percent of websites that advertised prescription drugs in 2006 did not actually require a physician's prescription (CASA, 2006b). From 2004 to 2007 there was an increase in websites offering prescription drugs for sale. However, in 2008 there was a decline in the number of websites offering prescription drugs without a physician's prescription, to 85 percent (CASA, 2008).

Hallucinogenic drugs have regained popularity among teenagers and young adults, and the Internet is proving to be a valuable resource in procuring hallucinogens (Halpern and Pope, 2001). Websites give information on how to obtain, synthesize, identify, and ingest hallucinogens. Some sites explain how to identify wild plants like mushrooms that are hallucinogenic. Information is easily accessible on ornamental botanicals, like the San Pedro cactus, that contain hallucinogenic properties and are readily available at garden stores. Up-to-date information on botanical and synthetic hallucinogens is available, with some sites having recipes for synthesizing hallucinogens. Internet-savvy teens can bypass the usual channels of information in textbooks and medical sources and learn what they need to know about acquiring drugs online.

Ryan Haight was an 18-year-old from California who purchased painkillers over the Internet and died of an overdose on February 12, 2001. In response to his death, Senators Dianne Feinstein of California and Norm Coleman of Minnesota proposed "The Ryan Haight Act." This legislation was intended to allow the continued use of the Internet to purchase legally prescribed drugs by adults but to close the loopholes that have allowed the illegal pharmacy sites to operate. However, the "Ryan Haight Internet Pharmacy Consumer Protection Act of 2005" was not passed into law.

LSD from 2002 to 2004, with a trend toward leveling off in 2005 (SAMHSA, 2007a). Alcohol use, however, is another story.

Alcohol

Alcohol remains the number-one drug used by children and adolescents in the United States. Of students reporting drinking alcohol within the last thirty days in 2006, 16 percent were eighth graders, 33 percent were tenth graders, and 44 percent were twelfth graders (Johnston et al., 2007). Overall, in 2006, of those who were current drinkers, 3.9 percent were 12 or 13, 15.6 percent were 14 or 15, 29.7 percent were age 16 or 17, and 51.6 percent were 18 to 20 years old (SAMHSA, 2007a). One report found that some teens were drinking five to six times a month (American Academy of Pediatrics, 2006). Both teenage girls and teenage boys reported drinking, although girls reported fewer drinks per occasion than boys. Girls averaged three drinks per drinking occasion, and boys about five. Older teens (18- and 19-year-olds) reported "blackout" drinking, where their memory of the drinking spree was impaired or missing. In the early 1990s, several authors noted that girls were catching up to boys in their substance use (Gfellner and Hundleby, 1994; Gullotta, Adams, and Montemayer, 1995). The gender gap in substance abuse narrowed over ten years ago for all ages and had nearly disappeared in the mid-1990s in the adolescent population.

Although the minimum legal drinking age (MLDA) was raised to twenty-one in each state, thousands of underage kids drink. Over time, national surveys by the NIDA indicate that there is heavy episodic drinking in the underage group and that the survey respondents reported very little difficulty in obtaining alcohol (Dunn and Goldman, 1998; Ellickson, Tucker, and Klein, 2003; Klitzner et al., 1992). In the early 1990s, research into preteen drinking showed that children thirteen years old and younger had access to alcohol and were experimenting with it (Faiia, 1991). Marjorie Faiia spoke with junior high and elementary school janitors, bus drivers, and teachers and found that evidence of the presence of alcohol was clear (e.g., empty "nips" in the school trash, an empty bottle of Southern Comfort under the seat in the back of the school bus). In one interview with a teacher from a parochial grammar school, the respondent reported that several girls were "throwing up" during a middle-school (sixth, seventh, and eighth grade) dance. A confiscated perfume bottle contained vodka instead of perfume. Many of the respondents stated they procured their alcohol from home or from older friends who worked in convenience stores and grocery stores.

Youth access to alcohol does not come only through pilfering from home or shoplifting. Some buyers use older kids or "adult strangers" as vendors. Evidence from police undercover "sting" operations show that merchants sell alcohol to minors. In one survey, 97 percent of the underage decoys were able to purchase a six-pack of beer (Preusser, Williams, and Weinstein, 1994). Since the late 1990s, tighter restrictions have been placed on the sale of alcohol to minors, with increased sanctions for liquor stores selling to underage drinkers.

Binge drinking is defined as four or more drinks on one occasion for girls and five or more drinks in one sitting for boys. In the early 2000s, binge drinking began early—at 13 years old—peaked around 18 years, and gradually declined after the age of 22 (National Institute on Alcohol Abuse and Alcoholism, 2002). Nearly 20 percent of young drinkers are described as "binge drinkers." In 2006 the rate of binge drinking was 1.5 percent for 12- or 13-year-olds, 8.9 percent for those 14 or 15, 20 percent for 16- or 17-year-olds, and 36.2 percent for those 18 to 20. Binge drinking in girls can be viewed as an act of rebellion and as a way to shed the "good girl" image and adopt the "bad girl" image (Best et al., 1995). "Bad girls" are seen as more of a "turn-on" than are "good girls." Since girls often hang out with boys who are older, they may start using alcohol and drugs at younger ages (Gullotta et al., 1995).

One study found that binge drinking in adolescents showed incredible diversity in drinking patterns, depending on exposure to pro-drug environments, deviant behaviors, and demographic differences (Tucker, Orlando, and Ellickson, 2003). Despite the diversity, binge drinking universally affects these adolescents in adverse ways. It lowers academic performance, impairs memory, causes verbal skill deficiencies, and alters the ability to perceive reality (Brown, Tapert, Granholm, and Delis, 2000). Additionally, the social costs of binge drinking by teens are very high, especially when it results in dangerous and foolish behaviors. The four main accidental death categories (car accidents, falls, fires, and drowning) are related to substance use and abuse. Further, much youth vandalism and crime, along with suicide, is related to alcohol and drug use. Heavy use is related to increases in violent offenses for both boys and girls (Bachman and Peralta, 2002).

The social background of the children and adolescents is a crucial variable in substance use and abuse. Children living with substance abusers have easier access to alcohol and drugs, have less supervision, and also have role models who are substance abusers themselves.

Gaining social status with one's peer group or social entrée into a group through drinking is another important factor. For many young drinkers, imbibing is a way to demonstrate adult status and for boys a way to display their masculinity (Broom, 1995). Getting drunk is seen as a rite of passage and has replaced traditional puberty rites in many cultures (Peake, 1994). Binge drinking, even including vomiting together, is an aspect of this transition into adulthood and is seen as part of a social bonding experience (Bui, 1993). The use of alcohol and drugs creates an image for the young drinker, and it may accompany entrance into a peer group (Odgers, Houghton, and Douglas, 1996). Young people drink to make social encounters go smoothly, to reduce stress and tension in their lives, and to make it easier to "hook up" with the opposite sex (Thomas, 1995). Early drinkers and nondrinkers have been compared on the prevalence of behavior problems and school problems at grade seven, grade twelve, and finally at age twenty-three (Ellickson et al., 2003). Problems for early drinkers included academic difficulties, substance abuse problems, and deviant and violent behavior. By early adulthood, the early drinkers had employment problems and substance abuse problems, and had developed criminal behavior.

Anyone familiar with college social life can describe Thursday nights in the residence halls. These events, referred to as "Thirsty Thursdays," have caused concern and alarm on many campuses nationwide. It used to be that weekend partying began on Friday night, usually taking place off campus or in a fraternity house. In the 2000s, the weekend can begin on Thursday night with partying going on within the residence halls. Many educators and college administrators are very concerned about "Thirsty Thursdays," although few intervene. The practice is an extension of high school drinking behavior, known as "Thursday night" or "group party" night. Students coming from all over the country arrive on college campuses with knowledge of these social drinking norms. Absenteeism and poor performance in Friday morning classes is a topic discussed by many a college professor. For further discussion of college drinking, see Chapter 9.

Unfortunately, adolescents—like adults—drink and drive. The fact that they are inexperienced drivers puts them at higher risk of accidents, further exacerbated by underage drinking and the potential for arrest. Traffic traumas and daily headlines recounting youth deaths tied to drinking are commonplace (Vaznis, 2007). Indeed, motor vehicle accidents are the number-one cause of death for 15- to 20-year-olds (National Highway Traffic Safety Administration, 2007). In 2005, of young drivers killed in a car accident, 28 percent had been drinking. Gender differences are seen here, with boys much more likely to be involved in fatal crashes. In 2005, of 15- to 20-year-old males involved in fatal crashes, 24 percent had been drinking at the time of the crash, double the number (12 percent) of female drivers.

Marijuana

Very popular with junior high and high school students, marijuana is identified by many students as their drug of choice. It is by far the most widely used illicit drug by youth and adults. Many young people consider marijuana harmless and see no long-term effects.

Patterns of marijuana use show a slight decline in the 2000s. Results of the Monitoring the Future survey (2007) indicate a drop in marijuana use by tenth and twelfth graders. The prevalence of marijuana use was 10 percent of eighth graders, 25 percent of tenth graders, and 32 percent of twelfth graders.

The marijuana grown in the 2000s is not the same as the "weed" that was smoked by the young people at Woodstock, the famed 1969 concert. In the 1960s and the 1970s, marijuana was frequently grown in home gardens. Marijuana of the 2000s is far more potent, due to hydroponic farming techniques and selective-seed plantings. The potency of marijuana is determined by the level of tetrahydrocannabinol (THC) present. Levels of 3.5 percent are found in average marijuana, 7–9 percent can be found in higher-grade "dope," and as much as 8–14 percent is in hashish, or "hash" (Hahn, Payne, and Mauer, 2005). This strain of marijuana is more harmful to users, yet most children and many of their parents believe that marijuana is relatively harmless. Early and consistent marijuana use has been associ-

©iStockphoto.com/jabejon

ated with medical problems in later life, including intestinal problems and a loss of sense of smell (Ellickson, Martino, and Collins, 2004).

Marijuana is very easy for teens to access. In 2006, of those 2.1 million people who used marijuana for the first time within the past year, 63.3 percent were younger than age 18 (SAMHSA, 2007a). For those 12–17 years old, 4.7 percent had used marijuana for the first time. "Pushers" and sellers are readily available, approaching boys older than 15 more often than girls or younger students.

For many years it has been suggested that marijuana is a "gateway" drug, that is, one that opens the door to more serious drug abuse, as in heroin and cocaine addictions. While marijuana may operate as a gateway drug, it is not necessarily a cause of later, hard drug use (Morral, McCaffrey, and Paddock, 2002). Factors besides marijuana use may be more predictive of young people beginning to use hard drugs. The opportunity to use drugs and individual interest in hard drug use may be better predictors. It is more likely that tobacco and alcohol are gateway drugs to a greater extent than marijuana.

Inhalants

Despite the "War on Drugs" and all efforts to reduce substance use, the young continue to use drugs. Among many young people, there is a naiveté about the nature of drug use and an attitudinal minimization of the potential harmful outcomes. Ordinary household products like glue, nail polish, and cleaning sprays also are considered to be harmless by young people. This contributes to a growing problem involving children inhaling these products.

In 2006, of the 783,000 who used inhalants for the first time within the past year, 77.2 were under the age of 18 (SAMHSA, 2007a). The average age of first use of inhalants in 2006 was 15.7 years. In 2007, inhalant use for first-time users dropped to 775,000 persons, with 63.3 percent under age 18 at first use. The average age of first use was 17.1 in 2007 (SAMHSA, 2008). "Huffing" and "sniffing" have also been reported as activities of middle- and high school students. Huffing is when the inhalant is taken in through the mouth; and sniffing, through the nose. Inhaling these substances can cause serious medical conditions, including sudden death. Inhaling glue or other toxins shuts off the oxygen supply to the brain and poisons the users. Inhalants may be the first substance that children experiment with to get high. Children who live in home situations where there is alcohol or substance abuse are more likely to experiment with inhaling fumes (American Academy of Pediatrics, 1996; Anderson and

Loomis, 2003). It is possible that this very youthful substance abuse can later lead to adult substance abuse. Illicit drugs like cocaine and heroin may be more attractive to individuals with some previous experience with getting high.

In the early 2000s, by the time students were in the seventh grade, one out of five reported that they had tried huffing (National Institute of Health, 2004). Since the substances that are inhaled are legal and do give pleasurable feelings, they may not be thought of as drug abuse by young users (see Box 4.2). Most of these substances depress the central nervous system and produce a relaxed feeling. However, these substances are toxic and contain chemicals that can produce serious medical problems.

Box 4.2   Huffing or Hide-and-Seek?

"Huffing," the practice of inhaling fumes to get high, is attractive to adolescents because the products that are inhaled are readily available and cheap. A nationwide survey by the National Institute on Drug Abuse (2001) found that children twelve years old and younger reported that they knew someone, a fellow classmate or a friend, who "huffed." The peak years of inhalant use by eighth, tenth, and twelfth graders were the mid-1990s. After a decrease in use in 2001, inhalant use again spiked in 2005 and then declined in 2007 (Johnston et al., 2007; SAMHSA, 2008).

Most children are unaware of the deadly consequences of inhaling fumes from these toxic substances. Cloths are soaked in inhalants and put into the mouth, or paper bags and plastic bags are sprayed with aerosol products, and the users breathe in freely from the bags. Paint thinner, correction fluids, felt-tip markers, and gasoline are inhaled to get high. There are literally thousands of common household supplies that can be abused as inhalants—gases from butane lighters, whipped cream aerosols, spray paints, deodorant, and upholstery protection sprays.

In one case, several children (as young as eight years old) were observed hanging around a local dry-cleaning establishment. The owners were concerned about vandalism, so they closely watched the kids. To their amazement, they saw that the kids were taking turns breathing in the fumes that were being vented out of the dry-cleaning machines. Members of the group of playmates (all under thirteen) were questioned and freely admitted that they were "getting high" and "having fun." Unfortunately, huffing or sniffing inhalants has replaced hide-and-seek as an after-school pastime for some children.

Steroids

Another area of concern regarding young people and drug use involves a student population that is not typically identified in drug abuse discussions. High school athletes and student leaders are usually admired and respected; however, some of these students use anabolic steroids. Anabolic steroids function like the male sex hormone, testosterone. Injected or taken orally, steroids can cause a teenager to gain weight, strength, endurance, muscle, and aggression. Female athletes who take steroids face the same side effects as males, including liver cancer and high blood pressure. As early as 1990 the American Medical Association warned against the nonmedical use of steroids by young people and urged an increase in penalties for distributing steroids to minors.

Student athletes use these drugs to aid in competitions by bolstering their physical performance (Bahrke and Yesalis, 1994; Zickler, 2000). Anabolic-androgenic steroids (AAS) can cause both behavioral and personality changes. Mood and attitude toward self and others can also be affected. Although many users are dedicated weight trainers, the use of AAS is not confined to professional athletes. One study found steroid use among girls was strongly associated with female fighting, and the use of smokeless tobacco by boys was strongly associated with risky sexual behavior (Miller et al., 2005).

Steroid users engage in many harmful activities as part of their drug use (Miller et al., 2005; Peters, Copeland, and Dillon, 1999). These include self-taught injection procedures; injecting specifically into muscles like those in the calves; "stacking," which is concurrent use of different steroids; and use of other drugs such as diuretics and insulin.

Steroid users face many of the same health risks as other drug users. Among the negative physical health effects are retention of fluid, acne, hypertension, and painful injection sites. As always, with illegal injections there are risks of hepatitis and HIV. For women who are steroid users, there is often a change in the voice and onset of menstrual irregularities. Personality changes and negative effects for both sexes include more aggressive attitudes, including violent behaviors (Miller et al., 2005). After prolonged use, tolerance develops for the drugs and symptoms of withdrawal occur when trying to stop (see Box 4.3). These negative health risks can be motivators for individuals to stop using steroids (Peters et al., 1999). The 2007 Monitoring the Future survey showed greatest use in the late 1990s and early 2000s. At this writing, use is 1.1 percent among eighth graders, 1.7 percent among tenth graders, and 2.3 percent in twelfth graders (Johnston et al., 2007). This can be attributed to reduced supply—

Box 4.3   Is the High School Quarterback on Anabolic Steroids?

Anabolic steroids are used by bodybuilders and athletes to "bulk up" and to build muscle mass. Steroids can be taken in pill form or injected right into the muscle. Nonmedical use of steroids to improve appearance and to improve muscle growth is illegal and dangerous. Despite their danger, these drugs remain popular because they give users the stamina to train harder. Users also claim steroids help them to relax after strenuous exercise, and because steroids can increase the athlete's level of aggression, they make the athlete more competitive. When the levels of aggression are raised too high, however, the result is known as "roid rage." Brand names include Sustanon 250, Deca-Durabolin, and Anavar, among others.

The long-term effects of steroid use with exercise can build muscle. However, when used during puberty, they can impede normal development. The sex drive is initially enhanced in steroid users, but over time it decreases and becomes depressed. Men may have lower sperm counts and may develop enlarged breasts. Side effects include high blood pressure, trembling, liver tumors, jaundice, and more. Many substances sold as steroids are fake or contaminated, further compounding the dangers. Moreover, steroid users are also involved with other drug use and frequently use painkillers (Wines et al., 1999).

Young people who use steroids generally get them from friends, coaches, other athletes, and drug dealers. Friends, nonmedical handbooks, and fitness magazines are the primary sources for information regarding anabolic steroids. These sources are not always accurate, and there is much false information available to young people.

The 2007 Mitchell report on the widespread use of steroids among professional baseball players may give the message to young athletes that steroid use is acceptable and even required to excel in sports.

---

the Anabolic Steroid Control Act of 2004 added more drugs to the Schedule III list, expanded the authority of the Drug Enforcement Administration, and increased penalties. Education also may be a factor in reducing steroid use.

Designer Drugs and Club Drugs

One way to measure substance use by children and adolescents is to examine hospital admissions. Emergency room hospitalizations have increased for overdoses of the drug ketamine. Ketamine, or "Special K," is one of the popular club drugs, usually snorted and done in groups. While it is commonly taken intranasally, ketamine is emerging as a popular drug among a hidden population of injection drug users (Lankenau and Clatts, 2004). It produces dissociative sensations, and users report dreamlike, hallucinatory effects. Injecting ketamine either intravenously or intramuscularly produces a very intense high known as the "k-hole." In the k-hole, time is suspended and the person experiences hallucinations. The hidden population of ketamine injection users is found in street youths, runaways, and homeless youths. This population survives by the "hustle" (getting needs met by deceitful means) and by selling sex. This poses the same threat of health risks, disease transmission, and problems as for any illegal injection drug use.

Designer drugs are synthetic drugs developed in home laboratories. Often designer drugs have controlled-drug counterparts. For example, ecstasy (MDMA or XTC) produces positive feelings, mild hallucinogenic experiences, and enhanced alertness, which contribute to their popularity with young people. Amphetamines do not occur in nature and are completely lab created. Once prescribed for dieters because they decrease hunger and speed up the metabolism, amphetamines have been found to be very addictive and to contribute to increased heart rate and blood pressure. Known also as "speed," "crank," "ice," and "zip," amphetamines are also popular with the young. Phencyclidine (PCP, or angel dust) is a depressant, a stimulant, a hallucinogen, and an anesthetic, so the effects of PCP will vary. Many users report feelings of paranoia and extreme aggressive behavior. PCP can accumulate in cells, causing brutal and bizarre behavior long after initial use (Hahn et al., 2005).

Tranquilizers such as Valium, Quaalude, and Librium are frequently combined with alcohol for the synergistic effect. The date rape drugs like gamma hydroxybutyrate (GHB, "G," "liquid ecstasy," "Georgia home boy"), Rohypnol ("roofies"), and ketamine (Special K, "cat") discussed above show up at many parties and gatherings of young people (NIDA, 2006). "Roofies" combined with alcohol are attractive to young people who enjoy the depressant effects and the social image of the drug (Thio, 2001). In 1996 the Drug Induced Rape Prevention and Punishment Act made it a federal crime to slip someone a drug in order to carry out a sexual assault (Hahn et al., 2005).

Lysergic acid diethylamide-25 (LSD, or "acid"), popular in the 1960s, showed a sharp decline from 2001 to 2006. The annual prevalence rate at this writing is between 1.1 and 2.1 percent of students in the eighth, tenth, and twelfth grades (Johnston et al., 2007).

Experimentation with alcohol and drugs is a very likely occurrence for teens. As noted above, many who experiment will stop using alcohol and drugs as they mature, but even experimentation can lead to problems. This exposes users to the harmful and health-threatening realities of substance abuse, such as, in the extreme, death by alcohol poisoning from a single episode of excessive drinking. Polysubstance abuse (the use of two or more substances at a time), not unusual for the adolescent population, is a very dangerous pattern of drug use that tends to get established in late adolescence (Collins, Ellickson, and Bell, 1999). Combining different drugs and different doses can result in a synergistic drug effect that exaggerates the effects of each drug (Hahn et al., 2005).

Indicators of Substance Abuse

There is some difficulty in determining the extent of childhood and adolescent alcohol and drug use. Since it is illegal and therefore a deviant behavior, it is hidden. It comes to our attention when there is an accident or some serious problem. The media may alarm the public with exaggerated claims or continued coverage of one event. However, any use of alcohol or drugs by youth can be considered problematic.

Problem substance abusers may not always be heavy users or addicted. They may not drink or take drugs regularly; however, when they do, they have problems. Moreover, the likelihood of problems developing from substance abuse is greater for them than for adults.

Some common symptoms among substance-abusing adolescents is a change in sleep patterns—needing much more or much less sleep than in the past. A decline in school performance and interest in completing homework can be another sign. Changes in adolescent behavior toward family, friends, and teachers can be hints as well. While no one change in behavior may signal substance use, a range of different behaviors can signal a problem. Family members may engage in denial of the problem in the same way as the substance abuser. Clinical practitioners working with adolescent substance abusers report that it may take many months before parents recognize the signs of substance abuse in their children.

Society is ambivalent about substance use, encouraging substance use in many different contexts and defining abuse differently for different populations at different times. This can be seen in the marketing of alcohol to children and teens. A powerful industry entices the youth market. "Zippers" are 24-proof (12 percent alcohol) gelatin shots much like homemade "jello-shots" that are popular with teens. They are packaged like snack packs that are made by large food corporations. The sale of zipper shots in grocery and convenience stores began in 1999. Zippers are advertised over the Internet with the use of soft pornographic images, and this advertising is not limited to those over the age of twenty-one (National Association of African Americans for Positive Imagery, 2007).

Clearly, the government needs to address the marketing and promotion of alcohol and drugs to minors (see Box. 4.4). More programs need to be developed for families and children, as well as increased media outlets on the harmful effects of substance abuse.

Box 4.4   Selling of Alcohol and Drugs to Minors

Legal drugs and alcohol are advertised and promoted heavily with many advertising campaigns aimed at young people. Previous research found that images of teens using alcohol on television were prevalent, with more than 40 percent of programs portraying drinking teenagers (Lang, 1998).

The alcoholic beverage industry markets to young people through websites and trendy youth-oriented commercials. The images in these ads suggest that you will find a sexy mate, have good times, and, with the right brew, forget the hassles of work and study (Hahn et al., 2005). Alcohol advertisements frequently depict a world of freedom, usually a world without women or wives, one very attractive to male adolescents. Risk taking and meeting new challenges are also associated with beer advertisements.

The industries that produce alcohol and legal drugs are always looking for new markets. Through packaging, advertisement, and sales tactics, new drinkers or new legal drug users are sought. Wine coolers are marketed to drinking youths, and low-calorie alcoholic beverages appeal to many young girls. Aggressive ad campaigns use beach parties, athletic events, and celebrity rock stars to promote alcoholic products (Hahn et al., 2005). This is not a recent strategy; it has been suggested that Anheuser Busch bought Sea World in order to promote its beer. The park contains an extravagant beer museum, and free beer is given to adults. Data from the Center on Alcohol Marketing and Youth at Georgetown University in 2007 show alcohol advertising is shifting from magazines to television. From 2001 to 2006, alcohol ads fell by 22 percent, while the number of television ads grew by 33 percent (Center on Alcohol Marketing and Youth, 2007).

Everyone exposed to the advertising campaigns, including policymakers, internalizes the benign and attractive image created by advertising. A multibillion-dollar industry exists around alcohol and legal drugs, and one can only guess at the billions of dollars that are generated by the illegal drug industry. Clearly, the government needs to address the marketing and promotion of alcohol and drugs to minors in the media.

Treatment and Prevention

Treatment and prevention efforts for substance use and abuse among children and adolescents are broad and ongoing. The legislature, the school system, the family, and the community can offer important strategies to discourage or prevent underage drinking. These strategies involve implementing various programs and building alternative opportunities for substance-free activities. Some examples of legislative strategies to curb underage drinking and driving are raising the age of licensure, provisional licenses, and graduated licenses.

School strategies to control underage drinking can be built into the curriculum. These programs usually take a very wide view of substance use and abuse and include efforts at building self-esteem and self-confidence. Family strategies concentrate on educating parents; stronger parenting skills affect communication and interpersonal relations. An example of a partnership between schools and families is a situation in which parents host overnight parties at school after the prom to avoid underage drinking, driving, and horrific car accidents. Another example is that of schools arranging bus transportation for all prom attendees (Vaznis, 2007). Finally, community strategies emphasize community mobilization to stop illegal sales and advertising as well as community-based coalitions to provide a coordinated effort to prevent underage drinking and drug use.

Approaches to adolescent alcohol and drug use should be therapeutic and not punitive (Gans and Shook, 1994; Morral et al., 2006). A public health approach that emphasizes reducing access to alcohol and drugs, encouraging adolescents to learn refusal skills, and promoting close parental supervision should be emphasized. Parents, teachers, peers, community organizations, nurses, social workers, primary care professionals, physicians, and counselors play key roles. Alcohol and drug testing should be avoided on a routine basis. Preferably, alcohol and drug screening should be incorporated into a routine health history by pediatricians. There should be school-based prevention strategies. The government should increase restrictions on access to alcohol and its marketing, including advertising. Counteradvertising showing the negative facts about substance use and abuse should be programs that can be funded by taxing alcohol.

A critical issue is to distinguish "experimentation" with substances from the problematic use and abuse of substances by children and teens. Youthful experimentation can be treated within a school setting or by outpatient group counseling. Adolescents with a physical dependence on alcohol or another drug, estimated to be 8 percent of those who use substances, are likely to need inpatient treatment that begins with medication to help with withdrawal (SAMHSA, 2007a).

Conclusion

Alcohol and marijuana remain the substances most frequently used by youth, although patterns of their consumption can vary widely depending on the diverse environments in which children and adolescents live. In any case, the cultural and social foundations of the United States encourage the use of alcohol and drugs. The availability and access to alcohol and drugs are constant and easy, even for minors. Underage drinkers can procure alcohol in many creative ways, including buying alcohol over the Internet.

In addition to the marketing of alcohol and drugs, there are many social-policy issues that need to be addressed. An alcohol and drug strategy at the national level can establish guidelines for dealing with substance abuse issues among children and adolescents. Standards need to be developed to distinguish between youthful experimentation with substances and problematic alcohol and drug use. Young people consume alcohol mostly on weekends, and much of their consumption goes on in public. It is a social activity allowing drinking youth to feel more comfortable in social settings (Oostveen, Knibbe, and de Vries, 1996).

Further research needs to focus on the connections between substance use and juvenile delinquency, domestic violence, mental illness, and school problems. More educational programs are needed to alert the public and professionals in the field about the harmful effects of substance abuse. These programs should be integrated into the curriculum from the earliest grades. Substance abuse among children and adolescents is not only a personal or family problem, it is also a public health issue that requires developing solutions to the many social problems linked with alcohol and drug use.

5 Women and Substance Abuse

Women's substance abuse problems have been with us throughout history, yet it is only since the 1970s that professional attention has focused on helping women with drug and alcohol problems. This chapter provides a brief history of women's drinking, reviews indicators and correlates of women's substance abuse problems, and provides a comparison of the substance abuse problems of women and men. Special attention is given to the problems associated with prenatal substance abuse and children of alcoholics and addicts. The chapter concludes with a discussion of the treatment and prevention needs of substance-abusing women.

Historical Recognition

Historically, drug use was considered acceptable for women, to help them cope with daily stress and tension (Broom, 1995; Rienzi et al., 1996). Elixirs and tonics such as "Aunt Emily's Tonic," containing cocaine, were sold to women to build up their "weak" constitutions and help with fighting off the "vapors," fainting spells that upper-middle-class Victorian women were believed to suffer.

It was acceptable for women to drink at home and at social events in colonial America. While it was frowned upon for women to go to taverns, it was acceptable for women to work in the bars. Those women who drank to excess were branded promiscuous. By the middle of the eighteenth century, approximately one-half of bars were owned by women (National Center on Addiction and Substance Abuse [hereafter, CASA], 2006a). Following an English tradition, women who lived in cities and were widows were most likely to be granted a tavern license (Salinger, 2002). In 1771 in Charlestown, South Carolina, almost two-thirds of liquor licenses were held by women.

Women of the 1880s hid their opiate use from family and friends. Indeed, the majority of those addicted to opiates in the nineteenth century were educated and wealthy women who were given opiates to cope with melancholy and irritability (White, 1998). By the end of the nineteenth century, alcohol abuse by women was seen as a by-product of their greater independence from men. Greater social freedom and an emphasis on equality set the scene for greater alcohol and drug use by women. Alcohol and drug use became a symbolic indicator of the emancipation of women (CASA, 2006a). After the end of Prohibition in 1933, drinking among women increased. By 1939 approximately 39 percent of women drank; this rose to 60 percent in 1945 (CASA, 2006a).

As early as the end of the nineteenth century, it was known that the alcohol problems of women were qualitatively different from the drinking problems of men. It was thought that women had lower genetic vulnerability to alcoholism and a different progression, findings that years of research have borne out.

Description of Women's Substance Abuse Problems

Women's use and abuse of drugs and alcohol have fluctuated over time. While drinking increased among women after the end of Prohibition and into the 1990s, a decrease has been the case in the 2000s. In the early 1990s, 60 percent of US women were reported drinkers (Wilsnack, Wilsnack, and Hiller-Sturmhofel, 1994). At this writing, approximately 46 percent of women drink alcohol (SAMHSA, 2008). The overall decline in drinking among women may be related to the greater awareness of the problems women experience because of their drinking (CASA, 2006a). However, there are hundreds of medications available and marketed to women in order to help them cope with tension and daily stress, opening the door to different kinds of substance abuse problems. By 2003, 5.2 million women were abusing alcohol or considered alcohol dependent (SAMHSA, 2005b). In 2007, 12.5 percent of men were considered substance abusers, more than double the 5.7 percent of women with substance abuse problems (SAMHSA, 2008). The rate of illicit drug dependence in 2006 was 3.7 percent for men and 2.0 percent for women. Overall, white women from the ages of twenty-one to twenty-nine, single or living with a partner, and with an income of over $40,000 are at greater risk for heavier drinking (Caetano et al., 2006). Alcohol dependence in women is increasing among younger generations (Holdcraft and Iacono, 2002).

Differences Between the Substance Abuse Problems of Women and Men

Social norms have always directed women toward a higher standard of conduct, so that the rules that apply to women are different from those that apply to men. This "double standard" has been noted in every area of conduct, from dress codes to sexual behavior, with no exception for substance abuse. Societal attitudes and sanctions are harsher on the woman who breaks the norms surrounding alcohol and drug use than on males who do— perhaps because of women's association with parenting. Women's behavior is watched more closely, and there is less tolerance for norm breaking.

Male drinking often takes place in public with crowds of other drinkers, while female drinking is more likely to be hidden. Thus, norms sanctioning the drinking behavior of women have been stronger, and some cultures have very strong prohibitions against women drinking alcohol. While males are expected to drink, females are more likely expected to remain abstinent. Females are more likely to use alcohol and drugs to deal with the underlying tensions and stressors in their lives, in contrast to men, who drink more to feel uninhibited and deal with external pressures such as work and finances (Buelow and Buelow, 1995; National Institute on Alcohol Abuse and Alcoholism [hereafter, NIAAA,] 2006). Women who are married to problem drinkers often enable them and become codependents, making excuses for their husbands and helping to cover up the substance abuse. On the other hand, most men do not want their wives to be "lushes" and often respond to problem drinking with shaming and abandonment. In short, women must bear the stigma of addiction much more than men (Blume, 1991; United Nations Office on Drugs and Crime [hereafter, United Nations], 2004).

Attempting to avoid this stigma results in secretive alcohol and drug use that makes the problem "invisible" (Broom, 1995; CASA, 2006a). For a full-time homemaker, substance use can be easily hidden. When a woman does not have coworkers or does not leave the house, there are fewer opportunities to be recognized as a substance abuser. Women are often referred to as "closet drinkers," preferring the safety of drinking at home rather than in bars. As important, drinking alone at home reduces the chance of being stigmatized by the label "alcoholic." Of course, for all the drinking problems that we know about, there are certainly many women with alcohol and drug issues that remain hidden, and they therefore never receive help. However, with increasingly more women entering the workforce, the more likely they are to drink in public.

Stigma can be the most important psychosocial factor in distinguishing the substance abuse problems of men and women (Covington, 2002). Not surprisingly, substance-abusing women tend to have low self-esteem.

Additionally, some men view drinking women as, in their eyes, fair targets for sexual aggression, including rape (Tjaden and Thoennes, 2006). Stigma can also become attached to the family of a substance abuser, something families, especially those of financial means, seek to avoid (see Box 5.1).

Alcoholic women may find the alcohol helps them cope with experiences and situations of powerlessness with partners (Lammers, Schippers, and VanderStaak, 1995). The notion of an imbalance of power between men and women, and how this links with substance abuse issues and issues of treatment, has been the focus of some feminist thinking. Feminism questions research findings that are primarily based on men and challenges methods and treatments that do not address the specific needs of women. It is well-known that women are often introduced to substances by their partners and are unwittingly put in situations where they can become ensnared in the illegal behavior of their partners (see Box 5.2).

The idea that women are passive and powerless participants in the world of illegal drugs, exploited by men, has been challenged. Anderson (2005) ar-

---

Box 5.1   Janet's Alcoholism

Janet was a woman in her mid-fifties living in an expensive resort community. Her husband was an executive in a large national business firm. Owing to her family's wealth, Janet was asked to serve on the board of trustees of the local hospital. There were whispers at the hospital that Janet had a drinking problem. On one occasion at a hospital meeting, Janet seemed to see mice running across the floor—something no one else had observed.

Janet was admitted to the hospital with a diagnosis of gastritis, an inflammation of the stomach. Reviewing Janet's medical record, the social worker found that she had a history of numerous diagnostic procedures and hospitalizations for stomach problems. The social worker was amazed by the amount of medical intervention Janet had received, yet there was no indication that any professional had talked with Janet about her drinking. The social worker approached Janet's physician. He acknowledged that he had not intervened because he was not comfortable talking with Janet about drinking because of her family's high status in the community. The physician agreed to the social worker talking with Janet. Janet readily agreed to treatment for alcoholism and was admitted to a highly regarded inpatient treatment program in a neighboring state. Janet completed the monthlong program but returned to drinking very soon after discharge. She was found dead a short time later in her own front yard.

Source: Case reported by Sylvia Mignon, former director of social service at a community hospital in Massachusetts.

Box 5.2   Heroin and Mom

A five-year-old boy was found on a highway in Massachusetts. His mother, aged twenty-eight, had not reported her son missing even though four hours had passed. She thought her son was with another relative. Instead, she was left with trying to explain how heroin could have been found at the feet of her son.

The day after her son was returned home to her, police pulled over the mother as she made an illegal U-turn and noticed a bag of heroin (about the size of a softball) in the car at her son's feet. The mother explained that the car belonged to her boyfriend who was at her home caring for her two older children, ages six and eleven. She sobbed, "I'm not a bad mother." The family was known to the child protection agency in Massachusetts, the Department of Social Services (DSS), since the mother had left an abusive relationship. The commissioner of the DSS stated: "It's been four days since the incident; she has not been arrested. We have no evidence that she is a drug user or seller, and right now, we don't have any evidence that the children are at risk. If there is evidence that the child is at risk, we will then act. If she is arrested, we will act" (McPhee, 2006).

gued that women play an important role in the world of illegal drug sales and use. Women often purchase and sell drugs, provide housing and meals for those with drug problems, and support male drug dependency.

Biological Differences Between Women and Men

Significant biological dissimilarities exist between women and men with substance abuse problems (Brady and Ashley, 2005; CASA, 2006a). Differences between female and male drinkers include women's greater physical vulnerability to alcohol—that is, women experience earlier physical consequences of their drug and alcohol use than do men (Ackermann et al., 2005; Nelson-Zlupko, Kauffman, and Dore, 1995).

Women metabolize alcohol very differently from men. Female drinkers are also more likely to develop liver disease more quickly than men who drink. Alcoholic cirrhosis and alcoholic hepatitis are found in women after fewer years of daily drinking than in men. This is explained by the fact that a woman will have a higher concentration of alcohol in her blood than will a man drinking the same amount of alcohol as the woman, even though both are of comparable weight (Brady and Ashley, 2005). Women are more likely to develop specific problems earlier in their problem drinking, including cognitive deficits, alcoholic cardiomyopathy, and alcoholic liver disease (Ackermann et al., 2005). Degenerative diseases of the musculature and of the heart muscle develop more quickly in female drinkers. Women who drink are also more vulnerable to brain damage than male drinkers. More-over, mortality rates are higher for female drinkers than for their male coun-terparts (El-Guebaly, 1995; NIAAA, 2000a). One review of the literature found that death rates of female alcoholics were 50 to 100 percent higher than the death rates of alcoholic men (Walter et al., 2003).

Women are less likely than men to be cocaine addicts. In the 1980s, 30 to 40 percent of cocaine addicts, including crack, were women (CASA, 2006a). As with alcohol, women metabolize cocaine differently from men. Recent evidence shows that cocaine affects women's brains differently from the brains of men (Kilts et al., 2004). Hormonal changes over the course of the menstrual cycle also affect the use of cocaine. Women are less sensitive to cocaine and experience less euphoria and dysphoria. Without the extreme highs and lows, women are less likely to experience the rushes of cocaine use. Men notice cocaine's effects sooner than women and have greater phys-iological responses (e.g., increases in blood pressure). Lower sensitivity to the drug and the high cost of cocaine may explain why women are less likely to become cocaine addicts (Bowersox, 1996). However, in the early 2000s, more women became cocaine dealers (Anderson, 2005).

There are a host of other factors at play in the substance abuse prob-lems of women. Physicians more frequently prescribe tranquilizers for women that are, in fact, specifically marketed for women (Bowe, 1992). More frequent suicide attempts using substances are reported for female than for male substance abusers (CASA, 2006a). In addition, the rates of incarceration for drug-related offenses, rates of drug-related prostitution, violent crime, and reports of child neglect and abuse have all increased for women (Lex, 1994; CASA, 2006a).

Indicators of Substance Abuse in Women

A number of factors correlate with substance abuse among women, includ-ing parental substance abuse, a trauma history, and psychological problems. Studies note a link between female substance abuse and early childhood abuse, including sexual abuse (Covington, 2002; Johnsen and Harlow, 1996). In reality, the strongest predictor of substance abuse for females is a history of physical and sexual abuse (Girls and Substance Abuse, 2006). Substance-abusing women have high rates of trauma and repeated trauma in their lives (Brady and Ashley, 2005; McHugo et al., 2005). The reluc-

tance of women to acknowledge their trauma and the inability and unwill-ingncss of treatment programs to address trauma are added difficulties. Since childhood sexual abuse, including incest (sexual relations between relatives), is so deeply hidden, the relationship between substance abuse and a history of sexual abuse may not receive the attention of treatment pro-fessionals. Further, for women, there is a higher risk of sexual encounters with strangers, which puts women in possibly dangerous situations.

The actual relationship between alcohol and drug use and female sex-ual activity has not been studied as much as that of the association between male sexuality and substance use. Not surprisingly, a complex set of situa-tional variables and individual characteristics determines the effects of al-cohol on behavior. Women who drink are at a greater risk for sexual assault. It is well-known that alcohol and drugs, used by the man or woman or both, are predictors of rape, including date rape of teens (Benson, Charton, and Goodhart, 1992; CASA, 2006a). Relatively little alcohol can change a per-ception of force, and inebriation can result in an inability to respond to an assault. Women who use alcohol and drugs may have no control over their partners in the relationship, making them vulnerable to unsafe sex and un-wanted pregnancies (Rasch et al., 2000).

The National Violence Against Women Survey found that two-thirds of women who were raped as adults said their rapist was using drugs or al-cohol at the time (Tjaden and Thoennes, 2006). Twenty percent of female victims said they were using drugs or alcohol at the time of the rape.

Combining alcohol with sexual activity increases risk taking (Norris, 1994). This can lead to infection with sexually transmitted diseases (STDs) and, as mentioned, ratchets up the likelihood of unwanted pregnancies. Not surprisingly, substance-abusing women have an increased risk of HIV/ AIDS (Benson, Quackenbush, and Haas, 1996; United Nations, 2004). Overall, alcoholic and addicted women are likely to have negative experiences with men and decreased trust in intimate relationships (Schmid, 2002).

Prostitution can be both a cause of addiction and a likely result of addiction. Estimates are that between 18 and 72 percent of women drug users have been prostitutes (CASA, 2006a). Many prostitutes have been childhood victims of sexual abuse.

Substance-abusing women have high rates of dual diagnosis, considerably higher than for men (Campbell and Alexander, 2006). Women with substance abuse problems have much higher rates of post–traumatic stress disorder (PTSD) than women who do not have substance abuse problems. PTSD and substance abuse are strongly correlated. Rape is a devastating experience and most likely to lead to PTSD in both women and men (Najavits, Weiss, and Shaw, 1997).

Eating disorders such as bulimia and anorexia are found far more often in girls and women than in boys and men (Herzog et al., 2006); they are frequently hidden and are co-prevalent (existing or occurring together) with alcohol and drug abuse (CASA, 2006a). Clinical eating disorders have been overrepresented in women in treatment for alcoholism (Peveler and Fairburn, 1990). Overall, up to half of those who have an eating disorder abuse alcohol or illicit drugs (CASA, 2003). Approximately 35 percent of those with substance abuse problems have an eating disorder. The coexistence of alcohol and drug abuse with eating disorders must be addressed in treatment (Gordon, 2007).

Cocaine and Crack Cocaine

Dramatically altering the drug scene was the arrival in the 1980s of crack cocaine. The problem of crack is clearly intertwined with the problems of the inner city (CASA, 2006a; Fagan, 1990; Williams, 1990, 1992). The lower cost of the drug, the clear connection to lower socioeconomic groups and minorities, and the highly addictive nature of crack cocaine combine to make this a significant social problem. Use of crack cocaine has contributed to the significant increase in the incarceration of women, especially minority women (CASA, 2006a).

The bartering of sex for crack completely changed the picture of prostitution in urban areas and greatly augmented the spread of HIV and other sexually transmitted diseases. Socioeconomic aspects of crack use and the important role of sex as a means to acquire crack combine to pose a serious threat of increased sexually transmitted diseases (Baseman, Ross, and Williams, 1999; SAMHSA, 2007b). See Box 5.3 for a picture of the realities of crack houses and "shooting galleries."

A study of middle-class female cocaine users found that women were introduced to cocaine by friends "just for fun" (Sterk-Elifson, 1996). Initially, cocaine use can be part of interpersonal relationships and recreation. Eventually, however, the use becomes more solitary, with women spending more and more time trying to "score" (acquire) the cocaine and pay for it. One study found that while women felt that they were in control of their use of cocaine due to financial limitations and responsibilities, the nature of cocaine use, including the time, energy, and money spent on scoring, indicated addiction (Sterk-Elifson, 1996).

Cocaine use by women can increase susceptibility to addiction, eating disorders, and weight loss. Family drug use, age at onset of sexual abuse, age at onset of depression, and illegal drug use correlate with crack cocaine use (Boyd, 1993). Cocaine users are especially vulnerable to prostitution (CASA, 2006a).

Women and Children

A critical difference between men and women is that women are far more likely than men to have responsibility for children. Pregnant substance-abusing women are subject to even greater social stigma than other women with alcohol and drug problems, leading to delays in seeking prenatal care. In reality, very often prenatal care is sporadic or absent for substance-abusing women (United Nations, 2004).

The amount of alcohol consumed and the pattern of use impact the kinds of problems for the baby, with binge drinking especially harmful (Maier and West, 2001; National Center on Birth Defects, 2004). Pregnant white women are more likely to engage in binge drinking than other racial groups (Caetano et al., 2006). Pregnancy also increases the risk of physical abuse, with perhaps as many as one-fifth of women experiencing abuse during pregnancy (CASA, 2006a). The increase in physical abuse by male partners when a woman is pregnant, coupled with binge drinking by the pregnant woman, can lead to very serious consequences.

The 1980s brought reduced alcohol use during pregnancy in the United States, with concerns that even a drink each day would affect the development of the fetus (Day, 1995). Findings of the 2007 National Survey on Drug Use and Health reflect that approximately 11.6 percent of pregnant

Box 5.3   Inside the Crack House and "Shooting Galleries"

Crack houses offer a fascinating but disturbing glimpse into the social relationships of crack addicts (Williams, 1990, 1992). People come together for
erotic stimulation and cocaine smoking. The places are overcrowded, noisy,
and smoky and smell of a mixture of sweat, semen, filth, and crack. In this
nauseating atmosphere, people relate to each other as objects.

Terry Williams offers a searing portrait of the realities of crack houses
for young girls and women and the desperation within:

> It was full of young girls—fourteen, fifteen, sixteen year olds. Some of
> these girls stayed for days at a time, getting high and having sex with these
> guys. But most of them would f— just to keep getting high: when they ran
> outta money to cop, they would go to the first man who would give them
> another hit and do whatever he asked—blow jobs, suck on other girls, you
> name it. (Williams, 1990, 108)

In the shooting galleries, drug users pay a cover charge to get into the
place and then rent needles. After the drug users shoot up, they return used
syringes to the manager of the shooting gallery. Clearly, shooting up with
used needles is very risky for HIV infection. Not only are needles rented and
shared in these settings, but other drug paraphernalia, such as cookers used
to mix drugs, are also shared.

In the shooting gallery, just as in the crack house, there are different social roles that are played out. Some drug injectors do not want to, or cannot,
inject themselves, so they enlist the help of "injection doctors" or "hit men";
the drug user may be afraid of needles or does not yet know how to inject
himself or herself. In other instances, injectors cannot easily hit a vein and
need help. Injection doctors are usually paid a fee in drugs. Some women
who are sexually involved with other drug users may want their sex partners
to inject them as part of the relationship; boundaries between these partners
over the risks of infection are occasionally established.

Sheigla Murphy and Dan Waldorf (1998) offer, through the words of a
twenty-seven-year-old Hispanic woman, a description of a shooting gallery
run by an elderly woman:

> At this shooting gallery, people smoke [crack] there so it is real dark.
> There's people on the floor, the table, and standing around. Half of them
> are smoking, the other half are shooting up. People are in the bathroom. It's
> kind of dark, some of the windows are broken. It smells stinky. And most
> of the people . . . some of them are kind of moody. It's a scary place to go,
> but they know me. (Murphy and Waldorf, 1998, 127)

women drank alcohol, 3.7 percent reported engaging in binge drinking, and 0.7 percent reported being heavy drinkers (SAMHSA, 2008). Binge drinking in the first trimester was 4.6 percent in the years 2005–2006, having dropped from 10.6 percent during the years 2003–2004. This decline in binge drinking may be a response to increased educational efforts geared to pregnant women.

Women using cocaine while pregnant experience negative consequences for themselves and the child; among these for the mother are risk of heart problems, high blood pressure, stroke, and sudden death. For the fetus, this may mean a premature birth (Burns, Mattick, and Cooke, 2006), which in turn can mean low birth weight and the potential for separation of the placenta from the uterus, causing fetal death (United Nations, 2004). Heroin users risk miscarriage, early delivery, a smaller baby, and withdrawal syndrome for the baby. Women who smoke marijuana while pregnant risk premature birth; visual problems and tremors have been noted among these newborns (Burns et al., 2006).

Some jurisdictions have tried to convict and imprison pregnant drug users (Paltrow, 1992; Surratt and Inciardi, 1998). Even at this writing, some incarcerated women brought to the hospital to deliver their babies can be chained to the bed. In July 1989 in Florida, Jennifer Clarise Johnson was the first woman in the United States convicted of exposing her baby to crack while pregnant (see Box 5.4 for a discussion of her case).

Box 5.4 Jennifer Clarise Johnson

Jennifer Clarise Johnson, a twenty-three-year-old, poor, black crack addict, was the first woman to be convicted in a court of law for exposing her baby to drugs in utero. After her babies both tested positive for cocaine at birth, Johnson was charged with two counts of delivering a controlled substance to a minor. Florida drug laws did not apply specifically to fetuses, but prosecutors were able to obtain a conviction on the grounds that Johnson passed a cocaine metabolite to her babies during the one minute after birth, before the cutting of the umbilical cord. This allowed her to be convicted under a drug delivery law, with the umbilical cord as the method of delivery. Johnson received a sentence of fifteen years of probation. The Florida Supreme Court overturned the decision in 1991, on the basis that the drug delivery statute was not intended for application to a case of transmission by umbilical cord.

Sources: Roberts, 1991; Surratt and Inciardi, 1998.

The strategy most often used to address prenatal substance abuse is legalistic rather than oriented toward treatment (Surrat and Inciardi, 1998). Hundreds of women in the United States have been arrested since 1985 on the grounds that they were placing their unborn fetuses at risk owing to drug abuse. There have been no parallel arrests for women who use tobacco or alcohol. As of 2005, substance abuse by pregnant women was considered child abuse in fourteen states, and nine states required health professionals to report suspected cases of pregnant women abusing substances (Figdor and Kaeser, 2005). Unfortunately, fear of imprisonment may prevent some pregnant substance abusers from getting appropriate, or any, prenatal care.

In the early 2000s, two pregnant women were prosecuted for the deaths of their fetuses on the grounds of drug use during pregnancy (Stoesen, 2008). In South Carolina, in a case before the state supreme court, a woman was convicted of homicide and received a sentence of twenty years; the case is, at this writing, under appeal. In Oklahoma a woman was charged with murder when her child was stillborn, allegedly owing to the woman's use of methamphetamine during her pregnancy. In filing a friend-of-the-court brief, the National Association of Social Workers (NASW) argued that no scientific link has been established between "meth" use and pregnancy loss.

The alcohol-dependent or drug-addicted mother experiences greater difficulties in meeting the demands and responsibilities of the parenting role than do other women (Smyth and Miller, 1998). For example, although some cultures have encouraged drinking of alcohol while breast-feeding a newborn, milk production can be reduced and can affect the baby's sleep and motor development (Mennella, 2001). Child abuse and neglect may result from alcohol or drug dependency in mothers (Widom and Hiller-Sturmhofel, 2001). While it is often assumed that all substance-abusing women have significant parenting problems and greater risk of abusing their children, this is not necessarily the case (Hogan, Myers, and Elswick, 2006). That is, some women are able to meet their parenting responsibilities despite problems with alcohol and drugs.

It is inaccurate as well to assume that substance abuse is the sole cause of problems in caring for and providing for children. Poverty can be correlated with parenting difficulties. A survey of twenty-one rich nations ranked the United States at the bottom for addressing child welfare needs (McHugh, 2007). Despite great wealth in the United States, its low rank has been attributed to significant economic inequality and low public support for families.

Whether children have a positive or negative influence on women seeking treatment is a mixed picture. More efforts need to be made to document living arrangements of children and mothers during treatment (Knight and Wallace, 2003). It is commonly believed that children provide an incentive for women to seek recovery; however, the loss of custody of children can diminish motivation (Wilke, Kamata, and Cash, 2005).

The next section reviews potential physical effects on children whose mothers drink during pregnancy. Additional issues for children include emotional problems, stress, depression, attention deficit disorders, and slower cognitive processing (Burden, Jacobson, and Jacobson, 2005; Kulaga, 2006). There may be a connection between prenatal exposure to alcohol and breast cancer in later life; studies with rats indicate that even modest alcohol use while pregnant may leave a child more vulnerable to adult cancer as well as diabetes and osteoporosis (Lock, 2004). Evidence now suggests that those exposed to alcohol in utero have a higher risk of developing psychiatric disorders in early adulthood (Barr et al., 2006).

Fetal Alcohol Spectrum Disorders

Fetal alcohol spectrum disorders (FASD) refers to the range of effects on a child when the mother drinks alcohol during pregnancy. These include fetal alcohol syndrome (FAS) and fetal alcohol effects (FAE). FAE refers to children who have cognitive and behavioral problems but have fewer or less severe problems than those with FAS. The Institute of Medicine in 1996 dropped the term *FAE* in favor of *alcohol-related neurodevelopmental disorder* (ARND) and *alcohol-related birth defects* (ARBD). ARND refers specifically to functional or mental problems. For example, ARND children can have a difficult time memorizing or focusing attention (Lupton et al., 2004). ARBD refers to problems with hearing, the kidneys, bones, or heart (Centers for Disease Control [hereafter, CDC], 2006a).

FAS was first identified in France in 1968 and in the United States in 1973 (CDC, 2006a; NIAAA, 2006). One of the major causes of birth defects and retardation in the United States, it is the leading cause of preventable mental retardation (NIAAA, 2000b). This syndrome results in permanent damage to the child who was exposed to prenatal alcohol. FAS can affect a child born to any woman from any social, cultural, or economic background who drinks while pregnant. The National Institute on Alcohol Abuse and Alcoholism (NIAAA, 2000b) estimates that one out of six women who are potential mothers drinks enough to threaten her unborn baby. There is no safe amount of alcohol that can be consumed while pregnant. Women who drink five or more drinks on one occasion or who have seven or more drinks a week are at very high risk of delivering FAS babies (Women's Health Weekly Staff, 2003). Sometimes women are drinking before they realize

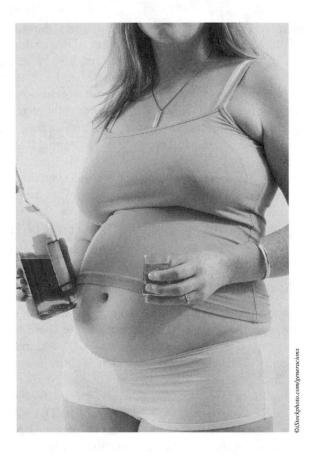

©iStockphoto.com/generacionx

that they are pregnant, and the first trimester of pregnancy is a critical period for development (Cornelius et al., 1993; Jacobson and Jacobson,
1999). Brain damage is most likely to occur during the last trimester of
pregnancy (CASA, 2005). Alcohol is more toxic to the fetus than heroin,
cocaine, or marijuana (CASA, 2006a).

The Substance Abuse and Mental Health Services Administration
(2003) estimated that each year about 40,000 babies are born to alcohol-
dependent mothers. The difficulty in making the diagnosis as well as the
stigma preventing women from admitting their dependency may keep estimates lower than the actual number of cases (CASA, 2005). Most of the
children suffer lifelong problems that are very expensive to treat. The cost in
the United States for care and treatment of children with prenatal exposure
to alcohol approaches $5 billion a year (Lupton, Burd, and Harwood, 2004).

Children growing up with FAS have many secondary disabilities,
often involving problems at school and with the law. Antisocial behavior,

hyperactivity, cognitive-processing and learning disorders, language and speech problems, cerebral palsy, depression, and epilepsy are linked to FAS (Burden et al., 2005; CASA, 2005). Further complications and problems associated with prenatal alcohol exposure and FAS include slower growth; central-nervous-system damage; poor muscle tone and coordination; facial abnormalities; abnormalities of the ears, liver, and palate; and "invisible disabilities," manifested in being self-centered, being unable to make friends, and having difficulty in knowing right from wrong (CDC, 2006a).

FAS is diagnosed based on observations and tests of newborns and children. Frequently included signposts are physical and facial deformities, low weight and small stature, and neurological problems. FAS children may have very small heads (microcephaly) and may exhibit hyperactive behaviors. A good social history of the mother that includes alcohol intake during pregnancy is necessary for a physician to make the medical diagnosis of FAS (National Center on Birth Defects, 2004). The problem is of sufficient magnitude that the American Academy of Pediatrics has recommended that physicians increase their knowledge of ARND (Preboth, 2001). Children with FAS do not outgrow it and have lifelong difficulties. Poor judgment and inability to distinguish between right and wrong can leave a child vulnerable to physical, sexual, or emotional abuse.

Fetal alcohol spectrum disorders are lifelong conditions that require early identification and intervention. As indicated, they may manifest as physical, behavioral, academic, and any combination of these characteristics. Because of these disabilities—including impairment of linguistic and motor-skill development—early intervention with a focus on teaching social skills and communication skills along with functional skills is crucial (Burgess and Streissguth, 1992). Research in the early 2000s points to the effectiveness of brief motivational interventions by health professionals in an attempt to prevent FASD by reducing pregnant women's drinking and increasing the use of effective contraception (Floyd et al., 2007).

Crack Babies

The 1980s brought concern for "crack babies" and dramatic and sensationalized stories of the catastrophic effects on these newborns (Jones, 2006; Surratt and Inciardi, 1998). In 1985 an article in the *New England Journal of Medicine* warned of the devastating impact on babies with prenatal exposure to cocaine. Some have found this to be a medical myth rather than a reality, so that, in reality, crack babies may not face the lifelong problems of those babies born with FASD (Blake, 2004). However, efforts to remove the term *crack baby* from the media have not been especially successful (Blake, 2004). In hindsight, while fears of an epidemic of severely and permanently disabled crack babies have not been realized, clearly it is appropriate to try to reduce harm to crack-addicted women and their babies. As important, some research in the early 2000s points to deficits among crack babies related to lack of prenatal care, malnutrition, and other problems associated with poverty (Ornes, 2006).

Heroin use by pregnant women is associated with miscarriage, early delivery, low birth weight, and higher risk for sudden infant death syndrome (SIDS). The newborn may experience withdrawal symptoms including irritability, disrupted sleep, and considerable crying, and require special medical interventions (CASA, 2005).

The impact on the public child welfare system of drug using and abusing parents is staggering. In the early 1990s, Toshio Tartara (1992) observed that the numbers of drug-dependent infants in foster care placements were rising because of drug-dependent mothers. The Bureau of Justice Assistance Drug Court Technical Assistance Project at American University (2003) estimated that foster care costs between $3,000 and $5,000 annually per infant for basic care. There is an additional $750,000 cost per each drug-exposed child from birth through age eighteen for special health and educational needs. Thirty percent of drug-exposed babies need foster care.

The Adoption and Safe Families Act (ASFA) was designed to ensure that decisions are made in a timely way so that children may be placed in permanent living situations. Research has found that, under ASFA, women can enter substance abuse treatment more quickly and remain in treatment longer, although treatment rates may not be higher (Green, Rockhill, and Furrer, 2006).

Prescription and Legal Drugs

A multibillion-dollar business, the pharmaceutical industry enjoys the largest profits of any business in the world. Pharmaceutical companies are clearly creating "needs" for their drugs by advertising tranquilizers and antidepressants. Approximately 19 percent of girls and women have taken prescription drugs for nonmedical reasons. Women who abuse prescription medication are more likely to be young, white, and unmarried, and live at a low socioeconomic level (CASA, 2006a).

Specific kinds of alcohol are aimed at women drinkers. Fruit-flavored alcoholic drinks, including wine coolers, were developed for the female market. Independence, romance, and self-fulfillment are the fantasy these ads try to create for women (Budden, 2008; Moog, 1991). Low-calorie alcoholic beverages have been created to attract weight-conscious women and underage drinkers. These products blur the difference between soft drinks and alcoholic drinks. Mike's Hard Lemonade, Doc Otis' Hard Lemonade, Tequiza, and Hooper's Hooch all disguise the taste of the alcohol in their products. These products are sometimes referred to as "starter brews" and are aimed at young drinkers and women. They are seen as increasingly important to advertisers of alcohol, not only because of their consumption but also because they are more likely to pass on recommendations to others (Budden, 2008).

Treatment and Prevention

The roots of treatment geared specifically for women grew from the temperance movement and the establishment of the Martha Washington Societies of the 1840s (White, 1998). However, many years had to pass before women were seen as an important group deserving of treatment. The treatment needs of women have been getting attention only since the 1970s, and in the early 2000s, one-third of clients in treatment were female (Brady and Ashley, 2005). It is estimated that over 6 million women from the ages of 18 to 49 need substance abuse treatment, yet only 10.4 percent receive treatment at a substance abuse facility (SAMHSA, 2007b). An important consideration in treatment is the context of what it means to be a woman in a male-dominated society (Covington, 2002).

Women entering treatment have more severe substance abuse problems than men, including more psychological and medical problems (Campbell and Alexander, 2006). Challenges in women's treatment include limited financial resources and coexisting problems such as family responsibilities, which can involve child care, depression, and lack of transportation (Fendrich, Hubell, and Lurigio, 2006).

Women receive less support from partners for entering treatment than do men (Amaro and Hardy-Fanta, 1995; Brady and Ashley, 2005). Overall, compared with men, women stay a shorter amount of time in treatment, are younger, have responsibility for children, are less likely to have jobs, and live on less money.

Reproductive and social services for women with substance abuse problems are not readily available (Campbell and Alexander, 2006). Only an estimated 13 percent of substance abuse facilities offer child care, and only about 12 percent offer prenatal services (Brady and Ashley, 2005). However, brief interventions for pregnant women can significantly lessen alcohol use during pregnancy (O'Connor and Whaley, 2003).

Reducing substance abuse among women can also reduce other problems, such as child abuse, although it does not appear to affect abortion decisions (Martino et al., 2006). Programs specifically designed for women can have a salutary, favorable effect on substance abuse, mental health problems, health status, HIV risk, and employment (Brady and Ashley, 2005). Family therapy can be beneficial except in situations where there is ongoing family violence (Center for Substance Abuse Treatment, 2004). Services that integrate substance abuse treatment (such as methadone maintenance) with that for intimate-partner violence, known as relapse prevention and relationship safety (RPRS), reduce both problems (Gilbert et al., 2006).

A review of thirty-five studies found support for female-specific treatment. Treatment should be provided by a supportive staff that emphasizes individual counseling. As discussed previously, because women are more likely to have responsibility for children, this can have a significant impact on their ability to access appropriate treatment options (Hardy-Fanta and Mignon, 2000).

Group therapy is a highly regarded form of substance abuse treatment that can be made more effective for women by focusing more on women's attitudes, relationships with others, and their own specific needs (Beyer and Carnabucci, 2002). Parenting programs and child-friendly treatment environments can be beneficial (Plasse, 1995; United Nations, 2004). Women need a strengths-based comprehensive and integrated treatment approach that can develop their sense of empowerment (Covington, 2002). Home visits for substance-abusing pregnant women appear to be a promising intervention tactic (Grant et al., 2005). Overall, access to services that directly respond to the needs of women with children must be improved (Marsh, D'Aunno, and Smith, 2000).

Women for Sobriety was founded in 1975 as an alternative to Alcoholics Anonymous by Jean Kirkpatrick (Schmid, 2002). The history of AA is clearly male-dominated, and Kirkpatrick felt that for women the concept of powerlessness over alcohol espoused by AA was detrimental to the recovery of women. A more positive approach to encourage self-esteem, lessen guilt and shame, and promote empowerment of women underlies the Women for Sobriety program.

Conclusion

This chapter contrasted the substance abuse problems of women and men and revealed greater physical consequences for women. Children of substance-abusing women can pay a heavy price, including significant physical and psychological consequences attributable to their mothers' drinking or drug use or both.

The fact that FASD is preventable speaks to the importance of developing alcohol prevention programs for women. Prevention efforts generally focus on social, behavioral, and medical referrals for the woman who is using alcohol, but these prevention strategies need to be studied to determine their effectiveness (NIAAA, 2000a). Overall, prevention outreach to women is critical and includes going into women's homes or engaging them on the streets (United Nations, 2004).

Gender issues in treatment need to be included in national drug policy development (United Nations, 2004). A national policy must address pregnancy, with an eye toward treating pregnant women with alcoholism and addiction rather than subjecting them to criminal justice responses. Expanded educational programs to alert the public and professionals about the harmful effects of substance abuse are also needed. These programs should be integrated into school curricula from the earliest grades.

Much more attention needs to be focused on education, prevention, and treatment of substance abuse among women. Well-known women, including Betty Ford, Kitty Dukakis, and Jeane Kirkpatrick, have served as important beacons of hope for substance-abusing women. Programs specifically geared for women using a variety of treatment approaches have been shown to be effective in women.

6 Race and Ethnicity

Ethnic groups are subcultures within a larger society that derive from a particular national or cultural origin. In the United States and Canada, with the exception of Native Americans and First Nations peoples, the entire population consists of ethnic groups that have immigrated, voluntarily or not, at one time or another, from another continent.

The history of each ethnic group has been marked by assimilation ("joining up" with the economic, political, and educational institutions), and acculturation, or acquiring the cultural patterns of the majority. Ethnic groups share a territory, biological characteristics, a kinship system, and belief systems (Inglehart and Becerra, 1995). While historically the term *race* has been applied to biological characteristics, most biologists in the twenty-first century agree that it is a socially constructed concept. The term *ethnicity* acknowledges distinct cultural and "racial" groups and has been used to refer to both racial and ethnic groups. The similarities and distinctions of race and ethnicity are complex; for example, the US Census Bureau utilizes 126 racial and ethnic categories (Winker, 2004).

In this chapter, we will consider the historical recognition of drug use as an aspect of ethnicity, and ethnicity as an aspect of drug use, both in early ethnographic descriptions and cross-cultural surveys. We then survey important aspects of alcohol and drug use among Hispanics, African Americans, Native Americans, and Asians in the United States. Finally, we consider how substance use affects ethnic families differently.

Historical Recognition of Drug Use Among Ethnic Groups

The first public "awareness" of a relationship between ethnicity and substance use was in temperance and Prohibitionist politics from the mid-nineteenth century through the 1930s. Puritan-derived Protestants and nativists identified immigrant groups as drunkards, starting with the arrival of Germans and Irish in 1840, right up to Prohibition enactment in 1920, and repeal in 1933. Urban ethnics against Prohibition squared off against "dry," rural, southern Protestants. Southern Prohibitionism was also tied into racist imaginings of African American males as hypersexualized by alcohol (Lender and Martin, 1982). Finally, there was racist imagery of Chinese immigrants as opium-smoking "dope fiends," the so-called Yellow Peril. All of this fits the tendency to stigmatize and demonize outsiders as threats to native purity (Kinder, 1992).

Moving to relatively nonbiased, scientific examination of ethnicity and drugs, at the dawn of the twentieth century, explorer-ethnographers cataloged the customs they encountered. In these accounts are some of the earliest considerations of ethnic-specific use of mind-altering chemicals. A century ago, Waldemar Jochelson (1906) published the results of his late nineteenth-century fieldwork among the Turkic-speaking Yakut tribe of Siberia, focusing on the myth and ritual surrounding the avid consumption of fermented mare's milk in festivals dedicated to the deities. A deity, according to their beliefs, had in fact provided fermentation instructions to the Yakut. Anthropologists saw many societies in which drinking and shamanistic drug use were seamlessly woven into the fabric of society, generating no social problems.

One of the earliest threads of research into drugs and ethnicity was anthropological observations of hallucinogen use in shamanistic ritual and in religious revitalization. As early as 1921 a very few researchers had even sampled hallucinatory brews themselves (Harner, 1973). Paul Radin's 1923 study of peyote religion among the Winnebago showed leader John Rave introduced to the Winnebago a blend of shamanism and Christianity in which peyote was both a libation and a healing medication (Radin, 1970). In the following decade, Weston La Barre (1938) published his famous work on the peyote cult among Mexican, southwestern United States, and Plains tribal cultures. Radin and La Barre saw that peyote religion served as a quasi-revolutionary protest against deculturation and oppression. Morris Edward Opler (1938) chronicled peyotism among Apache tribes in the official *American Anthropologist* journal. Conversion to a new religious perspective, even by the use of peyote, often pulled the alcoholic into sobriety. Native Americans offered many examples, perhaps most famously the New York Seneca; living in depressing "slums in the wilderness" at the end of the eighteenth century, they were led by the 1799 visions of their prophet, Handsome Lake, into a plan for sobriety and economic advancement.

Robert Bales, author of *Cultural Differences in Rates of Alcoholism* (1946), was the pioneer in comparing patterns of drinking among ethnic groups. Bales contrasted Irish and Jewish drinking patterns. Irish agricultural economics and inheritance patterns kept men at home as bachelors and "boys" well into their forties, during which time they consorted in same-sex tavern groups, where it was normative, if not encouraged, to engage in heavy drinking to facilitate conviviality, as well as to reduce their sexual and economic frustration. Bales then observed that Jews drank at home, with families, in a ritualistic context and developed temperate habits. Religiosity and animosity toward drunkenness also played a large part in Jewish sobriety. Finally, Bales cited a low level of alcohol abuse among the Balinese, who released tension through trance states.

Explanatory models of the relationship between substance use and ethnicity began with Donald Horton, author of *The Functions of Alcohol in Primitive Societies: A Cross-Cultural Study* (1943). Horton postulated that alcohol use functions to relieve anxiety, which can arise from feuding, warfare, marginal subsistence techniques, and disruptive culture contact with Europeans and Americans. As a rule of thumb, the amount of drunkenness obtained via drinking is proportional to the strengths of dangers facing the society. However, alcohol use creates a new problem, that of dealing with drunken aggression and unleashed sexual impulses; these societies create institutions to channel and limit aggression and sexuality.

Horton's model, which became known in the mid- and late 1940s, was not systematically challenged for another decade, until Edwin Lemert (1954, 1956) objected to jumping from technology to anxiety right over sociological considerations while also failing to explain why people would turn to drunkenness as an anxiety reliever rather than, say, the equally famous anxiety-reducing mechanism of ritual magic.

In 1962 Peter B. Field published *A New Cross-Cultural Study of Drunkenness,* wherein he lambasted Horton's methodology, such as his attempts at measuring drunkenness and anxiety. Cross-cultural studies, including those that attempted to link culture and personality, had now become grounded in statistical indexes and scales not available at the time to Horton, studies associated with George Peter Murdock and with J. W. Whiting and I. L. Child (1953). Field recalibrated Horton's raw data and concluded that the correlation of alcohol abuse with anxieties is not a powerful, overarching paradigm to which we should submit. Field's calculations pointed to the lack of social structures that are reliable, stable, permanent, and well defined—this lack being a wellspring of drinking; in other words, his findings showed that sobriety was based on social solidarity, as well as child-rearing that controlled aggression.

Drunken Comportment: A Social Explanation (1969) by McAndrew and Edgerton is a fascinating study of the wide variety of drunken behavior in different cultures. This important work revealed that it is not the properties of alcohol that are responsible for specific intoxicated behaviors; rather, cultural expectations determine how drunk people act. See Box 6.1 for a description of drunken comportment in Truk.

Horton (1943) not only gave us the first attempt at a scientific theory of drunkenness but was also one of the first to consider acculturative stress in substance abuse. The other earliest mention of the latter came the year before, in the work of the three Chopras (1942), who described the weakening of strictures against drunkenness as people left traditional rural communities of India. Bales (1946) chronicled the transition from a ritualistic,

---

Box 6.1   Drunken Comportment in Truk

Some of the classic observations of drunken comportment were made in the 1970s in Truk, a cluster of the Caroline Islands in Micronesia, by Mac Marshall, a preeminent ethnographer of drinkers. Young men in Truk get as drunk as possible on weekends, and engage in aggressive, defiant, brawling displays. They are considered to be temporarily insane, beyond reason, and crazy (any mentally deranged person, including a drunk, may be labeled a "sardine," headless like tinned fish). For example:

> X started pounding heavily on the thin walls of his parents' dwelling, before racing outside where he groveled for rocks to throw at the house. . . . [H]e wove back into view, staggered in an exaggerated fashion for a while in front of the audience that had begun to gather[,] . . . rushed at a young woman and a younger boy (who simply grinned and walked away a little faster) [,] . . . picked up rocks which he began throwing at his grandfather's house, the family cookhouse, his parents' house, and at the bystanders who were enjoying his antics from a prudent distance. All the time X whooped, staggered, and shouted his anger to all listeners. (Marshall, 1979a, 70–72)

X took a break from his "running amok" to have a cut bandaged by Marshall, get a glass of water, and ask questions about Elvis, the Beatles, and Bruce Lee. X also studiously avoided the anthropologist's house as a target when flinging rocks in every other direction (Marshall, 1979a, 70–72).

controlled use of alcohol into problem usage by the Hopi and Zuni following the arrival of Spanish liquors. See Box 6.2 for a summary of early ethnographic research and cross-cultural studies.

The Complexity of Ethnicity

Researchers on ethnicity continually grapple with its intricate, "fuzzy" nature. In a volume on research into ethnic and multicultural drug abuse,

---

**Box 6.2   Summary of Early Ethnographic Research
and Cross-Cultural Surveys**

Overall, there is a huge amount of ethnographic research and cross-cultural surveys on alcohol and drug use. Marshall concluded an edited volume of this research (1979b, 451–457) with this summary:

1. Solitary, addictive drinking behavior is rare in small-scale, traditional societies.
2. When societies have had time to develop shared values and customs concerning drinking and drunkenness, this protects against disruptive drinking behavior.
3. The amount of alcohol in a beverage has little connection to the drunken comportment that results; "rowdiness" is shaped by culture more than blood alcohol concentration.
4. All societies allow for relaxed rules of social behavior in situations where alcohol is consumed.
5. Alcohol is usually defined as a social facilitator, despite some evidence to the contrary.
6. Disruptive drinking occurs only in secular settings.
7. Alcohol is used in celebrations the world over. (We add here that "toasting" rituals are found worldwide.)
8. Availability of recreational opportunities is inversely related to drinking—the "boredom rule."
9. In any society, the main consumers of alcohol are likely to be young men.
10. Violence accompanying drinking is much more likely when drinking with strangers.
11. Drinking is seldom disruptive in societies where alcoholic beverages are considered foods or medicines.

Howard Rebach (1992) reminded us that ethnicity is a marker for a host of variables, including family structures, male-female relations, child-rearing practices, and, of course, a host of issues regarding alcohol and drug use. Rebach (1992), Collins (1992), and Chavez and Swain (1992), all writing in the same volume, confirmed that it is difficult to generalize about an ethnic group due to huge intragroup variation, comprising factors such as pre- and postimmigration, degree of acculturation, socioeconomic status, gender, age, and urban-rural and regional differences, which Peter Myers (2002c) has dubbed "five-dimensional epidemiology."

Culture change, including acculturation of immigrant ethnic groups, is not a one-way, one-dimensional process. In fact, acculturation is a multi-dimensional process.

1. Culture change proceeds unevenly; family structure and alcohol use patterns may lag behind adopting the latest clothing styles, slang, and so on. The different realms of culture proceed at different rates as they are "dragged" by the magnet of acculturation.

2. People often are "in the middle"; this may be a healthy bicultural or transnational identity, or both (e.g., Dominicans and Haitians residing in New York City easily and happily switch languages in midparagraph), or a case of failed assimilation. Ethnologists have documented alcoholism attendant to "acculturative stress," which may affect both individuals and entire communities, where traditional culture is fragmented, undermined, diluted, or devalued. Two early ethnographic portraits of this phenomenon were by William Madsen (1967) among Mexican Americans in south Texas and George and Louise Spindler (1971) among the Menomini. They identified subgroups that abandoned traditional culture but were not successfully acculturated, existing in limbo and at risk for addictions. The Texas subgroup was reviled by traditionalists as "agringados" ("gringo-fied").

3. People may have a blended, or creolized, culture. To provide a graphic example, Puerto Rican clients with whom Myers worked in New York City used many words that blended Spanish and English. "Spanglish" words include *rufo* for "roof," *elevador* instead of *ascensor* for "elevator," and *daime* for "dime." A classic study of how acculturation can produce a blended form of drinking pattern was Howard Blane's (1977) study of Italian immigrants to the United States. Blane compared those born in Italy with those who were US-born for at least ten years, including children of immigrants and grandchildren of immigrants. There was a dramatic change among males: daily drinkers went from 92 percent (Italy-born) to 15 percent (US-born) over the trigenerational span. Among women, daily drinking declined from 73 percent (Italy-born) to 9 percent (US-born). While wine and cordial consumption was

cut in half, this "Italian" trait still stood out, although now accompanied by some whiskey consumption, an American trait. Overall, Italian Americans blended drinking norms of Italy and the United States, resulting in lower rates of cirrhosis of the liver in the United States than found in Italy.

Descriptions of Substance Abuse

This section examines the patterns of use and issues of Hispanics, Native Americans, African Americans, and Asian Americans. For the purposes of comparison, whites aged twelve or older are more likely than any other racial or ethnic group to use alcohol (56.1 percent) (SAMHSA, 2008). The rate of binge drinking among whites is 24.6 percent. Overall, the rate of substance abuse and dependence for whites is estimated at 9.4 percent (SAMHSA, 2008).

Hispanics

The term *Hispanic* is used to refer to a culturally, socially, and economically diverse group of Spanish-speaking people that includes Mexicans, Puerto Ricans, Colombians, Cubans, Central Americans, and Dominicans. There is so much heterogeneity among people of Spanish-speaking populations that it is difficult, if not dangerous, to attempt generalizations. Often these groups do not have many other characteristics in common beyond language and perhaps religion, an important consideration when discussing the existing literature on Hispanic substance use or abuse.

The *2006 American Community Survey* found close to 42 million Hispanics living in the United States (US Census Bureau, 2007). Forty-two percent of those aged twelve and older reported current alcohol use, with 23.4 percent reporting binge drinking (SAMHSA, 2008). Overall, the rate of substance abuse or dependence for Hispanics is estimated at 8.3 percent (SAMHSA, 2008).

Some Hispanics may be in the United States illegally or as part-time migratory workers. This is particularly evident in the Mexican and Guatemalan population. The illegal status and the nature of legal, migratory, part-time work makes it difficult to study the substance abuse patterns for this group. Often Mexican and Guatemalan migrant workers are hidden or "invisible" to the larger society. The social isolation of the Mexican or Guatemalan migrant worker and the illegal alien is a significant factor, along with peer influence, that is associated with heavy drinking in this population (Garcia and Gondolf, 2004).

Andrew Gordon studied different Hispanic nationalities in a Connecticut city in the late 1970s (Gordon, 1978, 1981). Dominicans drank less after migration, which they related to their efforts to integrate into the local economy, abetted by a kind of work ethic. Men were expected to correspond to the ideal of the *hombre serio,* conscientious and responsible, concerned about the future. Drinking comportment was expected to be "suave," that is, slow, genteel, not drunken, with fine brands of liquor. Gross drunkenness was considered *indecente,* failing to show respect. In addition, the increased authority and independence of women postmigration curbed the excesses of heavy drinking; they simply would not stand for it.

In contrast, about one-third of Guatemalan males drank to excess and drunkenness, and drank more than they did in Guatemala. Weekends were typically a "time-out" binge. Guatemalan bars re-create the cantina of the home country. The pace of drinking renders most participants in the Friday evening revelries incapacitated to one extent or another. Within this subculture, drunkenness is glamorized and sentimentalized; the drinker is roguish, sad, and picaresque. The sentimentalized self-destructiveness of heavy drinking is also a theme that reverberated through various bohemian and student subcultures in the United States from the 1930s to the 1950s, with drinkers identifying with the generation of expatriate writers, who frequently drank themselves to death (Room, 1984). The high valuation on the drunken role among Guatemalans is seen in the exchange "Como esta?" "Un poco jodido de chupar" ("How are you?" "A little wrecked from drinking"). Puerto Ricans in Providence, Rhode Island, fell across a spectrum of socioeconomic and acculturative groups. One subgroup mixed alcohol with drugs; family violence occurred to a much greater extent than among other Hispanic ethnicities.

Dominican upward mobility, described by Gordon (1978, 1981) in Providence, is also found in New York City, where, for example, 80 percent of bodegas are Dominican owned, but it also has led many into the pathway of drug dealing (Shedlin and Deren, 2002). This drug economy has ensnared many youth, as chronicled by ethnographer Terry Williams in his book *The Cocaine Kids: The Inside Story of a Teenage Drug Ring* (1990). Over twenty years after Gordon, Michelle Shedlin and Sherry Deren (2002) conducted ethnographic research in the Dominican community of Washington Heights, New York City. They found that "getting ahead" for economic stability and family support were still important values. Moreover, "control and self-control . . . emerged as the most important attribute to be maintained in life . . . control of the family[,] . . . future[,] . . . behavior[,] . . . resources[,] . . . mind and body, are all seen as necessary for success and the respect of the family, of friends, and the community here and in the Dominican Republic" (78). What was intriguing was that these values persisted even among drug users. A common expression among drug users was "I am trying to dominate [or 'control'] the drug[s]." Crack use in particular was seen as loss of control, but even crack users evaluated themselves as relatively in or out of control in their use of that substance. It is important to note that treatment providers working with clients totally immersed in addictive lifestyles can appeal to cultural values in their facilitation of clients' motivational and decisional balance.

In the early 2000s, epidemiological data found lifetime prevalence of alcohol abuse and alcohol dependence at 22 percent for Dominicans, 41 percent for Central Americans, and 47 percent for Puerto Ricans (Baez, 2005). In her review of research findings, Annecy Baez referred to the transnational identity of Dominicans—their ambivalence about national identity, their visits to the Dominican Republic, and financial attachments there. Their settlement in a small number of close-knit communities can slow acculturation and assimilation, and form a protective barrier against alcohol abuse and addiction among Dominican adults. Still, there are high rates of poverty among Dominicans, and there is a subset of depressed, unemployed males, who have "dishonorably" failed to provide for their families, in the proclaimed goal of upward mobility and respectability, and who then separate from their families and drift into alcoholism. Many of these same factors exist for Puerto Rican crack users in Spanish Harlem, New York (see Box 6.3).

Box 6.3 Puerto Rican Crack Users in Spanish Harlem, New York

Philippe Bourgois's picture of Puerto Rican crack users in Spanish (East) Harlem, New York City, in *In Search of Respect: Selling Crack in El Barrio* (1995) showed that these addicts, demonized by society and stigmatized even within the world of substance abusers, have normal feelings and aspirations. Many of the residents of El Barrio (Spanish Harlem) had pursued the typical immigrant working-class dream in their early teen years, dropping out of high school with their mothers' permission to work in local factories. As factories moved out of the city, they had no education or social skills to compete in the service economy and drifted into the underground economy.

Bourgois describes the wish of crack addicts for a normal job. One of his key informants, Primo, the denizen of a crack house, exclaims: "It makes me feel f——d up, not being able to get a job. Because sometimes it seems like I like to be lazy. But you get tired of sitting around and not doing shit. I like to make myself useful, really—like I'm worth something" (121–122).

Native Americans

Native Americans and Alaskan Natives number close to 2.5 million, according to the *2006 American Community Survey,* and make up 300 different tribal groups (US Census Bureau, 2007). In 2007, of those aged twelve or older, 44.7 percent reported current use of alcohol, with 28.2 percent engaging in binge drinking (SAMHSA, 2008). Native Americans have the highest rate of substance abuse and dependence, estimated at 13.4 percent (SAMHSA, 2008).

The diversity among Native Americans is as great as the diversity that has been noted with Hispanic and Asian populations. There were over 200 different Native groups in North America when European contact occurred. Indigenous peoples did not use alcohol in their culture before their exposure to Europeans. Each group had its own culture, including its own language and specific social structures. A discussion of the alcohol and drug problems for this population is very complex, since adult drinking varies widely over time and from culture to culture. Alaska Natives have a different pattern of intergroup relations with the US government and a different history than other Native American groups (Beauvais, 1998). The Brokenhead Ojibwa of Canada have drinking rates far higher than the US average, while the Standing Rock Sioux have reported lower rates than the US average (Longclaws et al., 1980; Whitaker, 1982). See Box 6.4 for a description of problem drinking among northern Canadian ethnic groups.

Alcoholism and other drug abuse have been particularly devastating to Native American communities. Jeaneen Grey Eagle, the Native American

---

Box 6.4   Problem Drinking in Northern Canadian Ethnic Groups

Alcohol is a problem among the "circumpolar" ethnicities, with darkness, cold, and boredom the norm for large parts of the year. In the 1970s, author Peter Myers traveled up the coast of Labrador on a small packet with Inuit males returning from incarceration in the provincial capital of St. Johns, Newfoundland, to the northern Labrador Inuit settlement of Nain, still in their prison-issue garb. They had little or no memory of the events leading up to their arrest, due to alcoholic blackouts. Obtaining their first alcoholic beverages in some time, they came close to falling overboard. Then again, a local, intoxicated Caucasian mayor did manage to fall headfirst onto the rubber bumper between ship and dock!

coordinator of a tribal recovery program, estimated that one-quarter of the children in her community suffered from fetal alcohol syndrome or fetal alcohol effects, where three generations of FAS exist, with a devastating effect on the community (Dorris, 1989).

Aboriginal communities across Canada are rife with high rates of suicide, alcoholism, and in the case of youth, solvent abuse (Myers, 2001). Statistical summaries for the United States and Canada invariably note a hospitalization rate for alcoholic psychoses and alcoholic liver disease in Native American communities at many times that of the general population (Young, 1991).

One cannot imagine greater acculturative stress than that suffered by Native American adolescents forced to travel far away from the reservation to the Indian boarding-school complex, where they were stripped of their culture as if in boot camp, with astronomical suicide rates ensuing. In contrast, Native Americans who moved to Chicago and obtained stable employment drank considerably less (Garbarino, 1971).

Kaha:wi Jacobs and Kathryn Gill (2002) wrote of the urban Aboriginal (Native) population of Montreal. They found that addictive careers and lifestyles were rooted in powerful social networks of substance abusers, ties so strong that even culturally relevant treatment programs had a hard time making inroads. "Skid Row" becomes almost a counterculture away from the pressures of a middle-class value system. In the researchers' sample, almost half had attempted suicide and the vast majority of females reported emotional and physical abuse histories.

According to Canada's Royal Commission on Aboriginal Peoples (1996 [hereafter, Royal Commission]), the Innu (formerly known as Montagnais and Naskapi) of Labrador were relocated in the 1960s from their traditional lands and hunting areas to small, unattractive locations with poor housing and few meaningful activities in which to participate. Gas sniffing and alcoholism, domestic violence, and high suicide rates developed shortly after (Royal Commission, 1996). Cultural stressors contributory to self-injury and chemical dependency among the Inuit (Eskimo) and Innu of Labrador included despair over the loss of land and the traditional ways, dashed expectations (broken promises), powerlessness, restricted economic opportunity following relocation, and abusive treatment at residential First Nations schools. See Box 6.5 for further discussion of the consequences for the Innu.

Owing to the patterns of intergroup relations that resulted in many Native groups being forced onto reservations, a unique system of domination existed for many. This tremendous loss of freedom for Native Americans made for a difficult transition to life on reservations, certain to have serious

> ### Box 6.5 The Killing of the Innu
>
> The Innu were again in the news in late 1999, when Survival International published a report with the provocative title *Canada's Tibet: The Killing of the Innu* (Samson, Wilson, and Mazower, 1999). The report extrapolated from statistics to claim that the Innu community of Utshimassits had the highest suicide rate of any community in the world, thirteen times higher than the general Canadian population—approximately one-third of the population had attempted suicide (Samson et al., 1999). This report went further into the role of the school in contributing to acculturative stress:
>
> > While failing to equip most young Innu to function successfully in Euro-Canadian society, the school effectively separates them from their own cultural roots. Ironically—given that most children feel deeply alienated from Canadian society—older people complain that the young have already lost their own culture and "become Akanishau" (white). . . . The result leaves most Innu children "ashamed and confused" feeling that they belong fully in neither world. (Samson et al., 1999, 22)
>
> The Innu became visible to the United States when the *New York Times* and television newsmagazines publicized their plight (Rogan, 2001).

social and psychological effects. Most Indian reservations were located in rural areas and were clustered in the US West and Southwest. Access to health resources had been limited by lack of transportation and by the fact that few health facilities were available. Educational opportunities and employment training were sparse.

Historically, many reservations had prohibitions against alcohol, which meant that people had to leave their homes and their neighborhoods to drink. As a consequence, Native Americans have a high rate of alcohol-related fatal crashes. Since drinkers had to leave the reservations and drive across large areas of rural roads, drunk-driving injuries were common. The second highest rate of alcohol-related fatalities in the United States occurs in San Juan County, New Mexico. Stephen Kunitz and colleagues (2002) studied re-arrest rates for driving while intoxicated (DWI) in San Juan County and adjacent counties, as well as the Shiprock Navajo Reservation and the Jicarilla Apache Reservation in New Mexico, and the Ute Reservation in southern Colorado. Higher rates of re-arrest were attributed to the lack of culturally sensitive treatment programs.

An excellent example of the devastation wrought by alcoholism on a Native reservation is found in the movie *The Honour of All: The Story of Alkali*

©IStockphoto.com/ImagineGolf

Lake (1985). The movie documented the experiences of the Alkali Lake Indian Band of the Shuswap in British Columbia, Canada, between 1940 and
1985. Through the years virtually 100 percent of Natives on the reservation
became alcoholic, enduring many of the social problems associated with alcoholism, including family violence. Recovery started with one woman,
Phyllis, who quit drinking after her young daughter told her she did not want
to live with her anymore because of the drinking. Phyllis reached out to a recovering alcoholic clergyman from off the reservation. Through Alcoholics
Anonymous and Native teachings, her husband Andy joined Phyllis in recovery. Others who came into recovery went to Poundmaker Lodge in Alberta,
Canada, for inpatient treatment. By 1975, 40 percent of Alkali Lake Natives
were in recovery, and by 1985, 95 percent had achieved sobriety!

This poignant film had no well-known actors. It featured the residents of Alkali Lake as they played themselves in a reenactment of their experiences. Alkali Lake became a model of successful treatment for Native peoples in Canada.

African Americans

There are over 37 million African Americans in the United States, according to the *2006 American Community Survey* (US Census Bureau, 2007). Of those aged twelve and older, 39 percent reported current alcohol use, with 19.1 percent reporting binge drinking (SAMHSA, 2008). The overall rate of substance abuse and dependence among blacks is estimated at 8.5 percent.

African American alcohol and drug use patterns vary widely by social class, age, and gender. In the system of social stratification are homeless "bottle-gangs" at the first level, convivial heavy drinking at working-class festivities, and middle-class cocktail lounges, as per advertising for expensive brandies featuring African American models. If we break down the "lower" socioeconomic strata by gender, we find more heavy drinkers as well as more abstainers among African American women, in comparison with middle-class women of any ethnicity. And by age, drinkers are younger and abstainers are older and more likely to have a church affiliation (Collins and McNair, 2002; Gary and Gary, 1985).

There is an ancient tradition of temperance in African American communities. Temperance was part of the program in the founding of African American churches early in the nineteenth century, more as a public health than a morality issue. There was an overlap between temperance and abolitionism; the great abolitionist leader and orator Frederick Douglass proclaimed: "It was as well to be a slave to master, as to whisky and rum. When a slave was drunk, the slaveholder had no fear that he would plan an insurrection; no fear that we would escape to the north. It was the sober, thinking slave who was dangerous, and needed the vigilance of his master to keep him a slave" (Douglass, 1892, 133).

Risk factors for substance abuse in African American communities include the easy availability of alcohol, a liquor store on every block, easy availability of drugs, informal "corner" peer group usage and expectation of use, unemployment and economic frustration, and advertising campaigns targeting people of color. Barriers to prevention and treatment include concepts of substance abuse as a weakness or a moral failure rather than as a health problem, and fatalism about supernatural preordination of life situations (Wright, 2001).

For African Americans the black church is an important resource. The social support given to its members by churches is well documented

(Brown et al., 2006; Pattilo-McCoy, 1998; Resnicow et al., 2000). The role of the church in African American communities may not be as fundamental as it was in the past; however, these churches are still more involved in secular and community activities than most white churches (Brown et al., 2006; Cavendish, 2000). Outreach and support for local underprivileged groups and local community needs are central to the mission of black churches. These community activities often provide services related to substance abuse (Caldwell, Greene, and Billingsley, 1992). Churches help their members with socioeconomic deprivation and with discrimination and civil rights issues (Levin, Taylor, and Chatters, 1994).

In addressing substance abuse issues, the church can play multiple roles. It can serve as a place to house treatment programs and also as a source for referrals. The church can participate in substance abuse prevention efforts (Brown et al., 2006). Participation in AA and church involvement are predictors of sobriety in ethnic treatment populations (Roland and Kaskutas, 2002). Several authors have noted the positive effects that religious affiliation and church attendance can have on promoting good health by members (Drevenstedt, 1998; Musick, 1996). Ferraro and Albrecht-Jensen (1991) examined the relationship between health and religion and found that religion connects people to each other, often resulting in better health. The positive effect of religion on good health was indicated across all social classes. Social integration due to religion promotes good health, including abstention from alcohol and drugs. Thus, blacks are more likely to turn to the church when faced with health problems (Ferraro and Koch, 1994). This was not true for the white sample in the study.

Drevenstedt (1998) found that gender, race, and age were related to the health benefits of church participation and attendance. The social support hypothesis proved accurate for white men; however, among non-whites the benefit of church participation on subjective good health held only for younger black women. A study of rural black Baptist church members' moral position on the use of alcohol and drugs encouraged abstinence (Blazer, 2002). Frequent church attendance was strongly associated with abstinence. Overall, surveys of alcohol use among African Americans reflect that the greater the religious participation, the more likely African Americans are to abstain from alcohol (Collins and McNair, 2002).

Robert Beckford (2001) examined black theology in the Caribbean and the impact of its doctrine on substance use issues. Alcohol and drug misuse and abuse are viewed as a quick fix to the horrors of poverty and deprivation. The "gospel of prosperity," promoted in the black Christian churches of the Caribbean, is seen as insufficient to help with substance problems. A new theology of the present, one that focuses on current concerns, as a replacement for the gospel of prosperity, encourages churches to develop more creative solutions in changing the political and socioeconomic realities for its members. This role of activist and advocate encouraged for black Christian churches in the Caribbean is similar to the roles played by the black churches in the United States.

In comparing denominations that teach abstinence with those that do not, religious denomination is a factor in risk for alcohol dependency, especially in white adults (Ford and Kadushin, 2002). However, the normative and doctrinal beliefs of the denomination are not as significant a predictor of alcohol dependency as the integrative functions of church membership. Frequency of church attendance, which is an indicator for integration, is more important in predicting alcohol dependence in blacks. As indicated previously, the church, with its strong integrative dimension, significantly affects patterns of black alcohol use and abuse. Church attendance and integration are associated with positive health behaviors, including abstinence and moderate use of alcohol. Unfortunately, there is a missing link, that of referral into treatment from the church, due to supernatural paradigms concerning behavioral health issues and tendencies toward denial of substance abuse problems. However, in the first decade of the 2000s, author Myers noted the start-up of small addiction-referral operations within African American churches in Newark, New Jersey, a network of faith-based efforts called Bridge to Recovery, and programs benefiting from the federal administration's emphasis on faith-based initiatives. It remains to be seen how effectively faith-based initiatives will implement evidence-based prevention and treatment methods, or link clients to such resources.

Crack cocaine is used by all ethnic groups but is seemingly most common among poor inner-city African Americans (Wechsberg et al., 2007). One controversy involving African Americans and drugs concerns the disproportionate sentencing of crack offenders versus those caught with ordinary powder cocaine. Until 2007, federal sentencing guidelines considered any amount of crack as equivalent to 100 times the amount of powdered cocaine. Derrick Curry, a twenty-year-old college student in Washington, D.C., was a small-time crack courier caught in an FBI-DEA (Federal Bureau of Investigation–Drug Enforcement Administration) sting operation, and sentenced to nineteen years and seven months with no possibility of parole, nearly three times the prison sentence served by most murderers (Inciardi and Surratt, 1998).

African Americans have argued in the press and in court that such guidelines unfairly target and persecute them, as crack is predominantly found in African American communities (Wechsberg et al., 2007). However, according to calculations by eminent criminologist and drug expert James Inciardi and his associate Hilary Surratt (1998), crack use is only weakly correlated with African Americans; the association of being black, criminal, and a crack user is largely stereotypical, especially for males, among whom there is no statistically significant difference in crimes committed by crack users. African American female crack users, however, do have higher, statistically significant rates of violence-related crime and prostitution than their Caucasian counterparts. Crack usage and the crack-crime connection are socioeconomic rather than racial or ethnic, crack having been prevalent in all poor communities. See Chapter 11 for further discussion of sentencing practices for cocaine-related offenses.

Asian Americans

There were 12.5 million Asians Americans living in the United States in 2006, according to the *2006 American Community Survey* (US Census Bureau, 2007). In 2006, among Asian Americans twelve or older, 35.2 percent reported current use of alcohol, with the lowest rate of binge drinking (12.6

percent) of any ethnic group (SAMHSA, 2008). Substance abuse or dependence for Asian Americans is estimated at 4.7 percent (SAMHSA, 2008).

People of Asian origin, other than Japanese, have the most moderate drinking patterns of all the races. Asians have the lowest death rate due to alcohol and drug use compared with blacks, whites, or Hispanics. Genetic differences in some Asian populations may affect the rate and patterns of alcohol and drug use. Even small amounts of alcohol can cause a reaction called "flushing" in many Asians. Flushing involves burning and reddening of the neck and face. This is often accompanied by feelings of nausea and headaches. This is a metabolic reaction caused by the absence of certain metabolic enzymes (more specifically, erythrocyte aldehyde dehydrogenase). Doris Meier-Tackmann and associates (1990) discovered an enzyme in a Japanese sample that was associated with faster alcohol elimination from the body. This helps explain some observed differences within the Asian population.

In a comparison of Chinese, Filipino, and Vietnamese adolescents' drug use, patterns of use were uncovered that were unique to each ethnic group, gender, age, and immigrant status (Nemoto et al., 1999). Cultural differences explained different drug use patterns. Filipinos' first drug use was with marijuana, while the Vietnamese began with crack or regular cocaine. Cocaine and crack were used twice as often by the Chinese and the Vietnamese as by the Filipinos (Nemoto et al., 1999). Filipino substance abusers engaged in riskier behaviors as compared with Chinese and Vietnamese substance abusers. Specifically, Filipinos engaged in sex with injection drug users, engaged in sex while on drugs, and were themselves injection drug users. This can be explained by cultural factors, such as a stigma attached to injection drug use and a fear of needles for some groups (Nemoto et al., 1999).

Asian Americans are highly diverse, with over thirty different Asian groups and twenty-one different Pacific Island ethnic groups. As we have learned from other ethnic groups, the educational attainment, the economic status, and the level of acculturation into mainstream American culture vary dramatically for each group. The pattern of drinking problems among Southeast Asians may be affected by the fact that some Southeast Asians living in the United States are children of Southeast Asian mothers and American soldiers. Many of these children came to the United States to find their fathers. In some cases, the fathers were never found, and in others, the fathers rejected the children. This may have led to more depression and trauma, resulting in self-medication through alcohol for some Southeast Asian Americans (Makimoto, 1998).

Family history of alcohol and drug abuse is a consistent predictor of developing substance abuse. Asian Americans report the lowest rate of family alcoholism of all ethnic groups. Recent comparisons between Korean and Chinese subgroups of Asians revealed that Korean Americans reported higher rates of family history of alcohol abuse than did Chinese Americans, with great diversity in the vulnerability of Asian subgroups to substance abuse problems (Ebberhart et al., 2003).

Ethnicity, Drugs, and Families

When we think about cultural variation, we think of language, art, music, and food but sometimes overlook kinship and the family. But this can vary just as widely; cousin marriage, polygamy, and clan membership are all unfamiliar to most Americans but common in other societies. Immigrant groups bring with them kinship patterns, most commonly the extended family comprising three generations, or including an aunt or cousin, that may grow to be fairly robust or decline with assimilation.

Maxine Womble (1990) found that African American women were more encouraged to drink by spouses than was the case in other ethnic or racial groups, and those African American women drank more as a "social activity" than other ethnic women. However, black women had fewer alcohol or drug abuse problems than white women. Several authors have observed that blacks have lower substance abuse patterns than whites (SAMHSA, 1998, 2008; Vaccaro and Wills, 1998).

The powerful, resilient black family seemed to meet its match with the crack epidemic of the late 1980s, as portrayed in this quote from someone who lived it:

> It started getting bad, like, okay, this is '90, I can say '80. When . . . crack started. We didn't have drugs like that then . . . You had to venture out for drugs. Stuff like that. You ain't had pushers on every corner. . . . Mothers pushing, grandmothers pushing . . . It's just everybody selling cocaine. So, it's worse. Worse. Brothers cussing . . . you cussing your mother out. Beating your mother up if she don't give you money to get your hit and all that. . . . It never was like that. Never was like that. You still had a sense of, you know, you do respect your mother. You would not dare talk back to mother, right. That was a no-no. . . . A little boy, my girlfriend, her son "Get the —— outta my face." He sells drugs. He's 15. He's 15. It was a shock to me. Much as I seen and been through . . . still got the nerve to shock me. (Pettiway, 1993, 261)

Thus, the advent of crack had a disruptive effect on traditional African American family roles, in which respect for mother and grandmother is paramount. The economic power acquired by a teen drug dealer resulted, in this Philadelphia neighborhood, in role reversal, with power in the hands of the adolescent, as well as degradation of maternal respect by her descent into drug dealing. But the African American family is also highly resilient, and has backup mechanisms to keep it alive through adversity. These have served them well in the face of drugs' impact on the family. The eldest daughter is typically given executive authority and a caregiving role over younger siblings, making her a sort of coparent, or a "parentified" child. In the addiction field, it is common to ascribe the "parental child" or "family hero" role within addicted families, but, then, this can be a normal structure in the African American community.

Treatment and Prevention

In the early 2000s, more attention has been paid to the treatment needs of specific racial and ethnic groups. However, research on African Americans and Hispanics reveals they have less access than other ethnic groups to treatment for alcoholism, drug abuse, and mental health problems (Niv and Hser, 2006; Wells et al., 2001). One study of African American crack users found that difficulties entering treatment were related to unemployment, lack of insurance or money to cover the cost, and lack of transportation (Wechsberg et al., 2007). For Asian Americans, denial of substance abuse problems can be especially strong. The stigma and shame associated with "losing face," coupled with social isolation of individual families, are at the core of the difficulty in acknowledging substance abuse problems and seeking treatment (Fong and Tsuang, 2007).

There are important difficulties inherent in the treatment of Native Americans. The federal response to Native American substance abuse has been incarceration rather than treatment, and when treatment has been provided, it typically did not recognize cultural aspects. The cultural perspective in treatment for Natives began to develop in the 1980s, and a critical issue became the fostering of positive ethnic identity in the process of providing treatment (Beauvais, 1998; French, 2004). The so-called Red Road Approach is an adaptation of the Twelve-Step programs of Alcoholics Anonymous and Narcotics Anonymous for Native Americans who seek recovery from addictions utilizing traditional healing practices (White Bison, 2002).

Overall, factors that are associated with entering treatment are easy accessibility, the ability to acknowledge a substance abuse problem, strong religious beliefs, and support from family, friends, and the community. As noted, African American churches can provide important support for treatment.

Information is lacking about how racial and ethnic groups respond to drug prevention efforts (Resnicow et al., 2000). The federal Substance Abuse and Mental Health Services Administration has since 1999 stressed the importance of providing culturally competent services, but they are still in early development. These services need to include staff sensitivity to cultural issues of clients, the incorporation of cultural values and traditions into treatment programs, staff who come from the same cultural background, as well as client participation in policymaking and implementation of prevention and treatment services.

Conclusion

Early ethnography brought a lot of vivid images of cultures in which the use of drugs was ritually woven throughout the fabric of society, and was not associated with social problems as in major Western urban societies. Cross-cultural surveys sought to pinpoint which psychological traits were correlated with alcohol use and misuse. Many social scientists recognized the link of stressed migration and acculturation in weakening the social bonds and supports important for mediating drug and alcohol misuse.

Further research has shown that it is difficult and even misleading to try to paint a broad-brush picture of drug use among large ethnic categories. Dominican use patterns, for example, are distinctive and contrast with other Hispanic categories, and even within the ethnic group vary by city, age group, and other variables. Two of the worst scourges for Native American groups have been fetal alcohol syndrome and inhalant abuse. African American substance use risk factors are offset by preventive factors provided by church affiliation. Asian Americans are the least likely to develop substance abuse problems yet can have more difficulty acknowledging substance abuse when it does occur. Finally, drug use has different impacts on the different ethnic kinship and family constellations. Much more remains to be done to make treatment accessible to minority groups and to offer prevention programs.

7 Issues of Sexual Identity

In this chapter we continue the discussion of diversity in the world of alcohol and drugs with a focus on sexual orientation. We describe substance use and abuse in the gay, lesbian, bisexual, and transgendered (GLBT) population; consider the types of drugs abused; and examine treatment and prevention issues.

A sexual attraction to same-gender partners is known as homosexuality. Any homosexual may be referred to as gay, while female homosexuals are referred to as lesbians. Bisexuals are individuals who are attracted to both sexes (Hahn et al., 2005). *Transgender* is a catchall designation for anyone who challenges the traditional definitions of sex and gender. It can include drag queens, drag kings, transsexuals, transvestites, intersexuals (having biological characteristics that are both male and female), and gender benders (an informal term referring to transgressing or "bending" expected gender roles) (Leeder, 2004).

There is no one explanation for sexual orientation because it and identity result from a very complex developmental process. Theories have considered genetic, hormonal, environmental, and other factors in explaining homosexuality. The complexity and diversity themes that frame this text continue to be important in discussing the GLBT population.

Precisely determining the percentage of gays in the total population is far from easy. Homophobia leads some GLBT persons to remain "in the closet," choosing to hide their sexual orientation rather than be victims of prejudice and discrimination. Alfred Kinsey et al. (1998) estimated that 2 percent of females and 4 percent of males identified themselves as exclusively homosexual. Since then, estimates of the percentage of gays in the population increased the total number of gay females and males to 10 percent (Hahn et al., 2005).

GLBT groups are identified as a minority group within the United States. When sociologists use the term *minority,* they are referring to those groups in society that are treated unequally and who are victims of prejudice and discrimination. The United States has been described as a homophobic society, meaning that an exaggerated and irrational fear of homosexuality is characteristic. Living as a gay person in a homophobic society creates many obstacles, leaving the person open to acts of discrimination and victimization. Hate crimes are those that are motivated by hatred, prejudice, and fear of others. In the case of gays, who are frequently the victims, hate crimes are often referred to as gay bashing. Some of the violence at school and in the streets is linked to gay bashing and homophobia. And alcohol and drug use by GLBTs may be seen as a way to cope with this and other aspects of social inequality. These added strains must be considered when trying to understand substance abuse issues within this population (see Box 7.1).

Diana Fishbein and D. Perez (2000) examined the factors that contribute to high and low risk of involvement in deviant behavior, including substance abuse. Individual attitudes and personal relationships were identified as important influences in participation in deviance having potentially harmful results, such as drug overdosing. Strong bonds to family and community, as well as positive attitudes toward the norms and values of the community, protect the individual from engaging in deviance. GLBT persons are at a greater risk of losing strong bonds to family and to the dominant culture. Racism, discrimination, and social inequality increase the likelihood of drinking because they cause mental distress and lower self-esteem (Leason, 2003), thus placing such targeted groups at greater risk for substance abuse problems.

Historical Recognition

Historical and cross-cultural evidence reveals that homosexuality has been an approved pattern of sexual orientation in the social skein. Homosexuality was accepted in ancient times in both Western and Eastern cultures. Native American peoples practiced the *berdach* and gave legitimate status to "manly women" and "two-spirit men." Condemnation of homosexuality arrived with Christian missionaries. The strong prohibitions against homosexuality that became prevalent in Western societies draw from the Levitical laws of Judaism. By the time of the American Revolution, homosexu-

Box 7.1   Is Sexual Orientation Linked to Substance Abuse?

Much of the substance use and abuse in gay culture is related to social context, and the difficulties associated with a gay identity may also be related to substance abuse. Historically, bars, lounges, clubs, and public baths were common meeting places for GLBT individuals. Since World War II the gay bar has been the easiest meeting place for lesbians and gays to meet, and this increased the opportunities for drinking and taking drugs.

One example of the gay social scene is the gay "circuit party" (an ongoing series of dance events that extend through the day and night). Some of these circuit parties last for entire weekends (Lee et al., 2003). Attendees at circuit parties report that they want to "be uninhibited and wild" and also to "look and feel good" and may be seeking sexual activity. Circuit party attendees are typically educated and financially stable. Overuse and overdose of drugs are reported by attendees at circuit parties (Mansergh et al., 2001). Alcohol, "poppers" (volatile nitrates), ecstasy, Special K, GHB (gamma hydroxybutyrate), and Viagra have been reported as the most frequently used drugs (Ross, Mattison, and Franklin, 2003).

In addition to gay social venues that promote substance use, there may be other links between a gay lifestyle and substance abuse problems. For some gay men, "looking good" is a high priority. In an effort to develop an "ideal body type," gay men may use anabolic steroids (Bolding, Sherr, and Elford, 2002). Most steroid users report side effects such as insomnia, depression, hypertension, and testicular atrophy among other serious mental and physical consequences.

ality had been criminalized and serious sanctions applied to those found guilty of sodomy and "perversion."

Since homosexuality has been historically regarded as deviant behavior in the United States, much of the activity, including substance use and abuse, has been hidden. However, there was always anecdotal data that related homosexuality to drinking and drug taking. Many homosexuals found bars and private clubs as the only meeting grounds available to them.

In the 1950s, gays and lesbians were denied any legal protections. Senator Joseph McCarthy promoted antihomosexual sentiment and legislation. His campaign, the "Lavender Scare," against homosexuals in politics and government, was successful. It was around this time that Bill W. (cofounder of Alcoholics Anonymous) talked about how difficult it was for homosexuals to participate in AA and maintain their sobriety (Paul, Stall, and Bloomfield, 1991). In 1949 the first "special interest" gay AA group was formed in Boston. This group disbanded during the 1950s, and it was not until 1969 that another gay AA group was formed, in California. In 1974, AA started listing gay meetings in its world directory. As of this writing, gay AA is the largest special interest group in the AA fellowship.

By the 1960s, with the civil rights movements for minorities and women, the stage was set for a social movement for gay rights. In June 1969, police raided a homosexual bar, the Stonewall Inn, and a riot broke out. This event marked a turning point in gay politics. Shortly after the riots the Gay Liberation Front took shape, and through its activism, the first legislative hearings on gay rights convened in New York (Burgdorf, 2006). With all the political activity and the new visibility of the gay rights movement, a spotlight was shone on gay life. It was about this time that excessive drinking and drug taking became coupled with being gay.

In the decades after Stonewall, civil rights gains were made. Medical professionals no longer considered homosexuality a disease or a mental illness—the diagnosis of homosexuality was removed from the *Diagnostic and Statistical Manual of Mental Disorders* (DSM) in the 1970s. Sexual acts had been decriminalized in many states, and then in 1981 everything changed again. The country entered the era of the AIDS epidemic. Initially diagnosed in gay male populations, the disease was regarded as a "gay" disease. This epidemic once again focused significant attention on gays and the substance use and abuse patterns within the gay community. See Box 7.2 for a discussion of HIV/AIDS.

Descriptions of Substance Abuse by GLBT Persons

Higher proportions of the GLBT population use alcohol and drugs than the general population. In a comparison of patterns of drug use between gay and straight (heterosexual) populations, Susan Cochran et al. (2004) found there were consistent lifetime patterns of more drug use by gays than straights. However, in the early 2000s the gap closed somewhat. Additionally, the homosexuals in Cochran's study reported more cocaine, heroin, and marijuana use than did the heterosexuals. Overall, the study found moderate elevation of drug use and drug dependency in gay and bisexual populations as compared with straight populations.

Laurie Drabble and Karen Trocki (2005) examined the relationship between substance use problems and sexual orientation. Lesbians and bisexuals were compared with exclusively heterosexual women in relation to alcohol consumption, bar going, other drug use, and past substance abuse treatment. The patterns of substance use and abuse did vary among the different populations. The complexity of the findings led the researchers to

Box 7.2   HIV and AIDS

AIDS is identified more with male homosexuals in the United States than with any other group (Dolcini et al., 2003). Drug dependence is also a characteristic that is closely associated with AIDS in the United States. Men having sex with men who are intravenous drug users (MSM-IDU) are groups at the highest risk of contracting and transmitting HIV in the United States (Bull, Piper, and Rietmeijer, 2002). The links between alcohol, crack, and HIV are noteworthy (Rasch et al., 2000). Substance use is often accompanied by unsafe sexual activity. Unprotected sex, multiple sex partners, exchanging sex for drugs and money, and the incidence of sexually transmitted diseases are significant problems in the GLBT population. Like crack, alcohol is often associated with unsafe sexual activity and an increased chance of HIV. The complex interplay between HIV risk behavior and non-injection drug use focuses primarily on club drugs and gay social venues such as bars, dance clubs, and bathhouses. Participation in these gay social venues is associated with polydrug use, HIV status, and more frequent substance use. The drugs most frequently injected were cocaine and methamphetamine (Bull et al., 2002). Research in the early 2000s pointed to a reduction in perceived need for safe sex because of the effectiveness of highly active antiretroviral therapy. That is, AIDS was no longer perceived by some as a terminal illness but an infection that could be treated and controlled (Stolte et al., 2004).

Intravenous drug–using (IDU) women who have sex with other women also have higher levels of HIV-related risk behaviors (unprotected sex and injection practices that are riskier, such as sharing needles) than other IDU women (Young et al., 2000).

conclude that measures of sexual orientation and behavior need to be part of any population-based survey. They also noted the importance of taking sexual identity into account when developing treatment and prevention services, discussed later in this chapter.

An early survey of the gay and lesbian population found discrimination, orientation toward gay bars, and gay identification are important in understanding gay and lesbian substance abuse (McKirnan and Peterson, 1992). Homosexual men and women differed in their responses to the variables. Discrimination was stronger against gay men than against lesbians, yet lesbians reported more generalized negative effects and stress. Social norms of sexism, heterosexism, and male drinking patterns can cause lesbians to feel stigmatized and experience more shame and guilt over substance abuse issues than do male homosexuals. Descriptions of male gay life should not be generalized to female gay life, since there is significant diversity in these populations.

Substance abuse and family violence have also been researched and correlated in gay populations. In an exploratory study of twenty-five gay men, three different perceptions were found among the sample: (1) drugs and alcohol were perceived by the majority of men (thirteen) as the causes of relationship violence; (2) three respondents indicated they used alcohol and drugs to cope with their victimization; and (3) one respondent felt that the abuser was violent regardless of alcohol or drug use (Cruz and Peralta, 2001). In a study of 104 self-identified lesbians, 64 percent reported that drugs or alcohol were used before or during battering episodes (Schlit, Lie, and Montagne, 1990). Much more work needs to be done to understand the relationship between substance abuse and partner violence among gays and lesbians.

Ron Stall et al. (2001) looked at heavy and problematic use of alcohol and drugs in a population of men who had sex with other men (MSM). Heavy alcohol and drug use was prevalent in this population, and multiple drug use and alcohol-related problems were common. Important correlates included demographic factors, early childhood traumas and adversities, current mental health status, and social and sexual practices that are part of a male homosexual culture. These findings suggest that multiple levels of associations need to be considered when trying to explain substance abuse within the MSM population. The individual level, the group level, and the sociocultural level each add to the analysis (Stall et al., 2001).

Substances that are closely associated with substance abuse in the GLBT population include alcohol, methamphetamines, intravenous drugs, and designer and club drugs (Newman, Rhodes, and Weiss, 2004). A brief description of these forms of substance abuse highlights issues within the GLBT community.

Alcohol

A large national survey of alcohol consumption found that gay men spent much more time in bars than did other groups of men, yet this did not result in significant consumption of alcohol for all gay men. However, heavy drinking among men having sex with men is associated with risky sexual behaviors, with a higher probability of unsafe sex (Irwin, 2006). Heavy drinking was associated with HIV risk behaviors in non-HIV men.

Women who had sex with other women (WSW), including bisexuals and lesbians, spent more time in bars and drank more than did exclusively heterosexual women (Trocki, Drabble, and Midanik, 2005). Elizabeth Gruskin

et al. (2006) also found that lesbians who spent more time in bars were likely to drink more than those who did not frequent bars. They noted the psychological importance of the bar for reduction of stress, lesbian identity, social networking, and intimate relationships; however, the findings also noted the potential health consequences. Discrimination and depression are risk factors for alcohol and drug use in seeking to reduce tension. This may be more the case for lesbians, who face double discrimination—as homosexuals and as women. Substance abuse by lesbians and other sexual minorities may to a higher degree reflect the discrimination and harassment experienced from being gay than does attendance at gay social venues.

The few existing studies of alcoholism in lesbians suggest high rates. One study examined the prevalence of alienation in lesbian and heterosexual women and its relation to alcoholism. While alienation correlated with alcoholism for heterosexual women, it did not for lesbians, suggesting that other variables should be investigated to explain lesbian alcoholism (Jaffe et al., 2000). Susan Jo Roberts et al. (2005) also found very high rates of reported alcohol abuse among lesbian women. The Boston Lesbian Health Project II, a national health survey of 1,139 lesbians, found higher and heavier rates of alcohol intake than were found in women in the general population. Risk factors for alcohol abuse in the lesbian population were a family history of alcoholism, rape, or childhood sexual abuse, or a combination of these (Roberts et al., 2005). As noted in Chapter 5, these risk factors have been identified with substance abuse problems for all women.

Stephanie Nawyn et al. (2000) examined the workplace sexual harassment experiences of lesbians, gay men, and heterosexual women and men. The study found that lesbian and bisexual women did not experience more workplace harassment than heterosexual women. However, there were more alcohol-related problems for the lesbian and bisexual women as a result of workplace harassment. In contrast, gay and bisexual males experienced significantly more sexual harassment in the workplace than did heterosexual males. However, gay males did not report increased alcohol-related problems as a result of this harassment.

Methamphetamine and Designer and Club Drugs

Also known as meth, speed, crank, and crystal, methamphetamine is a relatively cheap and very potent stimulant. Feelings of euphoria, increased self-esteem, and increased sexual desire make meth a very popular drug among the GLBT population (Shoptaw and Reback, 2007).

Gay and bisexual men use stimulants such as meth at a rate ten times higher than other groups (Colfax et al., 2004). An affinity exists between the gay subcultures of MSM and the use of meth, since the pharmacological effects of the drug encourage the expected behaviors and norms of the subculture (Green and Halkitis, 2006). Studies report that meth use and abuse among MSM should be considered alarming (Shoptaw and Reback, 2007). Meth use increases the risk for HIV owing to greater risk of unsafe sex and the sharing of needles, which leads to unsafe injections. Some meth users also use Viagra, an erectile dysfunction drug. Gordon Mansergh et al. (2006) found evidence that Viagra was often combined with meth and associated with sexual risk behaviors in MSM.

Motivations for meth use include fears of being unattractive due to aging and illness, loneliness, and a desire to drop sexual inhibitions (Kurtz, 2005). Consequences can include loss of friends, loss of employment, and risk of HIV and other sexually transmitted diseases (STDs). Perry Halkitis and Michael Shrem (2006) examined meth use among gay men in New York City with a focus on psychological and psychosocial correlates of meth addiction. They found that among chronic meth users, it helped them cope with unpleasant feelings, avoid physical pain, and engage in good times with others.

Sabina Hirshfield et al. (2006) described meth use among a sample of MSM found online. Many were young, reported sex with many partners, had unprotected sex, and were HIV-positive (see Box 7.3). David Bimbi et al. (2006) examined the complex role of drugs, as well as alcohol, in relation to sexual behavior among gay and bisexual men. Not surprisingly,

Box 7.3   Use of the Internet to "Hook Up"

The GLBT community has taken advantage of the Internet to meet new people and to hook up. An hour spent online will turn up many gay websites and chat rooms. Graham Brown et al. (2005) studied gay men in Perth, Australia, who used chat rooms to meet sexual partners. They concluded that gay men use the Internet to engage with other gay men in ways that are very different from traditional gay social venues, with expectations for sex surfacing more quickly.

In a study of 609 gay men seeking sex, 34 percent reported meeting men for sex via the Internet (Benotsch et al., 2002). Respondents also reported higher rates of meth use and unprotected sex with multiple partners. Unsafe sex and sexual compulsivity were associated with MSM meeting online (Dew and Chaney, 2004). Online interventions may be useful for sensitizing professionals to these health issues and also as educational prevention sources for gay men.

Graham Bolding et al. (2005) found that HIV-positive men in London were meeting casual sex partners more often on the Internet than at settings like gyms and bars, increasing risks of HIV transmission. Sheana Bull et al. (2004) also found elevated risks of HIV and sexually transmitted diseases among MSM who met online. Older, white, college-educated men solicited sex on AOL in contrast with younger men who found sexual partners on Gay.com and Yahoo.

These findings suggest that the Internet is an important way to communicate within the MSM population. They also suggest that the Internet might be used as an educational tool for prevention of HIV and sexually transmitted diseases.

they found that sexual risk taking while under the influence of drugs (and alcohol) increased. Among gay men who travel as a leisure activity, many MSM report high rates of substance abuse and unprotected sex (Benotsch et al., 2006).

The use of ecstasy (MDMA) within the gay community appears to be on the rise (Klitzman, 2006). Straight and gay ecstasy users were compared, and findings indicated that risk behaviors such as unprotected sex and sharing needles did not differ in the two groups (Degenhardt, 2005). Gays did report more use of other drugs associated with the "dance scene," like ketamine and meth, and also reported having significantly more sexual partners and higher rates of injecting drugs.

Lesbians and gay men use recreational drugs more than other segments of the population. These drugs are used as part of "nightlife" partying, and include drugs like "Special K" and ecstasy (Halkitis, Palamar, and Mukherjee, 2007; Lee et al., 2003; McDowell, 2000). Adam Green (2003) noted the increase in the use and popularity of club drugs by gay men. In a study of forty-nine gay and bisexual methamphetamine users, it was reported that the use of club drugs made sexual encounters easier and also contributed to a sense of community. A study of patterns and contexts of meth use over one year for gay men found that meth use crossed every age, educational, and racial and ethnic group (Halkitis et al., 2005). Respondents reported using meth in combination with other prescribed and illegal drugs. The context of the drug use differed depending on the HIV status of the respondent; HIV-positive men reported higher levels of use in bathhouses and at sex parties, while HIV-negative men reported use in the context of a "club scene."

Gamma hydroxybutyrate (GHB) is a popular drug among the GLBT population (Halkitis and Palamar, 2006). In a study of 450 club drug users, older gay men and those who identified as gay rather than bisexual reported more frequent use of GHB and also reported more polydrug use. GHB was combined with alcohol, meth, and ecstasy and used at circuit parties, sex clubs, and nightclubs. Perry Halkitis and Joseph Palamar (2006) looked at the perceived stigma of GHB use, tolerance of potential adverse side effects, and reasons that GHB was preferred as a drug over other substances; respondents reported increased energy and libido, short duration of action, sleep assistance, and limited aftereffects as reasons.

Indicators of Substance Abuse in the GLBT Population

Young gay men are far more likely than their heterosexual counterparts to take drugs, including ecstasy, cocaine, and marijuana. Correlates of heavy substance use among male homosexuals and bisexuals include polydrug use, multiple sex partners, and frequent attendance at gay bars and clubs (Greenwood et al., 2000).

Club drug use among urban gay males has increased in popularity and use (Mansergh et al., 2001). Observers of the gay scene note that a lot of young gay people start clubbing on Thursday night and carry it through Monday morning. Drugs help the individuals to keep up with this long event.

Internalized homophobia—or self-hatred because one is a homosexual—is one of the greatest obstacles to sobriety and becoming drug-free. As long as individuals suffer from internalized homophobia and cannot accept themselves, the recovery process from substance abuse is stalled. In fact, internalized homophobia may prompt someone to want to change his or her sexual orientation. GLBT persons who are in denial about their sexual orientation may also be in denial about their substance abuse. The combination of societal homophobia and internalized homophobia leads to a higher incidence of substance abuse in the GLBT community (Cabaj, 2000).

Dean Amadio (2006) examined internalized heterosexism and alcohol problems and found that there was a relationship between internalized heterosexism and alcohol problems for lesbian women but no significant relationship for gay men. This research supports the position that gender differences within the homosexual population are significant and need to be a focus of research. Gay men lead lives as different from gay women as straight men's lives are different from straight women's. Gender roles and gender norms operate in both populations. Thus, there is great diversity within the GLBT groups in their patterns of alcohol and drug use and the consequences of that use.

Homelessness

Homelessness plays a critical role in drug use and sexual risk taking among young men who have sex with men (YMSM). One study compared three groups of YMSM persons: (1) those who were never homeless, (2) those who had been homeless but now had a home, and (3) those who were currently homeless (Clatts et al., 2005). Much higher levels of lifetime drug use and sexual risk were found in those YMSM persons who had experience with homelessness and who were currently homeless.

A study of homeless, adolescent sexual minorities compared these youths with heterosexual, homeless youths on mental and physical health difficulties (Cochran et al., 2002). Findings showed a much higher incidence of running away from home, use of highly addictive substances, experiences with victimization, and having more sexual partners among the GLBT youth. The authors concluded that homeless GLBT youth are at a higher risk for negative outcomes than their heterosexual counterparts.

Leslie Amass, Jonathan Kamien, and Cathy Reback (2007) studied the characteristics of homeless, substance-using men who had sex with men and their HIV risk behaviors. The men were mostly Caucasian and identified themselves as bisexual or gay. Most had exchanged sex for money and drugs within the last thirty days, and many in the sample met the criteria for mental health disorders, including mood disorders and depression. These men were considered high risk for contracting and transmitting AIDS.

Adolescent Issues

Research on GLBT youth indicate that substance abuse problems are more common in these groups than in other adolescent groups (Jordan, 2000).

Gay students are most often the victims of hate crimes and harassment at school, and that increases the risks of suicide and substance abuse in this population (Callahan, 2000). Feelings of marginalization and isolation that contribute to depression and low self-esteem have also been linked to substance abuse problems in GLBT youth (Jordan, 2000). Adolescents who are coming to terms with their sexuality and recognizing that their sexual orientation may be gay are at a higher risk for substance abuse and suicide (Batelaan, 2000; Hahm et al., 2008).

The role of the school in helping GLBT students is very important. The school culture tends to be heterosexist, that is, engaging in discrimination against homosexuals or bisexuals by heterosexuals. The day-to-day life of the high school student revolves around heterosexism, which the school can encourage or discourage. Because gender identity issues can contribute to serious psychological problems and substance abuse, schools might take a proactive position for students coping with these issues (van Wormer and McKinney, 2003). School districts that have not advocated for GLBT youth and have not tried to prevent harassment have been successfully sued (Callahan, 2000).

One examination of college students and health behaviors focused on the relationship between campuswide drinking and drugging norms and beneficial resources available on campus for GLBT students (Eisenberg and Wechsler, 2003). Where resources were available for GLBT students, there was less participation in substance abuse behavior.

Treatment and Prevention

There are many factors in considering the treatment needs of the gay, lesbian, bisexual, and transgender population. GLBT individuals who enter treatment tend to have greater psychopathology and more severe substance abuse problems than the general population (Cochran and Cauce, 2006).

As early as 1995, Karen Holmes and Robert Hodge pointed out that the single most important strategy for preventing alcohol and drug abuse in the GLBT population was to change society from one that is homophobic and heterosexist to one that is inclusive and egalitarian. Prevention efforts must address risk factors including victimization, attempted suicide, school dropout, low self-esteem and self-efficacy, inadequate social services, and the absence of healthy role models, more common among gay and lesbian youths. Health and social service providers who work with the GLBT communities need to be aware of the strong associations between substance abuse and sexual risk behaviors.

Existing programs can improve their delivery of services to the gay and lesbian alcohol- and drug-abusing clients. Professionals who provide substance abuse treatment need to understand the social and historical realities of GLBT life, including homophobia and other forms of discrimination (Center for Substance Abuse Treatment, 2001; Zhankun, 2003). Addiction counselors' attitudes toward the GLBT population are crucial to success in treatment (Mathews, Selvidge, and Fisher, 2005). Michele Eliason and Tonda Hughes (2004) compared the attitudes of treatment counselors toward GLBT clients in rural and urban settings. Clearly, the attitudes of the treatment professionals were crucial to the outcomes of the treatment plan. There was no significant difference in the effect of attitudes or knowledge of specific GLBT problems in rural versus urban settings. Counselors in both settings had very little formal education about GLBT issues, and approximately one-half of the counselors in both settings reported holding ambivalent or negative attitudes toward the GLBT client. Monitoring of programs is needed to ensure that discrimination on the basis of sexual orientation is not present.

Recent work suggests the need for gay-sensitive or gay-specific treatment programs, since nonspecialized treatment programs may not be addressing GLBT needs (Matthews, Lorah, and Fenton, 2006). A study conducted in the early 2000s found that although 11.8 percent (N = 911) of programs in a SAMHSA (Substance Abuse and Mental Health Services Administration) list of treatment services indicated they offered special services for GLBT clients, many were found to offer treatment no different from that offered to other clients. In reality, only 7.4 percent of treatment programs offered a service specifically geared for the GLBT population (Cochran, Peavy, and Robohm, 2007). There is no proof as yet that gay-specific treatment programs have a higher success rate with this population; however, gay Alcoholics Anonymous groups are growing. Age, ethnicity and race, and social class of the gay client are important in developing treatment plans (Halkitis et al., 2005). Mental health, drug use, sexual risk taking, and gay culture need to be central in developing treatment plans. Behavioral therapy approaches seem to be showing treatment effectiveness (Whitten, 2006).

Thomas Irwin (2006) recommends specific treatment programs for meth-addicted MSM. Paranoia and thought disturbances brought on by addiction to meth may set up barriers to engaging in treatment. When clients do enter treatment, there are many people who recover. The Matrix Model of treatment is beneficial for stimulant abuse disorders and includes twelve-step facilitation with cognitive therapy and community reinforcement. Treatment interventions for gay male meth users look especially promising if programs target both substance abuse and sexual behavior (Larkins, Reback, and Shoptaw, 2006).

Family and school are areas where GLBT students have difficulties. Tasks of adolescence include identity formation and emerging sexuality—tasks more complicated when a student is GLBT. This age group in general is at a higher risk for experimentation and use of alcohol and drugs. Risk factors associated with GLBT youth include emotional distress, internalized homophobia, social marginalization, sexually transmitted diseases, and family conflict (Morrow, 2004). If school policy and the environment are hostile to GLBT youth, then these students need counseling and advocacy. This role can be filled by school social workers, who should provide a safe atmosphere and promote freedom from harassment (Batelaan, 2000). Overall, sexual orientation needs to be a consideration in the design of substance abuse treatment programs (Hahm et al., 2008).

As we have seen, transgender women are at a very high risk for HIV, substance abuse, and mental health problems. One study of lesbian and bisexual women found that 16 percent of the women who reported significant drug use and severe health and life problems also reported wanting drug treatment; however, it was not available to them (Corliss, Grella, and Mays, 2006). The Transgendered Resources and Neighborhood Space (TRANS) programs have been successful in promoting health care for transgender women (Nemoto et al., 2005). In addition to education addressing problems of substance abuse and HIV, these neighborhood programs provide general health promotion and referral services. Future efforts need to address how to increase treatment for all substance abusers, including the development of programs geared specifically for GLBT populations.

Conclusion

Homophobia is a significant factor in the lives of gay people, and the role it plays in GLBT substance abuse is critical. Rejection by loved ones, victimization by hate crimes, discrimination in employment, and the general lack of any institutional supports for the GLBT life are all considerations in understanding gay substance abuse.

Social contexts such as gay bars in which GLBT individuals meet and socialize contribute to the heavy drinking patterns of gays. "Coming out" or "leaving the closet"—identifying oneself as a homosexual—is a very stressful process that can lead to abuse of alcohol and drugs, and the high school and college experiences of gay youth may contribute to use and abuse of alcohol and drugs. A further factor to be examined comprises gender differences within the GLBT population; for example, lesbians are more likely than gay men to have been victims of childhood sexual abuse, which can be a factor in substance use and abuse.

Overall, gays and lesbians are considered to be at very high risk for substance abuse problems, especially alcohol, methamphetamine, ecstasy, and other designer and club drugs. Urban gay and bisexual males report methamphetamine use as part of many sexual encounters. Polysubstance use is high, and drugs are frequently used in bathhouses and bars.

Roles that are open to GLBT individuals are more limited than the roles available to the general population. Marriage, parenthood, and secure employment work as safeguards against substance abuse. In our society these safeguards are not as open to GLBT individuals. Reduction in discrimination against the GLBT population can be one factor in reducing overall substance abuse.

8 The Elderly

Substance abuse among the elderly has historically been of little interest to health-care providers and researchers. This chapter reviews the alcohol and drug problems of the elderly, obstacles to identification, and treatment issues. We will see that the drinking and drug problems of the elderly arc descrving of the same level of intervention offered to younger people. Consider Mr. B., for example:

> Mr. B. is a sixty-seven-year-old man who has lived alone since the death of his wife two years ago. After a successful career in business, he retired at the age of sixty-two with the hope that he and his wife would do a lot of traveling. Mr. B. used to enjoy golf and reading, but now he finds he has a hard time concentrating. His favorite activities now are watching television and drinking four to five glasses of red wine daily. His daughter and grandchildren have noticed that he no longer has much energy or interest in life and that he has developed poor personal hygiene. Mr. B.'s daughter is aware that he has significantly increased his use of alcohol in the last two years but she feels this is one of his few pleasures and would feel uncomfortable talking about drinking with her father.

Historical Recognition

The elderly alcoholic received almost no professional attention until the 1970s (Mayer, 1979; Mignon, 1993/1994). Since the 1970s, greater research and clinical attention has been paid to the problems of the elderly, including alcoholism (National Institute on Alcohol Abuse and Alcoholism [hereafter, NIAAA], 2000a; O'Neill, 2003). Increasing interest in the elderly is justified by the fact that the elderly population is growing, and the lack of diagnosis of drinking problems (or misdiagnosis) can lead to inadequate and inappropriate social and medical responses (Gunter and Arndt, 2004; Patterson and Jeste, 1999). Since the early 1990s, however, more emphasis has been placed on diagnosing and treating the elderly with alcohol and drug problems.

There is lack of agreement about the definition of *elderly*. Some consider ages fifty-five and older to be elderly, others think age sixty is the beginning of the elderly years, while still others consider the traditional retirement age of sixty-five to be the beginning of the elderly years. The latter age is also when most become eligible for Medicare health insurance coverage.

There are a number of reasons more professional attention needs to be paid to the substance abuse problems of the elderly. The number of elderly in this country has been rapidly increasing and is expected to continue to rise—numbers alone justify concern about alcohol problems later in life (Coogle, Osgood, and Parham, 2001; Gunter and Arndt, 2004). Some researchers predict an increase in alcohol abuse later in life because younger people include more heavy drinkers and fewer who abstain from alcohol than older generations. The increase in alcohol problems in general, along with the aging of baby boomers, ensures a significant increase in elderly drinking problems, thus creating greater challenges to the health-care system (Hanson and Gutheil, 2004; Liberto, Oslin, and Ruskin, 1992).

Physicians are likely to mistake the effects of alcohol abuse in the elderly for irreversible dementia. These misdiagnosed patients may receive custodial care rather than treatment (see Box 8.1). It has been known for a long time that early identification and treatment of drinking problems in the elderly can prevent expensive long-term institutionalization and thus reduce health-care costs (Gurnack and Thomas, 1989).

The difficulty in identifying and treating alcohol and drug problems for the elderly stems from a number of sources. First, there is little consistency regarding definition. It is still true at this writing that the terms *alcohol abuse, alcohol problems, problem drinking,* and *alcoholism* are often used interchangeably. The substance treatment field has not yet come to grips with these inconsistencies and has used these terms in ways that are confusing. Therefore, the fact that there is no consistent terminology contributes to the difficulty in determining which level or type of intervention is most appropriate. The same lack of consistent definitions of alcohol and drug use and abuse among younger people extends to the elderly as well (Hanson and Gutheil, 2004).

A second reason it is difficult to identify and treat the elderly is that research has been based on dissimilar groups, making it hard to come up with general statements about the elderly with drinking and drug problems.

Box 8.1   Case Example of an Elderly Alcoholic

Mrs. S. was an eighty-eight-year-old woman admitted to the local hospital with a diagnosis of dementia of uncertain etiology. This diagnosis meant that she had mental confusion and no one knew the reason for it. Mrs. S. had been living alone. The director of Social Service in the hospital contacted the family, a son who lived at a distance and actually had little contact with Mrs. S. In reviewing Mrs. S.'s history with the son, he denied that she had a drinking problem.

One day during her hospital stay, Mrs. S. was quite agitated as she sat in a chair with a table in front of it in the hallway by the nurses' station. The director of Social Service approached Mrs. S. and asked why she was upset. Mrs. S. responded by banging her fist on the table in front of her and yelling: "I don't like this bar. I can't get these girls to serve me." Further investigation revealed that a neighbor (who thought she was being helpful) had been bringing alcohol to Mrs. S. at her home.

Mrs. S.'s confusion continued. After a lengthy hospital stay while an application was made for Medicaid insurance coverage, Mrs. S. was transferred to a nursing home.

Source: Case reported by Sylvia Mignon, former director of Social Service in a community hospital in Massachusetts.

A third reason also relates to problems with research—differences in ways data are collected make it difficult to compare findings (Blazer and Pennybacker, 1984; Katz, 2002). Interviews with elderly substance abusers will not likely reveal the same findings as interviews with their physicians, for example. Perhaps the most disconcerting reason it is difficult to identify elderly substance abusers is that many health-care practitioners, especially physicians, lack knowledge of and concern for the drinking and drug problems of the elderly (Hanson and Gutheil, 2004; Mignon, 1995, 1996).

Descriptions of Elderly Alcohol and Drug Problems

Much of the research on elderly drinking focuses on trying to determine how many elderly have drinking problems. For example, studies examine rates of problem drinking for those who are living at home, those who are in the hospital, or the elderly living in nursing homes. In a national survey, it was found that among those over age sixty, 52.8 percent of men and 37.2 percent of women were current drinkers (Breslow and Smothers, 2004).

The 2007 National Survey on Drug Use and Health found 38.1 percent of those aged sixty-five and older drink alcohol (SAMHSA, 2008). Estimates are that between 5 and 16 percent of the elderly living in the community have alcohol problems (Williams, Ballard, and Alessi, 2005; Zimberg, 1978). One review of research on elderly people living in the community found drinking problem estimates between 3 percent and 25 percent for "heavy alcohol use" and 2.2 percent to 9.6 percent for "alcohol abuse" (Liberto et al., 1992). Bowman (1998) found that among those aged sixty and older, medical problems due to drinking accounted for more trips to the hospital emergency rooms than did heart attacks!

Research studies show that elderly men are more likely than elderly women to have drinking problems (Breslow and Smothers, 2004). A 2003 study of those with Medicare insurance found 16 percent of older men and 4 percent of older women reported unhealthy drinking patterns (Merrick et al., 2008). This may be the case because men of all ages are more likely than women to have alcohol problems. It may also be related to the fact that women suffer more physical consequences of alcohol abuse than men and may die at younger ages. In addition, as discussed in Chapter 5, the drinking of women is more likely to remain hidden than the drinking of men, and older women are likely to underreport drinking (Katz, 2002).

Research results are not without controversy, since some studies encourage alcohol use by elderly women. The *New England Journal of Medicine* (2005) published a study that found, of 12,480 women ages seventy to eighty-one, those who drank "moderate" amounts of alcohol on a daily basis reduced their chances of suffering cognitive impairments (Stein, 2005). Women who had consumed one-half to one drink per day for four years were 20 percent less likely to have problems with their mental abilities. The results suggest that alcohol intake can improve blood flow and may have protective factors for the brain as well as the heart.

There is agreement in the research literature that hospitalized or institutionalized seniors have higher rates of alcohol problems. Five to 15 percent of the hospitalized elderly have alcohol-related problems (Patterson and Jeste, 1999). One older study found that 40–60 percent of the residents in nursing homes were alcoholic (Blose, 1978). Some nursing homes are unaware that patients have had alcohol problems and serve alcohol to their patients (Klein and Jess, 2002). In the mid-1990s, Hazelden (1996), a highly regarded treatment program in Minnesota, reported that 20 percent of hospitalized elderly were diagnosed with alcoholism and almost 70 percent of hospitalized elderly had alcohol-related problems.

There is not sufficient evidence to determine exactly how many elderly have alcohol problems (Hanson and Gutheil, 2004). The 2007 National Survey on Drug Use and Health found that 7.6 percent of those older

©iStockphoto.com/benedek

than 65 are binge drinkers, with the rate of heavy drinking of 1.4 percent (SAMHSA, 2008). In reality, more is known about the past drinking practices of the elderly in nursing homes or in other institutions than is known about the elderly still living in the community (Blazer and Pennybacker, 1984). The fact that there have been wide variations in estimates confirms the need to do more to identify the elderly with drinking problems. Diagnostic criteria for substance abuse were developed for younger populations and therefore underestimate prevalence in the elderly (Patterson and Jeste, 1999). Elderly problem drinking has even been referred to as a "hidden epidemic" (Hanson and Gutheil, 2004, 370).

There is no national picture of prescription drug use by the elderly (Moxey et al., 2003). However, it is known that the elderly consume more prescription drugs than any other age group (SAMHSA, 2002). One study found 78 percent of the elderly using prescription medications (Jorgensen et al., 2001). In another study, of elderly living at home, 58 percent were estimated to be taking three or more medications in a year (Moxey et al., 2003). Using conservative estimates, 70 percent of the elderly population in the United States take a minimum of one medication on a long-term basis and 30 percent take three or more long-term medications each year (Moxey et al., 2003). Further, they are known to have more adverse reactions to drugs (Hudson and Boyter, 1997). Moreover, the elderly are at risk for underuse, overuse, or inappropriate use of prescribed medications (NIDA, 2008; Patterson and Jeste, 1999; Schliebner and Peregoy, 1998). Women are at greater risk of abuse of prescription drugs than men.

Box 8.2   Appropriate Use of Medication by the Elderly

The American Geriatrics Society proposes the following recommendations to ensure appropriate use of medications by the elderly (Johnson, 2002).

1. Improve elderly patient access to essential medications through increased Medicare funding for prescriptions.
2. Improve the knowledge and skills of health professionals in geriatric pharmacotherapy through increased training.
3. Improve the ability of elderly persons to access medical professionals who can review the appropriateness of their medications.
4. Educate the elderly about the appropriate use of medications.
5. Develop systems that can identify elderly persons at risk for taking medications inappropriately, and devise interventions to reduce medication problems.

Management of prescription medications in the elderly is more complicated than in younger people (Moxey et al., 2003). Estimates are that the elderly have two to five times more adverse drug reactions than younger people (Carlson, 1994) and are three times more likely to need a hospital admission for an adverse drug reaction (Hudson and Boyter, 1997). Overall, a combination of insufficient information about the effects of drugs on the elderly, the fact that the elderly are often taking a number of prescribed medications, negative bias toward elderly patients, and high drug costs contribute to adverse drug reactions and problems with drug interactions (Rigler, 2000). Low-income elderly must balance the need to purchase medications with purchasing other life essentials (Murray and Callahan, 2003). In 2000, more than 2 million elderly with Medicare health insurance did not take medications as prescribed owing to high costs (Mojtabai and Olfson, 2003). When it comes to a choice between purchasing food and medications, it is hardly a surprise when the elderly do not opt for medications. See Box 8.2 for recommendations of the American Geriatrics Society to ensure appropriate medication usage. Much more needs to be learned about the use and misuse of medication by elderly people.

Indicators of Substance Abuse in the Elderly

In general, the elderly consume less alcohol than younger people, since alcohol consumption tends to decrease after the age of 50 (Williams et al., 2005; Wojnar et al., 2001). Older people may think alcohol has a negative effect on health. They may have less money to spend on alcohol. Another important factor is that the elderly may not accurately report how much alcohol they consume (Hanson and Gutheil, 2004). Since they have diminished physical tolerance for alcohol, focusing solely on the amount of alcohol they consume and how often they drink can be misleading (Moore et al., 2002). The National Institute on Alcohol Abuse and Alcoholism (NIAAA) recommends that those aged sixty-five and older have only one drink of alcohol per day (SAMHSA, 2002).

Early-Onset and Late-Onset Drinking Problems

Research and clinical literature typically divides elderly persons with drinking problems into two groups (Beechem, 2002): early-onset alcoholics have had a long history of alcoholism and just happened to survive into old age; late-onset alcoholics are those who develop drinking problems later in life, often thought to be in reaction to the stresses of aging and the loss of important roles in society. Two-thirds of elderly problem drinkers constitute the early-onset group, while one-third are considered late-onset (Benshoff and Harrawood, 2003; Williams et al., 2005).

Early-onset problem drinkers are more easily identified and tend to have more severe drinking problems, since they are likely to have received intervention from legal or human service agencies, or both (Beechem, 2002; Williams et al., 2005). See Box 8.3 for an example of an early-onset problem drinker.

Box 8.3   Example of an Early-Onset Elderly Drinker

Mr. F., aged sixty-two, is a Vietnam war veteran who served two tours of duty. While he did not want to talk about his combat experiences in the 1960s, when he returned home to his family, his wife acknowledged that he was never the same. Mr. F. began drinking heavily and used heroin. While it had been his dream to complete college after the service, he did not. After supporting Mr. F. for many years, his wife divorced him. His two children, who had lived with much fighting between their mother and father and were victims of Mr. F.'s verbal abuse, had little sympathy for their father. They were embarrassed that he became homeless and would turn up every year or two to ask them for money. Through the years Mr. F. was admitted to detoxification programs between twenty-five and thirty-five times. He always refused a referral to a halfway house where he could begin rebuilding his life. This past year, however, Mr. F. was diagnosed with cirrhosis of the liver due to alcoholism. It was then that he agreed to enter a rehabilitation program for veterans.

Late-onset problem drinkers are less likely to come to the attention of health and human service agencies owing to social isolation, lack of willingness to seek help, and physical limitations. For the late-onset alcoholic, typically drinking problems are attributed to loneliness, social isolation, death of loved ones, loss of status due to retirement, and physical illness (Beechem, 2002). See Box 8.4 for an example of a late-onset problem drinker.

Box 8.4   Example of a Late-Onset Elderly Drinker

Mrs. P., aged sixty-six, retired last year from her challenging and lucrative position as the chief operating officer of a community hospital. She and her husband thought of themselves as happily married for thirty-eight years. However, Mrs. P. typically had worked twelve- to fourteen-hour days and did not spend much time with her husband after their children were grown. Her work was so demanding that Mrs. P. had not developed any hobbies or engaged in activities beyond work. Since her retirement, Mr. P. has noticed that his wife leaves the house only infrequently and then just to go to the liquor store. While she drank at social functions during her working years, Mr. P. is surprised that his wife is now drinking two bottles of red wine each day. When he has tried to express concern about her drinking, Mrs. P. becomes defensive and tells her husband that she can do what she wants now that she is retired. Mr. P. is struggling to help his wife and telephoned their family doctor to seek assistance.

Alcohol and other drugs can combine to have negative consequences for the elderly person (Oslin, 2006). Even relatively small amounts of alcohol can cause problems for the elderly with chronic illnesses who are taking medications (NIAAA, 2000a). They are at higher risk for medical problems and have more abnormal laboratory test results than younger alcoholics (Moore et al., 2002). Some problems that might result are depression, heart or respiratory problems, and high blood pressure. Elderly drinkers are also more likely to fall and fracture a hip than those who do not drink (Gambert, Newton, and Duthie, 1984).

Illicit Drug Use by the Elderly

Little is known about the use of illegal substances by the elderly. However, it is not considered a substantial problem (Blow and Barry, 2002). One explanation is that illicit drug users and addicts may die before they reach elderly status. However, although it is uncommon, a few are able to maintain an illicit drug addiction for fifty or more years (Courtwright, Joseph, and Des Jarlais, 1981). Sophia ran away to New York City when she was seventeen. She became a prostitute working in an expensive New York brothel. In 1934 she was introduced to opium smoking by the madam's boyfriend. Sophia continued smoking opium through the 1930s but World War II cut off smuggled opium in the early 1940s. She began using morphine, first orally and then by injection because it was cheaper and a better high. Sophia became one of the morphine addicts she had once looked down upon. Like others who maintained their addictions over many years, she had the financial resources to take care of herself (Courtwright et al., 1981). Another example is Ike Turner, a musician and ex-husband of singer Tina Turner, who died in his seventies in late 2007 from a cocaine overdose, after a lifetime of drug abuse.

Elderly illegal drug use is expected to rise because baby boomers used more alcohol and illegal drugs than previous generations and can bring these patterns of use into their elderly years (Marks, 2002). For example, illicit drug use by those aged fifty to fifty-nine climbed from 1.9 percent in 2002 to 4.1 percent in 2007 (SAMHSA, 2008). While little research addresses elderly illicit drug use, it is becoming more common to see news accounts of elderly illegal drug activity (see Box 8.5).

Box 8.5   Grandpa Sells Drugs!

Wilfred "Willie" Lacombe, aged sixty-three, was arrested on drug trafficking charges for allegedly selling crack cocaine from his apartment in an elderly housing complex in Taunton, Massachusetts (Rosinski, 2004). Neighbors suspected his involvement with drugs because many people were entering and leaving the apartment in the middle of the night, especially on weekends. Some elderly residents said that while they suspected Mr. Lacombe was selling drugs, they were too scared to call the police. While Mr. Lacombe had previous assault convictions, he had no previous drug charges. A resident of the elderly complex apparently alerted police, and it was there that he was caught selling cocaine to a well-known prostitute.

Richard Picardi, Sr., aged seventy-six and known as "Pops," was arrested for selling OxyContin, Roxicet, and Percocet from the Chelsea, Massachusetts, taxi firm where he worked (Underwood, 2008). Police recovered seventy-four Roxicets in a bottle and $11,646 in a case. The spokesman for the district attorney's office had this to say: "It is certainly brazen to be dealing drugs so openly from a commercial establishment. He is much older than our usual drug defendants" (Underwood, 2008, 19).

Obstacles to Identification and Treatment

Negative attitudes on the part of health professionals toward alcoholics of any age are well documented (Jeffery, 1979; Mignon, 1995, 1996). There is also evidence that health professionals show less interest in elderly patients (Coccaro and Miles, 1984; Greene et al., 1987). Like the rest of society, physicians have been socialized into a negative view of aging and the elderly. It is no surprise that they carry these views into their medical practice. Emil Coccaro and A. Miles (1984) found, in a review of seventeen studies, that medical students, educators, and practicing physicians held indifferent or negative attitudes toward geriatric education and geriatric medical care. These negative attitudes translate into spending less time with elderly patients than with younger patients and making less effort to define and treat medical problems in older patients (Ford and Sbordone, 1980; Gunderson et al., 2005; Patterson and Jeste, 1999). This may be changing, given that gerontology, the study of the elderly, has grown as a field in recent years.

Negative attitudes on the part of physicians and other health professionals toward alcoholics can be attributed to "derived stigma" (Straus, 1976). This means that health professionals prefer to avoid treating alcoholics for fear they will become labeled as treating undesirable patients and will lose favor with patients or other professionals if they become known as the doctor who treats alcoholics. In addition, physicians may regard alcoholics as "messy" patients who do not follow instructions and do not show up for appointments (Mignon, 1995, 1996).

A patient who is both alcoholic and elderly faces two sources of stigma, which can contribute to the reasons drinking problems of the elderly are more often unsuspected and undiagnosed than are the drinking problems of younger people (Mignon, 1993/1994). For older women, there is ageism plus sexism (Katz, 2002). Studies also show that physicians' negative attitudes toward the elderly are fostered by their involvement with only the sick and debilitated elderly; see Box 8.6 (Bernard et al., 2003; Adelman and Albert, 1987; Linn and Zeppa, 1987). Attitudes toward the elderly seem to be moderating, with research in the 2000s showing a neutral attitude toward older adults by medical students (Bernard et al., 2003).

Methods used to identify people with drinking problems may not be appropriate in identifying the drinking problems of the elderly (see Box 8.7). Younger problem drinkers are likely to be identified through family, job, social, and legal problems. The elderly are not likely to be identified as problem drinkers in the same ways because they are less likely to be

---

Box 8.6   Case Example of Physician Treatment of an Elderly Alcoholic

Mrs. T. was an eighty-eight-year-old woman who resided in an extremely wealthy area of a resort community in Massachusetts. She suffered from mental confusion and was admitted to the hospital for a medical workup. Her physician, Dr. B., was chided on occasion for being the doctor of the "rich and famous." Dr. B. wrote an order in Mrs. T.'s medical chart that she could have a daily aperitif, an alcoholic drink taken before dinner as an appetizer.

Within a day or two Mrs. T. showed physical signs of withdrawal, a strong indicator of a serious alcohol problem. On Dr. B.'s day off, Mrs. T. was examined by Dr. B's junior medical partner, who recognized the symptoms of withdrawal. The junior physician discontinued Dr. B.'s order for a daily aperitif and ordered medication to help Mrs. T. through the physical withdrawal from alcohol. Mrs. T. remained in the hospital until she was transferred to a nursing home.

Was Dr. B. unaware of Mrs. T.'s drinking problem? Should he not have been concerned when Mrs. T. asked to drink alcohol while hospitalized—a very uncommon request except among those who have alcohol problems? Did Mrs. T.'s status as a wealthy woman in the community have some bearing on the situation?

Substance abuse treatment professionals know that giving a small amount of alcohol to alcoholics under controlled circumstances is highly inappropriate and contributes further to the craving and discomfort the alcoholic is experiencing.

Source: Case reported by Sylvia Mignon, former director of social service in a community hospital in Massachusetts.

---

married, employed, or arrested for driving under the influence of alcohol (NIAAA, 2000a; Blazer and Pennybacker, 1984). The elderly who do have substance abuse problems report more stress, more financial problems, and more relationships characterized by conflict, and have fewer social resources (Brennan and Moos, 1996).

One study of hospitalized elderly persons found that medical staff recognized only 25 percent of patients who abused alcohol, tobacco, or benzodiazepines (Blow, 1998). Only 10 percent of those with substance problems were referred for treatment. The criteria for substance abuse and dependence in the *Diagnostic and Statistical Manual of Mental Disorders* (DSM-IV), devised for the drinking problems of younger people, may not be appropriate criteria for the elderly.

Box 8.7   Indicators of an Alcohol Problem in the Elderly

1. Falls
2. Accidents
3. Poor nutrition
4. Poor hygiene
5. Poor living conditions
6. Lack of exercise
7. Social isolation

Sources: Graham, K. (1986), Identifying and measuring alcohol abuse among the elderly: Serious problems with instrumentation, *Journal of Studies on Alcohol, 47*(2), 322–326; Rigler, S. K. (2000, March 15), Alcoholism in the elderly, *American Family Physician, 61*(6), 1710–1715.

The diagnosis of mental impairment raises further difficulties. Even physicians who are interested and trained in the problems of elderly alcoholics find it difficult to distinguish the dementia of the elderly caused by alcoholism, known as Wernicke-Korsakoff syndrome, from other forms of dementia such as Alzheimer's disease (Blake, 1990). While it is known that Wernicke-Korsakoff syndrome is a major cognitive impairment due to long-term drinking, it remains unclear whether cognitive decline is caused or made worse by drinking (Beresford, 1995). In a review of the literature on the relationship between elderly alcoholism and psychiatric problems, Richard Finlayson (1995, 58) concluded, "There is ample evidence that both alcoholism and aging contribute to the risk of cognitive impairment." Of patients who have a diagnosis of dementia, it is estimated that 21 to 24 percent have alcohol-related mental impairment (Smith and Atkinson, 1997).

Attitudes of the elderly themselves can make diagnosing and treating an alcohol problem more difficult. One reason is that alcohol problems may be considered a more stigmatizing condition by the elderly than by younger people (Rathbone-McCuan and Triegaardt, 1979; SAMHSA, 2002). There is evidence that only an extremely small minority of elderly are able to acknowledge they have a drinking problem (Abrahams and Patterson, 1978/1979; Guttman, 1978; SAMHSA, 2002). Women may have even more difficulty than men acknowledging a drinking problem, the stigma being stronger for women (CASA, 2006a). Relying on the elderly themselves to acknowledge a problem may not be appropriate because they may have difficulty remembering how often or how much they drink and may not have a daily schedule that helps with recent memory.

Possibly contributing to the problem are family reactions to the drinking behavior of the elderly person. Family members may not talk with their elderly relative about drinking because they may feel they are being disrespectful, or they may think that drinking provides one of the few pleasures available to the elderly individual. Those who have this perception reveal that they know little about drinking problems and the suffering drinking problems cause. The result of these family attitudes is that the elderly can develop drinking problems with little interference from others, and the protective attitudes of family members, including children, can make the problem even worse.

The elderly can also have a psychiatric diagnosis in addition to substance abuse problems (Benshoff and Harrawood, 2003). Rudolph Moos and colleagues (1993) found that 29 percent of elderly men in veterans' hospitals had psychiatric diagnoses. Heavy drinking and depression are closely associated, and it can be difficult to determine which came first; drinking may begin to bring relief from depression, and depression may result from drinking. Older men and older women are at higher risk of depression if they are heavy drinkers (Manninen et al., 2006). With the loss of health, a job, or a spouse—or all of these—some elderly may seek relief through substances (Benshoff and Harrawood, 2003). Substance abuse can be a significant risk factor for suicide in the elderly (Beechem, 2002). One-quarter to one-half of the elderly who commit suicide are substance abusers (Waern et al., 2002).

Treatment and Prevention

There is more research done on determining the prevalence of elderly drinking problems than for examining how the elderly enter substance abuse treatment and appropriate treatment alternatives. In a study of 171 men older than fifty-five, 104 were in a Veterans Administration substance abuse treatment program, while 67 of the men were not receiving substance abuse treatment (Gomberg, 1995). Gomberg found that the elderly men most likely to enter treatment identified themselves as being alcoholic or problem drinkers and had a strong physical dependence on alcohol. The respondents were more likely than the men not in treatment to be still working or seeking a job and to have family and friends who urged them to seek help for their drinking.

Few studies have examined treatment of the elderly alcoholic (Williams et al., 2005). The small body of literature on treatment focuses on whether it is preferable to mix the elderly with other age groups, or whether it is preferable to have special programs for the elderly. This literature also examines whether treatment is more or less successful for the elderly than for younger people (Graham et al., 1995). There appears to be general agreement that elderly patients are just as successful as, and perhaps even more successful than, younger patients in treatment (Lemke and Moos, 2003). Early research found that early- and late-onset problem drinkers responded equally well to treatment (Zimberg, 1978). A study conducted in the early 2000s found that older problem drinkers in inpatient rehabilitation programs had less-severe drinking problems and fewer psychiatric problems but more medical problems (Oslin et al., 2005). In this sample, older drinkers were less likely than middle-aged clients to participate in follow-up treatment.

Roland Atkinson's (1995) review of research on the treatment of older alcoholics concluded that programs specifically for older patients are preferable to treatment settings for mixed ages. However, some researchers have found that the elderly respond as well as younger patients to the same treatment approaches. In a study done in the early 1980s that used data from 550 alcoholism treatment programs, no support was found for the view that the elderly need special programs (Janik and Dunham, 1983). Other, later researchers concluded that there was not much evidence that the elderly require some special type of treatment (Williams et al., 2005).

Of the research supporting special treatment programs for the elderly, one undertaken in the late 1980s found that elderly substance abusers treated in special groups remained in treatment longer and were more likely to complete treatment than their peers in a mixed-age group (Kofoed et al., 1987). Another study of veterans in a substance abuse inpatient program designed specifically for the elderly found that those treated in their own programs were 2.9 times more likely to be abstinent after six months than those treated with younger patients (Kashner et al., 1992). There is evidence that suggests that elderly individuals may need a slower-paced, less confrontational, and more supportive treatment environment than do younger patients. This may be especially the case for older women (Katz, 2002). Joseph Liberto and David Oslin (1997) recommend more structured treatment programs, including comprehensive assessment, flexible rules that relate to discharge from the program, and follow-up counseling when the person has completed a treatment program.

A primary care setting is likely to be more convenient for those who have transportation or mobility problems (SAMHSA, 2002). Elderly people may feel less stigmatized in the primary care setting where ranges of health problems are treated. However, some elderly may require the more intensive services of a substance abuse treatment program.

Brief interventions by physicians, as described in Chapter 12, can be effective with elderly alcohol abusers (Hanson and Gutheil, 2004). The 153 elderly participants in a study by Michael Fleming and Linda Manwell (1999) received two short counseling sessions regarding alcohol from their physicians. In comparison with the control group, the elderly participants who were counseled reduced the frequency of excessive drinking. These findings are considered the "first direct evidence" that primary care physicians in the community can successfully assist the elderly in reducing their drinking (NIAAA, 2004, 437). Thus, the findings underscore the importance of physicians' intervention in the primary care setting with elderly patients' drinking problems.

Older patients may require longer periods for detoxification, the medical treatment needed for those who are likely to experience physical signs of alcohol withdrawal (Rigler, 2000). In addition, elderly patients may need more intensive medical treatment, owing to major medical problems. For these reasons, treatment of older patients may be more complex and expensive than treatment for younger people (Hettinger, 2000).

Motivational interviewing, as developed by William Miller and Stephen Rollnick (1991, 2002), focuses on a cooperative therapeutic relationship with well-defined goals, and has also been recommended as an especially helpful approach in the treatment of the elderly (Barry, Oslin, and Blow, 2001). However, further testing of the motivational interviewing model is needed (Hanson and Gutheil, 2004). The emphasis here is on supportive counseling rather than a confrontational approach, which assists the elderly in seeing the risks in continuing with their current level of drinking. Since spouses influence the drinking of the elderly, it is important for family members to be included in treatment (Graham and Braun, 1999; Hanson and Gutheil, 2004).

The reality is that elderly problem drinkers have traditionally been excluded from alcoholism treatment programs owing to age, and have been excluded from programs for the elderly due to drinking ("Older Problem Drinkers," 1975). While this picture has changed in the early 2000s to a greater willingness to offer treatment to the elderly, there is no consensus as to whether inpatient or outpatient treatment alternatives are preferable. Notwithstanding this open debate, the lack of treatment programs for the elderly continues to be an issue (Schultz, Arndt, and Liesveld, 2003). There is little evidence that elders struggling with an alcohol problem seek assistance through AA (Mosher-Ashley and Rabon, 2001).

The Center for Substance Abuse Treatment encourages treatment programs for the elderly to include the following recommendations outlined by Schonfeld and Dupree (1996):

1. Age-specific group treatment that is supportive and nonconfrontational and aims to build or rebuild the patient's self-esteem;
2. A focus on coping with depression, loneliness, and loss (e.g., death of a spouse, retirement);
3. A focus on rebuilding the client's social support network;
4. A pace and content of treatment appropriate for the older person;
5. Staff members who are interested and experienced in working with older adults;
6. Linkages with medical services, services for the aging, and institutional settings for referral into and out of treatment, as well as case management (Blow, 1998, 73).

The National Institute of Alcohol Abuse and Alcoholism is now encouraging special efforts regarding prevention of elderly problem drinking. NIAAA suggests studies of large populations of the elderly to determine the prevalence of drinking problems, the risk factors, as well as factors that may prevent elderly persons from developing drinking problems. It encourages examination of interventions with the elderly, including screening and assessment, and identifying the barriers to intervention and treatment. NIAAA (2004) also encourages substance abuse training for those who provide services to the elderly, such as homemakers and home health aides.

Conclusion

Researchers and clinicians interested in drinking problems of the elderly need to give more attention to identification and referral of the substance abuser. Since it is unlikely that elderly drinkers will request help with their drinking, the responsibility can fall to family members and health-care practitioners. This is especially important, since younger alcoholics are more apt to receive legal referrals for treatment, while elderly drinkers are more likely to be referred by family and medical professionals. Since elders are not likely to seek treatment on their own, community outreach programs can be helpful in locating elderly problem drinkers and referring them for treatment.

Historically, physicians have shown little interest in treating alcoholic patients. Also, they may not have the knowledge to diagnose alcoholism, and even if they do, they may not be motivated to do anything about it. More likely to refer younger patients for treatment, doctors often offer less-intensive treatment or no treatment to elderly problem drinkers.

Physicians and other health-care practitioners are in an excellent position to identify the elderly who misuse medications and are problem drinkers. It is a hopeful sign that the American Medical Association published guidelines for primary care physicians in preventing, diagnosing, and treating elderly with drinking problems. Patients do expect their physicians to assist them by appropriately prescribing medications and encouraging them to closely follow the medication regimen. Much more needs to be done to ensure that prescription drugs are used in the intended ways and, of course, that the elderly can afford them.

The elderly person will likely take a physician's recommendation for assessment and treatment of a drinking problem seriously. Chapter 12 examines ways in which people, including the elderly, can be screened and assessed for their drinking and drug problems. Overall, much more remains to be done to acknowledge elderly substance abuse, identify those with problems, and devise appropriate interventions.

PART 3

Social Consequences of Substance Use and Abuse

9 College Drinking

Since the late 1970s, college drinking has become a major concern. Although alcohol consumption declined among the population aged twenty-five and older during the 1980s, it rose among those aged seventeen to twenty-four. More people within the latter age group were students in college, and more of them were drinking alcoholic beverages. Once again, parents, college administrators, public health authorities, reformers, and researchers had become concerned about another "epidemic of drinking" among the nation's college students. Shortly after repeal of Prohibition in 1933, temperance reformers complained about alarming increases of drunkenness at football game rallies as well as at the games themselves and lax enforcement of statutes against public drunkenness (Warner, 1970). Complaints by the diehard "drys" went unnoticed, and the "wet" majority prevailed.

In the 1980s, accounts of underage drinking, alcohol-related accident fatalities, and hazing deaths through overdrinking alarmed parents, college officials, and public health authorities. When researcher Henry Wechsler coined the term *binge drinking,* he gave people a handle on the situation and a social problem was born. In the early 2000s heavy drinking by college students has been considered an important public health problem (Martens, Ferrier, and Cimini, 2007). Interestingly, up until the 1980s the term *binge drinking* had a different meaning—it referred to those who had periods of days and weeks of intense drinking followed by abstinence.

This chapter examines the rise, development, consequences, and responses to binge drinking in college. It first examines the antecedent conditions of binge drinking, the campus conditions under which it flourishes, the kinds of problems that attend binge drinking, and the responses it evokes in students and college administrations.

Wechsler first introduced the term *binge drinker* in a 1992 Massachusetts college survey (Wechsler and Isaac, 1992). A few years later he conducted a national survey of 119 four-year colleges with a sample size of some 14,000 students (Wechsler, Isaac, Grodstein, and Sellers, 1994b). For the next ten years, Wechsler published national surveys on various aspects of binge drinking. His 1994 *Journal of the American Medical Association* (*JAMA*) article brought Wechsler's work to national attention. Within a few short years, others made use of his concept in other surveys, including studies of college alcohol problems and collegiate alcohol education and treatment. In the meantime the term had gained general acceptance and increased usage in all media.

According to Wechsler's classification, the standard still used as of this writing, male binge drinkers are those who have had five or more drinks in one sitting at least once in the past two weeks. Women, because they are usually smaller and metabolize alcohol differently from men, are binge drinkers if they have had four drinks at one time during the past two weeks. Wechsler's surveys established that binge drinkers constituted 40 percent of the general college student population. His concept gave a numerical measure, a name for the basic alcohol problem besetting the collegiate world, and an estimate of the size of the problem. In the early 2000s, it has been suggested that it is limiting to define binge drinking within a two-week time period, that it may be more accurate to identify risky-drinking college students without the two-week restriction (LaBrie, Pedersen, and Tawalbeh, 2007). Further, some have taken issue with the definition of *binge drinking,* considering five drinks for men and four drinks for women too low a threshold (Weitzman and Nelson, 2004). Clearly, the definitions of this kind of drinking, also known as heavy episodic drinking, affect our perceptions of the problem and the conclusions we draw about how to deal with it (Presley, Meilman, and Leichliter, 2002).

The Antecedent Conditions of Binge Drinking

Early signs of binge drinking can occur in either or both elementary and high school years. Binge drinking is the most common pattern of alcohol use among high school students (Miller et al., 2007). Underage drinking contributes to unintentional injury, homicide, and suicide, the three leading causes of death among those aged twelve to twenty. In analyzing data from the 2003 National Youth Risk Behavior Survey, Jacqueline Miller and colleagues (2007) found that 45 percent of high school students reported drinking alcohol within the past month. Of drinking students, 29 percent were binge drinkers, with similar rates among boys and girls. Binge drinkers had higher rates of low school performance and risky behaviors, including sexual activity, sexual victimization, smoking, use of illegal drugs, and suicide attempts. While most attention is placed on college drinking, the risk for drinking problems and alcohol dependence is actually higher among high school dropouts and those who do not attend college (Harford, Yi, and Hilton, 2006).

The basic assumption here is that the presence, absence, or variation in both conduct and controls of drinking situations are essential to the making of binge drinkers. Heavy episodic drinking is more apt to occur when there is a weakening of social controls combined with an excess of definitions favorable to heavy drinking, such as spending time with other heavy drinkers (Hirschi, 1969; Sutherland, 1970).

Early exposure to uncontrolled drinking increases one's chances of becoming a binge drinker. Collegiate drinking studies report that binge drinkers are more likely to have experienced their first drunkenness before the age of 16, especially at age 12 or younger. Also, having an alcoholic parent increases the chances of becoming a heavy drinker. An early study comparing 150 moderately drinking Tufts University undergraduates with 150 imprisoned chronic drunkenness offenders was suggestive on this very point (Ullman, 1953). Most Tufts undergraduates had their first drinking experience at age 15 at home with their parents as instructors, and recalled nothing special about their first drinking occasion. Most of the chronic drunkenness offenders had their first experience at age 12, in a public drinking place, with an older friend or stranger as companion. All recalled getting drunk.

Researchers find that adolescents who drink heavily are much more likely to have friends who are heavy drinkers. Their and their friends' tolerance for drunkenness has often been connected with absent or erratic parental regulation. Binge drinkers are more likely to come from families of fairly high socioeconomic status. If their parents drank or if one of them had a drinking problem, adolescents stand a much better chance of becoming binge drinkers.

People typically learn how to drink in intimate groups. Adolescence is the period when peer-group influences become stronger, along with parental influences. When one's peers' drinking pattern agrees with one's parents, no conflict exists. When peers' drinking patterns conflict with parents' drinking patterns, conditions for clandestine drinking have been established. Adolescents drink with friends at times, places, and circumstances that decrease the chances of being caught by parents or other authorities. Subsequent drinking generally takes place in the absence of social controls. If clandestine drinking proves rewarding, repetition follows. Youths have learned that drinking is fun in the absence of personal and social controls and the presence of like-minded friends.

Given alcohol's role as social facilitator when people gather—as well as its physical and mental feel-good effects—its popularity with the collegiate population is quite understandable. Social, along with personal, identity is being further developed, and students spend much of their time with peers. Their parents are absent; their contact with faculty is both highly specific and infrequent. The people with whom they are in the most frequent, nonspecific contact of considerable duration and intensity are their peers. Peer control is a significant condition of undergraduate life. The extent and degree of peer influences on binge drinking over the course of the college years become an important developmental issue.

Undergraduates face a variety of problems of adjustment when beginning college (Becker, Geer, and Hughs, 1968; Gorsline, Holl, Pearson, and Child, 2006). Study habits, getting good grades, finding a place in the collegiate organizational scheme, deciding on a major, and learning and adapting to student culture are only some of the problems they face. The solution to many of these problems comes from their peers. Chance as well as choice figures in the process of selecting new friends. Whether through proximity (roommate, floor mate, teammate, or classmate) or shared social characteristics or interests or values, drinking with peers facilitates the process of acquaintance. Drinking not only facilitates contact and the chances of making friends, it also adds yet another basis for selection of friends. Thus, in time, students tend to develop friendships with those who have similar drinking patterns, whether abstainers or light, moderate, or heavy drinkers.

College students learn or perfect the art and practice of binge drinking in specific and typical drinking situations with a group of regular drinking partners. Undergraduate drinking involves participants in face-to-face contact. Drinking groups of a particular social composition are more likely to participate in binge drinking (Harford, Wechsler, and Muthen, 2003). Thus, binge drinking is both a process and a product of social interaction.

Heavy episodic drinking, while seen by the larger culture as deviant behavior, may also be seen as acceptable behavior that should be promoted (Leppel, 2006). Those who engage in heavy drinking in college can encourage heavy drinking among their peers. Students who can "hold their liquor" (meaning they can drink significant amounts of alcohol and not appear intoxicated) can be considered "cool" by others. Binge drinking varies according to the culture, demography, organization, and environment of colleges, structural conditions that influence drinking. Before examining drinking groups and drinking patterns, a brief summary of the structural conditions of binge drinking follows. College culture includes its traditions and rituals, and the varieties of drinking habits shared by faculty, staff, and students are part of its subcultures. Demography includes the number and distribution of students by sex, age, and racial and ethnic groups. Organization refers to such characteristics of colleges as public or private, four-year or two-year, coed or women's, military or denominational, and so on. Environment includes region, ecology (urban, suburban, or rural), and housing.

National surveys of alcohol consumption find significant variations in drinking in the United States. The rank order of drinkers of alcohol by region, from most to least, is the Northeast, Midwest, West, and then the South. Similarly, most drinkers are found in urban areas, with fewer drinkers in suburban areas. And the fewest drinkers are located in rural areas (SAMHSA, 2008). Colleges in the Northeast have the highest percentage of binge drinkers. While public colleges have the highest percentage of drinkers, private colleges have the highest percentage of binge drinkers (Presley et al., 2002). Students at public colleges consume more alcohol than students at private colleges. This may well be because most public colleges are located in urban areas, whereas more private colleges are situated in suburban or rural areas. Four-year colleges have almost twice the number of heavy episodic drinkers as two-year colleges.

Few studies have compared schools with various heavy drinking rates. In the CORE Alcohol and Drug Survey, conducted in the 1990s, schools with various heavy episodic drinking (HED) rates were divided into three categories: high HED, medium HED, and low HED (Presley et al., 2002). This secondary analysis of the CORE Alcohol and Drug Survey found specific demographic and environmental influences on college drinking. Compared with students from medium and low HED schools, more students from high HED schools were white, male, underage, living on campus, and members of a fraternity or a sorority (Presley et al., 2002).

This study suggested that peer pressure, long used in explanations of collegiate drinking, actually has two facets: the pressure of face-to-face contact and the pressure of assumed or actual conduct of other members of an organization (Presley et al., 2002). Two examples of the second variety come from comparisons of black and women students under two different campus conditions. Black students attending black colleges generally have low HED rates. Black students attending white colleges have much higher HED rates although lower than white rates. Similarly, women attending women's colleges have low HED rates. Women attending coed schools have much higher HED rates.

©iStockphoto.com/REKINC1980

Some major studies have provided descriptive generalizations of the various social characteristics of heavy episodic drinkers. The CORE Survey, as noted above, found that white males under twenty-one and fraternity members were much more likely to be heavy episodic drinkers. The CORE Institute (2006a) reported over 81 percent of college whites are drinkers, compared with African Americans at 6.8 percent and Hispanic college students at 4.1 percent.

Peer Control and Living Arrangements

A well-known generalization states that students who live on campus are much more likely to become binge drinkers than students who live off campus. But why is it that students who reside in fraternity or sorority houses or college residence halls have a much greater probability of becoming heavy episodic drinkers than those students who live at home or in apartments? After all, light, moderate, and problem drinkers as well as abstainers can be found in all types of residences. However, the extent and degree of peer influence are greatest in dormitories, fraternities, and sororities. Peer influences can be reduced if college students are living at home with their parents. As has been known for some time, commuters are least likely to be heavy episodic drinkers.

Becoming a college student involves a process of major status change. First-year students experience changes in the number, frequency, duration, and intensity of contact with parents and other students. Three stages mark this rite of passage: acquaintanceship, routine, and group affiliation. During acquaintanceship, face-to-face contact with parents disappears for some time, to be replaced by a wide variety of contacts with fellow students, faculty, and staff. Routine begins to emerge with the beginning of classes, classroom contacts with faculty at specific times and places, residence hall staff and administrative personnel, and a variety of specific and diffuse contacts with roommates, residence hall mates, and students taking the same courses. A good deal of time is spent in the company of residence hall mates and roommates at meals and before and after classes in the residence hall. If students reside in a fraternity or sorority house, the frequency, duration, and intensity of contact with peers are at their highest levels.

Students affiliate with campus groups according to common interests and values. They join study groups, play groups, and work groups. Or they concentrate on one of the three. Membership in a variety of groups produces the well-rounded and educated young adult.

College freshmen learn about drinking and drinking expectations, sometimes with deadly results. The likelihood of indoctrination increases markedly if students live in fraternities or residence halls. And one central feature of the campus "fun culture" is heavy drinking. The frequency of partying and drinking increases with each year in college (CORE Institute, 2006a; Harford, Wechsler, and Seibring, 2002). Residence hall parties get broken up if they get out of hand. Fraternities have not always had resident assistants making rounds and writing residents up for infractions of college alcohol policy. Residence hall residents attend both fraternity and off-campus parties. Hence, heavy episodic drinkers are more likely to be found in residence halls and most likely to be found in fraternities. And since 1984, when twenty-one became the legal age for purchasing alcoholic beverages, many binge drinkers are underage freshmen and sophomores (see Box 9.1).

The routine activities of binge drinkers show how they spend a good deal of their time on and off campus, and how the patterns of regular social interactions can be at the expense of scholarly and other values. Binge drinkers are much more likely to drink in larger groups and to have four or more roommates and four or more friends. They are much more apt to

Box 9.1   The Death of Scott Krueger

Scott Krueger, an eighteen-year-old freshman at the Massachusetts Institute of Technology (MIT), died in 1999 as a result of alcohol poisoning. Krueger passed out while involved in an initiation rite at the Phi Gamma Delta fraternity, where he lived. Krueger and his pledge class were expected to finish alcohol left for them while other fraternity brothers watched the movie *Animal House*. After Krueger passed out, he was taken to his room and placed on his stomach with a trash can near his head. Later, it was the fraternity brothers who called campus police. Krueger lay in a coma for three days before he died.

Three years later MIT paid $6 million to settle a civil suit filed by Krueger's family. The family used $1.25 million to create a new scholarship for MIT students. MIT president Charles Vest stated: "The death of Scott as a freshman living in an MIT fraternity shows that our approach to alcohol education and policy, and our freshman housing options, were inadequate. I am deeply sorry for this" (Emery, 2000).

Changes at MIT since the death of Krueger include not allowing freshmen to live in fraternity houses. All fraternities and sororities on campus must have a resident adviser. Students now receive instructions in the responsible serving of alcohol, and MIT requires registration of parties where alcohol will be served. For gatherings larger than seventy-five people, third-party cash vendor services are required. Consequences of violating alcohol policies range from reprimand for first offenders to expulsion in the most severe cases.

Sources: Herper, 1999; Ray, 2004; Emery, 2000.

drink in bars, at off-campus parties and at drinking games, or on or off campus (Knight et al., 2002).

A well-established generalization states that the larger the drinking group, the longer they stay in the drinking situation and the more they drink (Storm and Cutler, 1981). Belligerence is one of the outcomes of drinking in these kinds of situations. When altercations develop, male students are more likely to be the instigators, whereas binge-drinking women are much more apt to be victims of aggression (Harford et al., 2003). Two studies, done in the late 1990s, showed that leaders in fraternities and in athletic teams set the tone in those drinking groups (Cashin and Meilman, 1998; Leichliter et al., 1998). Findings from research conducted in the early 2000s showed that binge drinkers spent four hours socializing, one hour in intramural or intercollegiate sport, and three hours watching television. As might be expected, that leaves just one hour for study time (Knight et al., 2002).

Fraternity Drinking

Fraternity members are known to have higher rates of alcohol consumption than other college students. One study of a national college fraternity found that 97 percent of fraternity members drank alcohol and 86 percent were binge drinkers, with 64 percent being frequent binge drinkers (Caudill et al., 2006).

Fraternities support heavy drinking, and their widespread protection from oversight due to their status as private organizations has contributed to the frequency and severity of alcohol-related problems. Indoctrination is more likely in fraternities because of hazing rituals, emphasis on masculinity and drinking, presence of bars in fraternities, lack of surveillance, and the encapsulation of fraternity life (Borsari and Carey, 1999). Major examples of problems include deaths, accidents from hazing, and sexual assault, including gang rape. Weekend keg parties at fraternities are important drinking places for freshmen that are pledging or just attending these parties. Minors are apt to be served in fraternities, which, as private organizations, are less subject to official scrutiny. More than 75 percent of hazing deaths from 1900 to 1999 occurred in the last three decades of the twentieth century, with 99 percent of drinking deaths occurring in the last two decades (see Box 9.2). The majority of students who died were first-year students (Nuwer, 2002, 2004).

While acquaintance or date rape may not be related to where college students live, gang rape is very much associated with fraternity house parties. Gang rape is likely to occur when there is strong concern for masculinity,

---

Box 9.2   Alcohol Poisoning: Fraternity Deaths on Campuses

Samantha Spady, a nineteen-year-old Colorado State University sophomore, died of alcohol poisoning September 5, 2004, in the Sigma Phi fraternity. Other students who thought she needed to "sleep it off" had placed her in a Sigma Phi storeroom. Spady had been the homecoming queen and senior class president, and had worked for the Drug Abuse Resistance Education (DARE) program in her hometown of Beatrice, Nebraska. In the eleven-hour binge before her death, Spady consumed the equivalent of thirty to forty beers.

Lynn "Gordie" Bailey, an eighteen-year-old freshman at the University of Colorado in Boulder, died of alcohol poisoning after participating in a Chi Psi fraternity ritual in which he had to drink whiskey and wine. After drinking the equivalent of twenty-two beers in a two-hour period, Bailey had a blood alcohol level of 0.328 percent (Cada, 2004).

where women are defined as sex objects, and where using alcohol is the easiest and quickest route to sexual conquest (Martin and Hummer, 1989; Sanday, 2007).

College Athletes

With higher rates of alcohol consumption and binge drinking, athletes thus have higher rates of alcohol-related consequences than nonathletes (Nelson and Wechsler, 2001; Presley et al., 2002). These findings come as a surprise to many, since it is often assumed that athletes take better care of their health and have less time to engage in drinking and drug use. One study found that athletes perceived their own alcohol use to be lower than that of nonathletes (Kueffler, Lim, and Choi, 2005). In examining types of athletes, wrestlers have significantly higher drinking rates than those who play volleyball, softball, or track (Kueffler et al., 2005). With respect to gender, male athletes have significantly higher rates of alcohol use than their female counterparts.

High rates of alcohol use by athletes may be related to the intense pressure of high-stakes intercollegiate sports. High school and college athletes may be combining steroid use with alcohol. More public attention has been given to this problem in the wake of Marion Jones and other athletes admitting to steroid use after lying about it (Shipley, 2007). While athletes are more likely to be the targets of alcohol prevention programs on campus, these efforts have not been especially successful (Nelson and Wechsler, 2001).

Binge Drinking and Its Troubles

Unfortunately, the "party hard" ethic can take a toll. Research on college drinking describes numerous negative consequences of heavy drinking (Wechsler et al., 1995; Westmaas, Moeller, and Woicik, 2007). Binge drinkers can make trouble for drinkers and nondrinkers alike due to obnoxious or offensive behavior, including vomiting—which someone must clean up. Substantial numbers of binge drinkers also break the laws (underage drinking, assaults, rape, vandalism). But heavy drinkers can be victims as well as offenders. As the quantity and frequency of drinking increase, the number and severity of alcohol problems similarly increase.

The troubles that drinking makes for college students include the following: missing class, getting behind in schoolwork, regretful behavior, forgetting where one was or what one did, arguing with friends, engaging in unplanned sexual activities, lacking protection when having sex, damaging property, trouble with the campus or local police, getting hurt or injured, requiring medical treatment for an alcohol overdose, and getting into an accident while driving after drinking alcohol (Wechsler et al., 1994b; Weitzman and Nelson, 2004). One study examined the troubles heavy episodic drinkers made for their fellow students and others. Students listed the following troubles that their heavy-drinking peers caused them: having been insulted or humiliated; had a serious argument or quarrel; been pushed, hit, or assaulted; had property damaged; had to take care of drunken student; found vomit in the hall or bathroom; had studying or sleeping interrupted; experienced an unwanted sexual advance; or been a victim of sexual assault or date rape (Wechsler et al., 1995).

College health personnel are generally advised to identify student problem drinkers. The *Diagnostic and Statistical Manual of Mental Disorders* (DSM-IV-TR) classifies problem drinking into two categories: alcohol abuse and alcohol dependence, as discussed in Chapter 12. Symptoms of alcohol abuse include drinking in hazardous situations, having alcohol-related problems, experiencing recurrent interpersonal problems, and recurrent legal problems. Symptoms of alcohol dependence include drinking more or longer, or both, than intended; drinking despite personal problems; and increased physical tolerance of alcohol. Researchers in the early 2000s sampled 14,009 students from 114 four-year colleges and diagnosed 31.6 percent as alcohol abusers and 6.3 percent as alcohol dependent (Knight et al., 2002). The percentage of abusers and those dependent on alcohol rose when they divided both types into low, medium, and high heavy episodic drinkers. This study added to the growing body of literature that has established the generalization that heavy episodic drinkers, when compared with other college students, are much more likely to live in fraternities and sororities or on-campus residence halls, spend much time socializing with a larger group of friends and roommates, drink in much larger groups, enjoy partying, and give as little time as necessary to studying.

The National Center on Addiction and Substance Abuse (CASA) estimated in 2005 that approximately 1,400 college students die each year from alcohol-related accidents, including car accidents. Other estimates are even higher. From 1998 to 2001, among college students aged eighteen to twenty-four, deaths increased 6 percent from approximately 1,600 to more than 1,700 from alcohol-related, unintentional injuries (Hingson et al., 2005). In the same years for the same college students, driving under the influence increased from 26.5 percent to 31.4 percent.

College students come to the attention of campus or local police for underage liquor-law violations. A fair percentage of those who come to police attention either as offenders or as victims of violent crimes are intoxicated at the time of the crime. African American students report that campus police more closely scrutinize their behavior than that of Caucasian students (Peralta, 2007). Also demanding the attention of campus or local police is the increasing percentage of freshman fraternity pledges dying from alcohol poisoning after fraternity hazing rituals (Nuwer, 2002). Violence against women, reported as well as unreported, seems to be a fairly common event, particularly for those who drink heavily. In the early 2000s, in a national sample of women attending college, researchers found that one in twenty had been raped. Women most likely to have been raped were under age twenty-one, lived in sorority houses, used drugs, drank heavily in high school, attended colleges with high HED rates, and were raped while intoxicated (Wechsler et al., 2002). Of female rape victims in this national sample, 72 percent were intoxicated at the time of the rape (Mohler-Kuo et al., 2004).

Responses to the Binge-Drinking Epidemic

Drink, drinking, drunkenness, and alcoholism have all been defined as social problems at different times and places in US history. The last quarter of the twentieth century was a time when excessive drinking by college students came to be seen as a social problem by many people. Rising consumption of alcoholic beverages among college students, an increased emphasis on health, a crackdown on drunken driving, and the growing conservatism of the country all have contributed to the increased public concern. The proliferation of large survey samples of college drinking and widespread media attention given to the concept of binge drinking provided the sufficient conditions.

From the mid-1970s until 1988, many states first lowered, then raised the legal drinking age to twenty-one. Researchers studied the lowering and then the raising of the drinking age to see if legal changes affected rates of alcohol consumption among college students. Consumption remained high during both changes. After the raised drinking age, most underage students drank in residence halls (O'Hare, 1990). As drinking in residence halls mounted, colleges could no longer ignore on-campus drinking and its aftereffects. Responses took place in two areas: campus alcohol policy and enforcement and efforts to reduce alcohol consumption by all types of drinkers in the student body.

For the more than 4,000 colleges in the United States today, increased numbers as of this writing have clearly stated policies; 955 of them established specific alcohol policies in response to the problems that age-specific prohibition made for them. Yet for most colleges, enforcement of alcohol policy has been highly variable. Enforcement can be strict, selective, erratic, lax, or nonexistent (Schuh and Shore, 1997). Twentieth-century field research shows how enforcement varies with the culture and social organization of university housing as well as a college's administrative bureaucracy (Riggs, 1970).

An anthropologist made a field study of one floor in a Rutgers University residence hall with respect to alcohol policy (Moffatt, 1989). He found that the resident assistant (RA) permitted drinking during the fall term, only to report every drinking violation during the spring term. An experiment in two University of New Hampshire residence halls compared standard university disciplinary procedure with student court adjudications of alcohol violations, finding the student court excessively tolerant (Cohn and White, 1990). A three-year study of three Northeastern University freshman residence halls yielded three generalizations: the swifter the application of sanctions for violating rules against drinking in the dorms, the fewer the violations; residence hall directors set the tone for their RAs; and RAs adopted one of three enforcement styles—"by-the-book," "in-between," and "laid-back" (Rubington, 1997).

Employee assistance programs (EAPs) in industry work when supervisors confront employees when their drinking impairs their work performance. One university's attempt to develop a residence hall EAP failed (Williams and Knox, 1997). RAs, trained to report drinking-impaired residents to the residence director, were reluctant to get students in trouble. Writing incident reports only added to their already considerable workload, and residence directors failed to see any consequences after they filed reports.

In contrast with the vast amount of research on college student drinking, there are only a handful of studies on the effectiveness of college alcohol policy. One study reported on the responses of college administrators to campus alcohol problems (Wechsler et al., 2000). A second study compared rates of heavy drinking on campuses that ban alcohol with campuses having no alcohol ban (Wechsler et al., 2001a). The third study compared heavy drinking on campuses with alcohol-free dorms with campuses without alcohol-free dorms (Wechsler et al., 2001b); college administrators, 714 in all, completed open-ended questionnaires and listed the variety of programs that their colleges were in the process of instituting. While all administrators had much to say about the programs on their campuses, they were silent on the question of whether the programs were actually functioning. None of the administrators reported any studies of their program's effectiveness.

The comparison of nineteen alcohol-ban colleges with seventy-six no-ban colleges produced only suggestive results (Wechsler et al., 2001a). Heavy drinking occurred on both campuses. There was, however, 30 percent less binge or heavy episodic drinking on the alcohol-ban campuses. The alcohol-free dorm study found that residents drank as heavily off campus as students living in dorms that permitted drinking. But since they did not drink in the alcohol-free dorm, the authors concluded that college administrators might well want to consider extending the idea of the alcohol-free dorms to their own campuses (Wechsler et al., 2001b).

A study of the campus alcohol policy of eleven Massachusetts four-year state colleges added further support to the notion of variable enforcement (Knight et al., 2003). After Massachusetts required all of its state colleges to adopt a uniform alcohol policy in 1999, researchers administered detailed questionnaires to a random sample of students from all of the colleges. Two years later, students answered questions about their drinking practices, experiences with punishment for violating the new alcohol policy, and their evaluations of the policy's enforcement. Deans and heads of campus security answered questions on the stringency of enforcement and any modifications they would make in the alcohol policy. The researchers first divided the eleven schools into no heavy episodic drinkers, occasional heavy episodic drinkers, and frequent heavy episodic drinkers. Then they divided the 1,251 students into nondrinkers, occasional drinkers, and frequent heavy drinkers. Heavy drinkers were more often men and on-campus residents. Student perceptions of enforcement derived from their own personal experiences with enforcement. Thus, heavy drinkers were more likely to say that the alcohol policy was strongly enforced. More than 80 percent of the infractions were for disturbing the residence hall peace. The above-mentioned three-year freshman residence hall study reported similar findings (Rubington, 1997). These studies suggest that when students "drink responsibly" in residence halls, they will not be written up by RAs or campus security.

College campuses have a variety of policies for eliminating, restricting, or reducing consumption of alcoholic beverages. Colleges can be totally prohibitive when they disallow members of the administration and the faculty and student body from possessing or serving alcohol in either buildings or on grounds. Some colleges have an age-specific policy that prohibits underage students from possessing, serving, or drinking on campus. These colleges may well have an on-campus pub for students of legal drinking age. The pub will have officials checking identification at the doors and may even have trained bar personnel who monitor student intake. Keg parties are banned, while student parties are subject to numerous restrictions (number of guests, preregistration, hours, and required service of nonalcoholic beverages). Some colleges permit only beer and wine in rooms for students of legal drinking age. Others may limit upper-level undergraduate possession to 64 ounces of distilled spirits. College administrators may encourage neighborhood bars to discontinue happy hours and reduced prices during certain periods, outlawed in Massachusetts in the late 1980s. In its review of 2000–2004 CORE data, the CORE Institute concluded that "awareness and enforcement of campus alcohol and other drug policies and awareness of prevention and treatment programs have a low impact on the drinking behaviors of students" (CORE Institute, 2006b, 11).

A program called Marketing Social Norms, developed in the 1990s, spread rapidly to a number of colleges. It has been well-known for a number of years that college students generally exaggerate the amount of drinking on their campuses. Alan Berkowitz and H. Wesley Perkins (1986) first commented on this discrepancy between belief and behavior. The discrepancy led them to devise a program for reducing alcohol consumption on campus (Perkins, 2002). According to the authors, soon after students arrive on campus, they assume that most students drink more than they do. Consequently, they increase their own intake in order to conform to what they take to be the drinking norm. It is this kind of misperception of the drinking norm that has contributed to the rising curve of collegiate alcohol consumption that began in the 1980s. Thus, the authors reasoned, if incoming students were provided with accurate information about the drinking norm on campus, they would be less compelled to join the ranks of the heavy drinkers. They might drink considerably less, and their alcohol consumption would then be in line with the true campus drinking norms.

Media presenting these data include newsletters, articles in the campus newspaper, posters, fliers, billboards, and radio programs. Programs marketing social norms have attained national popularity. Claims of success in reducing drinking on campus induced a number of colleges to adopt similar programs. In time, four articles—claiming that the marketing of social norms (MSN) campaigns had reduced drinking—were subjected to critical scrutiny. Three failed to meet accepted standards of scientific methodology, while the fourth reported that the MSN campaign failed to reduce high-risk drinking. A review article appearing in 2003 compared thirty-one colleges with MSN programs with sixty-one that had no such programs. The findings reversed social norms theory predictions. The no-program schools experienced slight *decreases* in heavy drinking whereas the MSN schools experienced slight *increases* in heavy drinking. The article concluded with a plea for more scientific research on social-norms marketing (random samples, comparison groups, and measures of intensity of exposure to MSN campaigns) (Wechsler et al., 2003).

Three years later a study meeting all these criteria was published (DeJong et al., 2006). This study randomly assigned nine colleges to the treatment condition (an MSN campaign) and another nine colleges to the non-treatment group. It had collected baseline data on 2,538 students in 2000 and post-test data on 2,939 students in 2003. Findings supported MSN predictions. The study reported a 30 percent reduction in alcohol consumption in the nine treatment schools. It also found that the more intense the exposure to norms marketing, the greater the reduction in alcohol consumption (DeJong et al., 2006).

Given the inordinate amount of time that well-designed evaluation studies require, another evaluation of MSN is not likely to appear in the next couple of years from this writing. In the meantime, more colleges will adopt MSN campaigns without rigorous evaluations.

One traditional response to drinking, alcohol education, continues to be present in at least one-third of the nation's colleges. The intent of alcohol education on campus was originally designed to get students thinking about not drinking at all. Abstinence was its goal at the start. Since the late 1970s, responsible drinking has been the goal. Despite a vast body of research attesting to its ineffectiveness, alcohol education continues to be a favorite campus technique for reducing alcohol consumption ("College Drinking," 2005). Evaluation studies find that alcohol education adds knowledge, changes some attitudes, but does not change drinking patterns. It always ends up "preaching to the choir," since only light or moderate drinkers sign up.

When a campus enforces federal, state, and local ordinances as well as its own alcohol policy, it changes how students act. The passage of the twenty-one-year-old drinking age markedly reduced car crashes involving young people aged eighteen to twenty-five. It also reduced the alcohol consumption of youth in the same bracket (Toomey and Wagenaar, 2002). Unfortunately, there have been few data on underage possession of alcoholic beverages on college campuses. The general point seems to be that once the law was passed, most people affected by it obeyed the law. Effectiveness of the enforcement of age-specific prohibition on undergraduates has yet to be properly evaluated. Once again, variability in the enforcement of alcohol policy is an issue.

Brief intervention with motivational interviewing, as described in Chapters 12 and 13, has shown effectiveness with college freshmen ("College Drinking," 2005). Treatment participants reported fewer drinking occasions and fewer drinks when indulging in alcohol (Michael et al., 2006).

In reality, there are far more moderate-drinking college students than binge drinkers. Elissa Weitzman and Toben Nelson (2004) advocate a "population approach" in which all college drinkers are targeted by prevention programs. It may be more realistic to reduce drinking among the majority of college drinkers than to have a significant impact on the frequent heavy and problem drinkers. This approach encourages media advocacy and policy controls to raise the prices of alcohol, reduce the number of alcohol outlets, and reduce alcohol advertising.

Another new strategy in reducing college drinking is showing effectiveness with students who were previously heavy drinkers. CollegeAlc is an online alcohol-misuse prevention course. One study showed a reduction in the number of episodes of heavy drinking, reduction in drunkenness, as well as a reduction in alcohol-related problems (Bersamin et al., 2007). See Box 9.3 for a description of alcohol-free dormitories specifically for students in recovery from substance abuse problems.

Conclusion

Heavy drinkers, like social problems, are made, not born. Generally the news media either coin or adopt a snappy, short term that characterizes the

---

Box 9.3   Substance Abuse Recovery on Campus

"If I had been able to get into one of these recovery dorms, maybe I wouldn't [have] had so much trouble getting through my first two years of college," said twenty-three-year-old Randy C. of the University of Central Florida, as he pointed to a newspaper article on recovery dorms at Case Western Reserve University in Cleveland. A first-semester junior, Randy fell victim to his taste for alcohol, marijuana, and other drugs in high school. "It got worse when I entered college at Miami." Poor grades, missed classes, arrest for driving under the influence (DUI), and interpersonal problems with college friends led to his withdrawal from college.

In addition to the special attention to binge-drinking practices among students, college-life professionals are taking an additional step: recovery dorms for students with histories of substance abuse. Originally pioneered by Rutgers University, the idea of a special dormitory is catching on slowly at other universities, such as Michigan's Grand Valley State University and, as noted, Case Western Reserve. Concerned with binge-drinking problems among its students, the recovery dorm program is part of a large effort to end substance abuse on campus. Located on a quiet street, the unmarked dormitory allows student residents to keep their efforts at recovery private and confidential. Each resident in the recovery dorm must have an approved treatment plan in place. Counseling or Alcoholics Anonymous meetings, or both, are the centerpiece of the treatment plan. House rules forbid alcohol or other drugs on the premises. Relapses are dealt with on a case-by-case basis. As with other recovery dormitories, a buddy system helps to create a supportive environment toward sustaining sobriety and long-term recovery.

Source: Adapted from Associated Press (2005, Jan.), Recovery dorms help some students, *Florida Today,* 19A.

situation, and a social problem is "born." The battery of surveys tracing the characteristics of heavy drinkers on college campuses in the 1990s defined the situation succinctly with the catchy term *binge drinking*. Despite the criticism that the term had primarily been used to describe alcoholic drinking bouts that went on for days, it succeeded in focusing public attention on excessive drinking on college campuses. Eventually, the term *binge drinking* also became known as heavy episodic drinking, but by that time the existence of a severe campus problem had been well established.

This chapter sketched the signs of adolescent heavy drinking, its growth in high school, and the conditions under which it is most likely to flower in the college years. After examining the troubles binge or heavy episodic drinkers make for themselves and others and the dire negative consequences that follow such excess, it looked briefly at some of the major responses of college administrations in their attempts to regulate and reduce a variety of campus drinking problems.

For years, Ivy League colleges defined heavy drinking as just a phase and followed a policy of laissez-faire. Research demonstrates that after graduation, adult responsibilities make moderate drinkers out of former heavy drinkers (Bartholow, Sher, and Krall, 2003). Exploratory studies tracing stability and change in campus drinking careers might shed some light on the social circumstances under which students change their drinking styles. Similar studies might also study a cohort of students who are diagnosed as substance abusers and compare them with those diagnosed as substance dependent according to DSM-IV-TR criteria. Considerable progress has been made, a variety of programs have emerged, and more are very likely to appear.

10 Alcohol, Drugs, and the Family

Cecelia and Ben met when they were in their late twenties. Ben had a terrific sense of humor, and his talents, honesty, and attention to her impressed Cecelia. They married after dating for over a year. Ben had told Cecelia that he was an alcoholic, but she didn't believe him. Cecelia knew that he drank wine almost daily but didn't see it as a problem. After all, she had grown up with an alcoholic father, and Ben didn't behave at all like her father. Ben came to drink more and started smoking marijuana every day. Their relationship deteriorated over several years, and they couldn't resolve whether to have children or not. Ben was no longer willing to work, and Cecelia was supporting him. After almost nine years of marriage, Cecelia and Ben divorced.

It is well-known in the substance abuse treatment field that the suffering and damage extend beyond the addict or alcoholic and have a tremendous impact on family and friends. Yet it can take a considerable amount of time before family members are able to acknowledge a substance abuse problem. The denial that addicts and alcoholics engage in, indeed one of the hallmarks of addiction, extends to others as well.

This chapter examines the effects of alcoholism and drug addiction on spouses and children in the United States. It describes and critiques the concept of codependency. Reviewing the literature on children of alcoholics, it also explores issues they can confront in their adult lives. The chapter examines as well the more recent efforts in the field to acknowledge the resiliency among children and partners of alcoholics and addicts.

Most of the literature on marriage and alcoholism focuses on the husband as the alcoholic because much more is known about this relationship than about that of a man with an alcoholic wife. Wives often stay with their alcoholic husbands much longer than husbands stay with alcoholic wives. This is often connected to economic realities, since men are more likely to have financial independence than women. There is also the case of both partners having substance abuse problems. Research in the early 2000s reveals that men and women at risk of alcohol problems are more likely to choose partners who are also at risk (Dawson et al., 2007; Dawson, Li, and Grant, 2007). Another recent study found that one-third of substance abusers' spouses are substance dependent as well (Low, Cui, and Merikangas, 2007).

Historical Recognition

Up until the early 1970s, it was common for treatment programs to focus only on the client who was working on his or her recovery. It is certainly frustrating for wives, after years of living with an active alcoholic who then achieves sobriety, to see their husbands still unavailable because of their commitment to a Twelve-Step program or other program of recovery. Many role adjustments must be made for the recovering alcoholic and family members. We now know that the needs of the family are every bit as important as the needs of the alcoholic or addict (O'Farrell and Fals-Stewart, 2006).

In the treatment field, everyone knows the story of the "elephant in the living room." This refers to the drug or alcohol problem of someone in the home that remains unacknowledged (the elephant), with family members tiptoeing around it. The problem is huge, yet no one is able or willing to talk about it. The idea of actually talking with a person about his or her substance abuse problem can seem overwhelming to others in the family. It is easier to deny than to risk the unpleasantness (and perhaps rage) of the addict or alcoholic. Family members who deny and perhaps unwittingly engage in behaviors that allow the substance abuse to continue are referred to as codependents, a term we will discuss shortly.

Families can adapt to alcoholism or addiction in the home in a variety of ways. A typology of family reactions to alcoholism (see Box 10.1) is revealed in the classic work of Joan Jackson (1954). Many in the treatment field are impressed by how relevant this typology continues to be as of this writing. Jackson was a participant-observer over a three-year period in Al-Anon, where she found most members were wives of alcoholics. (Al-Anon is the Twelve-Step program for families and friends of alcoholics.)

Box 10.1   Stages in Family Adjustment to an Alcoholic Husband and Father

Joan Jackson (1954) described the stages the family goes through when a husband and father is an alcoholic.

Stage 1. Attempts to Deny the Problems

Excessive drinking begins, and, although incidents are occasional, strain is placed on the marriage. Marital issues, not related to drinking, are not discussed in an effort to minimize the husband's drinking.

Stage 2. Attempts to Eliminate the Problems

As excessive drinking grows more frequent, the family begins to experience social isolation. The wife wants to minimize her husband's embarrassing behavior by limiting contact with friends. The marital relationship deteriorates, tension increases, and alcohol becomes the central issue for the family. The wife's self-confidence decreases, since she feels she has failed to stabilize his drinking. While the original family structure is still intact, the strain on the wife and children is showing, and the stress, and even desperation, deepen with each new episode of drinking.

Stage 3. Disorganization

The wife no longer tries to control her husband's drinking, and there is no effort to support him in his roles of husband and father. Family members behave in ways to relieve existing tension with little thought for the future, with the wife recognizing that his drinking may be a permanent problem. The wife finds she is unable to control her nagging and worries about her own sanity.

Stage 4. Attempts to Reorganize Despite Problems

A crisis such as no money or no food in the house brings the family to Stage 4. The wife takes over control of the family, and the husband comes to be seen as an unmanageable child. The self-esteem of the wife improves when she finds she is capable of taking care of the family on her own.

continues

Box 10.1   continued

Stage 5. Efforts to Escape the Problems

The wife separates from the husband and may end the marriage at this point. At times the marriage is reentered if the husband has a period of sobriety. If there is relapse, the marriage may be terminated. The pressure is enormous, since the wife must consider what is best for the children, whether she has the resources to leave, and where to go. The wife must deal with her own feelings about herself, her husband, and their marriage.

Stage 6. Reorganization of Part of the Family

The family reorganizes without the husband and father. Even though there may be divorce, the husband may not be able to acknowledge this and still may try to get back with the family.

Stage 7. Recovery and Reorganization of the Whole Family

The husband achieves sobriety whether there has been a separation or not. This can be a challenging period because the wife has managed the family and now the husband wants to be reinstated in his roles of husband and father. The wife may find it difficult to let go of the control, yet she realizes the importance of reinstating him into the family.

The Changing Family

Many changes in the family have taken place over time. The family of the twenty-first century is not the ideal family of the mid-twentieth century, when dad went to work and mom took care of the children and the household. Since 1960 there has been a decline in marriage rates and an increase in divorce rates (National Center on Addiction and Substance Abuse [hereafter, CASA], 2005). In recent decades we have seen an increase in single-parent families and more grandparents taking on parenting roles (Abbott, 2004a). Unfortunately, US society has also seen an increase in those struggling at the lower rungs of the economic ladder. In the early 2000s, we have seen greater understanding of the importance of fathers as well as greater attention to cultural and racial or ethnic differences in families. All of these factors have an impact on the use of substances and the consequences of substance use and abuse.

While the family issues of alcoholics and addicts tend to be treated as the same, there can be real differences in the issues families must cope with. Families of addicts can suffer more difficulties than families of alcoholics, with good reason—alcoholics have a legal source for their drug, while heroin addicts, for example, must locate an illegal source for heroin. In addition, addicts are more likely to need considerable amounts of money and are more apt to steal from family members in order to be able to buy their drugs. Family members may try to protect the person because of legal consequences. Since alcohol is much more accepted in society than drugs (especially illegal ones), family members are more likely to intervene with the person at a later point than if it is a drug problem (Curtis, 1999).

Overall, it is clear that family members have a difficult time coping with alcoholism or addiction in the home. The person who is abusing substances can become increasingly isolated from family members (Center for Substance Abuse Treatment, 2004). Financial problems are an inevitable result of the inability to work or of the loss of a job, as are concerns over the high cost of treatment (CASA, 2005). Many family members remain silent and stay within the difficult family situation. Others, although fewer, will seek professional help, will attend Al-Anon meetings (see Box 10.2), or will leave the family.

As family members struggle to cope, their survival strategics can be seen by others as actually helping the alcoholic or addict to maintain his or her addiction, known as codependency. Al-Anon encourages family members of alcoholics to try to emotionally detach and deal with their own issues but discourages those who are victims of violence from remaining in the relationship. An early 2000s approach offered by Hazelden, a highly regarded treatment program in Minnesota, promotes family members' staying engaged, to try to make the relationship work (Meyers and Wolfe, 2004). However, no support group or treatment program recommends staying in a relationship where violence is present.

Codependency

Codependency is a term commonly used in the 1980s and 1990s. Codependency calls attention to the fact that addiction affects the family of the addict while, at the same time, the family can affect the substance abuse of the individual (Rotunda and Doman, 2001). In general, a codependent is a person in an inappropriate, controlling, caretaking role with an alcoholic or addict. The codependent has low self-esteem and can experience a loss of

Box 10.2   Faustina Goes to Al-Anon

Faustina, aged thirty-eight, had been married to Duncan for ten difficult years. Off and on through the years, she had been concerned about her husband's beer drinking and marijuana use. Duncan had difficulty completing tasks and holding on to a job. He decided on his own to start attending Alcoholics Anonymous meetings. Faustina noticed that her husband seemed to like going, although he told her little about what went on in the AA meetings. At one point, Duncan suggested that Faustina attend an Al-Anon meeting.

The number of people attending the Wednesday night Al-Anon meeting surprised Faustina. There were approximately twenty women and four men. Faustina was amazed and a bit upset by the difficult situations they discussed. Some participants had family members who had been sober for years, while others were living with spouses or other family members who were still drinking. Faustina heard a term that was unfamiliar to her, "emotional detachment." Al-Anon members talked about how they were trying to take care of themselves and not allow the alcoholic's behavior to have a major impact on their lives. Faustina wondered how it was possible to live with an active alcoholic and not let it affect her. She decided to attend the weekly meetings in the hopes of making new friends and to see what she could learn.

Months later Faustina and Duncan decided to divorce. Nonetheless, Faustina continued to attend the Wednesday night Al-Anon meeting. She was grateful to have a place to go and always be welcomed. She appreciated the support she both received and gave to others.

self, defining him- or herself only in relationship to others. The term can be used as a negative description of or an insult to another person. (For example, Susan is such a codependent she even tells her husband how to eat his food!) In a more kindly way, it can also be used to refer to someone who is especially helpful to others. (For example, Jim canceled his golf game to shop for curtains with his wife.)

A codependent is usually closest to the alcoholic or addict, most often the spouse or partner. In the 1960s and 1970s, spouses of alcoholics were often referred to as "co-alcoholics," and myth had it that these spouses were even sicker than the alcoholic. Clearly, the label was a harsh judgment about spouses, and later the term *co-alcoholic* fell out of use. However, the notion that the codependent has the *need* to be in the relationship and to *enable* the alcoholic is still with us. In addition to the spouse or partner, the codependent can be a parent, sibling, other family member, friend, or coworker of the substance abuser.

Descriptions abound regarding the term *codependency*. The concept was developed in the mid-1970s, although the roots of the concept can be found in the work of psychoanalyst Karen Horney in 1950 (Horney, 1950; Martsolf et al., 1999). Horney described "morbid dependency," which includes, in simplest terms, the giving up of oneself to another. It is the desire to have an intensely close or symbiotic relationship with a partner that results in "alienation from the self" (Crothers and Warren, 1996, 232). In subordinating an individual's needs to those of others, codependents may feel helpless, may stay in failed relationships, and may feel powerless to leave (Gross, 2004).

Melody Beattie wrote what many consider to be the classic work on codependency, titled *Codependent No More* (1987). Bcattie offered a long list of characteristics of codependency that include caretaking behavior, low self-worth, repression, obsession, controlling behaviors, denial, poor communication skills, weak boundaries, lack of trust, and anger.

Codependency has been referred to as "a common mental health problem" (Martsolf et al., 1999, 97) and a learned feeling of helplessness (O'Gorman, 1993). Codependency has also been referred to as a "primary disease," occurring in all members of a family where addiction is present, and can bring with it physical problems (Anderson, 1994). Timmen Cermak (1986) argued that codependency is such an important problem that it should be included in the *Diagnostic and Statistical Manual of Mental Disorders*. At the extreme is Sharon Wegscheider-Cruse (1985), who referred to codependency as a "toxic brain disease"—it goes through stages and is characterized by stress-related illness and even death!

While there may be differences in definitions of *codependency*, there are common themes. These include an overinvolvement with the alcoholic or addict, and attempts to control that person's behavior, to the detriment of the codependent. All of this is done with the best of intentions. However, the loss of self-confidence and the shame felt by codependents can be significant (Lindley, Giordano, and Hammer, 1999; Wells, Glickauf-Hughes, and Jones, 1999). While reliance on a partner is certainly an important part of a healthy relationship, codependency blocks genuine intimacy, since the codependent experiences a loss of self (Gross, 2004).

The hallmark of codependent behavior is that the codependent shields the addict or alcoholic from the consequences of his or her behavior. This is the wife who calls her husband's boss to say that he has the flu when, in reality, he is passed out on the couch from drinking. If alcoholics or addicts were made to feel the consequences of their behavior, perhaps recovery would begin earlier.

The concept of codependency developed and was popularized without a theoretical or scientific basis, primarily by those who grew up in alcoholic homes themselves (George et al., 1999). However, codependency has been considered so important that efforts have been made to measure it.

Questionnaires have been developed specifically to do this. The Spann-Fischer Codependency Scale (SFCDS) was developed in 1991 to assess three characteristics: whether a person has extreme focus outside of the self, lacks the ability to express feelings, or uses control and denial to maintain a sense of purpose in relationships (Fischer, Spann, and Crawford, 1991). Another questionnaire, the Codependency Assessment Tool (CODAT), measures codependency based primarily on issues related to the focus on others and self-neglect (Hughes-Hammer, Martsolf and Zeller, 1998; Martsolf et al., 1999). Later in time, the Holyoake Codependency Index was devised to measure self-sacrifice, a focus on the external, and feelings of being overwhelmed by the problem behavior of another person (Dear, 2004; Dear and Roberts, 2005).

Criticism of the Concept of Codependency

While discussions of codependency became popular in the 1980s and into the 1990s, not everyone agrees that the label of "codependent" is a useful one. The early theories that focused on the pathology of spouses or partners of alcoholics have been replaced in the 1990s and 2000s by theories that focus on psychophysical stress (Hurcom, Copello and Orford, 2000). A review of the literature by Collins (1993) found no compelling evidence that codependency exists as a psychological problem for spouses of alcoholics or for children of alcoholics. Collins took issue with seeing relationship problems as disease, perceiving codependency as "both a social movement and big business" (1993, 470), referring to the number of self-help books, workshops, and seminars spawned by the codependency movement. Others see the concept of codependency as morally wrong, to the point of inviting attack on its existence; for example, a wife is showing signs of health rather than sickness in coping with an alcoholic spouse who is destroying himself and his family (Kokin, 1989).

The literature focuses on women as those most likely to become codependent (Anderson, 1994; Dawson et al., 2007; Harkness and Cotrell, 1997). From a feminist perspective, the concept of codependency can be another tool by which to subordinate women in society:

> The codependency movement encourages women to define themselves as relationship addicts who are powerless over their disease unless they actively involve themselves in a 12-step process. This model does not encourage women to be empowered in their lives and to make constructive change. Rather, it asserts that like the addict, the codependent individual will be in recovery forever. (Collins, 1993, 473)

Sandra Anderson found that the concept has "no diagnostic usefulness in that it does not inform about prognosis or what intervention will be most effective" (1994, 679). Self-labeling can exacerbate problems, since those who label themselves codependent are likely to gain more symptoms as a result (George et al., 1999). Codependency is not sensitive to cultural differences, and some women who are hesitant to break away from their families could be considered codependent. Yet another criticism is that children can blame parents for their own problems and emotionally withdraw from their parents rather than trying to reconnect with them in healthier ways (Anderson, 1994). Donna Martsolf et al. (1999) summarized the objections that have been raised regarding the concept of codependency: "the clinical use of a poorly defined concept, the effects of labeling, the victimization and blame of women for assuming a previously viewed normal social role, the rise of sexism leading to medicalization, and the failure to examine the issue in a social and cultural context" (1999, 98). While the heyday of codependency as a concept appears to be over, the concern for children and the spouse of alcoholics as well as behaviors associated with codependency are very much alive today.

Parenting Issues

The ages at which people marry and have children, typically late teens into the thirties, are when the risk of substance abuse is highest (Gruber and Taylor, 2006). Therefore, the opportunity for substance abuse to affect children is great. Almost half of children under age eighteen live with a parent or adult who drinks heavily, uses tobacco, or uses illegal drugs. Almost one-quarter of children live in a home where there is heavy drinking (CASA, 2005).

Substance abuse in a parent can mean that a child's needs are not met and children can be placed at risk of neglect or abuse (Anda et al., 2002; Peleg-Oren and Teichman, 2006). While some research questions whether substance abuse necessarily impairs parenting ability, other research confirms that it does (Anda et al., 2002; Lundgren, Schilling, and Peloquin, 2005).

Research in the early 2000s with methamphetamine abusers found that mothers tried to keep their children away from their drug use (Brown and Hohman, 2006). Also, it was difficult for respondents to acknowledge that their parenting had been impaired by drug use. In fact, the self-deceptions of good parenting can reinforce drug abusers' self-esteem and protect them from the guilt and shame resulting from poor parenting. However, deepening substance abuse does lead to declining parental abilities.

©iStockphoto.com/tomazl

Literature reviews suggest a higher risk of social maladjustment, lower self-esteem, greater self-depreciation, hyperactivity, suicide attempts, and legal problems among children of alcoholics and addicts (Schneider Institute, 2001; VanDeMark et al., 2005). Children of alcoholics can have higher rates of anxiety, depression, and poor academic skills (Johnson and Leff, 1999). Research on children of alcoholics and opiate addicts has found significantly higher rates of psychological, academic, and social problems than were experienced by families without an addicted parent (Wilens et al., 2002).

Women are at higher risk of marrying a substance abuser than are men. Further, and not surprisingly, the effects on children can be harsher if both mother and father are substance abusers (Center for Substance Abuse Treatment [hereafter, CSAT], 2004). The risk of substance abuse and depression and other forms of mental illness is higher if it is the mother who is alcoholic (Anda et al., 2002). The fact that the mother is most often the primary caregiver can mean a child is more strongly affected the mother's substance abuse.

It should be mentioned as well that it is very difficult to parent an adolescent who has a substance abuse problem. As discussed in Chapter 4, adolescent substance abuse has been correlated with family conflict, along with absence of parental limit-setting (Wu et al., 2004). It was estimated in the early 2000s that overall, one-half to two-thirds of substance abuse can be accounted for by adverse experiences in childhood (Dube et al., 2003).

An important factor in parental substance abuse is that children can serve as motivators for mothers to seek treatment. On the other hand, the presence of children can make it more difficult for women to obtain treatment (Hardy-Fanta and Mignon, 2000). At this writing, it is still the case that women are seen as the primary caretakers of children, although it is clearly appropriate and important to ask men who are entering inpatient substance abuse treatment the question who is caring for their children. Chapter 5 offers more discussion of mothers and children and their needs.

In general, the addicted parent is not likely to get help with parenting skills. However, there are exceptions. Beatrice Plasse (1995) reported on parenting groups for recovering addicts in a day treatment center in New York City. Sixty of sixty-eight recovering addicts remained drug-free for the duration of the program, an average of two years. The services included individual and family counseling, vocational training, and high school equivalency courses. Reported benefits were help in staying free of drugs while increasing their knowledge of child development and, as important, improving communication skills with their children. While the integration of family therapy and substance abuse treatment is used infrequently, this form of treatment seems to be helpful (CSAT, 2004).

The Family Strengthening Program of the Center for Substance Abuse Prevention assists communities in developing programs to support families at risk from substance abuse. Through behavioral couples therapy, family therapy, and parent and family skills training, families become stronger and substance abuse problems can be treated and prevented (CSAT, 2004; O'Farrell and Fals-Stewart, 2006). Residential substance abuse treatment programs for mothers and children are also showing effectiveness in helping both mothers and children (Connors et al., 2001; Wong, 2006). Group counseling for children whose parents are in substance abuse treatment can help children improve their confidence and self-reliance (Reinert, 1999). Ala-Teen, modeled after Alcoholics Anonymous, is a support group available to teenagers of alcoholic parents.

Children of Alcoholics and Addicts

At this writing, it is well-known that alcoholism runs in families and that children of alcoholics are at higher risk of developing alcoholism themselves (Bierut et al., 1998; Gruber and Taylor, 2006). The literature reflects that children of alcoholics are four to nine times more likely to become alcoholics than are those without alcoholic parents (National Institute on Alcohol Abuse and Alcoholism, 2000a; Windle, 1997). It is accepted today that both biological and environmental factors contribute to alcoholism in children, and thus that many factors are in play in determining whether alcohol or drugs will become a problem for individuals.

Coping with an alcoholic parent can be especially difficult, since children's coping mechanisms have not fully developed. Claudia Black (1981, 2002) and Sharon Wegscheider-Cruse (1985) described typologies that address ways that children adapt to the alcoholic home. This comes from the popular clinical literature designed to help those with alcoholism in their families, rather than from scientific evidence. Myers (2002a) pointed out the importance of giving credit where it is due: Wegscheider-Cruse's roots are found in the pioneering family therapy of Virginia Satir, and descriptions of birth order are based on the pioneering work of psychoanalyst Alfred Adler in the early 1930s. See Box 10.3 for a description of the roles children play in alcoholic homes.

There are no specific rules about which role a child will play in a family. It could be that a child will play one role and then move into another role. While there is no scientific research that can state how many children of alcoholics belong in each category, this is a typology that can be personally meaningful to students taking a substance abuse course and to counselors working with family members.

Despite the adversity children cope with in a substance-abusing home, and the risk of present and future problems, children can be very resilient (CASA, 1999). *Resilience* here refers to being able to overcome adverse situations and develop a positive self-image despite a difficult situation. Resilience is more likely to be found among children of substance abusers who have received treatment (VanDeMark et al., 2005). Recent prevention and treatment approaches focus on resilience by encouraging use of community services and supporting family bonding through shared activities (Gruber and Taylor, 2006).

The 1970s saw the development of the adult children of alcoholics movement (ACOA). The seeds were sown for coming to appreciate that children of alcoholics could have difficulties as a result of parental alcoholism—indeed that they are four times more likely to become alcoholic themselves.

One early 1990s study found ACOAs to have a higher divorce rate and lower emotional satisfaction, and 21 percent were "highly concerned" about their own drinking (Ackerman and Gondolf, 1991). Overall, 47 percent of the ACOAs responded that they were "highly affected" by parental drinking problems. Moreover, it has been suggested that ACOAs may be hypersensitive to natural disasters such as hurricanes, since it brings back feelings of helplessness (Dayton, 2004).

Box 10.3 Children in Alcoholic Homes

Black (1981) and Wegscheider-Cruse (1982, 1985) identify roles that children play in alcoholic families.

1. The *Responsible One* (Black) or *Hero* (Wegscheider-Cruse). This is usually the oldest child in the family, especially if the oldest is female. She is likely to perform the functions associated with being a parent. She will cook and clean and supervise the younger children. She can help her siblings do their homework. Parents of other children may say to them: "Why can't you be more like _____?" In the jargon of the child welfare system, this is the *parentified* child—the child who becomes the parent. Because this child appears to handle these responsibilities so well, it is very unlikely that adults will see the emotional pain this child may experience.

2. The *Adjuster* (Black) or *Lost Child* (Wegscheider-Cruse). The Adjuster or Lost Child goes along with whatever happens in the family and adapts without trying to change the family situation. This child tends to be withdrawn, not calling attention to him- or herself at home or at school. He or she is shy, lonely, and isolated.

3. The *Placater* (Black) or *Mascot* (Wegscheider-Cruse). The Placater or Mascot is usually the youngest child in the family and considered the most sensitive. She or he tries to reduce the anxiety or pain of other siblings in the home by trying to dispel anger and tension, often through the use of humor. He or she is a good listener and a good friend to others.

4. The *Acting Out Child* (Black) or *Scapegoat* (Wegscheider-Cruse). The Acting Out Child or Scapegoat is the child who gets the most attention and whose behavior most accurately illustrates the chaos of the home. Often a boy, this child engages in problem and even delinquent behavior. Typically there are behavior problems at school and even legal encounters. If this child is a girl, she may experience teenage pregnancy. Because this child's behavior is most visible in the community, he or she is the family member most likely to get professional attention, although that help may be offered only to the child and not the entire family.

As the ACOA movement developed, there was an acknowledgment that while we hope we can leave behind the pathology of childhood in the alcoholic home, the reality is that children of alcoholics can carry the dysfunction of early family life into their own adult lives. Children learned to keep the "secret" of the alcoholism. Contributing to dishonesty and lying, this encourages the child to feel shame about the situation. Alcoholism has been the hidden family problem that discourages children of alcoholics from sharing their experiences with others and receiving help (Ackerman, 1983). It is important to remember that while adult children of alcoholics are at higher risk of alcoholism, it is certainly not inevitable (Windle, 1997).

We have already said that growing up in an alcoholic home can set the stage for adult difficulties. The classic work by Janet Woititz (1983) can be described as an important part of the mini–social movement focusing on adult children of alcoholics. Woititz devised a list of thirteen characteristics that adult children of alcoholics used to describe themselves (see Box 10.4). Like the work of Black (1981) and Wegscheider-Cruse (1985), Woititz's work is based on anecdotal evidence rather than scientific research. Lay recovery programs are in the forefront of treatment efforts, while scientific inquiry has lagged behind in ACOA issues (Anda et al., 2002).

Woititz (1983) observed that the first characteristic, "guessing what normal is," is the most profound of the ACOA characteristics. Growing up in an alcoholic home distorts perceptions of what other "normal" families are like and how to appropriately interact with others in social situations. ACOAs can feel ill at ease in social situations, having little opportunity to learn social skills, since the family did not have these experiences.

Some may argue that "difficulty with intimate relationships" can be the most profound characteristic, with long-lasting and very negative consequences. If children have not had healthy role models for loving adult relationships, they may be at a loss as to how to have a healthy relationship with another adult. It is known that women with alcoholic fathers can be attracted to men with substance abuse problems. While no scientific research has uncovered the cause of this dynamic, it might be the desire to have a different and much improved outcome. That is, a woman with an alcoholic father may unconsciously decide this: "I couldn't help Dad with his drinking problem, but maybe I can help my boyfriend." Unfortunately, women can have a succession of relationships with addicted or emotionally unhealthy—or both—men. One dynamic at play is low self-esteem that encourages a woman to think she does not deserve any better. Of course, unhealthy relationships are not limited to women and men with alcoholic parents.

Achieving and maintaining a healthy relationship with a partner can be a serious struggle for some. In AA, newly recovering people are encouraged not to begin a new relationship for at least a year. The point is that a person cannot achieve a healthy relationship with another until that person is emotionally healthy himself or herself. One middle-aged woman, a recovering

Box 10.4   Characteristics Associated with Adult Children of Alcoholics

1. Adult children of alcoholics guess at what normal is.
2. Children of alcoholics have difficulty in following a project through from beginning to end.
3. Adult children of alcoholics lie when it is just as easy to tell the truth.
4. Adult children of alcoholics judge themselves without mercy.
5. Adult children of alcoholics have difficulty having fun.
6. Adult children of alcoholics take themselves very seriously.
7. Adult children of alcoholics have difficulty with intimate relationships.
8. Adult children of alcoholics overreact to changes over which they have no control.
9. Adult children of alcoholics constantly seek approval and affirmation.
10. Adult children of alcoholics feel they are different from other people.
11. Adult children of alcoholics are either superresponsible or super-irresponsible.
12. Adult children of alcoholics are extremely loyal, even in the face of evidence that the loyalty is undeserved.
13. Adult children of alcoholics are impulsive. They tend to lock themselves into a course of action without giving serious consideration to alternative behaviors or possible consequences. This impulsivity leads to confusion, self-loathing, and loss of control over their environment. In addition, they spend an excessive amount of energy cleaning up the mess (Woititz, 1983).

alcoholic herself, gave a good illustration of how difficult this can be: "Put me in a roomful of men. I'll find the sickest man in the room and he's the one I'll be attracted to" (Mignon, personal communication, 2005).

Efforts have also been made to objectively determine who may or may not be a child of an alcoholic, as well as specific behavioral characteristics. The Children of Alcoholics Screening Test (CAST) ascertains feelings, attitudes, and experiences with parental drinking to identify children of alcoholics from age nine through adulthood (Pilat and Jones, 1984/1985). The ACOA Behavior Profile addresses eight measures: feelings, relaxation, loyalty, control, relationships, drug and alcohol history, fears, and parental behavior (Ruben, 1999).

Traits ascribed to adult children of alcoholics can be seen as meaning-ful by some and not meaningful by others. Some adult children of alco-holics find relief in this self-identification and find it a source of a mean-ingful identity. A cautionary note should be stated: generalizations about "typical" ACOAs should not be made (Vanicelli, 1989). While some find relief here, this label can foster a negative self-image. In reality, ACOAs can be well-functioning adults not in need of treatment (Anderson, 1994). Carolyn Hurcom et al. point out that "more recent research has highlighted the possibility of neutral or even some positive outcomes" (2000, 495). That is, children of alcoholics can possess greater sensitivity to the prob-lems of others. Also, it is important to remember that there is much more to the relationship and shared history between parents and children than substance abuse (Abbott, 2004b).

Substance Abuse and Family Violence: What Is the Real Connection?

The relationship between substance abuse and family violence is a murky one. Substance abusers can be perpetrators of family violence or victims. Overall, estimates are that one-half to two-thirds of family violence perpe-trators were using alcohol or drugs at the time of abuse. More specifically, substance abuse is involved in 40 to 60 percent of partner violence (Easton, 2006). Before the 1970s, assumptions were made that substance abuse causes family violence. Although alcohol and drug abuse are frequently as-sociated with family violence, the relationship cannot be considered a causal one. In reality, the connection between substance abuse and family violence is one of the most difficult issues to understand in the family vio-lence literature (Leonard and Jacob, 1988). Previously, the assumption was made that intoxication causes violence and the violence will disappear if the perpetrator remains abstinent (Gorney, 1989). As of this writing, we know that these are two serious problems, each of which needs intervention.

The study of the connection between substance abuse and family vio-lence began in the late 1970s. Spouse battering has received the most atten-tion, with the majority of studies reporting findings obtained from female victims. Family violence includes spouse battering, child and adult sexual abuse, emotional abuse and neglect, and physical abuse and neglect—problems that cannot easily be lumped into one category. It is as difficult to define these specific forms of family violence as it is to define the terms *substance abuse, alcoholism,* and *drug addiction.* Sorting out the relation-ship between substance abuse and family violence is very complicated because many other factors are involved. Individual factors such as the personality of the substance abuser, including the presence of mental illness, are important. Specific properties of the drugs used may be factors; alcohol and cocaine, for example, are more associated with aggressive behavior than are drugs such as marijuana and heroin. Situational factors such as financial problems or physical illness can place a strain on the family. Sociocultural expectations regarding drinking and drugging behavior can be strong, with inappropriate behavior being excused by saying, "He was drunk when it happened."

Some research addressing the interrelationship between substance abuse and partner battering asks women about the substance use of their partners. As early as 1977, Bonnie Carlson, in interviews with 101 women, found that 60 percent of male perpetrators abused alcohol and 21 percent abused other drugs. An extremely strong association was found by Elaine Hilberman and Kit Munson (1978): out of a sample of 609 poor women referred by a rural health clinic for psychiatric evaluation, 93 percent stated alcoholism was a significant problem for their partners. Albert Roberts (1987) found that 60 percent of battered women stated their partners were under the influence of alcohol at the time, while 32 percent of their partners used other drugs and 22 percent used both alcohol and drugs. Brenda Miller et al. (1990), in a sample of 82 battering parolees and their spouses, found that alcohol was a problem for 76 percent of parolees and that 73 percent of parolees used some type of illegal drug on a regular basis. Hutchison (1999) found that frequent drunkenness on the part of the male perpetrator of spouse abuse was highly correlated with both threats and battering behavior.

Surveys of substance-abusing men and surveys of batterers confirm the relationship between substance abuse and family violence. For men who are enrolled in battering programs, often court mandated, the majority have alcohol problems (Stuart, 2005). A late 1990s study of eighty male alcoholics, both before and after treatment, measured self-reports of partner violence (Maiden, 1997): of these respondents, 94 percent indicated they had engaged in verbal aggression, 71 percent engaged in moderate physical violence, and 56 percent engaged in severe physical violence prior to treatment. After treatment, 75 percent reported verbal aggression, 20 percent reported moderate physical violence, and 1.6 percent engaged in severe physical violence. The researcher, R. Paul Maiden, concluded that while alcoholism treatment can be a factor in reducing family violence, it may not eliminate violence in the home.

Angela Browne's (1987) classic study of battered women who killed their abusers found that 78 percent of the deceased men were intoxicated every day or almost every day, while 40 percent of men in the comparison group were intoxicated daily. Close to one-third of the men in the homicide group used street drugs almost daily, while only 8 percent of the comparison group did. In another study, Frederick Rivara and colleagues (1997) found that alcohol and illegal drug use by the perpetrator increased the risk of homicide for family members without substance abuse problems.

There is evidence that alcohol-abusing batterers are more physically violent than nonalcohol-abusing batterers (Barnett and Fagan, 1993; Eberle, 1982; Flanzer, 1982). Miller and colleagues (1990) found that alcohol problems by either abuser or victim increased the level of violence. Injuries to women who have been victims of partner abuse are more severe when perpetrators have been drinking (Thompson and Kingree, 2006). In their study of police response to family violence, Sylvia Mignon and William Holmes (1995) found that offender use of alcohol increased the probability of arrest. When alcohol was absent, arrest occurred in 35 percent of cases; when alcohol was involved, arrest occurred in 45 percent of cases. In an early 2000s study of female alcoholics, 61 percent of women and their partners reported some level of violence in their relationship within the past year (Drapkin et al., 2005); 27 percent of the violence was considered severe. The woman was considered more severely violent in 23 percent of the couples, while men were considered more violent in 11 percent of the couples.

There is support for the proposition that physical abuse of women can be greater among perpetrators who use drugs only, in contrast to those who use alcohol only (Willson et al., 2000). In a sample of women attending a methadone maintenance clinic, 46 percent reported they had been victims of intimate partner violence within the past six months (El-Bassel et al., 2005). Women in this sample who used crack at least once a week were two to four times more likely to report physical or sexual abuse. It was also noted that women who were victimized may have been self-medicating with the use of illicit drugs.

A particularly difficult area to study is the relationship between family violence and substance abuse of the victim. Alcohol problems by either the abuser or the victim can increase the level of violence. Miller et al. (1990) found in their study of battering parolees that 56 percent of female victims had alcohol problems and 40 percent used some type of illegal drug on a regular basis. Research in the early 2000s has shown that although substance use may not increase risk of partner violence, the violence does put women at greater risk of heavy drinking (Martino, Collins, and Ellickson, 2005).

Fewer studies examine the relationship between substance abuse and child maltreatment. Families that do come to the attention of child protection agencies are not necessarily screened for substance abuse problems (Anda et al., 2002; Ritner and Dozier, 2000). States do not typically have formal policies in place that require children to be placed out of the home specifically because there is substance abuse present (Lundgren et al., 2005).

Substance abuse treatment programs and child protection agencies have historically made few efforts to work together. Few child protection workers have expertise in substance abuse, and "substance abuse labels tend to be loosely applied in child welfare investigations" (Anda et al., 2002, 132). Child welfare and substance abuse are separate bureaucracies, and this has hindered efforts to address the intertwining of these problems (CASA, 1999). Child welfare workers are not trained in substance abuse, nor are substance abuse clinicians attuned to child protection issues in the way they should be. The lack of treatment programs for women also impairs the efforts of child welfare professionals and courts to intervene in cases where substance abuse is present. In addition to these issues is the fact that women may not get the substance abuse treatment they need because of their child-care responsibilities (Stewart, Gossop, and Trakada, 2007).

Reviews of child protection agency records confirm the relationship between substance abuse and the greater likelihood of being referred to a protection agency for child abuse or neglect. MacMurray (1979) found that one-third of protective service case records mentioned the use of alcohol. In cases where alcohol was involved, abuse or neglect was more likely to be substantiated (84 percent) than if alcohol was not involved (65 percent). Parental substance abuse has also been correlated with higher risk of child maltreatment and placement of children in foster care (Smith et al., 2007).

The literature examining the connection between substance abuse and child maltreatment is not entirely consistent. In general, the lack of pertinent research makes it difficult to reach any definitive conclusions (Glover, Janikowski, and Benshoff, 1996; Widom and Hiller-Sturmhofel, 2001).

In her review of the literature, Charleanea Arellano concluded, "Studies continue to show a significant connection between child maltreatment and subsequent substance use" (1996, 930). Joanna Moncrieff and Roger Farmer (1998) reviewed fifteen studies of clients in substance abuse treatment facilities, showing that clients there have a higher rate of incest (sexual activity between a relative and a child, most often father to daughter) than the general population. In a study of 194 admissions to an adolescent substance abuse treatment facility, those with a history of having been sexually abused developed more severe substance abuse problems than those who hadn't been abused (Blood and Cornwall, 1996). Those who experience physical abuse as children may also develop more problems as adults than would those who as children weren't similarly abused (Westermeyer,

Wahmanholm, and Thuras, 2001). Christine Walsh and colleagues (2003) found that parental substance abuse was associated with significantly higher rates of child physical and sexual abuse than rates of abuse by parents without substance abuse problems.

In a study conducted in the early 2000s among patients in a detoxification program, 20 percent of men and over 50 percent of women acknowledged they were survivors of physical or sexual abuse in childhood (Brems et al., 2004). Also important to note is that men and women in detox began drinking at a younger age and with greater consequences than those without an abuse history. One study of 181 intravenous-drug-using women found that 60 percent had been sexually abused as children, 55 percent had been physically abused, 46 percent had been emotionally abused, 83 percent had been emotionally neglected, and 60 percent had been physically neglected (Medrano et al., 1999).

A national study of 1,099 women found that a history of childhood sexual abuse was "significantly linked to higher adult incidences of drug and alcohol abuse, sexual dysfunction, and depression" (Wilsnack et al., 1997, 264). In a study of clients in thirty-five treatment facilities, 36 percent stated they were victims of incest—29 percent of men and 55 percent of women (Glover et al., 1996). These findings speak to the importance of assessing for a trauma history. On a positive note, Gil-Rivas et al. found that a history of sexual or physical abuse did not result in "lower levels of treatment completion or lower levels of counseling participation" (1997, 355).

The relationship between substance abuse and victimization is complex, with the potential for many contributing factors (Logan et al., 2002). The majority of the literature on women with substance abuse problems examines the role of women as victims. In general, it is known that approximately 95 percent of serious partner abuse is perpetrated by men, with about 5 percent perpetrated by women (Mignon, 1998). While women usually have higher rates of abusing children than men, this may be attributable to women spending more time with their children (Mignon, Larson, and Holmes, 2002). Overall, economic dependence by a woman and emotional dependence by a man are strong contributors to partner abuse (Bornstein, 2006).

Conclusion

The study of alcohol, drugs, and the family is a complex topic concerned with many issues: the effects of substance abuse on the spouse, on the children when they are young and living at home, and on adult children as they try to make their own way in the world. Although not the cause of family violence, addiction and substance abuse can certainly aggravate family abuse situations. Those who were victims of childhood abuse, especially women who were sexually abused, are at greater risk of developing substance abuse problems in adolescence and adulthood. Thus, the prevention of child abuse can help to prevent substance abuse (Brems et al., 2004).

The good news today is that increasingly, family members are aware that help is available to them. Rather than blaming spouses for the alcoholism or addiction, we are more likely to emphasize the key role they can take in helping their addicted partners. Vernon Johnson (1980, 1986) pioneered the development of interventions to help alcoholics get into treatment. Johnson is credited with helping to destroy the myth that alcoholics could not be helped until they hit "rock bottom," losing family, friends, and job (Picard, 1991). A family intervention can be empowering for family members, since it gives them hope that they can help the alcoholic or addict make positive changes. As of this writing, more health professionals are willing to take their obligation to intervene more seriously, and the pediatrician's office can be a good place to begin.

Family members can get information about how to help a loved one by attending Al-Anon meetings, adult children of alcoholics meetings, Ala-Teen, and calling their local mental health clinic or the social service department at the local hospital. Taking a high school or college course on substance abuse is one way for students to learn about resources that can help them. Colleges also offer counseling services to students and typically have a substance abuse specialist on staff.

11 Alcohol, Drugs, and Crime

For years, myths have clouded public discourse on the link between drugs and crime. In the 1890s the city fathers of San Francisco feared that Chinese opium dens would corrupt the morals of their daughters. In the 1920s, New Orleans politicians claimed Mexican immigrants' marijuana caused the recent crime wave (Brecher et al., 1972). At the same time, the deep South feared that blacks crazed by cocaine would attack their men and rape their women. Cities in the 1960s cried out about "crime in the streets" where street junkies robbed pedestrians to get money for drugs. Yearly press spotlighting of crime waves gave rise to the simple proposition that drugs cause crime. In time, the myth became a social fact for many.

Drugs differ in their effects on individuals, and people hold a variety of beliefs about drug use. The same drug can sometimes have the same, different, or no effect on persons. Drugs also differ in their legal status. The situations in which people produce, distribute, and use drugs all vary in time, place, and circumstance. Useful generalizations about the drug-crime link need to take into account how drugs, their effects and legal status; individuals and their beliefs; and the situations of production, distribution, and use combine to produce a drug-crime event.

This chapter offers a sociological explanation for the drug-crime link. It examines links between crime and major drugs, including alcohol, marijuana, heroin, and cocaine. The chapter also reviews the impact alcohol and drugs have had on the criminal justice system, including law enforcement, courts, and corrections.

The classic work by Paul Goldstein (1985) organized the link between drugs and violent crime around three major issues. The three-part framework focuses on *psychopharmacology*, the *system* of drug markets, and *economics*. The psychopharmacological path deals with how individuals respond to the specific drugs used. As we will see in this chapter, the type of drug used can be associated with specific behaviors, with alcohol and cocaine most closely associated with violent crime. Goldstein's concern with the system refers to competition in drug markets, including fights and assaults between buyers and dealers. The third way in which drugs and crime are interrelated focuses on the economics of being able to afford the drugs, especially an issue with cocaine, for which there is frequent use. Developments in the 1990s and early 2000s generated controversy in understanding the economic issues. While the 1990s saw a doubling in the number of those incarcerated for drug offenders, when adjusted for inflation, the prices of heroin and cocaine fell by half (Boyum and Kleiman, 2003).

Thus, the most important correlations between drugs and crime are the behavioral effects of the specific drugs used, the need for addicts to get money so they can purchase drugs, and the "side effects" of the illegal drug market, such as financial and territorial disputes among dealers and users (Boyum and Kleiman, 2003). Person(s), drug, and setting must combine for there to be a drug-crime link. While the link between drugs and crime is most often associated with poor inner cities, drugs have permeated all layers of American society, including small towns (see Box 11.1).

Alcohol

The general public does not regard alcohol as a drug because it has long been seen as a social beverage and, more important, because it is legal. Yet

---

Box 11.1   Drugs and Crime in "America's Hometown"

Hannibal, Missouri, birthplace of Mark Twain, is now known for more than the escapades of Tom Sawyer and being "America's hometown." Twenty-six robberies in 2004 in this small town represented a fourfold increase over 2000. Overall, Hannibal's property crime rate is 56 percent higher than the country's average. With few jobs and a higher than average rate of poverty, the increase in robberies has been blamed on individuals seeking money for drugs. A professor of rural sociology at Ohio State University, Joseph Donnermeyer, noted that midwestern towns have seen increases in crime owing to poor economic conditions, while national figures fall (Leonard, 2005).

it is the most commonly used drug in the United States. The high rates of alcohol abuse and alcoholism document its standing as the drug with the greatest potential for abuse. Alcohol is involved in more crimes than all illicit drugs combined (Boyum and Kleiman, 2003).

Heavy drinkers are those who are more apt to commit crimes after drinking. As with crime, the highest proportion of heavy drinkers is in the eighteen to thirty-nine age range (Clark and Hilton, 1991; Substance Abuse and Mental Health Services Administration, 2007a). The kinds of alcohol problems they experience are more likely to be alcohol abuse rather than physical dependence on alcohol. Problem drinkers are characterized by social support for drinking, alienation, low social control (social mechanisms that regulate individual and group behavior), and impulsivity. A principal component of abuse is belligerence, more characteristic of heavy drinkers of poor socioeconomic status (Cahalan, 1970). And once again most criminals who commit major violent crimes evince these same characteristics. This sharing of characteristics by heavy drinkers and criminals strongly suggests that when found in the same persons, the risk of drug-related crime increases.

The most frequent drinkers in public drinking establishments are men in the 18–39 age range (Harford and Gaines, 1981). This dovetails very nicely with the finding that men in the 18–39 age range rank highest in the frequency of weekly intoxication (Clark and Hilton, 1991). It is both common knowledge and established fact that public drinking establishments such as bars and taverns are frequent sites of violence (Quigley and Leonard, 2005). An early 2000s observational study of 1,025 incidents of aggression in 118 bars found that as the level of intoxication increased, so did the frequency and severity of aggression (Graham et al., 2006). But the great preponderance of heavy drinkers who frequent bars and taverns do not commit any violent crimes when there. So the question remains, what conditions must be present in the person-drug-setting triangle to trigger violence?

The two conditions that make violence possible are the presence of a dispute and the absence of social controls. Disputes arise in public drinking places when disputants believe the disagreement can be solved only by violence and when companions, patrons, and bar workers fail to intervene. Further, assaults are most likely to occur if disputants share a culture of violence in public drinking places that have a low standard of decorum; a noisy, crowded clientele of people who are mostly strangers to one another; and a bar staff that permits intoxication (Graham et al., 1980). In contrast, domestic violence is more apt to occur in private places. Drinking may bring a long-standing dispute to the surface, with one participant deciding to resolve the conflict by violence. Violence is much more likely if an audience is absent, or if those present fail to intervene.

Considerable attention has been paid to drunk driving in recent years. All fifty states address drunk driving based on two statutory offenses (Alcohol Alert, 2007). The first offense is driving under the influence (DUI), or driving while intoxicated (DWI). Police officers make this charge based on observations of the car while traveling and driver roadside sobriety tests. The second possible drunk driving offense is known as illegal per se. This means that the driver has a blood alcohol contact (BAC) of 0.08 percent or higher. It has been illegal to drive with a BAC of 0.08 or higher since 2002. Many people mistakenly think that since they do not feel intoxicated, they will not be subject to a drunk driving arrest. In 2006, 32 percent of traffic fatalities involved a driver who had been drinking (Alcohol Alert, 2007). In 1996 there were 13,451 alcohol-related fatalities, compared with 13,470 in 2006, revealing little progress in reducing drunk driving.

Alcohol's implication in violent crime surpasses other drugs combined, somewhat less so in the case of property crime. The more liquor stores there are in a neighborhood, the higher the rates of violent crime (Gorman et al., 2001). However, the public and policymakers have been much more focused on illicit drugs in the crime connection and need to focus more on alcohol (Martin et al., 2004).

Alcohol's legality guarantees its preeminence as the United States' most commonly used drug. Drinkers have access to thousands of outlets purveying alcohol by the drink or by the bottle. Thus, compared with other drugs, the drinking population has more opportunity to drink with considerably less trouble and expense. Very few people who want a drink need to rob or steal in order to get money to pay for one. Except for some people who are skid row residents, drinkers are not likely to break the law in order to buy a drink. As might be expected, the alcohol-robbery link ranks at the very bottom. Nonetheless, a small but significant segment of the drinking population makes trouble for themselves and others after drinking occasions. These postdrinking troubles can eventuate in violent crimes such as assault, rape, robbery, and murder.

Alcohol, though linked with violent crimes, exhibits its greatest influence in assaults, simple assault (an attempt to cause bodily injury that results in little or no injury) as well as aggravated assault. Moderate drinking and mistaken consensus can set the stage for acquaintance and date rape. Heavy drinking by the victim is one of the precipitating conditions of fraternity rape (Martin and Hummer, 1989; Sanday, 2007). Underreporting and absence of true measures of alcohol consumption characterize all varieties of rape and sexual assaults.

Homicides are either acts of rational choice or acts of passion. A general assumption is that alcohol is more apt to be present when homicides are driven by passion. The setting for homicide is more often residences than bars and more often between intimates. Males in these relationships usually consume more alcohol than women, who generally drink less than men. In turn, the women who kill men in these relationships both drink less and kill men less frequently than men kill women (Browne, 1987).

A major concern in the study of violent incidents turns on the question of whether or not both assailants and victims had been drinking at the time of the offense. A classic study from the late 1950s of 500 Philadelphia homicides found that alcohol was involved in 60 percent of the killings. In 20 percent of the murders, the offender had been drinking; in 20 percent the victim had been drinking; and in another 20 percent, both offender and victim had been drinking (Wolfgang, 1958). The amount of alcohol consumed by all parties as well as the degree of alcohol influence becomes another important issue. William Wieczorek and colleagues (1990), in a study of convicted homicide offenders, found that approximately 50 percent were under the influence of alcohol at the time of the crime. Overall, 36 percent used alcohol alone, 7 percent used drugs alone, and 13 percent used both alcohol and drugs.

Marijuana

Marijuana has been known in the United States since at least the time of George Washington, who grew hemp on his plantation. The nation has also known legitimate medical use during its history. However, for much of its history, marijuana has been associated in the public mind with immigrants, minority-group use, and unconventional people, in general. In the last third of the nineteenth century, immigrants from India brought hemp with them, to the consternation of the San Francisco natives (Musto, 1987). In the 1920s, press and police attributed crime waves in New Orleans and prison riots in Colorado to Mexican immigrants (Brecher et al., 1972). In the 1930s Henry Anslinger called marijuana the "killer weed" and frightened Congress into increasing its appropriation to the Bureau of Narcotics, which he headed. The movie *Reefer Madness* engendered the popular belief that marijuana increased sexual behavior, violence, and madness. Blacks, members of the underworld, and black jazzmen adopted the Mexican immigrants' custom of smoking marijuana. Jazz musicians took their adopted custom with them when they migrated to Chicago and New York

(Polsky, 1969). In time, the beat subculture of the 1950s became notorious in the press in their undisguised praise for and use of marijuana. The hippie culture of the 1960s made the news, inspiring the 1970s epidemic of marijuana smoking among college students.

Marijuana is the most commonly used illicit drug in the world (United Nations, 2006). Always a controversial drug, it has been subject to conflicting definitions by the criminal justice system, the medical community, and the population of users.

Since the 1920s, marijuana spread throughout American society. It went from the poor and the underclass until it is, at this writing, found in segments of the working class, the middle class, and the upper class. For the most part, the persons who continue to use marijuana are more apt to be somewhat unconventional people, adventurous, and risk takers. Smuggling, growing, selling, and smoking marijuana are not very public activities, since transparency increases the risk of arrest. Discretion reduces those risks, and smugglers, dealers, and growers continue to take considerable precautions to conceal their activities and avoid arrest. Thousands of current and former college students can recall burning incense and covering the doors to their residence hall rooms so resident assistants could not smell the odor of marijuana. Some people put on sunglasses to disguise reddened eyes. And, of course, for many people the thrill of engaging in ostensibly illegal activities was a major inducement. For the most part, smoking marijuana was a social occasion. Three elements tightened the social group's bonds: partnership in illicit activities that required secrecy, experiencing marijuana intoxication, and observing its effects on their companions.

Marijuana is a drug that is more likely to induce euphoria rather than aggression (Grinspoon and Bakalar, 1997). Smokers, whether alone or together, experience its effects in private settings. How is it possible for marijuana to induce people in specific social settings to commit violent crimes? People who hold such a marijuana-crime linkage only demonstrate how popular beliefs can still triumph over social facts. Undoubtedly, a significant minority of the American public continues to link marijuana with violent crime.

Data compiled from convicted offenders such as probationers and jail and state prison inmates indicate that marijuana is the drug of choice of all convicted offenders. A large proportion claim that they were using marijuana at the time they committed the offense for which they were incarcerated. In the 2004 Survey of Inmates in State and Federal Correctional Facilities (produced every five years), 26 percent of federal prisoners and 32 percent of state prisoners stated they committed the crimes they were incarcerated for while under the influence of drugs (Mumola and Karberg,

2007). Thirty percent of persons queried in the 2004 National Victimization Survey and 27 percent in the 2005 survey said the offender was using alcohol or drugs, or only drugs (Mumola and Karberg, 2007). Aside from the problems with recall data, neither the offenders nor the victims specify the offense committed. Problems exist with drug testing of arrestees. Since marijuana remains in the bloodstream much longer than most other drugs, it is difficult to prove that its use was connected in any way with commission of the offense. And, in all cases, no specific offense is ever listed.

So, all things considered, it seems inappropriate to make any statements on the degree to which marijuana use is linked in any way with violent crime. Marijuana is less likely than heroin and cocaine to be related to crime and is less expensive (Boyum and Kleiman, 2003). Marijuana, as we have seen, has gone from being a menace to being mainstream, when compared with all other illicit drugs combined.

Heroin and Morphine

Heroin stands out as a particularly good example of how its use has changed over time. The drug experienced three stages of changes in definition, characteristics of users, and typical settings of use. All three periods made for changes in the frequency and types of crimes. From 1865 to 1914, opiates could be obtained by prescription from physicians, with or without prescription from pharmacists, at general stores, or through mail order. Drug use took place in physicians' offices or in users' residences. Typical users were middle-aged, middle-class women who lived in rural areas. There was little crime to speak of. In 1914, Congress, through the Harrison Act, prohibited the manufacture, sale, purchase, and possession of narcotics. From 1914 to 1965, users, market, and setting all changed. Heroin could be obtained only on the black market. Users, now defined as criminals, had to use the drug in secrecy. Inner-city youth living in low-income neighborhoods became the typical users. After some of them became addicted, they mostly committed property crimes in order to obtain money for drugs (Musto, 1987).

Since 1965, more and more addicts supported their drug habits by violent crime. Pathways to addiction had reversed. New users now came from young criminals. They fused two deviant careers. First, they became career criminals. In the course of that career, they came upon heroin and tried it out. Some of them became addicted. These addicts were much more likely to employ violence to obtain drugs. Consequently, rates of violent crimes committed by chronic heroin users mounted, violence taking place much more frequently at drug transactions (Goldstein, 1985).

When definitions of drugs change, enforcement also must be adjusted. Both changes took place sooner with heroin than with morphine. Physicians began using morphine in the 1840s. After 1865 the hypodermic syringe came into general use among physicians. Morphine became a wonder drug. Physicians saw it as a cure-all and treated most illnesses with it. For example, many thought it would cure alcoholism. In time, of course, many patients had become medically addicted after treatment overuse by physicians (White, 1998).

Morphine was derived from opium. In 1874 a chemist synthesized heroin from morphine. It soon became clear that heroin, ten times stronger than morphine, was a most addictive drug. While morphine continued to have medical use, physicians discontinued heroin treatment long before its prohibition.

Politicians and moral reformers concerned about the international traffic in narcotics and the presumed increase in addiction, particularly among minority groups, lobbied for federal narcotics control. Though many states had already passed statutes prohibiting cocaine, the reformers' law did not come into being until 1914. The Harrison Narcotic Control Act, though actually a tax act, resulted in the prohibition of narcotics. Treasury Department agents enforced violations of the Act. Their interpretation of the Harrison Act ultimately had lasting effects. Physicians thought when they prescribed maintenance doses to addicts and counseled them, they were providing medical treatment. Agents defined their actions as violations of the Harrison Narcotic Control Act. Within a short period of time, physicians refused to treat addicts, addicts became defined as criminals, the black market became the only source of drugs for addicts, and the addict subculture was born.

The period 1914–1965 saw a series of revisions in definitions of all the opiates, but of heroin in particular; in the population of addicts; and in settings of use. Now illicit, heroin attained status as a "dangerous drug." Most heroin addicts found in cities like New York, Chicago, and Los Angeles were primarily low-income males. The illegal drug dealers were most often found in the same neighborhood in which the addicts lived. In the pre–Harrison Act period, numerous physicians worried that unrelieved withdrawal distress could cause addicts great physical harm, in some cases even death. A widespread belief by physicians and researchers during the 1914–1965 era was that both tolerance and the need for more drugs to relieve withdrawal symptoms drove most addicts into crime. The need for drugs, coupled with their exorbitantly high prices on the black market, forced addicts to commit crimes in order to obtain money for drugs (Goldstein, 1985). But for the most part, large segments of the medical and research communities believed that addicts committed property crimes like burglary and theft. Thus, according to the beliefs of most authorities during this period, users first became addicted and then turned to crime in order to support their drug habit. And most of their unlawful efforts to obtain funds were nonviolent crimes.

In the 1914–1965 period, heroin's effects predominate as the major influence on crime. During that period, most held to a pharmacological interpretation. Once addicted and tolerance increases, addicts need more drugs. Withdrawal distress drives addicts' search for the relief that comes only from more heroin. This addiction cycle continually forces addicts to steal in order to pay the inflated prices that the black market demands. Thus, the principal crime during this period is property crime. All observers recognize that addicts do not engage in criminal pursuits while under the effects of heroin, a narcotic that tranquilizes rather than energizes. Were drugs legally available, critics argue, there would be no crime at all.

By the mid-1960s, these beliefs came into question as a result of three significant changes. To begin with, there had always been some addicts who used violence to obtain money for drugs. Nevertheless, the dominant theory of the drug-crime link during this period was based on the characteristic effects of heroin. How could users under the influence of a narcotic engage in the energetic action that violent crimes require? Changes in the character of recruits into addiction, the classification of crimes, and new patterns of drug use were the source of increased violent crime by chronic users.

The classic pathway into addiction had reversed by the mid-1960s. First, young men embarked on criminal careers marked by their use of violence. In the course of adopting a criminal way of life, some of them experimented with drugs. Those who became addicted used their propensity for violence to obtain drugs. And rates of violent crime spiked. About this time, the Uniform Crime Reports of the Department of Justice changed the classification of crimes. For years the department had classified crimes as being against persons (assaults, rape), against property (theft, robbery), and against public order (drunkenness, disorderly conduct). It developed the category of violent crimes that included aggravated assault, rape or other sexual assault, robbery, and homicide. Since the threat of or actual use of force was important, the Department of Justice reclassified robbery as a violent crime. Patterns of drug use had also undergone a change in this period. In the earlier period, most addicts used heroin exclusively. By the mid-1960s, most addicts had become polydrug users. And those who combined cocaine with heroin were especially prone to violence (Boyum and Kleiman, 2003).

During the peak of this period, drug transactions became a frequent setting for violent crimes. Suspicion and distrust have always surrounded the black market for drugs. Once more violent users entered the market as buyers as well as sellers, violence increased as the principal means of obtaining drugs or of resolving disputes. The newcomers made their own rules about transactions. They robbed dealers. They staked out and defended their territory by means of violence. In some large cities, gangs fought for control of their territory. Numerous disputes led to violence.

In the 1965–1985 period, a focus on the individual users constituted the major influence. Experts revised the previous interpretations. A more "violent breed" of career criminals robs other addicts as well as dealers to obtain drugs. Robbery, now reclassified with aggravated assault as a violent crime, became a major technique of acquisition. Whereas previously addicts used heroin exclusively, now most addicts had become polydrug users. All of these changes increased rates of violent crimes committed by heroin addicts. However, heroin is less tied to crime than is cocaine, with heroin addiction requiring continuity of use (Boyum and Kleiman, 2003). Moreover, research has emerged showing that heroin addicts entering treatment engage in less crime. That is, reduction in heroin use is associated with reduction in crime (Gossop et al., 2000).

In periods since 1985, the major change has been preeminence of cocaine. Nonetheless, violence continues to predominate in drug transactions. The Uniform Crime Reports reflect that in 2005, 4 percent of homicides were considered drug related (US Department of Justice, 2006). The highest percentage of total US drug-related homicides was 7.4 percent in 1989. Heroin use decreased, although it seems to be on the rise once again. Violence accompanies two changes in drug transactions. At this writing, buyers and sellers can be either users or nonusers. Transactions can be retail or wholesale, for personal use or resale. News reports include the police cliché of shootings as "a drug deal gone sour," and gangs involved in the traffic of drugs fight with others over territory. The spate of drive-by shootings is reminiscent of the gang wars of Prohibition (1920–1933).

A proper assessment of the heroin-crime link requires an informed estimate of the relative contribution of persons, drugs, and settings to each period of use. The prohibition against the manufacture and sale, possession, and use of narcotics remains constant through all periods. Persons, drugs, and settings are also present in all periods. However, as the present analysis argues, each one of those aspects predominates in different periods.

Cocaine, Methamphetamine, and Ecstasy

In the 1920s, some members of the entertainment industry and the underworld elite used cocaine, known as the "champagne of drugs." Cocaine reappeared in the 1960s, achieved epidemic status in the 1980s, and experienced decreased use in the 1990s. Nevertheless, it was second only to marijuana as the most frequently used illicit drug. It also retained its status as the illicit drug responsible for more violent crimes than all the others combined.

Chronic heavy users of cocaine can spend considerable time obtaining money for drugs and then exchanging that money for drugs. This perpetual drug-money hunt under unstable mental conditions increases the already high risks for using violence to obtain drugs or for becoming a victim of violence. In New York in the late 1980s, 90 percent of robbery suspects tested positive for cocaine. The 1990 Drug Use Forecasting studies found that 41 percent of arrestees tested positive for cocaine, once again the most frequently detected drug. Clearly, cocaine had supplanted heroin as the leader in both use and violent, drug-related crime and is more expensive than marijuana (Boyum and Kleiman, 2003).

Cocaine is most particularly associated with criminal homicide. Drug, person, and setting all combine as is the case with the three other drugs. But the setting and its "crack trade" stand out as the most significant influence in the cocaine–violent crime link. Many chronic crack users went from juvenile delinquent to career criminal. Along the way they acquired the crack habit, using force and fraud as their principal method of drug acquisition.

The neighborhood and the drug transaction are reasons violence can occur. All drug transactions entail the possibility of violence. Unlike heroin, crack is a fast-acting, high-intensity, and short-lasting drug. As a result, it imposes a different schedule of acquisition and use. The heavy chronic user seeks to repeat the experience almost immediately. Neighborhoods in which crack is sold are usually run-down, with numerous abandoned buildings. Generally, they are poorly policed areas of high crime. Most of the neighborhood people, residents and transients alike, are strangers to one another. These are all the conditions of urban disorder that increase the chances of violence, which indeed often characterizes transactions between buyers and sellers of crack. The role of assailant can be interchangeable with respect to buyer and seller, whether they are users or nonusers. In the absence of clear-cut rules, all parties are free to employ force or fraud to obtain drugs or resolve disputes (stealing, selling adulterated drugs, or seeking revenge after being victimized, and territorial disputes).

As might be expected, just as there has been a drop in crime overall since the turn of the twenty-first century, so has there been a decline in drug-related crimes. The peak crack cocaine years were the late 1980s and early 1990s, also the time of peak homicide rates (Levitt, 2004).

Methamphetamine and ecstasy are newer drugs on the drug-crime scene. Methamphetamine is associated with aggressive behavior (Boyum and Kleiman, 2003). However, research in the early 2000s indicates that while a person is under the influence of methamphetamines, more aggressive behavior than usual may result; yet it does not seem to lead to violence (McKetin et al., 2006). It is controversial whether ecstasy is correlated with crime. An early 2000s study found ecstasy use was more prevalent among young men in the general population than in a group of young men who had been arrested (Hendrickson and Gerstein, 2005). For ecstasy, the link to crime may be more about participation in acquiring the drug. Further research is needed on methamphetamine and ecstasy and their relationship to crime.

Criminal Justice Responses to Drugs

The war on drugs has had a dramatic impact throughout the criminal justice system. Enormous resources are given to the criminal justice system to enforce drug laws (Boyum and Kleiman, 2003). Over the years it has become apparent that the war on drugs has led to very significant increases in arrest, conviction, and incarceration rates.

It is important to remember that drug users are not necessarily drug dealers and drug dealers are not necessarily drug users. However, it can be common practice for drug users to sell drugs to support their own habits. Drug dealers may not be using drugs themselves; they may simply have a financial motive for buying and selling drugs. While the relationship between drugs and crime is complex, involvement in crime provides society with one more opportunity to address substance abuse problems (Braithwaite, 2001).

Law Enforcement

Police often have the first criminal justice encounter with drug dealers and drug users. Over 10 percent of all arrests involve violations of drug laws (Boyum and Kleiman, 2003). Not surprisingly, the poorest neighborhoods can have the highest arrest rates.

Media attention to large drug raids is rather popular. As in the days of Prohibition, when the government touted its ability to root out alcohol, so, too, does the public get the message that sizable drug raids by the federal

©iStockphoto.com/walik

Drug Enforcement Agency (DEA) as well as local and state police are a good use of public safety resources. Police officers themselves are known to have a higher rate of alcoholism and substance abuse problems than laypeople (Woody, 2006), and their behavior can affect the drug cases of arrestees. In Massachusetts in January 2008, an investigation into the Boston Police Department found that 700 bags of drugs had been stolen or inappropriately discarded (Johnson, 2008). Another 265 evidence bags were tampered with, and prescription narcotics were replaced with aspirin tablets. Cocaine was the most prevalent drug found missing.

Police also have the opportunity to make positive changes in lives. Some recent efforts include police participation in harm reduction strategies and voluntary treatment diversion programs (Goetz and Mitchell, 2006). One study, conducted in the early 2000s, showed that the desire to avoid trouble with the police was an important reason for heroin addicts to enter treatment (Weatherburn and Lind, 2001).

Courts

Prosecutors are well aware of the major increase in drug-related crime since they have to determine which cases will go forward for prosecution and must manage the resulting huge caseloads that are a threat to a well-run court system. Drug-related crimes are complex for prosecutors to handle and include possession, sales, gang violence, and murders to control illicit drug markets; the biohazards of methamphetamine manufacturing sites; and the maiming and death resulting from driving under the influence (Also-brooks, 2002).

Sentencing for drug offenders has focused on incapacitating drug offenders, deterring others from drug use when they become aware of the sentences they may be subjected to, and punishing offenders in proportion to the severity of the crime (Kleiman, 2004). Concerns have been raised for years that race or ethnicity and type of drug use have been factors in the sentencing of drug offenders. This has been of special concern in federal sentencing where disparities exist in sanctions for specific types of drugs, such as longer sentences for crack cocaine than for regular cocaine, including environmental and procedural characteristics (Kautt, 2002; Kautt and Spohn, 2002). Crack-cocaine sentencing disparity has been a hot issue in criminal justice, with poor blacks the most likely to use crack cocaine and therefore more likely to receive a harsher sentence (McBride, VanderWaal, and Terry-McElrath, 2001). While powder cocaine use has been more associated with whites, Hispanics make up 60 percent of those facing federal cocaine charges (Jordan, 2008). Under federal laws a person with 0.04 ounce (1 gram) of crack cocaine receives the same sentence as a person with 3.5 ounces (100 grams) of powder cocaine (Saltzman, 2008). At this writing, a minimum mandatory sentence of five years is required for dealing 0.18 ounce (5 grams) of crack cocaine, with ten years required for dealing 1.8 ounces (50 grams) of crack.

Mandatory sentences for drug crimes have been especially controversial. While envisioned as having a deterrent effect on drug use, they have only dramatically increased the numbers of offenders (McBride et al., 2001). Minority women more often are sentenced to prison for a drug offense than are white women (Mauer, Potler, and Wolf, 1999). Effects on families can be devastating (see Box 11.2). Incarceration of felony drug offenders has been found to lead to higher rates of recidivism than for other types of offenders (Spohn and Holleran, 2002).

In late 2007 the United States Sentencing Commission recommended significant reductions in crack-cocaine drug sentences. Approximately 20,500 inmates could be granted early release; however, the George W. Bush administration fought this on the grounds that these offenders could pose a threat to the community (Saltzman, 2008a). For the future it is preferable to give more sentencing weight to crimes of violence rather than focusing on the amount of illegal drugs bought or sold, or both (Kleiman, 2004).

Drug courts have their roots in the 1950s, when municipal court judges, some of them recovered alcoholics, sought to use the power of the

Box 11.2   Enrique and Elaine

Enrique was a Hispanic man in his early thirties incarcerated in a medium-security prison in Massachusetts. He had been working in a factory for years, making little more than minimum wage. He worked as much as he could because he has a wife and two young children to support. Enrique recounted that his brother-in-law made huge sums of money dealing drugs. The brother-in-law taunted Enrique for working so hard for so little money. He repeatedly suggested that Enrique get into the business and make some real money. Enrique was busted on his second drug deal and is now serving a mandatory fifteen-year prison sentence (Mignon, personal communication, 1995).

*   *   *

Elaine was a young woman of twenty-six with four children when she was busted for selling cocaine. As a result of the harsh mandatory sentences New York is known for, Elaine spent sixteen years in prison. Her story is one of many obstacles, brutality, despair, and problems of reintegrating into society with meager assistance (Gonnerman, 2004).

bench to compel treatment. This trend increased in popularity from the early 1990s to this writing; drug courts now require probationers to attend meetings of Narcotics Anonymous, Cocaine Anonymous, or other treatment for drug addiction. Drug offenders can avoid incarceration and remain in the community, typically under probation supervision and with a plan for treatment, if the terms assigned by the drug court are met. Research shows that drug courts can save money, reduce recidivism, and promote positive functioning in the community. Not all clients are successful in drug courts; however, the opportunity is there for treatment and recovery (Harrell, 2003). See Box 11.3 for a discussion of drug courts. In the future, drug courts will have to address the most effective strategies for specific types of drug offenders (National Institute of Justice, 2006).

Corrections

Today it is commonly known that incarceration of drug offenders has led to the explosion of the correctional population (Goetz and Mitchell, 2006). In 2004, 30 percent of property offenders, 25 percent of drug offenders, 10 percent of violent offenders, and 7 percent of public-order offenders in state prisons committed their crimes for drug money (Mumola and Karberg, 2007). One-quarter of federal inmates convicted on drug charges reported

Box 11.3   Drug Courts

Drug courts are an effort to ensure that the treatment needs of criminal offenders are met by requiring involvement in substance abuse treatment. Developed in 1989, there are now over 2,000 existing or planned drug courts
that have served over 400,000 drug-using offenders (Facts on Drug Courts,
2008). Drug courts can provide closer supervision than is typical for offenders on probation alone. They help motivate individual clients to acknowledge and deal with substance abuse problems. Drug courts encourage criminal justice agencies and substance abuse and mental health agencies to work
in collaboration for the benefit of clients, families, and the helping systems.

Drug courts are known to have a much more positive and supportive approach than other types of courts. One drug court in Massachusetts gave
clients who graduated from the program a standing ovation, led by the
judge!

In a review of thirty-seven evaluations of drug courts, it was found that
drug use and criminal activity declined for participants. Overall, 47 percent
of participants graduated from drug court programs (Belenko, 2001). There
appears to be significant evidence that they are working.

they committed offenses to buy drugs, compared with only 11 percent of
federal property offenders. In 2004, 17 percent of prisoners in state custody
and 18 percent of prisoners in federal custody acknowledged they committed their current offense to get money for drugs (Mumola and Karberg,
2007).

Drug and alcohol treatment needs are enormous among the incarcerated population. One study found that over half of incoming inmates to a
county jail were in need of substance abuse treatment (Lo and Stephens,
2000). Another study found that most incarcerated women have substance
abuse problems and that greater addiction severity is correlated with
higher recidivism rates (Alleyne, 2006). Incarcerated offenders may also
gain access to drugs, including the opportunity to inject drugs, creating
further problems (Small et al., 2005); see Box 11.4.

With the increase of drug offenders in prison, drug treatment programs
have increased as well (Knight, Hiller, and Simpson, 1999). A 2004 survey
of inmates in state and federal correctional facilities found that for those
with substance abuse problems, 40 percent of state and 49 percent of federal inmates participated in a treatment program during their incarceration
(Harrison and Beck, 2005). Prison substance abuse treatment has been

Box 11.4   Manny in Prison

The following is an excerpt on the deviant, drug-using life of Manny, in his own words:

> Lots of people have a quaint notion about life in prison. They think that there's no dope or booze or sex in there. That it's just a place where guys in striped shirts break rocks all day and lock up all night. There's all kinds of dope in prison. The walls can't keep it out. I've known cons that have had it dropped by airplane. Usually it doesn't happen that dramatically.
>
> I remember the first time I scored a piece of dope in Sing Sing. They'd just started experimenting with the open visiting privilege. The phones and glass booths had been replaced with tables. You sat on one side, and your visitor sat on the other. No contact during the visit, but you could have some privacy of communication. My brother comes up to see me, and since I was young and they were trying to rehabilitate me they allowed us to visit the new way.
>
> The first thing that comes out of my mouth when I see Bobby is, "Do you have any dope? Can you score?" I'm not asking "how are you?" or saying "glad to see you." I've been in there for nine months and the important question is, "Do you have any dope?"
>
> And Bobby says, "No, I can't bring you any dope." I tell him, "Listen, before we talk or anything, I want some dope." But he ain't tuned to my frequency at all. "I didn't come all this way up here to jawbone about scag, and I ain't going to bring in no dope. You're crazy."
>
> So I say, "Now, brother, you listen. I like dope; I need dope; I ain't got no dope. You get me an ounce of dope. I know you can score it. So you do it, pronto. Understand? When you get the job done, come and see me. I'll tell you how we can get it in." (Rettig, 1977, 72–73)

Source: Rettig, R. P. (1977, reissued 1999), *Manny: A criminal-addict's story*, Prospect Heights, IL: Waveland. Reprinted with permission.

shown to reduce drug use and recidivism, as discussed in Chapter 13 (Harrison and Martin, 2001; Knight et al., 1999). Unfortunately, the vast majority of offenders have no opportunities for treatment.

Conclusion

Alcohol and cocaine are much more likely to be involved in violence than tranquilizing drugs such as marijuana and heroin. But the extent of violence in all cases depends most heavily on the lack of personal and social controls in the setting of use. Reduction in heroin and cocaine use brings with it a reduction in crime.

Uncontrolled use of substances constitutes a major element in the drug-crime linkage. One generalization is that the greater the quantity and frequency of drug use, the greater the prevalence of violent crime. However, lack of social control in the setting of use is required to complete the triangle of person-drug-setting. In terms of social policy, expanding drug and alcohol treatment can reduce crime.

Millions drink alcohol in a controlled manner in both well-controlled public and private settings. It is only in poorly controlled public and private settings that uncontrolled users under the influence of alcohol are most likely to commit violent crimes. By contrast, users of marijuana smoke in private settings without violence primarily because all are controlled users by definition, and they are not allowed to smoke it legally in public.

The criminal justice system has been overwhelmed by drug offenders, from law enforcement, to courts, to correctional facilities. It is certainly time to further expand and develop drug courts and, overall, to offer more drug and alcohol treatment for offenders.

PART 4

Diagnosis, Treatment, Prevention, and Policy Implications

12 Screening, Assessment, and Diagnosis of Alcohol and Drug Problems

How do we know if someone has a problem with alcohol or drugs? Since denial is a hallmark of addiction, it is not a surprise that the addict is often the last to know. Family members and friends may express concern about alcohol or drug use but the abuser or addict is unable or unwilling to hear. Since talking about substance use can be difficult and uncomfortable, it makes sense to seek a simpler and more objective way to learn whether a person has an alcohol or drug problem. Screening tools can accomplish this in just a few minutes. We devote an entire chapter to screening, assessment, and diagnosis because they are critical in determining if treatment is needed and, if so, the type of treatment that is most appropriate.

> Sally is a forty-year-old married woman with two young children. She often feels tired and overwhelmed by her responsibilities. It is very difficult to keep up with the demands of caring for her children, ages seven and nine. Meal preparation has become a very big chore. She is not able to sleep well. Increasingly, Sally has become resentful of her husband who does not help with any household tasks. She has come to look forward to the four or five glasses of wine she drinks each evening.

Sally makes the decision to go to a new physician for a complete checkup. In filling out the medical history forms, she is asked questions about her use of alcohol. Sally has just completed the AUDIT screening tool, discussed later in this chapter. The nurse finds that Sally has a score of eight on the AUDIT, an indicator that she may be developing a drinking problem. The doctor then talks with Sally about her drinking (brief intervention) and encourages her to drink no more than two or three times a week and to limit her intake to two drinks on any occasion. In a follow-up appointment with the doctor eight weeks later, Sally reports that she followed her doctor's advice and is feeling much less fatigue, her sleep has improved significantly, and she feels better able to handle her responsibilities. Sally is fortunate that her doctor took an interest in her drinking and spoke with her about it.

In reality, many health-care providers do not ask about alcohol use (Bush et al., 1998; Fleming, 2004/2005). Research has shown that physicians historically have held negative views of alcoholics and feel uncomfortable treating those with alcohol and drug problems (Mignon, 1993/1994). Physicians may not accept the disease concept of alcoholism, preferring to view alcoholism as a social or psychological problem, rather than a medical problem. Defining alcoholism as something other than a medical problem allows physicians to think that substance abuse problems are better treated by other kinds of professionals, such as psychologists, social workers, or counselors (Mignon, 1996). Other barriers to physicians offering routine screening include lack of training in medical school and residency, lack of commitment on the part of medical facilities, and inflexible health-care systems (Fleming, 1997, 2004/2005). Managed care and quality assurance professionals may not have much interest in substance abuse problems and therefore do not encourage the involvement of physicians. With few physician role models who do screen, physicians are given the message that this is not a priority (Fleming, 1997).

At this writing, substance abuse is so prevalent that primary care physicians need the expertise to assist alcoholics and addicts (Fleming, 2004/2005; Samet, Rollnick, and Barnes, 1996). Primary care physicians often see patients with alcohol problems and need to recognize and intervene with those who have drinking problems. Patients should be screened for this as a part of routine physicals, before the doctor prescribes medication that could have a negative interaction with alcohol, and, of course, when it appears that a patient may have an alcohol problem (Fleming, 2004/2005; Lucas, 1998). It is recommended that all adults and adolescents be screened for alcohol problems by their health-care providers (Ebell, 2004).

Screening Instruments

By focusing questions on the effects of alcohol and drug consumption, screening instruments offer a quick, easy, and objective way to learn if these present a problem (Maisto et al., 2000). Considerable research attests to the usefulness of screening tools (Hays and Revetto, 1992; McCabe et al.,

2006). Screening can be completed with the assistance of a professional or clerical person asking the questions, or they can be self-administered. They can cost very little—just the paper they are written on.

The tools consist of a battery of questions about alcohol and drug use, and are ideally suited for determining whether a person needs to be further assessed for a problem by a substance abuse professional. While a screening tool does not provide an accurate diagnosis of alcoholism or drug addiction, it is an important step in the direction toward this (National Institute on Alcohol Abuse and Alcoholism [hereafter, NIAAA], 2002).

Much time and effort go into determining how effective screening tools are at uncovering alcohol or drug problems. Most screening instruments are regularly reviewed and revised. The accuracy and effectiveness of a specific screening tool are usually measured by sensitivity and specificity.

Sensitivity refers to the ability of the screening tool to accurately measure whether individuals have drinking problems. That is, sensitivity is the ability to correctly determine those who have a drinking problem (NIAAA, 2000a). For example, if an alcohol screening instrument has a sensitivity of 85 percent, 85 percent of sample subjects will be correctly identified as problem drinkers. A tool with high sensitivity is very unlikely to suggest a person has a drinking problem when he or she does not.

Specificity measures how well the screening tool screens out those who do not have a drinking problem (NIAAA, 2000a). That is, specificity is the ability to correctly determine those who do not have a drinking problem. For example, if a screening instrument has a specificity of 85 percent, this means 85 percent of nonproblem drinkers will be correctly identified as not having a drinking problem. In general, sensitivity takes priority over specificity for screening since it is more important to identify those with drinking problems rather than those who do not (Cherpitel, 1997).

Screening tools rely on the self-report method, in which individuals reflect on their behavior and experiences and respond to questions about their substance use. Thus, screening tools rely on the respondent to be honest about alcohol and drug intake. With the possibility that underreporting substance use is a way to present a positive image of oneself, it is important that questions are asked in a nonjudgmental way, tied to health-care issues (Center for Substance Abuse Treatment, 1994b; Ruben, 1999).

A screening tool may be more useful with one group rather than another and speaks to the importance of research to compare the use of screening tools in different populations. Overall, screening tools may be more effective in uncovering the drinking problems of men rather than women (Aalto et al., 2006; Cherpitel and Borges, 2000). As discussed previously, women with drinking problems may consume less alcohol than men, and, therefore, whichever screening tool is used, the threshold should be lowered for women (Enoch and Goldman, 2002). Ethnic differences are also important in examining the accuracy of screening tools, with tools generally more accurate in screening for the substance problems of white males (Cherpitel, 1999; Cherpitel and Borges, 2000).

Some of the best-known screening tools for alcohol problems are reviewed below.

The Michigan Alcoholism Screening Test

A well-known tool developed by Melvin Selzer (1971), the Michigan Alcoholism Screening Test (MAST), asks twenty-five questions about alcohol consumption and its consequences. The Short Michigan Alcoholism Screening Test (SMAST) reduces the number of questions to thirteen. See Box 12.1 for the SMAST. There is no cost for its use because it is in the public domain (Center for Substance Abuse Treatment, 1994a). Sensitivity ranges from 30 to 78 percent and specificity from 80 to 99 percent (Cherpitel and Borges, 2000). Another variation of the MAST is the Brief MAST (BMAST), a ten-question screening tool developed in 1972. The MAST is one of the older, easy-to-use tools. It does well in identifying alcohol problems in psychiatric settings (Teitelbaum and Mullen, 2000). The Geriatric Michigan Alcoholism Screening Test (MAST-G) is a version of the MAST designed to specifically address the needs of the elderly.

While this is one of the older reliable screening tests, the MAST does not address the duration of substance abuse and tends not to pick up early or less-severe drinking problems very well (Ruben, 1999; Teitelbaum and Mullen, 2000). Nonetheless, it says a lot that thirty-five years after its development, the MAST is still in use.

The CAGE

The briefest of the screening tools, the CAGE, was developed in 1984 by John Ewing and is still frequently used (Buchsbaum et al., 1992; Bush et al., 1998). It can be easily administered orally or in writing and can be completed in less than one minute. One of the tools most often used in primary health-care settings, it was clearly designed with medical professionals in mind, having been first published in the *Journal of the American Medical Association* (Maisto and Saitz, 2003). Cheryl Cherpitel and Guilherme Borges (2000) reviewed available research studies and found that the CAGE has a sensitivity ranging from 61 to 100 percent and a specificity ranging from 77 to 96 percent.

Box 12.1   Short Michigan Alcoholism Screening Test (SMAST)

1. Do you feel you are a normal drinker?
2. Does your wife, husband, a parent, or other near relative ever worry or complain about your drinking?
3. Do you ever feel guilty about your drinking?
4. Do friends or relatives think you are a normal drinker?
5. Are you able to stop drinking when you want to?
6. Have you ever attended a meeting of Alcoholics Anonymous?
7. Has drinking ever created problems between you and your wife, husband, parent, or other near relative?
8. Have you ever gotten into trouble at work because of your drinking?
9. Have you ever neglected your obligations, your family, or your work for two or more days in a row because you were drinking?
10. Have you ever gone to anyone for help about your drinking?
11. Have you ever been in a hospital because of drinking?
12. Have you ever been arrested for driving under the influence of alcoholic beverages?
13. Have you ever been arrested, even for a few hours, because of other drunken behavior?

Scoring: Answer yes or no. "Yes" answers on questions 2, 3, 6, 7, 8, 9, 10, 11, 12, and 13 are worth one point each. "No" answers on questions 1, 4, and 5 are worth one point each. A score of 4 or higher indicates an alcohol problem.

Source: Selzer, Vinokur, and Van Rooijen, 1975.

The CAGE is in the public domain, and there is no cost to use it (Center for Substance Abuse Treatment, 1994a). See Box 12.2 for the CAGE questionnaire. The appeal of the CAGE is that it is easy to use as well as easy to score, making it a popular instrument. The CAGE has also been found to be effective in screening the elderly (Buchsbaum et al., 1992; Hinkin et al., 2001).

The CAGE is not without drawbacks, however. It focuses only on problems already experienced and is better at identifying chronic rather than early drinking problems (NIAAA, 2002). It does not differentiate between current drinking problems and past problems (Bush et al., 1998). It may be less sensitive in the case of women and minorities, although it is

---

Box 12.2   The CAGE Screening Tool

In the past year:

C Have you felt you should Cut down on your drinking?

A Have people Annoyed you by criticizing your drinking?

G Have you ever felt bad or Guilty about your drinking?

E Have you ever had a drink first thing in the morning to steady your nerves or get rid of a hangover (Eye opener)?

One or more "yes" answers indicate a drinking problem for both men and women.

Source: Ewing, 1984.

---

considered an adequate tool for screening women (Maisto and Saitz, 2003), and a variation of the CAGE has been used to screen pregnant women in prenatal care settings (Chang, 2004/2005).

The Alcohol Use Disorders Identification Test (AUDIT)

The AUDIT is an instrument initially designed for use in primary health-care settings. It was developed in 1989 by the World Health Organization to identify patients with current drinking problems and is considered one of the most effective of the screening tools (Maisto and Saitz, 2003). Its sensitivity ranges from 38 to 94 percent, and specificity ranges from 66 to 90 percent (Cherpitel and Borges, 2000). An important asset of the AUDIT is that it effectively screens those of different ethnicities and can be used cross-culturally. The AUDIT performed well in a study identifying alcohol and drug abuse in adults with severe and persistent mental illness (Maisto et al., 2000).

The AUDIT has been successfully used on a college campus as part of an effort to reduce alcohol misuse among college students (Hartwell, Mignon, and Lempecki, 1998). Fifty students constituted the sample, and 18 percent (nine students) screened positive for an alcohol problem. The study found that the AUDIT can easily and inexpensively become part of routine screening for those who seek medical and mental health services on a college campus.

An important advantage of the AUDIT over other tools is that it can identify early problem drinkers (Higgins-Biddle et al., 1997). It can be administered by another person or self-administered, and the computerized version is just as accurate as the paper-and-pencil AUDIT (Chan-Pensley, 1999). Seemingly free of gender and cultural bias (Aalto et al., 2006; Maisto and Saitz, 2003), the AUDIT has the potential to be used in cross-

Box 12.3 The Alcohol Use Disorders Identification Test (AUDIT)

1. How often do you have a drink containing alcohol?
2. How many drinks containing alcohol do you have on a typical day you are drinking?
3. How often do you have six or more drinks on one occasion?
4. How often during the last year have you found that you were not able to stop drinking once you had started?
5. How often during the past year have you failed to do what was expected of you because of drinking?
6. How often during the past year have you needed a drink first thing in the morning to get yourself going after a heavy drinking session?
7. How often during the last year have you had a feeling of guilt or remorse after drinking?
8. How often during the past year have you been unable to remember what happened the night before because of your drinking?
9. Have you or someone else been injured because of your drinking?
10. Has a relative, friend, doctor, or other health-care worker been concerned about your drinking and suggested you cut down?

Scoring:

Question 1 is scored: 0 (never); 1 (monthly or less); 2 (2–4 times per month); 3 (2–3 times per week); 4 (4 or more times per week)
Question 2 is scored: 0 (1 or 2 drinks); 1 (3 or 4 drinks); 2 (5 or 6 drinks); 3 (7 to 9 drinks); 4 (10 or more drinks)
Questions 3–8 are scored: 0 (never); 1 (less than monthly); 2 (monthly); 3 (weekly); 4 (daily or almost daily)
Questions 9–10 are scored: 0 (no); 2 (yes, but not in the last year); 4 (yes, during the last year)

Zero is the lowest score for nondrinkers, and 40 is the maximum possible score. A score of 8 or above needs some intervention as recommended below:
A score of 8–15: advice and brochure provided
Score of 16–19: advice, self-help manual, follow-up visit recommended
Score of 20 or greater: advice and referral for assessment

Source: Babor, de la Fuente, Saunders, and Grant, 1989.

cultural research and can be used effectively as part of a larger survey (Ivis, Adlaf, and Rehm, 2000).

The disadvantages of the AUDIT focus on the length of time it takes to administer, typically longer than primary health-care providers are willing to spend (Bush et al., 1998). As seen in Box 12.3, it does take some time to score the AUDIT.

The National Institute on Alcohol Abuse and Alcoholism (NIAAA) uses the AUDIT for the National Alcohol Screening Day (Enoch and Goldman, 2002). The first annual National Screening Day, in 1999, found that 43 percent of the 18,043 people who were screened at community and college sites had scores that indicated harmful or hazardous drinking. Close to one-third of the participants (5,959) were referred for treatment. Only 13 percent of the group had previously received alcohol treatment (Greenfield et al., 2003).

There are literally hundreds of tools available today to screen for alcohol and drug problems. The five-item TWEAK (*T*olerance, *W*orried, *E*ye opener, *A*mnesia, *K*ut down) was developed specifically in 1993 to screen pregnant women for drinking problems and can detect moderate and high-risk alcohol consumption (Bradley, 1994; Chan et al., 1993; NIAAA, 2002). The MacAndrew Alcoholism Scale, the Self-Administered Alcoholism Screening Test, and the Rapid Alcohol Problems Screen (RAPS4) are other examples (Allen et al., 1998; Cherpitel and Bazargan, 2003). Screening tools can be adapted for specific groups such as adolescents and the elderly.

For all the concern about screening and competition among the instruments, one study found a sensitivity and specificity of 86 percent by asking only one question (Williams and Vinson, 2001): for a man, "when was the last time you had more than five drinks in one day?" For a woman, the question is asked with four drinks rather than five. Definitions of binge drinking often focus on five drinks for men and four drinks for women. Patients who screen positive can then be given a more detailed tool such as the AUDIT and then, if necessary, a substance abuse assessment (Ebell, 2004).

Screening Adolescents for Substance Abuse

In general, adolescents are not likely to be screened for alcohol and drug problems, although they can easily be screened in a variety of settings, including health-care facilities, schools, legal settings, and vocational programs (Baldwin et al., 2006). All adolescents with mental health issues should be screened, as should those in the child welfare system and adolescents who are in shelters (Center for Substance Abuse Treatment, 1999a). The Committee on Adolescence of the American Academy of Pediatrics called for routine screening of all adolescents in 1989 (Bastiaens,

Francis, and Lewis, 2000). Since substance use and abuse often coexist with criminal activity, it is important to assess the substance use of juvenile detainees, many of whom have alcohol, drug, or mental disorders (Lapham, 2004/2005; Teplin, 2001). Regardless of the setting in which adolescents are screened, parents should not be present, since this can affect the truthfulness of responses (Center for Substance Abuse Treatment, 1999a). Research shows that parents tend to underestimate the substance use of adolescents (Bastiaens et al., 2000).

Typically physicians are not meeting guidelines for adolescent alcohol screening, and they are not using the most effective screening methods (Marcell and Millstein, 2000). While health-care providers may choose not to use them, there are many screening tools for adolescents that are readily available. All are designed to be completed in ten to twenty minutes and are easily scored. The Problem Oriented Screening Instrument for Teenagers (POSIT) uses 139 self-report items that screen for difficulties in ten areas, including family functioning. It is one of the better-known adolescent screening tools and is recommended by the Center for Substance Abuse Treatment (Santisteban et al., 1999).

The RAFFT (use to *R*elax, use *A*lone, using *F*riends, *F*amily member with problem, *T*rouble resulting from use) is very good at screening for substance abuse or dependence among adolescents. In a study of 226 adolescents referred to an emergency room or clinic, two positive responses on the RAFFT yielded a sensitivity of 89 percent and a specificity of 69 percent (Bastiaens et al., 2000).

The Client Substance Index–Short Form (CSI-SF) has been found to be useful for screening adolescents involved with the juvenile justice system and has been successfully used by probation officers, juvenile intake officers, and counselors in juvenile facilities. The fifteen items on the test can be completed in five to ten minutes. No special training is needed to score the tool, and it is in the public domain, so no fees need be paid (Thomas, 1993).

The AUDIT is useful in screening adolescents for alcohol and drug problems (Kelly and Donovan, 2001). In a study of 352 undergraduate students, the AUDIT was found to be both reliable and valid with this age group (O'Hare and Sherrer, 1999). Other tools for use with adolescents are the Adolescent Drinking Index (ADI), the Rutgers Alcohol Problem Index (RAPI), and the Adolescent Drug Involvement Scale (ADIS) (Alcohol and Drug Abuse Institute, 2007). The MAST and the CAGE are not especially effective in identifying alcohol problems in adolescents, since they tend to pick up more chronic drinking problems; however, a version of the MAST has been developed for adolescents (O'Hare and Sherrer, 1999).

Screening the Elderly

The Geriatric Michigan Alcoholism Screening Test, or MAST-G, contains questions relating to the special needs of the elderly, addressing issues of memory loss, physical responses to drinking, and social consequences of excessive drinking, including social isolation. A study of all residents over the age of sixty-five in a small town in Italy found that the CAGE and lab test results (discussed later in this chapter) identified two different groups as problem drinkers (DiBari et al., 2002). In the group of 377 elderly individuals, 53 were screened positive by the CAGE and 24 screened positive with the lab tests. Only 7 participants screened positive on both tests, with the CAGE better able to identify problem drinkers than lab testing alone. Thus, the CAGE and lab tests used together are preferable than either the screening tool or lab tests used alone.

In a study of older veterans, five tools were used to measure alcohol problems, including the CAGE and the AUDIT (Reid et al., 2003). Only modest levels of agreement were found among the tools used. M. Carrington Reid and colleagues (2003) concluded that individual screening tools may not be very successful in uncovering drinking problems of the elderly and may need to be used in combination.

Screening for Drugs Other Than Alcohol

Alcohol is certainly not the only drug of abuse and, as noted earlier in the textbook, most people with substance abuse problems abuse multiple substances. Therefore, there is the need to screen for more than just alcohol use. However, the best-known and most widely available screening tools focus solely on alcohol. While this may have been adequate thirty years ago, this is no longer the case. Several tools are available to screen for drug abuse; however, very few tools screen for both drugs and alcohol. Screening instruments designed for adolescents and newer screening tools are more likely to include both alcohol and drugs.

One instrument that screens solely for drugs (and not alcohol) is the Drug Abuse Screening Test (DAST) 20, developed by Harvey Skinner (1982). Drug abuse refers to over-the-counter drugs or prescription drugs used in excess of the directions as well as nonmedical use of drugs (Vanderbilt Addiction Center, 2001). See Box 12.4 for the DAST 20. In the 1990s, the DAST was reduced from twenty questions to ten. DAST 10 can be effectively used in mental health settings with clients who have a major mental disorder (Maisto et al., 2000). It is also a useful tool for identifying college students with drug abuse (McCabe et al., 2006).

Box 12.4   Drug Abuse Screening Test (DAST) 20

1. Have you used drugs other than those required for medical reasons?
2. Have you abused prescription drugs?
3. Do you abuse more than one drug at a time?
4. Can you get through the week without using drugs?
5. Are you always able to stop using drugs when you want to?
6. Have you had "blackouts" or "flashbacks" as a result of drug use?
7. Do you ever feel bad or guilty about your drug use?
8. Does your spouse (or parents) ever complain about your involvement with drugs?
9. Has drug abuse created problems between you and your spouse or your parents?
10. Have you lost friends because of your use of drugs?
11. Have you neglected your family because of your use of drugs?
12. Have you been in trouble at work because of your use of drugs?
13. Have you lost a job because of drug abuse?
14. Have you gotten into fights when under the influence of drugs?
15. Have you engaged in illegal activities in order to obtain drugs?
16. Have you been arrested for possession of illegal drugs?
17. Have you ever experienced withdrawal symptoms (felt sick) when you stopped taking drugs?
18. Have you had medical problems as a result of your drug use (e.g., memory loss, hepatitis, convulsions, bleeding, etc.)?
19. Have you gone to anyone for help for a drug problem?
20. Have you been involved in a treatment program especially related to drug use?

Scoring: Each question answered in the affirmative receives 1 point, with two exceptions; two questions, 4 and 5, receive a point each for a negative response. A score of 6 points or greater suggests a drug problem needing assessment. A score of 16 or greater suggests a very serious drug problem.

Source: Vanderbilt Addiction Center, 2001.

The Substance Abuse Subtle Screening Inventory (SASSI) is perhaps the best-known tool that screens for both drugs and alcohol. The SASSI can be completed in about fifteen minutes and scored in fewer than five minutes. A paper-and-pencil version is available, as are a PC-based program and a web-based version. There is a Spanish-language version of the SASSI as well as a version for adolescents.

According to the SASSI Institute in Springville, Indiana, the SASSI-3 (revised) has a sensitivity of 94 percent and a specificity of 93 percent. However, one study of the Substance Abuse Subtle Screening Inventory–Adolescent Version (SASSI-A) found that it was only moderately useful in identifying substance dependence among adolescents when used in a juvenile court (Sweet and Saules, 2003).

While many other screening tools are in the public domain, and therefore freely available for use, there are fees for the SASSI-3 tests and scoring materials. Depending on the quantity ordered, paper tests cost between $1.30 and $1.55 each, and computer tests between $4.00 and $7.00 each (SASSI Institute, 2008). These costs can make it prohibitive to use the SASSI for screening large numbers of people, such as all defendants in court cases.

The Michigan Alcoholism Screening Test/Alcohol-Drug (MAST/AD) is a new variation of the MAST designed specifically to screen for all substances of abuse (Westermeyer, Yargic, and Thuras, 2004). The CAGE was adapted in 1995 to include drugs as well (Center for Substance Abuse Treatment, 1997).

Screening instruments are readily available, and their simplicity and accuracy make them easy to use and can yield lifesaving information. It makes sense to use tools that screen for both drugs and alcohol. We hope for the days when substance abuse screening tools are used in every physician's office, hospital emergency room, and courtroom. Health services on college campuses are very likely to offer alcohol and drug screening. As you read this, take a break and go online to www.alcoholscreening.org for a personalized screening sponsored by Boston University and Join Together, a national organization fighting substance abuse.

Although there is much research and discussion in the literature trying to compare the tools and determine the most accurate one, the reality is that the majority of screening tools are useful. More attention needs to be paid to getting health-care providers and criminal justice agencies to use them rather than argue over which is best.

Physical Examination and Laboratory Test Results

Screening tools and family reports are not the only ways to learn that an individual has a drug or alcohol problem. Physical signs can alert health-care providers that a patient may have an alcohol problem. They include stomach complaints, headaches, diarrhea, fatigue, unexplained weight loss, insomnia, and abnormal laboratory test results (Kick, 1999; Lucas, 1998). Laboratory test results can detect biochemical changes related to excessive drinking (NIAAA, 2002). This speaks to the importance for physicians and other health-care providers, including college medical services, to have the knowledge and willingness to intervene with substance abuse problems (Baldwin et al., 2006; Fleming, 2004/2005). Many of us are familiar with breath, saliva, and blood testing. While these tests can be very accurate, they typically identify drinking within the past twelve to twenty-four hours (Maisto and Saitz, 2003). It is known that those with alcohol problems may "dry out" by not drinking for days or weeks before returning to alcohol use. Thus, breath, saliva, and blood testing may not reveal an alcohol problem in those who are in a short abstinence phase. Urine screening is often used for those who are known to have substance abuse problems and are under the supervision of a correctional agency. At this writing, urine testing can be considered a standard part of a job application process.

Blood tests include the serum gamma-glutamyl transferase (GGT), the mean corpuscular volume (MCV), aspartate aminotransferase (AST), and others. GGT is the most frequently used biochemical measure of drinking and is considered by some to be the most sensitive of the lab tests (NIAAA, 2000a). GGT, a blood protein, is raised after four or more drinks each day over a period of four to eight weeks. Typically, GGT levels return to the normal range after four to five weeks of abstinence. Liver disease that is not associated with alcoholism can also increase GGT levels. Carbohydrate-deficient transferrin (CDT), another blood protein, increases with heavy alcohol intake. CDT and GGT are considered equal in terms of being able to identify alcoholism.

MCV is an index of the size of red blood cells. It takes excessive alcohol consumption over a period of four to eight weeks to show up in this laboratory test. However, the sensitivity of MCV is not sufficiently high to justify its use as the sole indicator of problem drinking (NIAAA, 2000a).

Lab testing may be less reliable than screening tools in uncovering alcohol and drug problems because it is likely to take more intense drinking over longer periods of time for lab tests to be abnormal (Babor et al., 2000; Maisto and Saitz, 2003). Overall, lab test results identify between 10 and 30 percent of those with drinking problems, not a sufficiently high percentage to justify using lab test results alone. Although not specifically used for the screening of alcohol problems, these blood tests are useful for monitoring those with alcohol dependence. In general, screening instruments are more effective than physical examination and laboratory test results (Bradley, 1994).

At times, court and health-care professionals can claim to be able to recognize alcoholics and addicts simply by their appearance. One judge in

Massachusetts boasted at a professional meeting that he knew so much about alcoholism he could tell a defendant was an alcoholic just by looking at him! No substance abuse professional would claim to be able to diagnose alcoholism or addiction at a glance. However foolish that comment, the judge was not entirely wrong. It is true that some chronic alcoholics may develop a ruddy complexion, spider veins, a bulbous nose (like famed comedian W. C. Fields), and a frail build. However, it is very likely that when a person develops that "alcoholic look," the individual is very advanced in his or her alcoholism.

Assessment of Alcohol and Drug Problems

After a positive screening or when there is behavioral or medical evidence of a substance abuse problem, an assessment is needed. While screening can be done by any health-care professional, a person without training, or self-administered by the patient or client, an assessment can be completed only by a substance abuse professional. This includes social workers, psychologists, nurses, counselors, and psychiatrists, as long as the professional has training and expertise in substance abuse.

The purpose of the assessment is to determine if alcohol or drugs, or both, are a problem and whether there may be coexisting psychiatric disorders. Therefore, an assessment is critical before an accurate diagnosis of substance abuse or addiction can be made. The advantages of diagnosis are that treatment planning can be improved, since the intensity of treatment and the setting in which it is provided can be individualized. An accurate diagnosis has benefits beyond those to individual clients—accuracy in diagnosis contributes to the overall improvement in substance abuse diagnosis, encourages improvements in research, and can enhance communication among practitioners and researchers (Maisto and Saitz, 2003).

A thorough assessment provides an accurate and efficient way of determining treatment needs (Allen, Columbus, and Fertig, 1995; Vander Bilt et al., 1997). Some clinicians prefer the open-ended interview of the client, while others would rather rely on assessment tools. Whatever the clinician's preference, information must be gathered in order to formulate an appropriate treatment plan (see Box 12.5).

Widely used in studying homeless and veteran populations, the Addiction Severity Index (ASI) employs 161 items to facilitate a diagnostic evaluation of a client. The ASI focuses on identifying personal and family history and asks questions about current problems in six life domains: medical, employment, alcohol and drugs, legal, family and social, and psy-

Box 12.5   Key Elements in the Assessment of Substance Abuse Problems

1. Demographic information such as gender, age, race, marital status, and address.
2. Past history of substance use, including types of drugs or alcohol or both, quantity consumed, and duration of use.
3. Employment—both current job and previous work history.
4. Educational level, including academic problems such as learning disabilities and diagnoses associated with school problems such as attention deficit hyperactivity disorder.
5. Family constellation—with whom is the client living? Are there children the client is responsible for? Where are the children? Are the children in need of services?
6. Legal problems, including past arrest and confinement records. Are there current charges pending? If so, what are they? Does the client have a lawyer or need a lawyer?
7. Medical history. Are there past or current medical problems the client is experiencing?
8. Psychological functioning—does the client have any mental health problems? Is there a past history of problems? Is the treating clinician available for consultation?
9. Family history of substance abuse—parents, aunts, uncles, grandparents?
10. Client's perceptions of his or her problems.

chological status. It seeks to place the person's drinking within a broader social context. Considered the most widely used assessment tool, the ASI is, as of this writing, in its fifth edition (Alcohol and Drug Abuse Institute, 2007). One drawback is that substantial training is needed in order to appropriately administer the instrument and interpret the results (Allen et al., 1995). In addition, the ASI has been criticized for not being able to produce consistent research results (Makela, 2004). The team of researchers who designed the ASI offered several reasons that the ASI continues to be used over twenty-five years after its development: it describes and quantifies the many problems associated with substance abuse, it is available for use at no cost, and there have been continuous efforts through the years to revise and improve the instrument (McLellan et al., 2006).

Some clients have both a substance abuse problem and a mental health problem. Formerly known as dual diagnosis, the term *co-occurring dis-*

orders is frequently used to refer to individuals who may have a psychiatric problem in addition to substance abuse. Mood and anxiety disorders are the most common mental health problems among substance abusers (Franken and Hendricks, 2001; Kessler et al., 2005). Several tools have been developed to assist in screening and assessing clients who may have co-occurring disorders.

The Symptom Checklist-90 (SCL-90) is a self-report instrument of ninety items that examines the following areas of potential psychopathology: depression, anxiety, hostility, interpersonal sensitivity, paranoid ideation, somatization (physical symptoms as a result of emotional problems), agoraphobia (fear of open spaces), cognitive-performance difficulty, and sleep disturbance (Franken and Hendricks, 2001). The ASI-PSY is a version of the semistructured assessment interview. Ingmar Franken and Vincent Hendricks found the SCL-90 preferable to the ASI-PSY for diagnosing anxiety and mood disorders in substance abuse populations in treatment. More research on screening and assessment instruments for substance abusers is needed for those who also have psychiatric problems.

Assessment of Children and Adolescents

The assessment of a child or adolescent is especially critical because the results can have lifelong consequences for that individual. That is, the characterization of the substance abuse problem will determine whether or not the child is seen as experimenting with drugs and alcohol—a situation he or she is likely to outgrow. If the substance problem is determined by assessment to include physical addiction, this typically calls for a very different professional response. For example, a fourteen-year-old girl diagnosed as an alcoholic is most likely to be told by treatment personnel that complete abstinence from alcohol is the most appropriate treatment goal— in AA terminology, that the person can never "drink again in safety." This can be a lifelong label and holds the risk that the adolescent makes this a self-fulfilling prophecy, that is, the adolescent continues to drink because she feels others expect it.

It is important to remember not all adolescents who use substances will become dependent, and therefore adolescents should not be pressured to accept the disease concept (Center for Substance Abuse Treatment, 1999a, 1999b). The 2007 National Survey on Drug Use and Health found 7.7 percent of adolescents to be substance abusers or substance dependent (Substance Abuse and Mental Health Services Administration, 2008). Indeed, the diagnosis of alcoholism can create further problems for an adolescent.

The vast majority of adolescents can best be described as experimenters and perhaps abusers of substances rather than alcoholics or addicts (see Box 12.6). As we will see in our discussion of diagnosis, physical dependence on the substance is of critical importance in making the diagnosis of addiction. Adolescents are most likely to use alcohol, and marijuana is the most frequently used illicit drug. Adolescents can be more challenging to treat than adults and require assessment in more domains. These domains for adolescents include relationships with parents and school functioning.

Like adults, adolescents can receive an open-ended interview assessment from a clinician or can complete a substance abuse assessment instrument. There are many assessment instruments geared for the evaluation of adolescent substance abuse problems (Alcohol and Drug Abuse Institute, 2007). The Adolescent Drug Abuse Diagnosis instrument incorporates 150 items in ten problem areas. It is used for diagnosis and treatment planning as well as research (Santisteban et al., 1999).

It can take more time to complete an assessment of a child or adolescent than of an adult. Parents must be contacted, family involvement being a critical part of the youth's assessment. The school should be contacted for information about grades and school functioning. Peer relationships, sexual history, and juvenile justice involvement are important areas for assess-

---

Box 12.6 Does Jason Have a Problem?

Jason is a fifteen-year-old ninth grader at East Cippeebee High School. He had been an excellent student through the sixth grade. His grades began to decline in the seventh grade, and currently he is failing three of his classes.

Jason's father feels he has become increasingly disrespectful at home. Jason's mother has noticed that he is home very little and has stayed out beyond his 11:00 p.m. curfew on a number of occasions. She remembers that Jason came home drunk once, and she made him promise he wouldn't drink anymore. Jason's mother did not tell his father about this episode because she feared her husband would become extremely angry. Since both her parents were alcoholics, Jason's mother is very sensitive about alcohol use. She is also not happy about her son's choice of friends. Although concerned that they may be smoking marijuana, she doesn't think Jason is using illegal drugs.

Is Jason just experimenting with drugs and alcohol, or could he be developing a problem?

ment. A school social worker or psychologist can play a major role in the appropriate substance abuse assessment of an adolescent.

Definitions and Diagnosis of Alcoholism and Substance Abuse

What is an alcoholic? What is a drug addict? While these terms are often used, and there is considerable research on substance abuse problems, there is still no one conclusive definition. E. M. Jellinek, in his classic work, *The Disease Concept of Alcoholism,* acknowledged the many definitions of *alcoholism* and even discussed the "definition" of *definition* when examining alcohol problems (1960, 33–35)! Remember that there are varying levels of alcohol and drug problems. Sally, the forty-year-old woman we met at the beginning of the chapter, is an example of an early problem drinker, while someone who has lost his or her job and family and is homeless is likely to be a late-stage drinker who is physically dependent on alcohol. While there may be different definitions of *alcoholism* and *addiction,* most focus not only on the quantity of substances consumed but also—and especially—on the impact that substance use has on the person's family and social life, as well as medical consequences.

The substance abuse treatment field has long debated the best and most accurate definitions of *alcohol problems, alcoholism, substance abuse,* and *addiction.* Prior to 1940 there were at least thirty-nine diagnostic systems (ways to categorize and diagnose whether an alcohol problem was present) for alcohol problems (NIAAA, 1995). *The Big Book* of Alcoholics Anonymous addresses different types of alcoholics. William Silkworth, the physician for Bill W., the cofounder of Alcoholics Anonymous, wrote in his foreword to *The Big Book* (the "Doctor's Opinion"), "The classification of alcoholics seems most difficult" (1976, xxviii). Silkworth described the emotionally unstable psychopathic alcoholic, the manic-depressive alcoholic, the alcoholic who is "the type of man who is unwilling to admit that he cannot take a drink," and the "types entirely normal in every respect except in the effect alcohol has upon them" (1976, xxviii).

Jellinek's work in the 1940s, 1950s, and 1960s was another important effort to classify drinking problems and to distinguish the extent of social, psychological, and physical problems as a result of drinking. Jellinek defined *alcoholism* as "any use of alcoholic beverages that causes any damage to the individual or society or both" (1960, 35). In describing different types of alcoholic syndromes, Jellinek used the Greek alphabet for the express purpose of avoiding any controversy that might come about because of labeling. *Alpha* alcoholism focuses on the social and familial consequences of drinking. In *beta* alcoholism the person develops physical problems such as gastritis, neuropathy, or cirrhosis of the liver, although withdrawal symptoms are not present. *Gamma* alcoholism is characterized by increased tolerance, loss of control over drinking, withdrawal symptoms, and physical dependence on alcohol. In *delta* alcoholism the person has the above problems and an inability to abstain from alcohol. *Epsilon* alcoholism is characterized by what had been called the "bender" drinker, someone who may stop drinking for months but then returns to very heavy drinking. While these terms are no longer used, this typology is helpful in acknowledging the range of patterns of problem drinking.

At this writing, the closest we have come to agreement on definitions and diagnosis of alcohol and drug problems is presented in the *Diagnostic and Statistical Manual of Mental Disorders IV–Text Revised,* or DSM-IV-TR (American Psychiatric Association [hereafter, APA], 2000), long considered the bible of mental health diagnoses. An examination of this book reveals that the terms *alcoholism* and *addiction* are not used. Two previous editions, the DSM-I and DSM-II, included the term *alcoholism*; however, the 1970s brought greater recognition of the importance of devising more specific criteria for identifying alcohol problems. It was the DSM-III, published in 1980, that dropped the term *alcoholism* and replaced it with *alcohol abuse* and *alcohol dependence* (NIAAA, 1995).

The DSM-IV-TR (APA, 2000) identifies the two major categories of *substance abuse* and *substance dependence*. See Box 12.7 for a review of the criteria for substance abuse. The DSM-IV-TR addresses a range of abuse of drugs: alcohol abuse and dependence, amphetamine abuse and dependence, cannabis abuse and dependence, cocaine abuse and dependence, hallucinogen abuse and dependence, inhalant abuse and dependence, nicotine abuse and dependence, opioid abuse and dependence, and phencyclidine abuse and dependence.

Overall, the substance abuse criteria focus on the impact of alcohol and drug use on the individual's family, occupational, and social functioning. The category of "substance dependence" acknowledges the impact on daily functioning, but it emphasizes the aspect of physical addiction to the alcohol or drug and physical consequences if the drug cannot be obtained. See Box 12.8 for a review of the criteria for substance dependence.

While it may be possible for an individual to move from substance dependence back to substance abuse, it is unlikely. Over time we have learned that the concept of "progression" is important to the disease concept; that is, a drinking or drug problem gets worse if not treated or if the

Box 12.7 DSM-IV Criteria for Substance Abuse

A. A maladaptive pattern of substance use leading to clinically significant impairment or distress, as manifested by one (or more) of the following occurring within a 12-month period:

1. Recurrent substance use resulting in a failure to fulfill major role obligations at work, school, or home (e.g., repeated absences or poor work performance related to substance use; substance-related absences, suspensions, or expulsions from school; neglect of children or household)
2. Recurrent substance use in situations in which it is physically hazardous (e.g., driving an automobile or operating a machine when impaired by substance use)
3. Recurrent substance-related legal problems (e.g., arrests for substance-related disorderly conduct)
4. Continued substance use despite having persistent or recurrent social or interpersonal problems caused or exacerbated by the effects of the substance (e.g., arguments with spouse about consequences of intoxication, physical fights)

B. The symptoms have never met the criteria for Substance Dependence for this class of substance.

Source: American Psychiatric Association (2000), *Diagnostic and statistical manual of mental disorders*, 4th ed., text revised, Washington, DC: APA, 197–198. Reprinted with permission.

person does not stop using. A person can stop drinking or drugging completely on his or her own or can enter a treatment program.

One problem with the *Diagnostic and Statistical Manual* is that it categorizes and generalizes rather than exploring the unique characteristics and issues of alcoholics and problem drinkers (Ruben, 1999). Tolerance varies, and so quantity of consumption is not mentioned in the DSM-IV (Kick, 1999). The DSM-IV criteria include symptoms associated with chronic alcoholism such as physical withdrawal from substances and medical problems that develop only in those who have been heavy drinkers for many years (Martin and Winters, 1998).

As discussed previously, many practitioners who use a screening tool are not trained substance abuse clinicians and are not familiar with the DSM-IV. They are more likely to see through their own personal and professional experiences that some people have worse drug or alcohol problems than others. Thus, the screening tool reduces the subjectivity and sometimes biases that practitioners have in terms of alcohol and drug problems.

Box 12.8   DSM-IV Criteria for Substance Dependence

A maladaptive pattern of substance use, leading to clinically significant impairment or distress, as manifested by three (or more) of the following, occurring at any time in the same 12-month period:

1. Tolerance, as defined by either of the following:
   a. A need for markedly increased amounts of the substance to achieve intoxication or desired effect
   b. Markedly diminished effect with continued use of the same amount of the substance
2. Withdrawal, as manifested by either of the following:
   a. The characteristic withdrawal syndrome for the substance (refer to Criteria A and B of the criteria sets for withdrawal from the specific substances)
   b. The same (or a closely related) substance is taken to relieve or avoid withdrawal symptoms
3. The substance is often taken in larger amounts or over a longer period than was intended.
4. There is a persistent desire or unsuccessful efforts to cut down or control substance use.
5. A great deal of time is spent in activities necessary to obtain the substance (e.g., visiting multiple doctors or driving long distances), use the substance (e.g., chain-smoking), or recovering from its effects.
6. Important social, occupational, or recreational activities are given up or reduced because of substance use.
7. The substance use is continued despite knowledge of having a persistent or recurrent physical or psychological problem that is likely to have been caused or exacerbated by the substance (e.g., current cocaine use despite recognition of cocaine-induced depression, or continued drinking despite recognition that an ulcer was made worse by alcohol consumption).

Source: American Psychiatric Association (2000), *Diagnostic and statistical manual of mental disorders*, 4th ed., text revised, Washington, DC: APA, 197–198. Reprinted with permission.

Brief Interventions

While those who suffer from chronic alcoholism or physical dependence are likely to need inpatient treatment, those who are problem drinkers may benefit from a simple straightforward intervention by a physician or other health-care provider. The use of screening instruments is often coupled with what are called *brief interventions*—conversations with a patient about his or her alcohol or drug use that can be helpful to early problem drinkers and those with moderate problems. A brief intervention can be a health-care provider speaking with a patient for fifteen minutes after the patient has scored high on a screening tool. Brief intervention can also be three to five sessions of counseling and education of five minutes' to an hour's duration (Higgins-Biddle et al., 1997). Brief interventions can take place in a physician's office, hospital emergency room, and college health centers (Chezem, 2004/2005; D'Onofrio and Degutis, 2004/2005; Baldwin et al., 2006).

One study in the late 1990s found that a thirty-minute intervention with a client by surgical staff in an emergency surgical ward could be helpful in reducing alcohol intake (Forsberg et al., 2000). In two groups, one received a brief intervention, while the other group received "extensive alcohol counseling." Alcohol consumption decreased between 13 and 16 percent for both groups. Patients drank as often as they did previously but imbibed less on those drinking occasions. Upon a six-month and a twelve-month follow-up, 15 percent of those previously determined to be at risk were no longer in the risk category. There were no differences found between the two groups and the interventions; that is, a brief intervention was just as helpful as more long-term counseling. In their review of clinical trials addressing screening and brief intervention, John Higgins-Biddle and colleagues found "that a significant proportion of risky drinkers respond to brief interventions and that resulting reductions in drinking may average about 20 percent" (1997, 574).

While it is important to talk with patients about their drinking problems, many physicians find it awkward, reflecting their own discomfort with the topic (Mignon, 1996). Physicians need to talk about drinking with their patients and can do so in supportive, nonjudgmental ways. Steven Kick suggested that the physicians use the phrase "I am concerned that your drinking is causing problems." If the patient has an illness, the physician could say, "Your alcohol consumption is making this condition more difficult to treat" (1999, 97). For all the discussion about physician participation, training professionals who work with physicians, such as nurses, psychologists, and social workers, may be a more effective way to screen clients for substance abuse problems (Mignon, 1993/1994, 1996). While the American Medical Association designated alcoholism as a disease in 1956, there is still much work to be done to ensure that the majority of physicians consider it a disease and feel responsible for helping those with substance abuse problems.

In general, there is agreement that brief interventions are useful in decreasing problem drinking (Baldwin et al., 2006; Fleming, 2004/2005).

Still, they have not been adequately studied as yet and may not show consistency in being helpful to women (Chang, 2002). Brief interventions are useful in medical office settings and are not likely to be used in treatment programs where it has already been determined that a client needs substance abuse treatment. It is important to note that, effective January 2008, physicians can bill patients' health insurance companies specifically for substance abuse screening and brief intervention services (Office of National Drug Control Policy, 2008).

Conclusion

The proliferation of screening and assessment instruments in the last thirty-five years is a marked contrast with the past, when substance abuse problems were ignored or denied. Medical problems of alcoholics may have been treated without any acknowledgment of the role of alcohol. In the 1970s the introduction of employee assistance programs did much to raise consciousness about the importance of offering help to those with alcohol and drug problems.

Most people with substance abuse problems initially deny that they are having difficulty with alcohol or drugs or both. They may say, "I can stop anytime I want," and really believe it. They may not know they have a substance abuse or dependence problem until they have lost a job, friends, and family. It certainly can be helpful for family members and friends to talk with the substance abuser or addict about the problem. Routine use of screening tools discussed in this chapter offers a simple, straightforward way of learning whether there may be a problem and can offer earlier intervention than can family members. As we have seen in Chapter 10, family and friends often deny the problem and wait to express concern until the person is deep in the throes of the substance abuse problem.

A referral for a substance abuse assessment is made after a positive finding on a screening tool. The assessment completed by a substance abuse professional can assist the client in establishing a treatment plan. Thus, screening and assessment serve as an important entrée into treatment. The earlier the intervention, the less restrictive and less intense is the needed treatment, as discussed in the next chapter.

The oldest of the screening tools were devised for alcohol problems. Tools to screen for drugs other than alcohol were developed later, and it makes the most sense now to use tools that screen for both drugs and alcohol.

Considerably more needs to be done to see that screening instruments are used regularly in physicians' offices, emergency rooms, and all other health-care settings. Screening tools can help to inform judges and court personnel in making decisions about the appropriate disposition of court cases. The use of screening tools in the court system could do much to reduce crime and overall criminal justice costs if substance abusers received an early intervention with their problems.

13 Treatment and Recovery

A majority of Americans abstain from or are moderate users of mind-altering chemicals. But for some, chemical use patterns create problems for themselves and others; lives tend to spiral downhill into shambles, at horrific costs to society and user alike. Drunk- or drugged-driving accidents are but one stark example. In the United States a wide array of self-help movements and formal treatment programs has evolved to facilitate recovery. This chapter examines research on treatment outcomes, the historical roots of treatment and recovery programs, and the variety of treatment modalities, facilities, and interventions.

Benefits of Treatment

A major meta-analysis (a statistical technique for combining findings of separate studies) found that one-fourth of persons exposed to alcoholism treatment remained totally abstinent in the year following treatment and one-tenth drank moderately (Miller et al., 2001). The remaining clients reduced alcohol consumption by 87 percent on average, abstained three out of four days, and suffered 60 percent fewer alcohol-related health problems. Another study found that treatment is associated with a 67 percent reduction in weekly cocaine use, a 65 percent reduction in weekly heroin use, a 52 percent decrease in heavy alcohol use, and a 61 percent reduction in illegal activity, one year after treatment (Hubbard, Craddock, and Anderson, 2003). Thus, if our measure of success is total abstinence, treatment has only fair results, but from the perspectives of public health and harm reduction, treatment can be deemed successful. Later in this chapter, we will delve into how we can improve on these figures.

Many studies have shown that the costs of criminal justice, health insurance, and productivity are reduced by an investment in substance abuse treatment (Ettner et al., 2006; Holder, 1998). The California Drug and Alcohol Treatment and Assessment (CALDATA) study found that each dollar invested in addiction treatment was returned sevenfold to society, although the precise ratio varies widely by locale and population served (Gerstein et al., 1994). The history of treatment shows that it evolved separately from the fields of medical and psychiatric treatment (see Box 13.1).

Self-Help Wellsprings of Addiction Treatment

Temperance and sobriety have been social movements and have overlapped with other social movements. Abolitionists in the 1840s and 1850s and the Suffragists at the turn of the twentieth century made drinking one of their concerns. The Anti-Saloon League, the Union of Ex-Boozers, and the

---

Box 13.1   Addiction: A Segregated Discipline

It is a curiosity in the history of medicine that the study and treatment of addictive and psychiatric disorders evolved separately and stayed segregated until the early 1990s. Contributing to this were doctors' attitudes toward the alcoholic and addict as an impossible case, a financial disaster, and an unsavory noncompliant patient, and the emergence of addiction treatment from grass-roots, self-help movements. For decades, medical training devoted very little time to the study of alcoholism, despite its horrendous medical consequences, and conversely, addiction counselors knew little about psychiatric syndromes from which their clients suffered. An elderly physician who cared about alcoholics remembered the "ash-can syndrome." In the days of coal-fired furnaces, a homeless alcoholic would be found in an alleyway, among ash cans. The hospital would treat the drunk for infections, pancreatitis, and fluid in the abdomen, but never alcoholism per se. Twenty-two years ago, author Peter Myers had a student who was almost thrown out of his internship at an old-style rehab for suggesting that a (now sober) client who suddenly went from mute and bedridden to dancing naked in the snow was bipolar and having a manic episode!

Washington Temperance Society encouraged inebriates to "Get on the Wagon" and "Take the Pledge" a century before Alcoholics Anonymous (AA) was born. Washingtonians toured the nation, organizing over 100,000 into membership (Blumberg with Pittman, 1991).

The wellspring of modern addiction treatment emerged from a grassroots, religious organization in Ohio in 1935, when some members of the Oxford Group, a middle-class Protestant evangelical group, applied their principles of self-improvement, sharing, confession, and witness to alcoholism (Kurtz, 1988). Led by William Griffith Wilson (the famous Bill W.) and Dr. Robert Smith (Dr. Bob), they split off and established a separate organization, Alcoholics Anonymous, in 1935. Another influence on the evolving ideology of AA was the philosopher William James, who considered religious conversion crucial in the rehabilitation of drunkards (James, 1961). The "Five Procedures" of the Oxford Group were "Give in to God, Listen to God's Direction, Check Guidance, Restitution, and Sharing for Witness and for Confession" (Alcoholics Anonymous World Services, 1980, 54–55). One can see the influence of this on the Twelve Steps and Twelve Traditions of AA, found in Box 13.2.

AA is a system of support and fellowship for staying sober by sharing among alcoholics in meetings. Some meetings are open to all; others are closed, in the sense that individuals who are not struggling with alcoholism ("civilians" in AA parlance) do not attend. New members are encouraged to attend "90 in 90," that is, ninety meetings in ninety days, very early in their recovery. Meetings tend to follow a familiar and comforting format, where speakers tell their "story" of deterioration and progression of alcoholic disease until they experience a "spiritual awakening" and enter sobriety. But what goes on *between* meetings is just as important: coffee and conversation follow meetings; members are encouraged to get a friend and mentor, known as a "sponsor," for advice and support at any time; as well as get the phone numbers of other members for connection and support in tough times.

AA is much more than a self-help meeting. It is self-described as a fellowship, a support system, and a sober alternative to the bar or drug subculture. The fellowship of AA is founded on principles of anonymity, total abstinence, lifelong attendance at fellowship meetings (one is only "recovering or recovered, one day at a time," never cured), and reliance on a "Higher Power," which often, but not necessarily, corresponds to an idea of deity. Another important feature of AA is that it is fiercely independent of professional institutions, as well as completely democratic, unstratified, and nonhierarchical. AA can be described as a "folk psychotherapy" or as a therapeutic social movement (Alibrandi, 1987). At this writing, AA has

Box 13.2 Alcoholics Anonymous

Preamble

Alcoholics Anonymous is a fellowship of men and women who share their experience, strength, and hope with each other that they may solve their common problem and help others to recover from alcoholism.

The only requirement for membership is a desire to stop drinking. There are no dues or fees for AA membership; we are self-supporting through our own contributions.

AA is not allied with any sect, denomination, political organization, or institution; does not wish to engage in any controversy; neither endorses nor opposes any causes. Our primary purpose is to stay sober and help other alcoholics achieve sobriety.

The Twelve Steps

1. We admitted we were powerless over alcohol—that our lives had become unmanageable.
2. Came to believe that a Power greater than ourselves could restore us to sanity.
3. Made a decision to turn our will and our lives over to the care of God *as we understood Him.*
4. Made a searching and fearless moral inventory of ourselves.
5. Admitted to God, to ourselves, and to another human being the exact nature of our wrongs.
6. Were entirely ready to have God remove all these defects of character.
7. Humbly asked Him to remove our shortcomings.
8. Made a list of all persons we had harmed, and became willing to make amends to them all.
9. Made direct amends to such people wherever possible, except when to do so would injure them or others.
10. Continued to take personal inventory and when we were wrong[,] promptly admitted it.
11. Sought through prayer and meditation to improve our conscious contact with God *as we understood Him*, praying only for knowledge of His will for us and the power to carry that out.
12. Having had a spiritual awakening as the results of these Steps, we tried to carry this message to others, and to practice these principles in all our affairs.

continues

Box 13.2   continued

The Twelve Traditions

1. Our common welfare should come first; personal recovery depends on AA unity.
2. For our group purpose there is but one ultimate authority—a loving God as He may express Himself in our group conscience. Our leaders are but trusted servants; they do not govern.
3. The only requirement for AA membership is a desire to stop drinking.
4. Each group should be autonomous except in matters affecting other groups or AA as a whole.
5. Each group has but one primary purpose—to carry its message to the alcoholic who still suffers.
6. An AA group ought never endorse, finance, or lend the AA name to any related facility or outside enterprise, lest problems of money, property, and prestige divert us from our primary purpose.
7. Each AA group ought to be fully self-supporting, declining outside contributions.
8. Alcoholics Anonymous should remain forever nonprofessional, but our service centers may employ special workers.
9. AA, as such, ought never be organized, but we may create service boards or committees directly responsible to those they serve.
10. Alcoholics Anonymous has no opinion on outside issues; hence the AA name ought never be drawn into public controversy.
11. Our public relations policy is based on attraction rather than promotion; we need always maintain personal anonymity at the level of press, radio, and films.
12. Anonymity is the spiritual foundation of all our Traditions, ever reminding us to place principles before personalities.

Source: Alcoholics Anonymous, 1976.

at least 5 million members worldwide. For decades after it was founded, AA was the only place for an alcoholic to turn.

The Twelve Steps eventually became the model for a wide variety of self-help recovery organizations. After AA, Narcotics Anonymous (NA), founded in 1951, is the largest and most pertinent to chemical dependency recovery. NA stayed small until the 1980s, and has at least 100,000 members as of this writing. Its principles and values are basically identical to those of AA.

Photo courtesy of Kathleen Bronson.

In the 1940s, members of AA started the National Council on Alcoholism (NCA), which was a bridge to the medical and professional community. NCA spokespersons, writers, and their professional allies pioneered in viewing alcoholism as a chronic, progressive disease, a view that has been accepted in the United States. Treatment programs have been heavily, if not overwhelmingly, influenced by this strain of thought. Treatment programs began to flourish in the 1960s, based on AA principles but also incorporating systemic treatment methods borrowed from social work, including the individualized treatment plan, case management, and an interdisciplinary treatment team, usually in a residential twenty-eight-day program. Recovering, paraprofessional counselors as well as professionals were employed at such programs, whose approach was known as the Minnesota Model.

Lois W., wife of Bill W., started Al-Anon in 1951. In the early days, primarily wives of alcoholics attended Al-Anon meetings. At this writing, Al-Anon is considered an appropriate support group for families and friends of alcoholics. It operates according to the same Twelve Steps and Twelve Traditions as does AA and has a similar meeting format. Nar-Anon is the fellowship for significant others of drug addicts. Outside of the chemical realm, probably the largest Twelve Step organization is Gamblers Anonymous.

A number of alternatives to the Twelve Step model are available for group support of recovery from chemical dependency. The most widespread of these is Smart Recovery, formerly known as Rational Recovery. This is based on cognitive-behavioral psychology, particularly the Rational Emotive Behavior Therapy (REBT) of Albert Ellis (Ellis et al., 1988). REBT considers addiction more a complex maladaptive behavior than a disease. In Smart Recovery groups, individuals are taught to cope with urges and manage thoughts, feelings, and behavior. Individuals who are uncomfortable with the spiritual emphasis of AA are attracted to Smart Recovery as an alternative.

Clearly, self-help programs can provide enormous assistance to those seeking recovery from addictions. Alcoholics Anonymous is the best-known program in the United States for the treatment of alcoholism. Physicians who do refer their patients for help with drinking problems are most likely to encourage them to seek help from AA. For the alcoholic or addict initially trying to become sober or abstinent, however, professional intervention is important. Typically, clinicians will encourage participation in a self-help program as well.

Therapeutic Community

Another self-help model arose starting in 1958, itself an offshoot of AA, becoming the other major ideological influence on addiction treatment. In 1958 a charismatic recovering alcoholic named Charles Dederich led an AA club in California, which started to admit drug addicts, and operated a drop-in center. Dederich innovated a hard-hitting, confrontational style in his meetings, or "seminars." His practices rapidly propelled him out of AA. An addict mispronounced *seminar* as *synanon,* and the name stuck. Synanon developed into an addict-run, residential program, featuring a variety of harsh confrontational groups having quasi-punitive, status-degradation practices designed to make a point to the hardened "junkie," such as wearing a sign describing an infraction and having one's head shaved, to mention but two. A stratified system of privileges allowed addicts to move up a status ladder as they progressed in their recovery, taking on more responsible tasks and leadership roles. Synanon came to the attention of the psychiatric profession, which applied to it the term "therapeutic community," a reference to a system of patient government and milieu therapy that arose in British psychiatric hospitals after World War II (Jones, 1953).

The prototype of the modern therapeutic community was Daytop Village, originally located in Staten Island, New York City, in the mid-1960s. Daytop was founded by psychiatrist Daniel Casriel and former Synanon leader David Deitch (Casriel, 1966). Modifying some of the harsh methods of Synanon, Daytop added the element of loving support and affection and an exploration of all areas of emotionality, thinking, and behavior. It also developed the marathon group session, found at many therapeutic communities in the early 2000s. Whereas Synanon expected clients to be lifelong members, one graduated from Daytop after a reentry phase. The

Daytop model has been adapted to therapeutic community (TC) programs worldwide, including Europe and Asia.

The other major program that emerged in the mid-1960s was Phoenix House, also in New York City, followed by Integrity House, Inc., in Newark, New Jersey; Marathon House in Rhode Island; and Gaudenzia House in Philadelphia, at the end of that decade. The TC paradigm grew to dominate the drug treatment field, including approaches in other countries, such as Italy, Brazil, and Malaysia (Garrett and Anderson, 2003; Garrett, Gallon, and Earp, 2003). While TCs are still a "tough love" program, most facilities have greatly softened the harsh practices that were prevalent in the 1970s and 1980s. Literacy and vocational education, psychiatric screening and referral, and connections to Twelve Step groups as an aftercare component are other innovations over the past fifteen years. Modified therapeutic community approaches have been applied to correctional settings, day treatment of substance abuse, and facilities designed for the homeless, mentally ill, and chemically dependent women with children (De Leon, 1997; Melnick and De Leon, 1999).

Nuts and Bolts of Treatment

There are many types of treatment and in the best circumstances treatment is easily accessible at a reasonable cost. While some alcoholics and addicts choose to enter a treatment program willingly, others do so under family or legal pressure.

How and Why Treatment Comes to Pass

Initiation of addiction treatment involves some combination of the following:

- *Desperation:* bottoming out, or becoming "sick and tired of being sick and tired." Often some event serves as a tipping point that gets through the smokescreen of defenses and resistance.
- *Compulsion:* a large proportion of involuntary (mandated) clients sent by employers via employee assistance programs, schools, child welfare, welfare-to-work, and criminal justice systems. Alternatives to incarceration for addicted offenders are a major part of the treatment industry, since states see the reduction in recidivism afforded by treatment.
- *Natural recovery motives:* striving for normality, health and social reintegration, a job, and a supportive family. People realize that the addictive lifestyle prevents them from achieving those things they yearn for. A

fact often overlooked by professionals is that many such individuals recover without involvement in treatment or self-help groups, dubbed "natural recovery" by Robert Granfield and William Cloud (1996). Some simply "mature out" while many find solace and structure in religion. Facilitating natural recovery motives is now seen as an important task in treating chemical abuse.

Desperation, compulsion, and natural recovery are actually complementary. Strategies for recovery need to take advantage of every incentive, lever, yearning for normalcy, natural maturation process, and therapeutic help that can be brought to bear on addiction. They come together to create a window of opportunity when the addict is ready to accept help. We need to "keep a bag packed" for that specific moment, for tomorrow the addict may feel a little better by gaining access to more drugs or get a little more fearful of treatment, and the mix of motives is no longer as auspicious.

Addiction Treatment Compared with Counseling and Psychotherapy

Addiction treatment is more comprehensive, intensive, and directive than counseling for nonaddicted individuals. Many addicted individuals are confused and deteriorating (psychologically, socially, and medically) from years of chemical anesthesia and a lifestyle revolving around acquiring and using drugs. They require a wider scope of treatment than most, with the exception of the severely mentally ill. The functions of the addictions professional are in many ways similar to those of a social worker, who must master practice dimensions such as case management, treatment planning, referral, clinical evaluation, and service coordination, in addition to counseling skills. The counselor also provides a great deal of structure and direction for the client, especially in early recovery. The client is urged to concentrate on immediate, simple, and concrete steps to stay sober during early treatment.

Addicts resist and deny the need to accept therapeutic help for their problems, with vehemence and tenacity. The reasons for this are many: dislike of the stigmatizing label "addict"; reaction to the trauma of loss of control; fear of exposure, rejection, and change; impaired memory and reasoning; and a normal reaction to involuntary, compulsory treatment (Myers and Salt, 2007; Taleff, 1997). Counselors may unwittingly set up denial by adopting an adversarial and confrontational stance. Engaging a client, building a therapeutic alliance, and working around frightening core issues are the best strategies to adopt.

A large proportion of people willingly seek out counseling and psychotherapy for their difficulties. In contrast, most addicts enter treatment with some element of compulsion, perhaps from family or from the legal system. This is justified by the fact that the client has a life-threatening condition that he or she is not currently competent to assess, by virtue of the denial system and chemical impairment of cognitive processes. The authors have encountered hundreds of individuals who entered treatment through some mandatory, involuntary process and are now extremely grateful this occurred.

Most mental health practitioners are not themselves emerging from psychiatric syndromes. In contrast, many addiction counselors enter the field out of their personal recovery experience, or from a history of family addiction problems. They often wear "two hats," as counselors as well as members of self-help fellowships that include their clients as members.

Procedures and Routines of Treatment

The client "career" in addiction treatment follows a pattern borrowed from the standard routines of social work and social service programs:

1. Clients are formally admitted through an intake procedure, and oriented to services, expectations, and confidentiality requirements.

2. A comprehensive biopsychosocial assessment is made, as discussed in Chapter 12, and is updated regularly.

3. Based on an assessment of strengths, weaknesses, and problems, a treatment plan is drawn up on a collaborative basis between counselor and client. Again, it is reviewed and updated on a regular basis.

4. Interventions include individual, group, and family counseling, client education on substance abuse, as well as vocational and education preparation for reentry.

5. Careful discharge planning is needed for continuity and to appropriately move the client to the next level of treatment or social reentry, with provision for ongoing recovery support.

It is not within the scope of this chapter to describe the basics of individual, group, and family counseling. The majority of counselors do not operate out of one narrow theoretical perspective, but stress active listening skills and a working therapeutic alliance. Most treatment for addicts takes place in groups. Groups are economical and provide role-modeling opportunities, break down isolation, reduce shame and guilt, and utilize the power of a group to facilitate personal change (Myers and Salt, 2007). It is

also important to intervene, where possible, with client families who may be "enabling" addictive behaviors by their protective and "helping" behaviors, unhealthy role adaptations, and unhealthy communication patterns.

Where to Go for Help Depends on How Much Help You Need

The system of patient placement criteria promulgated by the American Society for Addiction Medicine (ASAM) is an attempt to rationally match the assessed severity of addiction with an appropriate intensity of treatment or level of care. The Patient Placement Criteria consider withdrawal potential, biomedical complications, emotional or behavioral complications or both, acceptance or resistance to treatment, relapse potential, and recovery environment in computing placement in one of five levels of care (American Society for Addiction Medicine, 2002):

Level 0.5. *Early intervention services:* for individuals with problems or risk factors, basically a proactive prevention program that might include alternative, drug-free recreational activities, educational and vocational counseling, and brief counseling.

Level 1. *Outpatient treatment:* that is, attendance at a clinic for one to nine hours per week for treatment that may include individual, group, or family counseling, or all three. This includes outpatient continuing care following intensive rehabilitation.

Level 2. *Intensive outpatient treatment:* a structured rehabilitation program that the client attends for at least ten hours up to most of the day. Similar terms are *partial hospitalization* and *day treatment*.

Level 3. *Medically monitored, intensive inpatient treatment:* a live-in, structured rehabilitation program, familiar to readers as "going to rehab." This includes the twenty-eight-day treatment for alcoholism popular in the late 1970s and early 1980s, the therapeutic community model that keeps clients for up to a year, and a residential halfway house program.

Level 4. *Medically managed intensive inpatient treatment:* a medical or hospital setting for those who need medication to manage withdrawal symptoms and those who have serious medical problems.

While recovery may be accomplished within a single agency environment, treatment typically involves a "continuum of care" using more than one agency setting. Depending on addiction severity, the client may be placed in any of the levels of care. Level 4 may be necessitated by the need for medically managed detoxification, after which rehabilitation may take place within the medical setting or, by careful referral, in another facility at a less intensive level of care.

There is tremendous misunderstanding about detoxification. This short, first step is often mistaken for treatment itself, while it is more appropriately seen as the entrée into treatment. "I know Bob is hopeless; why, he went into detox four times, and he is still drinking," or, "I don't know why we waste all that money on funding treatment programs; the bums are in and out of the county detox and they never get better." In simple terms, the detoxification phase refers to medical monitoring and treatment with prescription medication for those who are physically withdrawing from alcohol.

If a patient undergoes a formal rehabilitation program, this, too, is only the beginning of recovery. Rehabilitation programs are typically no more than a month to two months, with the exception of some long-term therapeutic community programs that require a stay of six to eighteen months. Clients need a continuing support system after completion of a rehabilitation program, help in relapse prevention, and a framework to try out the tools acquired in treatment. This is usually referred to as *aftercare* or *continuing care,* taking place in an outpatient setting and lasting from three to six months. In addition, a majority of programs encourage clients to get involved in AA or NA or both, get a sponsor, and find a "home group" before termination of care.

Patients who have no strong support system may need or wish to stay in a therapeutic environment following formal rehabilitation, in the form of a so-called halfway house. These facilities are a step back into the community, usually featuring a work requirement and a stay of about six months. Still others experience a level of psychosocial disability due to their addiction or concurrent psychiatric disorders, so that they may need to reside in so-called long-term residential care facilities such as those provided by the Salvation Army.

Treatment received by clients may in fact not correspond to an ideal system such as the ASAM-PPC-2R. Frequently, patients lack insurance coverage for substance-related disorders, or such coverage is limited to a short-term detoxification stay or a few outpatient sessions. Some alcoholics and addicts have no health insurance at all and therefore may have access to only very short-term, state-funded programs. This is the situation faced by many seeking help for any behavioral problem. Most insurance policies have treated mental health differently from physical health problems and have strict caps on mental health coverage, including medication. There have been many efforts to establish parity for behavioral health issues via national and local legislation. In October 2008, Congress approved and President George W. Bush signed into law addictions and mental health parity legislation. This law mandates insurance coverage equal to coverage for other illnesses for both mental health and addiction treatment (Mulligan, 2008).

Goals of Treatment

Assessment of clients' strengths and weaknesses drives a treatment plan that is collaboratively drawn up by counselor and client and periodically revised and updated. The long-term goals of this plan are geared to strengthened and continued sobriety and stability of behavior, emotion, and thought.

Relapse Prevention

Very few people, when trying to move away from substance abuse, just stop for good at their first try. Even with professional help, they seldom get it right on the first go-round. Going back to a drink or drug after initiating treatment is given the rather daunting label of "relapse" in the addictions field. Even the alcoholic who has a single drink and then stops would be called a relapser by some, although others dub this a "lapse" or a "slip" if the person was drinking for fewer than twenty-four hours. Some clinicians see danger in labeling that one drink as a regular relapse, in that it results in tremendous shame and guilt, and that sends the message that since one has relapsed, one might as well go whole hog and drink the night away, a self-fulfilling prophecy of a total, catastrophic relapse (Beck et al., 1993; Marlatt and Gordon, 1985).

Professional approaches to relapse prevention include learning coping responses for high-risk situations; increasing self-efficacy about sobriety efforts, such as correcting irrational, hopeless thinking about stress ("I can't cope"); and avoiding anxiety-generating conflict and stressors. These parallel the "folk" formula for relapse prevention advised by Alcoholics Anonymous: "Turn it over" (resentments); "Stay away from people, places, and things" (associated with drinking); and HALT: "Don't get too Hungry, Angry, Lonely, or Tired." Another contemporary view of relapse is described in the "Stages of Change" typology below. The emphasis on relapse prevention has developed since the 1990s and is considered an important subspecialty among substance abuse clinicians.

Managing Emotions

Living for years under chemical anesthesia, perhaps during crucial developmental periods, makes the addict somewhat of an "emotional illiterate," without skills in recognizing, identifying, accepting, or communicating emotions. Managing emotional states is crucial in maintaining sobriety. Common triggers for relapse include getting panicked by the new experience of emotion, feeling guilty about negative feelings, failing to distinguish emotions from thoughts and actions (fearing to act out negative feelings), and experiencing bottled-up pain and anger.

Changing Behavior

Most treatment models emphasize learning assertive, responsible, and effective behavioral strategies instead of impulsive, self-defeating, irresponsible, and destructive behavior patterns. A sense that what one does makes a difference, or "self-efficacy," is a factor in positive treatment outcomes (Bandura, 1997). Establishing priorities and breaking down long-term goals into manageable steps are a part of the treatment planning process.

Changing Thinking Patterns

Addiction counseling has been influenced by several related approaches that emphasize the role of thinking patterns—especially irrational beliefs and negative self-statement—in generating, maintaining, and relapsing into chemical dependency. These approaches include Rational Emotive Behavior Therapy (Ellis et al., 1988), the intellectual basis for the Smart Recovery groups, Cognitive-Behavioral Therapy (Marlatt and Gordon, 1985), and Cognitive Therapy (Beck et al., 1993). "Awfulizing" or "catastrophizing" is a thinking style that magnifies or exaggerates the bad implications of an event or situation. This can be a self-stimulating, panicky cycle that results in paralyzing anxiety and flight back into chemical use. Likewise, the irrational belief that one cannot tolerate negative feelings or discomforts without chemicals must be overcome in the attempt to avert relapse. Cognitive approaches find a parallel in the fellowships such as AA and NA. Aaron Beck and colleagues (1993) identified anticipatory beliefs that precede relapse, such as, "I won't be able to make it through the day without drinking," or, "I can't have fun without pot," which then trigger permission-giving beliefs such as "one drink won't hurt." AA calls this process "stinking thinking" or BUDing ("building up to drink"), accompanied by behavioral signs such as isolating, cutting down on meetings, anger, and resentment.

Facilitation of Movement Through Recovery or Stages of Change

We have alluded to natural recovery motives and their importance at several places thus far. James Prochaska and Carlo DiClemente (1982) showed how it worked in practice. They described an integrative model of change that cuts across all theoretical approaches in counseling and psychotherapy. They studied individuals who had quit smoking cigarettes on their own and found that they moved through characteristic stages during this process:

1. *Precontemplative* stage: problems are denied and change is resisted;
2. *Contemplative* stage: there is recognition of problems;
3. *Preparation* stage: there is some commitment to action;
4. *Action* stage: real action and healthy change take place;
5. *Maintenance* stage: gains are consolidated;
6. *Termination* stage: the person has moved past the problem entirely.

Just as important as the stages themselves is the realization that this growth is cyclical and spiral in form. At any of these stages, an individual may fall back temporarily, gain strength and knowledge, and move further ahead. According to this model, then, relapse is just another normal recycling action in the healing process (Prochaska, Norcross, and DiClemente, 1994).

New Models of Treatment

Evidence-based practices that are urged by the federal government include Rational Emotive Behavior Therapy, Twelve-Step Facilitation, and Motivational Interviewing. Motivational Interviewing, or Motivational Enhancement Therapy (MET), an integrative, generic model of counseling, has become popular in the addiction counseling field (Miller and Rollnick, 1991, 2002). MET acknowledges the constant fluctuation in motives and readiness for change experienced by the addict. It advocates the following:

1. Expressing empathy through reflective listening that builds a working relationship and client self-esteem.
2. Helping the client perceive the rewards of change as opposed to the costs of keeping the status quo, by developing a discrepancy between current behavior and goals clients have identified and by developing self-efficacy.
3. Avoiding common therapeutic "traps" such as arguing and battling over disagreements; confrontation of denial; being the "expert," which leaves the client in a passive position; and labeling, which brings out resistance.

Although much of MET will be familiar to those trained in clinical social work skills, with an added cognitive-behavioral emphasis, it is attractively presented and user-friendly. It has become very popular in a relatively short period of time in the addictions field, traditionally slow to adopt any new method or paradigm.

Methadone Maintenance Treatment

Although this chapter emphasizes a treatment of addiction that results in a drug-free lifestyle, the most extensive intervention pertaining to drug abuse involves dispensing a substitute drug for the drug of abuse. For those addicted to narcotic-analgesics (opioids) (heroin; morphine; codeine; brands of oxycodone such as Percodan, Percocet, and OxyContin; and brands of hydrocodone such as Vicodin), the most prevalent treatment is systematic dispensation of methadone, a synthetic opiate substitute. Ingestion of methadone prevents the acute withdrawal syndrome that follows discontinuance of narcotic use. It has a longer duration of action with less of a "buzz" than heroin (Center for Substance Abuse Treatment [hereafter, CSAT], 2006). Over 120,000 individuals are enrolled in methadone maintenance (MM) programs in the United States as of this writing (National Alliance of Methadone Advocates, 2008).

Maintenance programs may not be considered treatment per se, but rather part of the public health approach named harm reduction. The client is socially stabilized, removed from a criminal lifestyle, and ready to reenter society. When methadone is dispensed early in the morning, clients can proceed to a job or school or attend counseling services on-site. Certainly, the safety it affords from contracting HIV/AIDS from intravenous drug use involving needle sharing is an argument in its favor. Many studies found that MM does reduce illicit opiate use, HIV risk behaviors, and criminality (Marsch, 1998; Van Den Berg, 2007).

There is a tremendous variety among methadone maintenance programs. They vary in the extent that they provide ancillary counseling services, from those that provide virtually none to those that provide a therapeutic community milieu, parenting skills workshops, and support groups for HIV-positive clients or abused women. They also vary according to the strictness of monitoring for other drug use, by frequency of urinalysis, number of drugs screened for, and policy concerning positive results of a drug screen. Some clinics turn out predominantly responsible, functioning members of society, and others feature a client population the members of whom "hang out" nearby after receiving their dose, drinking and taking other drugs—indistinguishable from any other street addict subculture.

Unfortunately, detoxification from methadone is a long and difficult process. With the presence of this powerful opioid painkiller in the system for a decade or more, the body's own internal mechanisms for regulating and modulating physical and emotional distress are in disuse. Many users start to add alcohol or tranquilizers, or both, if and when they taper off from methadone.

Buprenorphine

In 2000 the Drug Addiction Treatment Act expanded the opportunity for physicians to prescribe medications for the treatment of opioid and heroin addiction outside of the traditional methadone clinic (CSAT, 2005). The waivers physicians receive from the requirements of the Controlled Substance Act allow them to prescribe the newer medication for heroin addiction, a combination of buprenorphine and naloxone (Suboxone).

Studies on buprenorphine show that it is effective in substituting for and blocking the effects of other opioids. It is considered a safe drug, it is acceptable to patients, and it can assist addicts with staying in treatment (CSAT, 2005; Greenstein, Fudula, and O'Brien, 1997). Federal and local entities concerned with addiction and treatment are making an effort to promote training in and dissemination of buprenorphine, and regulations are being progressively relaxed to allow physicians to privately prescribe it to addicts. Private for-profit rather than public treatment programs are more likely to prescribe buprenorphine (Knudsen, Ducharme, and Roman, 2006).

Newer drug treatments for substance abuse include acamprosate calcium (Campral) and naltrexone (Vivitrol) for alcoholism, naloxone (Narcan) to counter the effects of heroin or morphine overdose, and a vaccine for cocaine abusers that can block the effects of the drug.

Casting an Anthropological Eye: Moving from a Culture of Addiction to a Culture of Recovery

Contemporary authors William Fancher (1995) and William White (1996) point out that treatment is conversion to a new perspective, a framework within which to understand one's problems and a belief that this framework will help them. White describes the pathway from subcultures of addiction into recovery subcultures, and Fancher describes the enculturation (conversion) of psychotherapy clients into "cultures of healing," including psychoanalysis and cognitive therapy. Fancher contends that although psychotherapy is often efficacious, it has little to do with what is said to be the particular benefit of this or that treatment approach. People benefit from talking to an actively empathic listener and exploring their feelings, thoughts, and behavior not *because* it is psychoanalytic, or neopsychoanalytic, or cognitive behavioral therapy. As lives are changed and saved, counselors and therapists may adhere fiercely to rigid beliefs about specific forms of therapy and become inflexible and dogmatic (Myers, 2002b). Dogmatism in change strategies is ill-advised, since we must employ evidence- or research-based strategies rather than merely repeat faith- or tradition-based ritual. The twenty-eight-day inpatient treatment model was not an empirically based strategy for all addicts, and has given way to a large extent to a variety of outpatient rehabilitation options. We must, in addition, tailor treatment to the specific and unique needs of suffering addicts and their ethnicity, mental status, gender, and age, and offer a menu of treatment options that allow us to mount an appropriate and flexible response.

Professionalization of the Field

In the 1960s and 1970s, most addiction counselors were recovering paraprofessionals, lacking a college degree, and addiction treatment methods were an extension of self-help traditions. Since the 1980s the addictions treatment field has gradually and unevenly professionalized, both in terms of training and staffing patterns and in adopting professional standards and models of care. In this, it has followed a path similar to that of other helping professions such as nursing and social work. Educational requirements have continually increased; a tiered system has emerged in which professional preparation determines the level of responsibility and the place in the organizational hierarchy of treatment. Certification requirements involve comprehensive course work, a written examination, and an oral and written case presentation. Many states also have degree requirements; career and educational ladders are evolving. Increasingly, professional preparation takes place in higher education addiction studies and addiction counseling curricula.

Conclusion

There are a number of critical issues facing the addictions field at the end of the first decade of the twenty-first century. Although addiction is often described as a chronic condition, it has usually been treated as an acute-care episode, like antibiotics for strep throat. Clinical outcomes research supports the conclusion that substance abuse is likely to recur when recovery support is terminated, like any other chronic condition (McLellan, 2002). Duration and continuity of care are more significant than the sheer amount of treatment received. In line with the Recovery Community Services initiatives of the Substance Abuse and Mental Health Services Administration, low-intensity, telephonic case monitoring is an effective long-term recovery strategy (Moos, 2003; White, 2005).

There is a new abundance of opportunities to get help, as in treatment alternatives to incarceration and interventions within child welfare and social welfare systems (Young and Gardner, 2002). Clinicians seek to end the traditional isolation of addiction treatment and integrate it throughout the social services and public health sectors and in the natural environments of clients, rather than up in the "house on the hill." Even brief interventions, as discussed in Chapter 12, offered in many settings by many types of professionals, can significantly affect clients in need of help (Babor et al., 2004; Barry et al., 2004).

Individuals with both a psychiatric and an addiction diagnosis are suffering from co-occurring disorders, previously known as dual diagnosis. Formerly, such persons did not get the treatment they needed; they were unlikely to be accepted into any treatment program, or they were "ping-ponged" back and forth between psychiatric and addiction facilities. During the 1990s, integrated treatment programs for co-occurring disorders sprang up. Many hospitals, as of this writing, subsume addictive and psychiatric programs under the rubric of "behavioral health."

Addiction treatment stands at a crossroads. A distinct profession of addictions counselor has emerged with a system of training and credentialing. Treatment is increasingly science based as well as planned to meet individual needs. Yet coverage for addiction treatment has been declining under managed care since the early 1990s, and it is difficult to obtain appropriate levels of care for the substance abuser and the addict. Given the huge health and social costs of addiction, and the proven record of addiction treatment in alleviating chemical syndromes and in repaying society many times over, it is illogical to allow this situation to continue. The recovery community and addictions professionals need to mount education and advocacy campaigns to jump-start state and local legislation for treatment parity and for funding treatment programs at higher levels. With the passage of legislation for insurance parity in mental health and addiction treatment in 2008 it is likely health insurance coverage for addiction treatment will expand.

14 Policy, Prevention, and Practice

Substance abuse is a major social problem affecting many in the United States and throughout the world. While offering treatment to individuals with alcohol and drug problems is important, social policy, which focuses on controlling access to alcohol and drugs, is also of importance and has the potential to reach many more people. These are complex issues, since policy and practice must also consider cultural influences. This chapter reviews policy implications and examines the importance of prevention. Finally, the chapter considers issues facing the field and substance abuse professionals.

Policy

Social policy reflects a society's response to social issues and to social problems. It is created through a political and interactive process in the quest to solve social problems. With many dimensions involved in its creation, social policy begins with the definition of the specific social problem. As noted in earlier chapters, the debate over nature and nurture as primary explanations for human behavior always enters the process. If the social issue or social problem under consideration is believed to be the result of human nature or biology, then social policies will emphasize biology, genetics, hormones, and other physical responses. If the social issue or social problem is considered the result of environment, responses will focus on changing the environment, including people and their behavior. It is understood that both nature and nurture play a role in explaining human behavior; however, when it comes to the creation of social policy, usually one will take precedence over the other. Depending on which perspective is adopted, different strategies and tactics will be utilized to play a key role in social policy development and implementation. Strategies are broad plans that include goals and outcomes, while tactics are the specific methods that will be used to implement the strategy.

Social policy is dynamic and ever changing. It is dependent on current definitions and theories of social problems as well as funding and politics. Since research generates theories, current research on a topic will have significant implications for the development of social policy. Often this development falls under the auspices of a particular field or discipline. If the social problem is owned by law enforcement, then the social policy reflects legal and criminal justice solutions. If the medical field has prominence in addressing the social problem, then social policy will focus on health and illness. This book has shown that the definition of substance use and abuse has undergone many different constructions. There are complementary and competing approaches to the solution of social problems once they are defined. For substance use and abuse, much debate has focused on whether alcoholics and addicts are "sick" people in need of treatment or "bad" people in need of punishment.

Social policy in the United States, also referred to as public policy, is distinct from economic or foreign policy, although all of these attempt to control human behavior. US public policy is created to regulate a range of human behaviors, from substance use to euthanasia. Often there is a compelling moral and religious dimension to the development of social policy, as in the issues of abortion and birth control.

In Europe, social policy is more focused on the circumstances under which people live than on their behavior. National health insurance and unemployment insurance are more likely to be addressed in social policy than gay rights or abortion. And, with respect to substance abuse, some European countries are more apt to adhere to a behavior modification model of treatment rather than subscribing to a disease model.

US social policy related to substance use and abuse has focused on many areas, including (1) access to alcohol and drugs, (2) alcohol and drug sales, (3) use of alcohol and drugs while driving, (4) harm reduction, and (5) taxation of alcohol and drugs. When the taxes on alcohol and drugs are raised, prices for these commodities are also raised. Moderate drinkers have been found to respond to higher prices of alcohol by cutting back on alcohol purchases (Manning et al., 1991). Educated consumers also have been found to cut back on alcohol purchases when the price of alcoholic beverages is higher (Kenkel, 1996). Overall, problems associated with alcohol decrease if access to alcohol is limited (Holder, 1999). Thus, public policy that is directed at limiting quantities and availability of alcohol, or at punishing violations of alcohol norms, can be effective in reducing alcohol-related problems.

When public support exists for governmental control of human behavior, then implementing social policy is easier, as in the passage of the Federal Uniform Drinking Age Act of 1984, which set the drinking age at twenty-one. Moreover, consideration and sensitivity to certain traits of the population are key. For example, the passage of laws requiring warning labels for pregnant women on bottles of beer is a reminder that gender as well as age and ethnicity should be of primary concern when creating social policy (Wilsnack and Wilsnack, 2002).

If a general consensus does not exist with regard to the government's role in controlling human behavior, the development of social policy is more difficult. So, in the area of substance use and abuse, it has been easier to develop policies that target youth. Traffic accidents, suicides, homicides, accidental deaths such as drownings, rapes, and vandalism all contributed to the development of social policies around the minimum legal drinking age. Higher minimum legal drinking ages reduce levels of alcohol-related accidents and crime. Lowering the legal blood alcohol limits for traffic violations reduces the number of deaths on the highways. Laws that existed for driving while intoxicated (DWI) have been revised to laws defining driving under the influence (DUI) since intoxication is more difficult to assess than "under the influence" of a substance. According to the National Institute on Alcohol Abuse and Alcoholism (2006; hereafter, NIAAA), current social policy strategy on alcohol and drug use is aimed at reducing the consequences of substance abuse rather than on a reduction in alcohol or drug use. This emphasis on harm reduction rather than a reduction of consumption is apparent in social policy tactics.

Tactics employed in harm reduction strategies focus on reducing opportunities for heavy drinking or for heavy drug use. These tactics include (1) training servers at bars and taverns, (2) eliminating "happy hours," and (3) reducing the size of drinks. Many college campuses have prohibited keg parties or the presence on campus of kegs, as these lead to heavy drinking occasions. Research indicates that heavy drinking occasions may contribute more significantly to problems with alcohol than does overall consumption of alcohol (NIAAA, 2006).

Social policy is established by local, state, and federal legislatures. These legislatures establish guidelines and laws to respond to alcohol production, distribution, and consumption patterns. As discussed earlier in this text, the Eighteenth Amendment to the Constitution, known as Prohibition, was repealed by the Twenty-First Amendment to the Constitution in 1933 and gave states rights to legislate and control alcohol production, possession, sales, distribution, taxation, and consumption. Some states allow local governments to pass ordinances regulating alcohol and drugs within their communities. Other states maintain stricter controls at the state level. These are all examples of social policy.

The official responses to alcohol and drug problems are established within the limits of current social policies and laws. And laws vary with regard to alcohol and drug problems. Since there is so much variability from state to state and from local community to local community, classifying alcohol and drug policies is a complex topic.

The NIAAA (2008) developed an alcohol policy classification system (APCS) to help organize and explain the laws and regulations affecting social policy. Public policy affecting alcohol can be divided into nine categories and five crosscutting dimensions. The nine categories are as follows:

1. *Alcoholic beverage control,* including manufacturing, labeling, packaging, and distribution through retail sales outlets and transactions;
2. *Taxation and pricing,* including sales, coupons, rebates, and specials;
3. *Advertising, marketing, and the mass media,* including promotions, billboards, broadcasts, and print and online advertising;
4. *Transportation, public safety, and crime,* including vehicle operation, general crime, violence, alcohol-specific offenses, and public safety issues;
5. *Health-care services and financing,* including facilities, services, programs, providers, Medicare and Medicaid and other health insurance coverage, and medical records;
6. *Education,* including public information and prevention efforts at every level of public education, from primary school through college;
7. *Other public services,* including housing, child protection, public assistance, corrections, unemployment, worker's disability, and public lands;
8. *Workplace,* including alcohol in the workplace, employee assistance programs (EAPs), and professional and occupation-specific issues;
9. *Other alcohol policy areas,* including alcohol and pregnancy, death certificates, and coroners' reports.

The five crosscutting dimensions are these:

1. *Demographic groups,* including children, the elderly, racial and ethnic groups, prisoners, homeless, military, and people with disabilities;

2. *Beverage types,* including beer, malt beverages, wine, and distilled spirits;
3. *Penalties, liabilities, and incentives,* including incarceration, mandatory education or treatment or both, fines, civil and criminal liabilities, license restrictions, and community service;
4. *Special jurisdiction,* including Native American lands, military bases, and specified localities where substance abuse may be higher than the norm;
5. *Other dimensions,* including discrimination, accreditation, testing, screening, charitable and faith-based initiatives, and the public sector.

This classification system allows the researcher to focus on the various dimensions of a social policy analysis of alcohol issues. See Box 14.1 for examples of how social policy interconnects with law to control access to alcohol.

Box 14.1   Examples of Legislative Social Policy on Alcohol

Social policy with regard to alcohol and drug issues is vast and complex. The Alcohol Policy Information System (APIS) is a web-based resource that was devised to provide information on state and federal alcohol-related laws and regulations. It is primarily a tool to assist researchers in their work to study the effects and the effectiveness of policies related to alcohol use.

The following are some examples of how alcohol policy intertwines with law. A change in social policy specified that blood alcohol content (BAC) of 0.08 or greater constitutes driving under the influence and increases the license suspension period if someone refuses a breath or blood test for alcohol. This is a federal initiative that denies states access to federal funds if they refuse to lower the legal limit to 0.08 from the previous level of 0.10. In New Hampshire a bill enacted in 2003 (2003 N.H. Laws 61, Bill number S 66) changed social policy by limiting local churches' exemptions to meal and room taxes when they have a one-day license for a "beer tent" at their church fairs and fiestas.

In the states of Delaware and Tennessee in 2006, the BAC limit was lowered from 0.10 to 0.08 for operators of recreational watercraft. In Virginia in 2006, loss of driving privileges for alcohol violations by minors changed from both mandatory and discretional suspension or revocation to mandatory revocation of license. Mississippi in 2006 repealed a 1 percent surcharge on beer containing more than 5 percent alcohol by weight and on distilled spirits containing more than 4 percent alcohol by weight (NIAAA, 2007).

Social policy that is more directly focused on drugs rather than alcohol utilizes many different strategies and tactics. The US drug policy is aimed at prevention, education, research, supply reduction, and treatment (Office of National Drug Control Policy [hereafter, ONDCP], 2008). Specifically, the goals of the ONDCP drug policy are to educate young people to reject drugs and alcohol; to reduce crimes and violence associated with drugs; to reduce social costs and health problems caused by illegal drug use; to guard the boundaries of air, oceans, and land from drugs; and to stop sources of illegal drugs both at home and abroad. In his March 1, 2008, radio address, President George W. Bush touted the decline in drug use over the past seven years.

Drug policy in the United States has been greatly influenced by the "War on Drugs," which has its roots in history. As early as 1906 the Pure Food and Drug Act was passed as federal legislation to control the use of over-the-counter medicines. The opium wars resulted in the United States restricting the importation of opium in the Opium Smoking Act of 1909. The Harrison Narcotics Act of 1914 did not ban opiate use; rather, it required physicians to register with the Internal Revenue Service and pay a fee to prescribe these drugs. Thus, early social policy of the United States with regard to drugs was firmly established at the federal level. It set the standard of prohibition and control that still influences social policy on drugs.

Legislative action to prohibit drug use and sale continued to criminalize drug use. In 1930, Henry Anslinger was appointed head of the Federal Bureau of Narcotics (FBN), a position that he held until 1962. Anslinger's perspective on drug policy was that drug use was a criminal offense and that drug addicts should be locked away. In 1937 the Marijuana Tax Act was passed at the federal level—it did not officially ban marijuana but, rather, levied a tax. There is evidence that the populations using different drugs have had an impact on whether a particular drug is criminalized (Belenko, 2000). That is, drugs used by those considered "unsavory" in society can be the drugs that bring legal sanctions. A legal definition rather than a public health definition was established for drug policy from the inception of the FBN. Through regulations on trade and taxation, the federal government has been able to control drugs and affect drug policy. Passage of the federal Controlled Substances Act (CSA) in 1970 replaced the Harrison Act and the Marijuana Tax Act as the standard for drug policy.

The CSA established different drug schedules or categories of drugs. Drugs such as heroin, LSD, and marijuana cannot be possessed by anyone except certified researchers. These are Schedule I drugs, in that they are considered to have high abuse possibilities with no medical purposes. Decisions on which drugs are included in specific schedule categories are made under the CSA by the Drug Enforcement Administration (DEA). Petitions to reschedule marijuana from a Schedule I drug to a Schedule III drug have been rejected by the DEA owing to its determination that marijuana has significant abuse potential and poses a risk to public health. The process to reschedule a drug considers eight factors: (1) the drug's abuse potential, (2) pharmacological effects, (3) scientific findings on the drug, (4) patterns of abuse, (5) significance and amount of abuse, (6) risks to public health, (7) dependence and addiction potential, and (8) gateway drug potential for serious drug abuse. See Box 14.2 for a discussion of medical uses of marijuana.

Box 14.2   Medical Uses of Marijuana

Marijuana use has not always been considered a criminal offense. Marijuana (hemp) was grown and used in the making of ropes and fabrics. It was also inhaled and ingested for its medicinal effects by early users. Useful in chronic pain control, marijuana is also useful as an appetite stimulant, both of these properties making marijuana medically helpful in the treatment of cancer. Since the criminalization of marijuana use was instituted, there have always been supporters for the medicinal use of marijuana. Generally, a physician needs to determine that a serious medical condition exists and that other medications are not as effective for treatment.

The quantity of marijuana that a patient can use is dependent on different state laws, as are the provisions for caregivers' accountability (Seamon, 2006). State laws range from symbolic laws that allow medicinal use of marijuana but carry no protection from prosecution to state laws that permit research into the therapeutic use of marijuana. Although medical marijuana laws exist in several states, federal prohibitions make the state laws difficult to implement. Alaska, California, Colorado, Hawaii, Maine, and Nevada have passed laws to allow medical marijuana use and protect against arrest on federal charges. State police cannot be compelled to enforce federal laws, so there is less prosecution for medicinal use in these states.

Drugstores and pharmacies cannot supply marijuana even when a prescription is presented. In order to distribute medical marijuana, "clubs" or "buyer's clinics" have emerged and have been targeted by federal law enforcement to prevent marijuana distribution. This point of law was brought to the US Supreme Court. In *Conant v. Oakland Buyers Cooperative,* the Supreme Court held that buyer's clubs can be prosecuted and that marijuana is not exempt from the Controlled Substances Act because of its medicinal benefits.

In June 2005 the US Supreme Court, in *Raich v. Gonzalez,* decided that the US Justice Department, including the DEA, can prosecute medical marijuana patients for violation of the federal Controlled Substances Act, despite legal use under state laws (NORML, 2007).

Funding is another crucial element, since it allows for the creation of new positions and programs to implement social policy. With the passage of the Comprehensive Crime Control Act of 1984 and the Anti-Drug Abuse Act of 1986, funding was increased for drug policy implementation. In 1988 the National Narcotics Leadership Act established the Office of National Drug Control Policy. This demonstrated an upsurge in the tactics involved in the war on drugs. The crack epidemic that was discussed earlier in this text occurred during Ronald Reagan's presidency in the 1980s and was influential in the increased funding of drug policies. The fiscal year 2008 budget for drug control in the United States was $13.7 billion. For fiscal year 2009, President Bush requested $14.3 billion (ONDCP, 2008).

In addition to increased funding, these legislative acts established mandatory sentences and more severe penalties for drug possession, sale, and use. Legislative efforts to win the war on drugs include the proposed Drug Dealer Liability Act of 1999. The Act mandated that in addition to criminal liability, dealers are held to civil liability. This meant that dealers could be sued by anyone, including drug users, for harm that resulted from the use of a controlled substance. The Act has been used as a model in state legislatures, including those in Arkansas, California, Colorado, Georgia, Hawaii, Illinois, Indiana, Louisiana, Michigan, Oklahoma, South Carolina, South Dakota, and Utah. See Box 14.3 for a discussion of varying state laws regarding marijuana possession and use.

Just as with alcohol policies, drug control policies are easier to pass when children are the target population. The Controlled Substances Act was amended to include the federal Protecting Our Children from Drugs Act of 2000. This Act increased the penalties imposed on drug dealers who use children in their drug trafficking. Since minors may be treated more leniently under the law, children have been recruited into the illegal drug business. In some impoverished inner-city neighborhoods, children as young as five or six are used to carry drugs and money back and forth between drug dealers and customers. These young children earn money for their families and are relatively safe from prosecution. Children growing up in drug-infested environments can learn that substance abuse is a "normal" activity. The Protecting Our Children from Drugs Act of 2000 imposes mandatory minimum penalties on dealers found guilty of using children under age eighteen to distribute drugs (Dolin, 2001).

At this writing, drug policies have been criticized and debated on several fronts. Many critics of the US drug policy, with its emphasis on legal responses rather than medical responses, point out the problematic areas contained within these definitions. One oft-cited concern is that the poli-

Box 14.3 Examples of Penalties for Possession of Marijuana

Penalties for possession and use of marijuana differ from state to state. There is a difference in penalties between possession for personal use and possession with intent to sell. Generally, the amount of marijuana that a person is found holding determines which possession charge is imposed. Possession with intent to sell always carries stiffer penalties.

In some states there are conditional release options for first-time offenders, and in other states, laws have decriminalized possession for personal use. In the latter there is usually no prison sentence or felony record for first-time arrests. Location of arrest may also play a significant role in determining penalties. Possession on a school bus or near a housing project carries more severe penalties. In Massachusetts, sale of marijuana within 1,000 feet of a school can bring a two-year mandatory minimum sentence with the possibility of up to fifteen years in prison, depending on the amount of marijuana. Overall, there can be a wide range of criminal justice responses to marijuana, further evidence of societal ambivalence toward the drug (NORML, 2008).

A new law in Massachusetts that decriminalizes possession of small amounts of marijuana took effect on January 2, 2009 (Saltzman, 2008b). This followed a referendum of state voters, 65 percent of whom supported decriminalization. Those caught with one ounce or less of marijuana are charged with a civil offense (instead of a criminal offense) and subject to a civil fine of $100. Offenders under the age of eighteen are required to attend a drug awareness class. Failure to attend the class within one year increases the fine to $1,000. At this writing, police and prosecutors have many questions about the implementation of the new law (Saltzman, 2008b).

cies and drug laws have more of an impact on minorities than on members of the dominant group. This is clearly seen in the tougher sentences given to low-income blacks for crack cocaine, while lighter sentences are granted to middle-class whites for powder cocaine, despite the fact that crack and regular cocaine are pharmacologically the same drug (Coyle, 2003). As discussed in the previous chapter, these sentencing requirements are undergoing reform as of this writing.

The issue of the high financial costs associated with a criminal justice response to drug policies is also raised. Policing and incarceration are very costly. There is also the problem of police corruption in enforcing drug policies. Methods used to enforce the drug laws often require undercover police tactics and vice work, which present potential opportunities for the police to be tempted by drug use. In addition, the profits earned through illegal drug sales can have a seducing and corrupting influence on professionals who do not earn large salaries.

It is clear that current drug policies have not been successful in reducing drug use problems in the United States. Some suggestions for reconstruction of alcohol and drug policies include redefining the issues as health problems, not criminal problems, and eliminating mandatory minimum sentences for nonviolent drug users. Alternatives to incarceration need to be developed, with a focus on treating substance abusers and their families instead of punishing them. Harm reduction could be given priority over zero-tolerance policies, and needle exchange programs could be expanded. Prohibiting the sale of alcohol or drugs in state-supported institutions could discourage alcohol and drug abuse. The discussion of prevention will highlight how a redirection of social policies can bring positive results.

Prevention

Discussions of the prevention of substance abuse problems tend to focus on three types of prevention efforts. *Primary* prevention focuses on preventing substance abuse problems from developing at all. Programs of this nature are often aimed at children and adolescents. This is the type of prevention that most people are referring to when discussing prevention of substance abuse. *Secondary* prevention refers to intervening in a drug or alcohol problem at an early point with the goal of preventing the problem from becoming worse. Needle exchange programs for heroin addicts are an example of secondary prevention, since they seek to reduce the harm to addicts and curb the spread of HIV/AIDS. *Tertiary* prevention refers to actual treatment provided to alcoholics and addicts. Most people do not consider tertiary prevention as prevention at all. However, tertiary prevention makes sense in the context of reducing the medical and social consequences of addiction to the individual and preventing the spread of consequences to family and friends.

The Center for Substance Abuse Prevention of the Substance Abuse and Mental Health Services Administration has offered new terminology: *universal prevention, selective preventive interventions,* and *indicated preventive interventions* (Center for Substance Abuse Prevention, 2008). *Universal prevention* refers to efforts designed for everyone—the general public and those not identified as at risk for substance abuse problems. *Indicated preventive interventions* are strategies for those who have some signs or symptoms but whose substance use does not warrant a formal diagnosis. *Selective preventive interventions* are activities specifically designed for individuals and groups who are at high risk for substance abuse problems.

Substance abuse prevention efforts need to consider both individual and societal factors. Why it is that some people choose to use illicit drugs or to abuse licit drugs such as alcohol? People do make choices within the context of their social lives (Reinarman and Levine, 1997). What leads people to make the choices that they do? What is the role of socioeconomic pressures and social deprivation in these choices? Primary prevention efforts acknowledge the need to improve the socioeconomic status of those who are poor. Many substance abusers have very poor work histories and high levels of unemployment. Vocational training in rehabilitation programs is seriously lacking (Machlan, Brostrand, and Benshoff, 2004). Treatment settings that do focus on vocational training and employment opportunities help to prevent relapse.

Social policies that reduce inequality can also prevent substance abuse. Countries such as Japan and those in Scandinavia have made a priority of reducing inequality in their societies and have also lowered their crime and substance abuse problems (Kuure, 2002). Social development may well prove to be the best prevention strategy for substance abuse. However, the considerable diversity in the United States makes this a much more complex issue, requiring more complex approaches.

Prevention of substance abuse requires a multipronged strategy and flexible tactics. Major social institutions need to integrate prevention efforts with other social institutions, such as the family and schools. Prevention should begin early within the family. Parents, siblings, and other family members are critical as role models who teach responsible use of substances, since they set the foundation for an individual's drug or alcohol use patterns. In addition to the family, the peer group of children in school needs to be involved with substance abuse prevention. Religious, educational, legal, and medical institutions also emerge as significant social institutions in developing and implementing prevention strategies.

A brief overview of institutional efforts will demonstrate directions and initiatives in prevention and highlight the complexity of addressing substance abuse problems in the United States in the early 2000s. As discussed in earlier chapters, substance abuse issues can be identified by special populations, by economic-strata use patterns, by occupations, by historical periods, by geographic and cultural locations, by licit or illicit drug use, by type of drug, and by "audience" response to the drug use. In addition, social definitions that are constructed with regard to alcohol and other drug use always reflect power and diversity. For example, those without power in society are most likely to have poorer legal representation and receive harsher sanctions for drug crimes than those who have more financial resources and therefore more power.

Religious Institutions

From a sociological perspective, one of the main goals of religious institutions is the socialization of its members into a value system and a lifestyle that incorporate the religious beliefs and ethics of the faith. The major religions in the United States have all taken a position on substance use and abuse. Participation in religious organizations can serve as a safeguard against substance abuse. Often the younger members of the faith are identified as targets for the message that the religion wants to deliver. Sometimes these messages are given directly through sermons and homilies; sometimes they are given in more passive communication styles such as posters and music. A crucial component of a successful prevention strategy is to give accurate and believable information. Participation in religious communities creates role models and support groups to reinforce the message (Center for Youth Development and Policy Research, 2003).

Educational Institutions

Educational institutions play a very significant role in substance abuse prevention. Since laws mandate that children attend school from the ages of six to sixteen, schools have important, frontline opportunities to implement substance abuse prevention programs. Education and accurate information are critical in social policy strategy with regard to alcohol and drugs. There are many different interventions and programs utilized within the school system to educate and inform students about the dangers and health risks associated with alcohol and drug abuse. It is crucial to include students in the process and design of substance abuse prevention programs. Some programs hope to improve and enhance cognitive problem solving and others focus on life-skills training. Strategies may include science-based curricula that emphasize the consequences of alcohol and drug abuse, teaching skills for refusing alcohol and drugs, and helping students to cope with peer pressure. As discussed below, some of these approaches are more practical and effective than others.

One socialization approach that has been implemented in many different school programs involves peer group involvement with students who are identified as at risk. These programs generally comprise a discussion and sharing among a group of at-risk-identified students with a peer educator. However, the effectiveness of this approach to prevention has been questioned. A sample of over 1,200 students from two large, diverse, urban high schools found that the effectiveness of this peer program was doubtful (Cho, Hallfors, and Sanchez, 2005). The study indicated that in a six-month follow-up, "negative effects" on prevention were noted. These might be explained by the possibility that putting all the at-risk students together in groups reinforced one another's substance abuse patterns. The specific drugs of abuse may also determine the effectiveness of drug prevention programs in schools. School-based social programs focusing on alcohol and tobacco abuse prevention seem to provide the most benefit and cost less than programs addressing drug use (Caulkins et al., 2004).

Gilbert Botvin and colleagues (2003) looked at the effectiveness of prevention training in grades three through six in twenty schools. Nine of the schools received the prevention program and the other eleven served as control groups. Stronger antidrug attitudes, higher self-esteem, and less smoking were found in the nine schools that received the prevention training. These findings support school-based substance abuse prevention programs. Another study, also conducted in the early 2000s, of high-risk students for substance abuse (due to poor school performance and contact with substance-using peers) also supported these school-based programs (Griffin et al., 2003). Early life-skills training to prevent substance abuse—which included teaching social resistance techniques and enhancing social and personal competence—resulted in positive behavioral patterns that lasted through high school (Botvin and Griffin, 2004). Follow-up research reaffirmed the effectiveness of life-skills training and prevention of substance abuse (Botvin and Griffin, 2005). Overall, gaps in such school curricula must be closed so that kindergarten through twelfth grade offers a continuum of education and prevention efforts.

Legal Institutions

According to the Office of National Drug Control Policy, law enforcement has several initiatives aimed at preventing the use and spread of "club drugs" and other synthetic drugs. Since production of these synthetic drugs requires specific ingredients—for example, iodine and pseudoephedrine—there need to be stricter regulations on the availability of these products (ONDCP, 2008). Stricter controls imposed by Canada on pseudoephedrine in 2004 resulted in a reduction in methamphetamine production. Information sharing and open communication among the different arms of the criminal justice system, with the implementation of a nationwide database on methamphetamine production, distribution, and consumption, increase the success of prevention policies. See Box 14.4 for a discussion of an international effort to reduce drug supply.

Local legal initiatives to prevent substance abuse include enforcing current laws and increasing the accountability of those who supply drugs to abusers. Bar owners and servers of alcoholic beverages are more aware of their legal accountability if a customer is served alcohol to the point of intoxication. Threats of lawsuits and criminal charges help to reduce the likelihood of bar owners encouraging excessive drinking.

The US Food and Drug Administration (FDA) has encouraged labeling changes to prevent prescription drug abuse. The "black box" warnings on controlled-release, high-strength opiates serve to educate as well as to prevent inappropriate marketing of these addictive prescription medications. These warnings must cite all the serious risks to users in a clear manner. Since these long-acting opiates are intended for chronic, severe pain and are not needed for individuals with intermittent pain, the risks of addiction must be made clear. OxyContin labels follow this protocol, and the FDA is working with other major pharmaceutical producers to promote consistent labeling across products. Labeling should alert physicians to accurately assess patients for the possibility of abuse. Family histories of abuse or personal abuse patterns need to be considered before a physician

---

Box 14.4   Global Efforts at Controlling Drug Production

Approximately 200 million people worldwide are estimated to be drug users, about 5 percent of the total population (United Nations, 2006). Marijuana remains the most widely used drug, with some decline in opiate abuse due to declining cultivation.

"Project Prism" is an international initiative aimed at improving communication and developing strategies to impose stricter global controls on the ingredients needed to produce ecstasy and other synthetic drugs. The Netherlands has been identified as a major producer and distributor of ecstasy. As a result of collaboration between the Dutch government and the United States, greater restriction and control of needed ingredients for production have been implemented. Under the Foreign Narcotics Kingpin Designation Act, the president of the United States can identify individuals as drug kingpins and then restrict their access to banking and other financial systems in the United States. Countries that have been designated as drug-producing or drug-transit countries can be refused bilateral assistance by the US government under the Foreign Assistance Act (DEA, 2001).

prescribes an addictive medication. Labels can also alert physicians to the necessity of monitoring for signs of abuse.

Medical Institutions

The efforts at substance abuse prevention that are being initiated through medical institutions are diverse and comprehensive, ranging from research into the biology of addiction, to developing testing and diagnostic measures, to treatments and control of substance abuse through medicine and therapies. As discussed earlier, increased use of drug testing in athletics and workplace settings has affected the substance use and abuse in these areas (see Box 14.5).

Research activities have had a significant impact on social policy development and implementation. Technological advances have allowed for more in-depth research on human biology, and in particular, on human genetic compositions. Medicine, through its research activities into genetics,

---

Box 14.5   Cheating on Drug Tests

Since mandatory drug testing has been implemented in many work settings, concerns have been raised regarding the validity of tests and the potential for false outcomes. Technical and scientific guidelines for drug testing in federal workplaces were established in 1988. There have been revisions to the mandatory guidelines over the years to cover recent advances in the field, but cheating and falsified results still occur. Sometimes cheating is the result of corruption and payoffs in laboratory settings; sometimes it results from individual actions.

Most cheating on drug tests is accomplished by substitution of "dirty urine" with "clean urine" or with adulteration of the urine sample. The counterculture pro-drug movement in the United States brought about the use of chemical adulterants that can prevent detection of drugs in urine and hair samples. These chemical adulterants are readily available for purchase over the Internet, marketed under names like Klear, Whizzies, Urine Luck, and Sweet Pee's Spoiler, which are usually toxic.

Other products that are available to confound a drug test include prosthetic devices that can be strapped to the waistband of clothing. These devices distribute clean or synthetic urine contained within a reservoir, allowing illicit drug users to mask their use from employers. In addition to urine testing, drug testing can include tests on sweat, saliva, and hair (Substance Abuse and Mental Health Services Administration, 2004).

hormones, and body chemistry, is increasing knowledge and awareness of the roles played by biology in addiction. The quest continues for identifying, modifying, or controlling specific genes that contribute to addiction.

At this writing, vaccines are being developed to prevent drug addiction (Ridgely and Iguchi, 2004). These vaccines have potential to help individuals who are dealing with addictions and, overall, help society lower the cost of addiction. State laws might permit coercive use of these vaccines, thus the potential for coercive use of vaccines to control addiction exists and is likely to remain controversial.

Careful attention to the promotion and marketing of prescription drugs can also help prevent substance abuse of prescribed medications. Prescription drug advertisements have been closely monitored and regulated by the FDA for false advertising or inaccurate data since 1962. The medical field has supported this effort by the FDA.

A highly regarded example of prevention efforts is the MOST of Us marketing and research firm of Montana State University–Bozeman (MOST of Us, 2008). This was the first program in the country to use the marketing of social norms (MSN) approach on a statewide basis for smoking prevention. Another emphasis of the program is the prevention of driving while intoxicated. MSN is considered an innovative health promotion technique based on the hypothesis that human behavior is influenced by what we perceive to be normal behavior. Humans can certainly misperceive the behaviors and attitudes of others, falsely assuming that many others are drinking and using drugs, for example. The Montana Model of Social Norms Marketing is a seven-step process: (1) *Planning and Environmental Advocacy,* to guide the efforts, including creating a social, political, and economic climate in which change can take place; (2) *Baseline Data,* related to behavior and perceived norms; (3) *Message Development,* based on current behaviors and perceptions of the readiness for change; (4) a *Market Plan* that can effectively see the issues from the point of view of the target population and develop media approaches; (5) *Pilot Test and Refine Materials,* especially through the use of focus groups; (6) *Implement Campaign,* by using print and broadcast media messages and promotional items; and (7) *Evaluation,* the constant process of reviewing the effectiveness of the specific prevention campaign through the use of qualitative and quantitative data.

Overall, community health can be improved through appropriate substance abuse prevention programs (Chinman, Imm, and Wandersman, 2004). Collaborations between science and practice are important. The Strategic Prevention Framework (SPF) of the Substance Abuse and Mental Health Services Administration supports prevention approaches that include comprehensive assessment, planning, and evaluation (Imm et al.,

2007). Evidence-based practices are integrated with community needs with emphasis on cultural diversity and sustainability. The Getting to Outcomes model translates the SPF into practical prevention programs. The model includes a ten-step process that allows practitioners to improve their prevention skills as well as create ways for them to evaluate and modify their current programs. A new direction will emphasize blended research that is conducted in practice settings. An active collaboration between researchers and practitioners will be the focus of future prevention work.

Practice

The practice of providing substance abuse treatment services has changed considerably since the 1970s. In 2008, only a select few alcoholics or addicts with private funds or excellent insurance could receive twenty-eight-day inpatient rehabilitation that was once a popular treatment option. Funding cuts for human services in the 1990s and into this century have meant less money for state-funded substance abuse treatment programs. For example, in Massachusetts in 2004, more than half of state-funded detoxification beds, typically occupied by those without private funds, were cut. Now there is much greater emphasis on short-term, evidence-based practice, and research efforts to prove which types of treatment work or do not work.

Between 60,000 and 70,000 professionals from a broad range of disciplines provide services for substance-abusing clients. These professionals include physicians, nurses, criminal justice practitioners, mental health workers, social workers, clinical and counseling psychologists, and, of course, addictions professionals. The settings in which they work are also diverse, including educational, social service, correctional, medical, and various substance abuse treatment venues, such as detoxification centers, outpatient programs, and halfway houses. Individuals in these treatment settings typically have a host of medical, psychiatric, social, educational, vocational, and legal needs.

In 2007, people receiving some form of substance abuse treatment numbered 3.9 million (SAMHSA, 2008). However, it is also estimated that approximately 80 percent of substance abusers do not get the help they need (Northeast Addiction Technology Transfer Center [hereafter, NeATTC], 2004). In 2007, an estimated 20.8 million people (8.4 percent of the population over age twelve) needed treatment for an illicit drug or alcohol problem but did not receive it within a specialty substance-abuse facility (SAMHSA, 2008).

Substance use disorders are no longer considered disorders separate from the existence of other life problems. Professionals increasingly recognize that over 5.4 million people who suffer from at least one serious mental disorder also have a substance abuse problem (SAMHSA, 2008). Over 65 percent of those incarcerated in prisons and jails are estimated to suffer from a substance abuse problem (Karberg and James, 2005).

There are numerous opportunities for people who want to practice in the alcohol and drug prevention and treatment fields. According to Karen Matherlee (2003), there will be over 115,000 practitioners working in the field by 2010. However, much remains to be done to make jobs in the field a sought-after career. The rate of compensation for addictions professionals is near the bottom of the scale within human service and health professions, and career and educational ladders are not clearly delineated (Center for Substance Abuse Treatment, 2000). Recruitment and training of sufficient qualified professionals are a major challenge (Gallon, Gabriel, and Knudsen, 2003; NeATTC, 2004). Clinical supervision is lacking, and counselors are often on their own in working with clients (NeATTC, 2004). Addictions professionals themselves can experience stigma, a kind of negative aura that emanates from treating the stigmatized. Caseloads can be huge, and there is the stress of working with a high-risk, unstable, and relapsing population. Given the above, it is understandable that understaffing and insufficient treatment slots are ongoing problems (Therapeutic Communities of America, 2008).

There are at least three cultures involved in the provision of substance abuse services. Self-help and personal recovery, as exemplified by Alcoholics Anonymous, is the culture from which substance abuse counselors have evolved. The second culture is the world of professional addiction education—social work, psychology, and medicine, both influenced and tempered by AA ideology. In the 1970s it was typical for alcoholism counselors to be in recovery themselves with no expectations of educational or specialized training. The twenty-first-century picture is far different, with professional positions often requiring certification or licensure, to be discussed shortly. The third major culture is a new thrust, championed and funded by the federal government, emphasizing "evidence-based, empirically validated," and "science-based" treatment. This includes the new National Institute on Alcohol Abuse and Alcoholism support for the use of medications to curb cravings (Medication + Counseling, 2005). In December 2005 the FDA gave initial approval to the drug Vivitrol, the first injection for the treatment of alcoholism. This once-a-month injection has been shown to reduce heavy drinking in patients who are receiving counseling at the same time (Heuser, 2006).

The world of professional practice is ambivalent about "science-based" approaches because professionals cling to the counseling ideologies in which they were trained and because these approaches often involve short-term treatments and medication treatment. The concern also is that "science" is a mantra that ignores the fact that just about any treatment involving and motivating the client toward recovery and relapse prevention, regardless of theoretical bent, may be helpful.

Prior to the late 1970s, the addictions workforce was primarily composed of nondegreed paraprofessionals who were themselves recovering addicts and alcoholics. They came from AA or were graduates of drug-free therapeutic communities. The ideological gap between these dedicated counselors and nonrecovering professionals was immense. In the late 1970s, standards for certification of addictions staff were developed, with credentialing focusing on "core functions" that were borrowed from the routines of social services. These core functions included screening, assessment, intake, orientation, treatment planning, case management, client education, crisis intervention, and individual, group, and family counseling.

In the effort to professionalize, many states have a system of voluntary certification, which means counselors have attained a certain level of knowledge, experience, or education, or all of these, in substance abuse. The trend as of this writing is movement toward licensure, a state requirement that may include passing a written examination in addition to knowledge, experience, and educational requirements. This positive trend helps to elevate the status of substance abuse clinicians and can bring greater financial compensation. Licensing of substance professionals also requires adherence to a code of ethics.

A number of organizations have developed to advance substance abuse treatment and the professionalization of the field. The National Association of Alcohol and Drug Abuse Counselors (NAADAC), founded in 1972, is the largest organization for addictions professionals, with almost 11,000 members and 46 state affiliates (NAADAC, 2008). Its new name is "NAADAC, the Association for Addiction Professionals," to welcome professionals who specialize in gambling, tobacco, and other addictions. The International Certification and Reciprocity Consortium/Alcohol and Other Drug Abuse Association (ICRC), founded in 1981, is a nonprofit, voluntary organization made up of agencies that certify alcohol and drug counselors, prevention specialists, and clinical supervisors. At this writing, the ICRC comprises 72 agencies, representing over 36,000 certified substance abuse professionals (ICRC, 2008). There have been discussions regarding a merger of NAADAC and the ICRC.

The International Coalition of Addictions Studies Education (INCASE) is a professional association founded in 1990 for individuals, students, and educational programs to enhance substance abuse training and education. Annual conferences highlight what is new in the field of substance abuse and curriculum development. The Addiction Technology Transfer Center (ATTC), founded in 1993 and funded by the federal Substance Abuse and Mental Health Services Administration (SAMHSA), takes as its vision a unification of science, education, and services to treat the addictions. Through the national office and fourteen regional centers, the ATTC seeks to assist in transforming research findings into practice. The ATTC is in the forefront of "evidence-based" practices.

The diffusion of innovation in cultures always takes time. The Institute of Medicine (2001) found that it took from fifteen to twenty years for evidence-based practices in mental health and addiction to move from "science to service," if at all—clearly a pace unacceptable for other kinds of intervention, including cancer drugs (Bradley et al., 2004). The reason for this glacial rate of change in the treatment culture has several roots, among them the ideological dogma of both recovery cultures and professional practice, including the failure of training (technology transfer) models that utilize conventional workshops or conferences that briefly expose counselors to new methods, which are lost after several months.

While the emphasis, at this writing, is on counseling and treatment, it is necessary also to prepare addictions specialists with skills in policy creation and research methods. Addictions professionals should be trained and prepared to contribute to public debates such as those regarding the decriminalization of marijuana. In the future, addictions professionals will need, in addition to clinical skills, education on welfare reform, alternatives to imprisonment, allocation of funding, and criminal justice solutions to discrimination (de Miranda, 2004).

While much remains to be done, several suggestions can help to fortify and professionalize the substance abuse treatment field. First, the number of new professionals seeking entry into the field needs to increase. Recruitment of second-career and recovering individuals needs to be intensified. The number of graduates from academic and field-based training programs needs to increase to keep pace with clinical need. Incentives to bring more professionals into the field should be considered, including salary increases, benefit expansion, and loan forgiveness programs. A national workforce plan should address recruitment, incentives, and a set of career and educational ladders (McLellan, Carise, and Kleber, 2003).

Second, there is a need to reduce staff turnover rates in community agencies, estimated to be 20 to 25 percent annually (Knudsen and Gabriel,

2003). Agencies are in competition with each other for qualified personnel, and once workers gain experience, they are often recruited for positions outside of direct clinical service. Treatment agencies compete for staff with mental health and correctional agencies, which may offer better financial and career incentives.

Third, there is a need for uniform standards in the education and training programs that prepare substance abuse prevention and treatment specialists. Such programs exist in community colleges, four-year institutions, graduate schools, and community programs. However, there is no agreement on program standards, curricula, and how much, if any, supervised fieldwork is required. Coordination is needed to develop and facilitate career opportunities and to encourage recovering and nonrecovering workers to acquire core competencies and credentials that will help advance their professional contributions to the workforce. In short, much remains to be done.

Conclusion

The United States has the largest market for illegal drugs of any country. If the demand were not there for drugs, the market would decrease. However, once a culture has been exposed to alcohol and drugs, they remain a part of the culture.

As the twentieth century drew to an end, credentialing of addictions professionals was still evolving. States increasingly have adopted licensure similar to that for professional psychologists and social workers. A tiered system began to emerge, including lower-level credentials that reflected minimal training (e.g., the Chemical Dependency Associate in New Jersey), and certification under the ICRC or the NAADAC. Certification has increasingly upped the ante of educational requirements, engendering, for example, the necessity for associate's, bachelor's, and master's degrees. Approximately one-half of addictions counselors have master's degrees, roughly divided between those who migrated from social work and psychology and those who started out at the community college level. The movement toward unifying competing systems of certification has shown progress in the effort to establish agreed-upon standards, skills, and attitudes in professional practice.

The real world of limited resources, limited budgets, and managed care forces the addiction treatment field to adopt novel and empirically based techniques such as brief screening and intervention by health-care providers (Institute of Medicine, 1990; Pincus, 2003). New motivational incentives for clients to participate in treatment, such as clients earning prizes for meeting specific treatment goals, may be used (Center for Applied Behavioral Health Policy, 2004). As discussed in Chapter 13, new medications to cope with cravings for drugs will also become more available.

Overall, a multidimensional approach to substance abuse treatment is needed to address this important multidimensional problem. It must include commitments from parents, the family, local communities, as well as state and federal organizations.

Glossary

Abstinence: to refrain from using alcohol or drugs by choice

Acamprosate calcium (Campral): a drug approved by the Food and Drug Administration in 2004 to reduce cravings for alcohol and help maintain abstinence

Acute condition: a condition with a sudden onset and limited time of duration

Adderal: a brand-name combination of amphetamine and dextroamphetamine used to treat attention deficit hyperactivity disorder

Addiction: use of a habit-forming drug persistently to the point of developing physical tolerance and physiological symptoms upon withdrawal

Addiction Severity Index (ASI): a multidimensional assessment instrument used to measure alcohol and drug problems

Al-Anon: support group organized for family, children, and friends of alcoholics

Ala-Teen: a support group organized for adolescent children of alcoholics

Alcohol-related birth defects (ARBD): a term that refers to problems with hearing, the kidneys, bones, or heart in the children of women who drank alcohol during pregnancy

Alcohol-related neurodevelopmental disorder (ARND): functional or mental problems of children of women who drank alcohol during pregnancy

Alcoholics Anonymous (AA): a supportive fellowship that promotes abstinence and recovery "one day at a time"

Amotivational syndrome: a controversial concept referring to decreased motivation associated with drugs, especially marijuana.

Amphetamines: a central-nervous-system stimulant also known as "speed"

Anabolic steroids: substances used by athletes to increase muscle mass

Analgesics: drugs used for the relief of pain

Angel dust: a common name for phencyclidine (PCP), a dissociative anesthetic; it can have properties of a stimulant, depressant, hallucinogenic, and analgesic

Antabuse (disulfirum): a prescription medication used in early recovery to deter drinking; those who drink while on antabuse become violently ill within a few minutes of ingesting alcohol

Antidepressant: a psychiatric medication used to alleviate depression; examples include Lexapro, Prozac, and Cymbalta

Antihistamine: medication to inhibit the release of histamines to treat allergies; examples include Allegra, Benadryl, and Claritin

Antipsychotic medications (also known as neuroleptics): drugs used to control symptoms of psychosis; for example, Seroquel XR to treat schizophrenia

Assessment: an in-depth review of social and psychological factors, work history, family history, and education to determine the appropriate course of treatment

Attention deficit hyperactivity disorder (ADHD): a behavioral disorder characterized by trouble with mental focusing in school and extremely high energy; diagnosed in approximately 8 to 10 percent of school-aged children

AUDIT: the Alcohol Use Disorders Identification Test, a screening tool developed in 1989 by the World Health Organization to screen for alcohol problems

Ayahuasca: a drink containing four hallucinogenic alkaloids prepared from vines by Jivaro shamans

Baby boomers: members of the US population born between 1946 and 1964

Barbiturates: central-nervous-system depressants with a high abuse potential, infrequently prescribed today

Beer: one of the world's oldest alcoholic beverages, made from grains, hops, yeast, and water

Benzodiazepines: a type of minor tranquilizer that includes Librium and Valium

Binge drinking: the consumption of five or more drinks on an occasion for men and four or more drinks for women

Biopsychosocial: an approach that integrates biological, psychological, and sociological insights and theories

Black market: an illegal market operating outside of government regulation to supply goods and services that are in short supply or illegal

Blackout: after a period of heavy drinking, the drinker cannot remember what he or she did while drinking; not to be confused with loss of consciousness, or "passing out"

Blood alcohol level (BAL): the amount of alcohol found in the blood, with 0.08 as the level of legal intoxication; also known as blood alcohol content, or BAC

Boggs Act: the 1951 law that increased penalties and required mandatory minimum sentences for drug offenders

Buprenorphine: medication approved by the FDA in 2002 for the treatment of heroin and other opiate addiction; eliminates severe withdrawal symptoms that can occur during opiate detox

Caffeine: a naturally occurring chemical that acts as a central-nervous-system stimulant, often found in coffee, tea, and soda

CAGE: a well-known screening tool with four questions to screen for alcohol problems

Campral (acamprosate calcium): a drug approved by the Food and Drug Administration in 2004 to reduce cravings for alcohol and help maintain abstinence

Cannabis sativa: the most common form of marijuana

Child neglect: failure of a parent, guardian, or other caregiver to provide basic needs for the child—food, shelter, supervision, medical attention—or permitting the child to use drugs or alcohol

Chronic condition: a condition that lasts or is expected to last up to a year or longer

Cirrhosis: a very serious liver disease that can be caused by excessive alcohol use

Club drugs: a category of recreational drugs used by young adults at dance clubs and raves; examples include MDMA/ecstasy, Rohypnol, and GHB

Cocaine (also, "coke"): the most powerful stimulant, derived from the coca plant

Cocktail: an alcoholic beverage such as whiskey, vodka, or gin combined with other liquors or fruit juices; a combination

Codeine: a derivative of opium used to relieve cough and pain

Codependent: a person involved with or living with a substance abuser or addict who focuses mainly on the needs of others to his or her own detriment

Cognitive impairment: changes in the ability to learn or process information; reduction in the ability to perform tasks that require memory and planning; diminished capacity in thinking caused by disease or injury

Cold turkey: a slang expression referring to stopping the intake of drugs or alcohol and enduring withdrawal symptoms

Co-morbidity: two or more illnesses affecting an individual simultaneously, such as mental illness and alcoholism

Concerta (methylphenidate, MPH): a prescription stimulant for the treatment of attention deficit hyperactivity disorder

Controlled Substances Act: 1970 federal legislation that provided the system of drug classification used today

Co-occurring disorders (also known as dual diagnosis): a combination of mental health and substance abuse problems

Cookers: drug paraphernalia used to mix injectible drugs

Coping mechanisms: tactics and skills used to deal with stress

Criminal justice: the system that includes police, courts, and correctional programs associated with the defining, monitoring, and enforcing of law

Decongestants: medications used to relieve nasal congestion

Decriminalization: removal of criminal sanctions for possession of drugs, most often applied to marijuana

Delirium tremens (DTs): the most severe withdrawal symptoms suffered by chronic alcoholics, including fever, hallucinations, seizures, or all of these

Dementia: the loss of mental processing ability that may affect communication skills, abstract thinking, judgment, and physical abilities

Demographics: the study of characteristics such as age, race, gender, and socioeconomic status

Depakote (divalproex sodium): a prescription medication used to treat bipolar disorder and seizure disorders

Depressants: drugs that decrease the activity of the central nervous system

Designer drugs: newer drugs developed by altering the chemical composition of other drugs; they are often more potent than their unaltered counterparts

Detoxification: the elimination of toxic substances such as drugs from the body; can also refer to medical supervision and the giving of medication to alcoholics and addicts to help them physically withdraw from substances, an initial step in treatment

Deviant behavior: the breaking of a norm, but not necessarily bad or perverse

Dextroamphetamine: a form of stimulant that produces wakefulness, focus, and energy, marketed under the name Dexedrine

Diagnostic criteria: the combination of symptoms that aid the physician, psychologist, or other professional in making a diagnosis of a disease or injury

Diazepam: a prescription medication used to relieve anxiety, muscle spasms, and alcohol withdrawal symptoms, marketed under the name Valium

Discrimination: an action consisting of unfair treatment of a person or group on the basis of race, sex, sexual orientation, age, or ethnicity

DMT (dimethyltryptamine): a potent psychedelic drug whose effects may last for only five to thirty minutes yet are described as profound with kaleidoscopic images and sounds

Doriden: trade name for glutethemide, an addictive drug used to treat some sleep disorders

Drug Abuse Resistance Education (DARE): a school-based drug prevention program provided by local police departments

Drug Abuse Screening Test (DAST): a screening tool used to determine if an individual is in need of an assessment for a drug problem

Drug Free Workplace Act: the 1988 federal law requiring policies to ensure a drug-free work environment

Drug Induced Rape Prevention and Punishment Act: the 1996 federal law that made it a criminal offense to slip someone a drug for the purpose of carrying out a sexual assault

Drug misuse: the inappropriate use of prescribed or other drugs

Drug paraphernalia: equipment used to inject illegal drugs

Drug policy: the official state or federal government response to drug problems, implemented through social programs and law

Drug schedules: the five categories, or schedules, of drugs established by the Controlled Substances Act of 1970 that are based on medical use and abuse potential

Dual diagnosis: a combination of mental health and substance abuse problems found in an individual; also referred to as co-occurring disorder

Ecstasy (MDMA): a synthetic hallucinogen

Employee assistance program (EAP): program offered within an employment setting whereby employees can obtain assistance with personal or work-related problems, such as substance abuse

Ephedra sinensis (ma huang): an herb that has stimulating effects

Epidemiology: the study of the distribution of disease or social problems within society

Episodic drinkers: those who drink on occasion, with periods of sobriety in between drunkenness

Eszopiclone: a sleep medication marketed as Lunesta

Fentanyl ("drop dead," among many other street names): a synthetic narcotic

Fetal alcohol effects (FAE): cognitive and behavioral problems that result from a mother's alcohol use during pregnancy; fewer and less severe than those associated with fetal alcohol syndrome

Fetal alcohol spectrum disorders (FASD): a term that refers to the range of effects on a child when the mother drinks alcohol during pregnancy

Fetal alcohol syndrome (FAS): permanent birth defects that result from a mother's alcohol use during pregnancy

Flexeril (cyclobenzaprine): a muscle relaxer and pain reliever

Gamma hydroxybutyrate (GHB): an illegal club drug that can produce euphoric effects

Gateway drug: a drug that leads to the use of other more harmful drugs

Gender bender: an informal term referring to individuals who "bend" expected gender roles

Glutethemide (Doriden): an addictive drug used to treat some sleep disorders

Goofballs: a slang term referring to barbiturates that act as central-nervous-system depressants

Grassroots: local people who are the source of activity in a community, in contrast to that structured by organized central powers

Hallucinogens: drugs that act on the central nervous system, producing changes in perceptions and hallucinations

Hangover: the aftereffects of ingesting large quantities of alcohol, characterized by headache, nausea, and irritability

Harm reduction: an approach to social problems that emphasizes lowering the damage or harm rather than eradicating the problem

Harrison Narcotics Act of 1914: a federal law that restricted the sale of narcotics without a prescription

Hashish (hash): a drug made from the resin of cannabis, typically smoked in a pipe

Hazing rituals: subjecting individuals to harmful and degrading acts in order to initiate new members into a social group such as a fraternity

Heroin: an illegal derivative of opium

Heterosexism: a term that denotes bias and prejudice against homosexuals

Homophobic: prejudiced aganst homosexuals

Huffing: taking in an inhalant through the mouth

Hydrocodone (dihydrocodeinone): a semisynthetic opioid prescribed for cough and mild to moderate pain, marketed as Vicodin

Hypnotics: drugs that depress the central nervous system to produce sleep—for example, barbiturates

Ice: nickname for crystals of methamphetamine that are inhaled or injected

Illicit drugs: drugs that are illegal to possess or sell

Indoctrination: teaching a belief or doctrine completely and systematically with the goal of preventing independent thinking

Intersexual: a person with both male and female sex characteristics

Intervention: treatment or care given to improve or relieve behaviors; often refers to family members as a group, with the help of a professional, talking with an addict or alcoholic to try to convince him or her to seek treatment

Intramuscular (IM): a route of drug administration where the drug is injected into the muscle

Intravenous (IV): a route of drug administration where the drug is injected into the vein

Jello-shots: a mix of vodka and gelatin poured into ice cube trays or small containers and cooled

Ketamine (Special K): a veterinary anesthetic that produces symptoms that mimic psychiatric disturbances

K-hole: a slang term for a state of mental dissociation achieved through ingesting high doses of ketamine

Librium (chlordiazepoxide): a tranquilizer commonly prescribed to treat anxiety or withdrawal from alcohol

Lunesta (eszopiclone): a prescription medication for the treatment of insomnia

Lysergic acid diethylamide-25 (LSD): a semisynthetic psychedelic drug that is used recreationally to produce hallucinogenic effects

Managed care: a system of health-care delivery that controls costs, in which gatekeepers, often primary care doctors, determine who can access specialty medical care

Mandatory sentences: a legal decision that sets the minimum length of incarceration for specific crimes, established by prior law and taking discretion in sentencing away from the judges; mandatory sentences often apply to drug crimes

Marijuana (pot, weed, dope): a drug that is usually smoked, made from the leaves of the cannabis plant; the main psychoactive ingredient is THC

Marijuana Tax Act of 1937: a federal law that restricted the cultivation, sale, possession, and distribution of marijuana

Marinol (dronabinol): an appetite stimulant composed of tetrahydrocannabinol (THC), the major psychoactive ingredient in marijuana; it is FDA approved to treat nausea and vomiting in cancer patients receiving chemotherapy and to stimulate the appetite of HIV/AIDS patients

Mescaline: a hallucinogen derived from the flowering heads of the peyote cactus

Meta-analysis: mathematical and statistical analysis of existing studies to draw conclusions, produce estimates, and summarize results

Methadone: a synthetic narcotic prescribed for heroin and other opiate addicts to
block withdrawal symptoms; used in opioid substitution therapy

Methamphetamine (also, "meth," "speed," "crank," "crystal"): a highly addictive
central-nervous-system stimulant

Methylphenidate: a central-nervous-system stimulant used to treat narcolepsy in adults
and attention deficit hyperactivity disorder in children, marketed as Ritalin

Michigan Alcoholism Screening Test: a well-known alcoholism screening tool developed by Selzer in 1971; the original asks twenty-five questions and the Short
Michigan Alcoholism Screening Test (SMAST) asks thirteen questions

Milieu therapy: a form of psychotherapy that involves communities of twenty to
thirty people who stay in the group for several months and are encouraged to
take responsibility for their behavior

Mood stabilizers: psychiatric medications used to treat mood disorders, such as Depakote for the treatment of bipolar disorder

Morphine: a very strong narcotic derivative of opium used as a painkiller, anesthetic,
and recreational drug

Naloxone (Narcan): used to counter the effects of heroin or morphine overdose and a
vaccine for cocaine abusers that blocks the effects of the drugs

Naltrexone (Vivitrol): used as treatment for alcoholism

Narcotics: the most addictive of all drugs, blocking pain and producing a feeling of
euphoria

Opioids: painkillers that can provide a "dreamlike high"

Opium: an addictive narcotic derived from the seeds of the opium poppy

Oxcarbazepine (OXC): a prescription medication used to treat seizures and bipolar
disorder, marked as Trileptal

Oxycodone: an opiate used to treat moderate to severe pain; the active ingredient in
OxyContin

OxyContin: a prescription painkiller that is a highly addictive drug of abuse (generic:
oxycodone)

Pancreatitis: inflammation of the pancreas, often caused by heavy alcohol use

Pathology: a study of the nature of disease

Peer group: a group of equals usually sharing the same social status, age, and interests

Peyote: a cactus containing a hallucinogen that is used in religious rites by some Native American tribes

Phencyclidine (PCP, angel dust): a veterinary anesthetic used illegally as a hallucinogenic drug

Phenobarbital: a barbiturate used to treat sleep disorders and seizures

Polydrug use: the use of two or more drugs concurrently and in combination to
achieve specific effects

Poppers: a street term for an inhaled recreational drug that is used to enhance sexual
pleasure

Potency: a drug's ability to produce an effect

Potentiation: the ability of one drug to increase the effects of a second drug when
both are taken at the same time

Prejudice: a feeling or attitude, positive or hostile toward people, based on their race,
sex, sexual orientation, age, or ethnicity—judging someone without even knowing her or him

Prevalence: the total number of cases of a disease or condition existing at a specific
time within a specific population

Primary prevention: stopping the emergence of a problem before it begins through education or socialization

Prognosis: the prediction of the outcome of disease and the chances of recovery

Progressive disease: a disease that increases in severity or scope in an individual

Prohibition: the thirteen years from 1920 to 1933 when alcohol production and distribution were outlawed by the Eighteenth Amendment to the US Constitution

Pseudoephedrine (PSE): a medication used to relieve nasal congestion caused by colds or allergies

Psilocybin: hallucinogenic mushroom and the active ingredient; "shrooms" or "magic mushrooms"

Psychoactive drugs: those that affect the central nervous system and thoughts, moods, and behavior

Psychodelic: a term often used to describe hallucinogens

Psychopharmacology: the study of the development and effects of psychoactive drugs

Public domain: information, publications, products, and processes that are available to all and are not protected by copyright or patent

Pure Food and Drug Act of 1906: federal legislation that regulated the production and distribution of food and drugs and required that ingredients be listed

Pusher: a slang term for a dealer of illegal drugs

Quaalude (also, "Ludes" and "disco biscuits"): the trade name for methaqualone, a sedative-hypnotic drug of abuse popular in the 1960s

Recidivism: rate of re-arrest or re-imprisonment, or both, for similar crimes

Red devil (secobarbital): a barbiturate used for sleep and marketed as Seconal

Relapse: a return to drinking or drug use after a period of abstinence and recovery

Respondents: individuals who answer questions in research, usually on a questionnaire or in an interview

Reverse tolerance: a drug user's experience of a drug's effects with lower amounts of the drug

Risk factors: biomedical and social indexes that place an individual at risk of substance abuse or illness

Ritalin: a Schedule II drug prescribed for the treatment of attention deficit hyperactivity disorder (ADHD) in children

Rite of passage: a ritual or ceremony that marks an important event in the transition from one stage of life to another

Robo-tripping: the effects of drinking high doses of cough syrup such as Robitussin

Rohypnol: trade name for a depressant and tranquilizer flunitrazepam prescribed for the treatment of insomnia; commonly known as the "date rape" drug

Roid rage: violent behavior that results from using anabolic steroids

Role adjustment: a change, modification, alteration, or correction of the parts that people play in interactions

SASSI (Substance Abuse Subtle Screening Inventory): the best-known tool that screens for both drugs and alcohol

Schedule I drugs: those with a high potential for abuse and with no appropriate medical use, including heroin and LSD

Schedule II drugs: those with a high potential for abuse and some appropriate medical uses, including cocaine and amphetamines

Schedule III drugs: those used for medical purposes and with low to moderate risk for physical dependence but high risk for psychological dependence, including anabolic steroids

Schedule IV drugs: those used for medical purposes and with a low potential for abuse, including benzodiazepines such as Xanax, Librium, and Valium

Schedule V drugs: those used for medical purposes and with very low abuse potential, sometimes available without a prescription, such as cough medicines with
codeine

Screening: the effort to identify alcohol and drug abusers in order to refer them for an
in-depth assessment of their substance abuse problems

Secondary prevention: identifying a substance abuse problem in its earliest stages so
that intervention can occur

Sedative-hypnotic drugs: drugs that produce relaxation or sleep

Self-esteem: the value or worth a person places on himself or herself

Self-help programs: those that utilize the skills and abilities of the individual as resources to solve her or his problems, with support from a group of individuals
with similar problems

Serotonin: a neurotransmitter in the brain that regulates mood

Sexual identity: the degree to which individuals identify with the social and biological aspects of being a man or a woman

Sexual orientation: the sexual attraction to another person, with reference to the other
person's sex. It may exist on a continuum from same-sex attraction only, at one
end of the continuum, to opposite-sex attraction only, at the other end

Shaman: a person who acts as a medium between the visible and spiritual worlds and
who engages in healing practices

Shooting up: the act of injecting drugs such as heroin into the body with a syringe

Side effects: unintended effects from ingesting a drug

Sniffing: the act of inhaling a drug such as cocaine through the nose

Social facilitator: someone or something that reduces stress in a social situation

Social problem: a condition that is defined as a serious concern in society and that
needs action to resolve it

Social support network: an interconnection of people made up of relatives, friends,
and peers whom one can call on for help; different from a support group run for
therapeutic reasons

Socialization: lifelong learning process whereby individuals learn who they are and
what they need to know about their culture, including their place in it

Sonata (zaleplon): a prescription medication to induce sleep

Special K: a street name for the veterinary anesthetic ketamine, which is used as a
dissociative hallucinogen

Speedball: the injection of a combination of heroin and cocaine

Spirits: unsweetened alcoholic beverages that have at least a 20 percent alcohol content

Starter brews: beverages in which the taste of alcohol is disguised. Examples include
Mike's Hard Lemonade, Doc Otis' Hard Lemonade, Tequiza, and Hooper

Stimulants: drugs that stimulate the central nervous system, for example, cocaine and
amphetamines

Subcutaneous: a method of drug administration where drugs are inserted under the
skin

Suboxone: a combination of buprenorphine and naloxone used in the treatment of
heroin addiction

Synanon: the first therapeutic community, developed by Charles Dederich in California in 1958

Synergism: the interaction of two or more drugs to produce effects more intense than
the independent effects of each of the drugs

Target population: a group within society that is the focus of social policy

Temperance: moderate alcohol use rather than abstinence; the American Temperance
Society formed in the early nineteenth century; the concept of temperance developed into the Prohibition movement

Tertiary prevention: dealing with an established substance abuse problem through treatment and rehabilitation while trying to stem the effects of substance abuse on others

Therapeutic community: a live-in substance abuse treatment facility

Tolerance: repeated use of alcohol or drugs that results in a decreasing responsiveness to the drug and requires larger doses to obtain the original effects

TWEAK: a screening tool for substance abuse used primarily for pregnant women

Typology: a systematic classification of types or cases that share characteristics

Uniform Alcoholism and Intoxication Act: the 1971 federal law that decriminalized public intoxication and set up state- and federally funded alcohol detoxification programs

Uniform Crime Reports: reports regularly published by the Federal Bureau of Investigation that gives statistics on Index Crimes—murder, rape, robbery, burglary, arson, aggravated assault, and motor vehicle theft

Valium: trade name for the minor tranquilizer diazepam, in the class of benzodiazepines

Violent crimes: serious crimes, such as murder, aggravated assault, and rape, that cause physical harm and may involve a weapon

Vivitrol (naltrexone): a monthly injectible medication used in the treatment of alcoholics to reduce cravings for alcohol

Wernicke-Korsakoff syndrome: impaired memory that results from excessive alcohol use, and often associated with thiamine deficiency

Wine: an alcoholic beverage that is made from fermented grape juice

Withdrawal symptoms: physical and psychological reactions that follow the discontinuation of a drug that one is addicted to or dependent on, with symptoms that can include tremors, sweats, anxiety, insomnia, and vomiting

Xanax: trade name for the minor tranquilizer alprazolam, in the class of benzodiazepines

Zaleplon (Sonata): a prescription medication for the treatment of insomnia

Zolpidem tartrate (Ambien): a prescription medication for the short-term treatment of sleep disorders

Discussion Questions

Part 1　Alcohol, Drugs, and Society: An Overview

1. How do social and cultural factors influence drug-using behavior?
2. How are a drug user's expectations related to drug use?
3. Why are some drugs considered benign and other drugs considered destructive?
4. Should all drugs be legalized? If not, which ones?
5. How is drug scheduling related to federal drug policy?
6. Discuss four medical problems associated with chronic alcoholism.
7. Discuss the rise of the disease concept of alcoholism and whether the disease concept is relevant today.
8. Compare and contrast sedative and stimulant drugs.
9. What are the risk factors associated with becoming a substance abuser?
10. Define *dual diagnosis* and the implications for those who have it.

Part 2　Diverse Populations: Patterns of Use and Abuse

1. Discuss the impact of drug use on children and adolescents.
2. What are your own ideas for helping children and adolescents with substance abuse problems?
3. Compare and contrast the substance abuse problems of men and women.
4. What can be done to reduce fetal alcohol spectrum disorders?
5. Describe and explain the differences in patterns of substance abuse among different racial and ethnic groups.
6. In what ways are cultural issues important in providing treatment to diverse groups?
7. How are the drinking problems of the elderly different from those of younger people?

8. Discuss the obstacles to identifying and treating older persons with alcohol problems.
9. What is known about illicit drug use among the elderly?
10. What role should health-care practitioners have in helping their patients with drinking problems?

Part 3 Social Consequences of Substance Use and Abuse

1. Discuss conditions that increase the probability that college drinking will become a social problem.
2. Is it appropriate to have different binge drinking criteria for men and women? Why or why not?
3. Discuss the efforts of colleges to reduce college drinking. What are some of your own suggestions to reduce college drinking?
4. Define *codependency* and give some examples of codependent behavior.
5. Describe the potential effects that living in alcoholic families have on children.
6. Describe the relationship between substance abuse and family violence.
7. In what ways are substance abuse and crime interrelated?
8. What is the relationship between alcohol and crime? Does drinking cause crime?
9. What is the impact on society of mandatory sentences for drug offenders?
10. What can the correctional system do to reduce substance abuse among criminal offenders?

Part 4 Diagnosis, Treatment, Prevention, and Policy Implications

1. Discuss how people can learn if they have an alcohol or drug problem.
2. Compare and contrast screening tools with a substance abuse assessment.
3. Discuss the differences between substance abuse and substance dependence.
4. What should family members say to a relative with a substance abuse problem?
5. Discuss three types of treatment available to those with drug addiction.
6. What is the role of Alcoholics Anonymous in the treatment of alcoholism?
7. Discuss your own ideas for how to prevent children and adolescents from becoming substance abusers?
8. How effective is current drug policy in the United States?
9. Discuss several substance abuse prevention strategies.
10. Discuss your ideas for improving the field of substance abuse treatment.

References

Aalto, M., Tuunanen, M., Sillanaukee, P., and Seppa, K. (2006). Effectiveness of structured questionnaires for screening heavy drinking in middle-aged women. *Alcoholism: Clinical and Experimental Research, 30*(11), 1884–1888.

Abbott, S. (2004a, Summer). The grandparents and the COA. *NACoA Network.* Retrieved on January 26, 2007, from www.nacoa.org.

Abbott, S. (2004b, Winter). Parents of COAs. *NACoA Network.* Retrieved on January 26, 2007, from www.nacoa.org.

Abel, E. L. (1985). *Psychoactive drugs and sex.* New York: Springer.

Abrahams, R. B., and Patterson, R. D. (1978/1979). Psychological distress among the community elderly: Prevalence, characteristics, and implications for service. *International Journal of Aging and Human Development, 9*(1), 1–18.

Ackerman, R. J. (1983). *Children of alcoholics: A guide for parents, educators and therapists* (2nd ed.). New York: Fireside/Simon and Schuster.

Ackerman, R. J., and Gondolf, E. W. (1991). Adult children of alcoholics: The effects of background and treatment on ACOA symptoms. *International Journal of Addictions, 26*(11), 1159–1172.

Ackermann, K., Croissant, B., Diehl, A., Mann, K., Mundle, G., and Nakovics, H. (2005). Neuroimaging of gender differences in alcohol dependence: Are women more vulnerable? *Alcoholism: Clinical and Experimental Research, 29*(5), 896–901.

Adelman, R. D., and Albert, R. C. (1987). Medical students' attitudes toward the elderly: A critical review of the literature. *Gerontology and Geriatrics Education, 7,* 141–155.

Alcohol Alert (2007). *2006 drunk driving statistics.* Retrieved on July 22, 2008, from http://www.alcoholalert.com/drunk-driving-statistics.html.

Alcohol and Drug Abuse Institute. University of Washington (2007, Jan.) Substance use screening and assessment instruments database. Retrieved on February 8, 2007, from http://lib.adai.washington.edu/instruments/.

Alcoholics Anonymous (1939). *Alcoholics Anonymous.* New York: Works.

Alcoholics Anonymous (1976). *The big book,* 3rd ed. New York: AA World Services.

Alcoholics Anonymous World Services (1980). *Dr. Bob and the good old timers.* New York: AA.

Alibrandi, L. A. (1987). The folk psychotherapy of Alcoholics Anonymous. In S. Zinberg, J. Wallace, and S. B. Blume (eds.), *Practical Approaches to Alcoholism Psychotherapy,* 2nd ed. (239–257). New York: Plenum.

Allen, C. J. (1988). *The hold life has: Coca and cultural identity in an Andean community.* Washington, DC: Smithsonian Institution Press.

Allen, J .P., Columbus, M., and Fertig, J. (1995). Assessment in alcoholism treatment: An overview. In NIAAA (National Institute on Alcohol Abuse and Alcoholism), Treatment Handbook Series 4, *Assessment alcohol problems: A guide for clinicians and researchers* (NIH publication no. 95-375, 1–9). Washington, DC: US Department of Health and Human Services.

Allen, L. M., Nelson, C. J., Rouhbakhsh, P., Scifres, S. L., Greene, R. L., Korkinak, S. T., Davis, L. J., Jr., and Morse, R. M. (1998). Gender differences in factor structure of the Self-Administered Alcoholism Screening Test. *Journal of Clinical Psychology, 54*(4), 439–445.

Alleyne, V. (2006). Locked up means locked out: Women, addiction and incarceration. *Women and Therapy, 29*(3/4), 181–194.

Alsobrooks, D. P. (2002). Waging a battle against myths. *Corrections Today, 64*(7), 86–89.

Amadio, D. M. (2006). Internalized heterosexism, alcohol use, and alcohol-related problems among lesbians and gay men. *Addictive Behaviors, 31*(7), 1153–1162.

Amaro, H., and Hardy-Fanta, C. (1995). Gender relations in addiction and recovery. *Journal of Psychoactive Drugs, 27,* 325–337.

Amass, L., Kamien, J., and Reback, C. (2007). Characteristics and HIV risk behaviors of homeless, substance-using men who have sex with men. *Addictive Behaviors, 32*(3), 647–654.

American Academy of Pediatrics, Committee on Substance Abuse and Committee on Native American Child Health (1996). Inhalant abuse. *Pediatrics, 97*(3), 420–422.

American Psychiatric Association (1994). *Diagnostic and statistical manual of mental disorders,* 4th ed. Washington, DC: APA.

American Psychiatric Association (2000). *Diagnostic and statistical manual of mental disorders* (4th ed.–text revised). Washington, DC: APA.

American Society for Addiction Medicine (ASAM) (2002). *Patient placement criteria,* 2nd ed. revised (ASAM PPC-2R). Washington, DC: American Society for Addiction Medicine. Retrieved on July 21, 2008, from http://www.asam.org/Patient PlacementCriteria.html.

Ames, G., Grube, J., and Moore, R. (2000). Social control and workplace drinking norms: A comparison of two organizational cultures. *Journal of Studies on Alcohol, 61,* 203–219.

Amis, K. (1953). *Lucky Jim.* New York: Viking Press.

Anda, R. F., Whitfield, C. L., Felitti, V. J., Chapman, D., Edwards, V. J., Dube, S. R., and Williamson, D. F. (2002). Adverse childhood experiences, alcoholic parents, and later risk of alcoholism and depression. *Psychiatric Services, 53*(8), 1001–1009. Retrieved on January 30, 2007, from http://psychservices.psychiatry online.org.

Anderson, C. E., and Loomis, G. A. (2003). Recognition and prevention of inhalant abuse. *American Family Physician, 68*(5), 869–874.

Anderson, S. C. (1994). A critical analysis of the concept of codependency. *Social Work, 39*(6), 677–685.

Anderson, T. (2005). Dimensions of women's power in the illicit drug economy. *Theoretical Criminology, 9*(4), 371–400.

Arellano, C. M. (1996). Child maltreatment and substance use: A review of the literature. *Substance Use and Misuse, 31*(7), 927–935.

Associated Press. (2007, April 29). Panel backs lower crack sentences. *Boston Globe*, A13.

Associated Press (2008, May 3). Obituaries: Albert Hofmann, 102, Swiss chemist who invented LSD. *Boston Herald,* 21.

Atkinson, R. M. (1995). Treatment programs for aging alcoholics. In T. Beresford and E. Gomberg (eds.), *Alcohol and aging* (186–210). New York: Oxford University Press.

Babor, T. F., de la Fuente, J. R., Saunders, J., and Grant, M. (1989). *AUDIT: The Alcohol Use Disorders Identification Test: Guidelines for use in primary health care.* Geneva: World Health Organization.

Babor, T. F., De La Fuente, J. R., and Saunders, J. (1992). *AUDIT: Alcohol Use Disorders Identification Test: Guidelines for use in primary health care.* Geneva: World Health Organization.

Babor, T. F., Higgins-Biddle, J. C., Higgins, P. S., Gassman, R. A., and Gould, B. E. (2004). Training medical providers to conduct alcohol screening and brief interventions. *Substance Abuse, 25*(1), 17–26.

Babor, T. F., Steinberg, K., Anton, R., and Del Boca, F. (2000). Talk is cheap: Measuring drinking outcomes in clinical trials. *Journal of Studies on Alcohol, 61*(1), 55–63.

Bachman, R., and Peralta, R. (2002). The relationship between drinking and violence in an adolescent population: Does gender matter? *Deviant Behavior: An Interdisciplinary Journal, 23,* 1–9.

Baez, A. (2005). Alcohol use among Dominican Americans: An explanation. In M. Delgado (ed.), *Latinos and alcohol use/misuse revisited* (53–65). Binghamton, NY: Haworth.

Bahrke, M. S., and Yesalis, C. E., III. (1994). Weight training: A potential confounding factor in examining the psychological and behavioral effects of anabolic-androgenic steroids. *Sports Medicine, 18*(5), 309–318.

Baldwin, J. A., Johnson, R. M., Gotz, N. K., Wayment, H. A., and Elwell, K. (2006). Perspectives of college students and their primary health care providers on substance abuse screening and intervention. *Journal of American College Health, 55*(2), 115–120.

Bales, R. F. (1946). Cultural differences in rates of alcoholism. *Quarterly Journal of Studies on Alcohol 6,* 489–499.

Bandura, A. (1997). *Self-efficacy: The exercise of control.* New York: W. H. Freeman.

Barnett, O. W., and Fagan, R. W. (1993). Alcohol use in male spouse abusers and their female partners. *Journal of Family Violence, 8*(1), 1–25.

Barr, H. M., Bookstein, F. L., O'Malley, K. D., Connor, P. D., Huggins, J. E., and Streissguth. (2006). Binge drinking during pregnancy as a predictor of psychiatric disorders on the structured clinical interview for DSM-IV in young adult offspring. *American Journal of Psychiatry, 163*(6), 1061–1065.

Barry, K. L., Blow, F. C., Willenbring, M., McCormick, R., and Brockmann, L. M. (2004). Use of alcohol screening and brief interventions in primary care settings: Implementation and barriers. *Substance Abuse 25*(1), 27–36.

Barry, K. L., Oslin, D. W., and Blow, F. C. (2001). *Alcohol problems in older adults: Prevention and management.* New York: Springer.

Bartholow, B., Sher, K., and Kroll, J. (2003). Changes in heavy drinking over the third decade of life as a function of collegiate fraternity and sorority involvement: A multilevel analysis. *Health Psychology, 22,* 618–626.

Bartsch, A. J., Homola, G., Biller, A., Smith, S. M., Weijers, H. G., Wiesbeck, G. A., Jenkinson, M., De Stefano, N., Solymosi, L., and Bendszus, M. (2007). Manifestations of early brain recovery associated with abstinence from alcoholism. *Brain: A Journal of Neurology, 130*(10), 36–47.

Baseman, J., Ross, M., and Williams, M. (1999). Sale of sex for drugs and drugs for sex: An economic context of sexual risk behavior for STDs. *Sexually Transmitted Diseases, 26*(8), 444–449.

Bastiaens, L., Francis, G., and Lewis, K. (2000). The RAFFT as a screening tool for adolescent substance use disorders. *American Journal on Addictions, 9*(1), 10–15.

Batelaan, S. (2000). School social work with gay, lesbian and bisexual students: The case of Fairfax County. *Intercultural Education, 11*(2), 157–164.

Beattie, M. (1987). *Codependent no more*. Center City, MN: Hazelden.

Beauvais, F. (1998). American Indians and alcohol. *Alcohol Health and Research World, 22*(4), 253–259.

Beck, A. T., Wright, F. D., Newman, C. F., and Liese, B. S. (1993). *Cognitive therapy of substance abuse*. New York: Guilford Press.

Becker, H. (1963). *Outsiders*. New York: Free Press.

Becker, H. (1967). History, culture and subjective experience: An exploration of the social bases of drug-induced experiences. *Journal of Health and Social Behavior, 8*, 163–176.

Becker, H., Geer, B., and Hughes, E. (1968). *Making the grade*. New York: Wiley.

Beckford, R. S. (2001). Theology in the age of crack: Crack age, prosperity doctrine and "being there." *Black Theology in Britain: A Journal of Contextual Praxis, 4*, 9–24.

Beechem, M. (2002). *Elderly alcoholism: Intervention strategies*. Springfield, IL: Charles. C. Thomas.

Beeder, A. B., and Millman, R. B. (1997). Patients with psychopathology. In J. H. Lowinson, P. Ruiz, R. B. Millman, and J. G. Langrod (eds.), *Substance abuse: A comprehensive textbook,* 3rd ed. (551–563). Baltimore: Williams & Wilkins.

Belenko, S. R. (ed.) (2000). *Drugs and drug policy in America: A documentary history.* Westport, CT: Greenwood Press.

Belenko, S. (2001). *Research on drug courts: A critical review, 2001 update*. New York: National Center on Addiction and Substance Abuse (CASA) at Columbia University.

Benotsch, E. G., Kalichman, S., and Cage, M. (2002). Men who have met sex partners via the Internet: Prevalence, predictors, and implications for HIV prevention. *Archives of Sexual Behavior, 31*, 177–183.

Benotsch, E. G., Seeley, S., Mikytuck, J. J., Pinkerton, S. D., Nettles, C. D., and Ragsdale, K. (2006). Substance use, medication for sexual facilitation, and sexual risk behavior among traveling men who have sex with men. *Sexually Transmitted Disease, 33*(12), 706–711.

Benshoff, J. J., and Harrawood, L. K. (2003). Substance abuse and the elderly: Unique issues and concerns. *Journal of Rehabilitation, 69*(2), 43–48.

Benson, D., Charlton, C., and Goodhart, F. (1992). Acquaintance rape on campus: Literature review. *Journal of American College Health, 40*(4), 157–165.

Benson, J. D., Quackenbush, M., and Haas, D. K. (1996). HIV, women and alcohol recovery: Risks, reality and responses. In B. L. Underhill and D. G. Finnegan (eds.), *Chemical dependency: Women at risk* (109–127). New York: Harrington Park Press.

Beresford, T. (1995). Alcohol and aging: Looking ahead. In T. Beresford and E. Gomberg (eds.), *Alcohol and aging* (327–336). New York: Oxford University Press.

Berkowitz, A., and Perkins, H. (1986). Resident advisers as role models: A comparison of drinking patterns of resident advisers and their peers. *Journal of College Student Personnel, 27*, 146–153.

Bernard, M. A., McAuley, W. J., Belzer, J. A., Neal, K. S., and Reynolds, D. W. (2003). An evaluation of a low-intensity intervention to introduce medical students to healthy older people. *Journal of the American Geriatrics Society, 51*(3), 419–423.

Bersamin, M., Paschall, M. J., Fearnow-Kenney, M., and Wyrick, D. (2007). Effectiveness of a web-based alcohol-misuse and harm-prevention course among high- and low-risk students. *Journal of American College Health, 55*(4), 247–254.

Best, J. A., Brown, K. S., Cameron, R., Manske, S. M., and Santi, S. (1995). Gender and predisposing attributes as predictors of smoking onset: Implications for theory and practice. *Journal of Health Education, 26*(2), S52–S60.

Beyer, E. P., and Carnabucci, K. (2002). Group treatment of substance-abusing women. In S. L. A. Straussner and S. Brown (eds.), *The handbook of addiction treatment for women* (515–538). San Francisco: Jossey-Bass.

Bierut, L. J., Dinwiddle, S. H., Begleiter, H., Crowe, R. R., Hesselbrock, V., Nurnberger, J. I., Jr., Porjesz, B., Schuckit, M. A., and Reich, T. (1998). Familial transmission of substance abuse: Alcohol, marijuana, cocaine, and habitual smoking. *Archives of General Psychiatry, 55*, 982–988.

Bimbi, D. S., Nanin, J. E., Parsons, J. T., Vicioso, K. J., Missildine, W., and Frost, D. M. (2006). Assessing gay and bisexual men's outcome expectancies for sexual risk under the influence of alcohol and drugs. *Substance Use and Misuse, 41*(5), 643–652.

Bischof, G., Rumpf, H., Hapke, U., Meyer, C., and John, U. (2003). Types of natural recovery from alcohol dependence: A cluster analytic approach. *Addiction, 96*, 1327–1336.

Black, C. (1981). *It will never happen to me.* New York: Ballantine.

Black, C. (2002). *It will never happen to me: Growing up with addiction as youngsters, adolescents, adults.* Center City, MN: Hazelden.

Blake, M. (2004, Sept.-Oct.). Crack babies talk back. *Columbia Journalism Review, 5.* Retrieved on July 11, 2008, from http://cjrarchives.org/issues/2004/5/voices-blake.asp.

Blake, R. (1990). Mental health counseling and older problem drinkers. *Journal of Mental Health Counseling, 12*, 354–367.

Blane, H. (1977). Acculturation and drinking in an Italian-American community. *Journal of Studies on Alcohol, 38*, 1324–1344.

Blane, H. T., Overton, W. F., and Chafetz, M. E. (1963). Social factors in the diagnosis of alcoholism I: Characteristics of the patient. *Quarterly Journal of Studies on Alcohol, 24*, 640–663.

Blazer, D. G. (2002). Abstinence versus alcohol use among elderly rural Baptists: A test of reference group theory and health outcomes. *Aging and Mental Health, 6*, 47–54.

Blazer, D. G., and Pennybacker, M. R. (1984). Epidemiology of alcoholism in the elderly. In J. T. Hartford and T. Samorajski (eds.), *Alcoholism in the elderly: Social and biomedical issues* (25–33). New York: Raven.

Blood, L., and Cornwall, A. (1996). Childhood sexual victimization as a factor in the treatment of substance misusing adolescents. *Substance Use and Misuse, 31*(8), 1015–1039.

Blose, I. R. (1978). The relationship of alcohol to aging and the elderly. *Alcoholism: Clinical and Experimental Research, 2*, 17–21.

Blow, F. C. (1998). *Substance abuse among older Americans (Treatment Improvement Protocol [TIP]).* Series 26, DHHS No. SMA 98-3179. Washington, DC: US Government Printing Office.

Blow, F. C., and Barry, K. L. (2002). Use and misuse of alcohol among older women. *Alcohol Research and Health, 26*, 308–315.

Blumberg, L. U. (with Pittman, P. L.) (1991). *Beware the first drink: The Washington temperance movement and Alcoholics Anonymous.* Seattle, WA: Glen Abbey.

Blume, S. B. (1991). Women, alcohol, and drugs. In N. S. Miller (ed.), *Comprehensive handbook of drug and alcohol addiction* (147–177). New York: Marcel Dekker.

Bolding, G., Davis, M., Hart, G., and Elford, J. (2005). Gay men who look for sex on the Internet: Is there more HIV/STD risk with online partners? *AIDS, 19,* 961–968.

Bolding, G., Sherr, L., and Elford, J. (2002). Use of anabolic steroids and associated health risks among gay men attending London gyms. *Addiction, 97*(2), 195–199.

Bonnie, R., and Whitebread, C. (1974). *The marihuana conviction.* Charlottesville: University Press of Virginia.

Bornstein, R. F. (2006). The complex relationship between dependency and domestic violence: Converging psychological factors and social forces. *American Psychologist, 61*(6), 595–606.

Borsari, B., and Carey, K. (1999). Understanding fraternity drinking: Five recurring themes in the literature. *Journal of American College Health, 48,* 30–37.

Botvin, G. J., and Griffin, K. W. (2004). Life skills training: Empirical findings and future directions. *Journal of Primary Prevention, 25,* 211–232.

Botvin, G. J., and Griffin, K. W. (2005). Prevention science, drug abuse prevention, and life skills training: Comments on the state of the science. *Journal of Experimental Criminology, 1*(1), 63–78.

Botvin, G. J., Griffin, K. W., Paul, E., and Macaulay, A. P. (2003). Preventing tobacco and alcohol use among elementary school students through life skills training. *Journal of Child and Adolescent Substance Abuse, 12,* 1–18.

Bourgois, P. (1995). *In search of respect: Selling crack in el barrio.* New York: Cambridge University Press.

Bowe, C. (1992, March). Women and depression: Are we being overdosed? *Redbook,* 43–44, 47, 78.

Bowersox, J. A. (1996). Cocaine affects men and women differently, NIDA study shows. *NIDA Notes, 11*(1), 128.

Bowman, L. (1998, May 8). U.S. elderly widely abuse alcohol and medications. *Washington Times,* A7.

Boyd, C. J. (1993). The antecedents of women's crack cocaine abuse: Family substance abuse, sexual abuse, depression and illicit drug abuse. *Journal of Substance Abuse Treatment, 10*(5), 433–440.

Boyum, D., and Kleiman, M. A. R. (2003, Summer). Breaking the drug-crime link. *Public Interest,* 19–40.

Bradley, E. H., Webster, T. R., Baker, D., Schlesinger, M., Inouye, S. K., Barth, M. C., Lapane, K. L., Lipson, D., Stone, R., and Koren, M. J. (2004). Translating research into practice: Speeding the adoption of innovative health care programs. *Issue Brief.* New York: Commonwealth Fund.

Bradley, K. (1994). The primary care practitioner's role in the prevention and management of alcohol problems. *Alcohol Health and Research World, 18*(2), 97–104.

Brady, T. M., and Ashley, O. S. (eds.). (2005). *Women in substance abuse treatment: Results from the Alcohol and Drug Services Study (ADSS).* DHHS Publication No. SMA 04-3968, Analytic Series A-26. Rockville, MD: Substance Abuse and Mental Health Services Administration, Office of Applied Studies.

Braithwaite, J. (2001). Restorative justice and a new criminal law of substance abuse. *Youth and Society, 33*(2), 227–248.

Bray, R., Fairbank, J., and Marsden, M. (1999). Stress and substance use among military women and men. *American Journal of Drug and Alcohol Abuse, 25,* 239–256.

Brecher, E. M., and the Editors of *Consumer Reports* (1972). *Licit and illicit drugs*. Mt. Vernon, NY: Consumers Union.

Brems, C., Johnson, M. E., Neal, D., and Freemon, M. S. (2004). Child abuse history and substance abuse among men and women receiving detoxification services. *The American Journal of Drug and Alcohol Abuse, 30*(4), 799–821.

Brennan, P. L., and Moos, R. H. (1996). Late-life problem drinking: Personal environmental risk factors for 4-year functioning outcomes and treatment seeking. *Journal of Substance Abuse, 8,* 167–180.

Breslow, R. A., and Smothers, B. (2004). Drinking patterns of older Americans: National health interview surveys, 1997–2001. *Journal of Studies on Alcohol, 65*(2), 232–240.

Bretteville-Jensen, A. L. (2006). To legalize or not to legalize? Economic approaches to the decriminalization of drugs. *Substance Use and Misuse, 41,* 555–565.

Brook, J. R. (1993). Interactional theory: Its utility in explaining drug use behavior among African American and Puerto Rican youth. In M. R. De La Rosa and J.-L. R. Adrados (eds.), *Drug use among minority youth: Advances in research and methodology* (79–101). NIDA Research Monograph 130. Rockville, MD: National Institute on Drug Abuse.

Broom, D. (1995). Rethinking gender and drugs. *Drug and Alcohol Review, 14,* 411–415.

Brown, D. R., Lacey, K., Blount, J., Roman, D., and Brown, D. (2006). Black churches in substance use and abuse prevention efforts. *Journal of Alcohol and Drug Education, 5*(2), 43–65.

Brown, G., Maycock, B., and Burns, S. (2005). Your picture is your bait: Use and meaning of cyberspace among gay men. *Journal of Sex Research, 42,* 63–73.

Brown, J. A., and Hohman, M. (2006). The impact of methamphetamine use on parenting. In S. L. A. Straussner and C. H. Fewell (eds.), *Impact of substance abuse on children and families: Research and practice implications* (63–88). New York: Haworth.

Brown, S. A., Tapert, S. F., Granholm, E., and Delis, D. (2000). Neurocognitive functioning of adolescents: Effects of protracted alcohol use. *Alcoholism: Clinical and Experimental Research, 24*(2), 164–171.

Browne, A. (1987). *When battered women kill*. New York: Free Press.

Buchsbaum, D. G., Buchanan, R. G., Welsh, J., Centor, R. M., and Schnoll, S. H. (1992). Screening for drinking disorders in the elderly using the CAGE questionnaire. *Journal of the American Geriatrics Society, 40*(7), 662–665.

Budden, R. (2008, Jan. 31). Wine, women and strong spirits. *Marking Week*. Retrieved on February 6, 2008, from http://marketingweek.co.uk/cgi-bin/item.cgi?id=59477andd=259.

Buelow, S., and Buelow, G. (1995). Gender differences in late adolescents' substance abuse and family role development. *Journal of Child and Adolescent Substance Abuse, 4,* 27–38.

Bui, C. (1993, Sept.–Oct.). *Alcohol and sex: Some gender issues*. Paper presented at the Alcohol and Youth Seminar. Kew, Victoria.

Bull, S. S., McFarlane, M., Lloyd, L., and Rietmejer, C. (2004). The process of seeking sex partners online and the implications for STD/HIV prevention. *AIDS Care, 16,* 1012–1020.

Bull, S. S., Piper, R., and Rietmeijer, C. (2002). Men who have sex with men and also inject drugs: Profiles of risk related to the synergy of sex and drug injection behaviors. *Journal of Homosexuality, 42*(3), 31–51.

Burden, M. J., Jacobson, S. W., and Jacobson, J. L. (2005). Relation of prenatal alcohol exposure to cognitive processing speed and efficiency in childhood. *Alcoholism: Clinical and Experimental Research, 29*(8), 1473–1483.

Bureau of Justice Administration Drug Court Technical Assistance Project. (2003, Oct. 3). *Information relevant to female participants in drug courts: Summary overview memorandum.* Washington, DC: American University.

Burgdorf, D. C. (2006, June 8). A brief overview of GLBT history. Retrieved on January 29, 2007, from http://awsd.com/burgdorf/glbthistory.pdf.

Burgess, D. M., and Streissguth, A. P. (1992). Fetal alcohol syndrome and fetal alcohol effects: Principles for educators. *Phi Delta Kappan, 74*(1), 24–30.

Burns, L., Mattick, R., and Cooke, M. (2006). The use of record linkage to examine illicit drug use in pregnancy. *Addiction, 1001*(6), 873–882.

Bush, K., Kivlahan, D. R., McDonell, M. B., Fihn, S. D., and Bradley, K. A. (1998). The AUDIT alcohol consumption questions (AUDIT-C): An effective screening test for problem drinking. *Archives of Internal Medicine, 158,* 1789–1795.

Cabaj, R. P. (2000). Substance abuse, internalized homophobia, and gay men and lesbians: Psychodynamic issues and clinical implications. *Journal of Gay and Lesbian Psychotherapy, 3,* 5–24.

Cada, C. (2004, Nov. 1). Two alcohol poisoning deaths on Colorado campuses stir change. *Boston Globe,* A2.

Caetano, R., Ramisetty-Mikler, S., Floyd, L., and McGrath, C. (2006). The epidemiology of drinking among women of child-bearing age. *Alcoholism: Clinical and Experimental Research, 30*(6), 1023–1030.

Cahalan, D. (1970). *Problem drinkers.* San Francisco: Jossey-Bass.

Caldwell, C., Greene, A. D., and Billingsley, A. (1992). The black church as a family support system: Instrumental and expressive functions. *National Journal of Sociology, 6,* 21–40.

Callahan, C. (2000). Schools that have not protected and worked with gay and lesbian students have been sanctioned by the courts. *Education, 121*(2), 313–326.

Campbell, C. I., and Alexander, J. A. (2006). Availability of services for women in outpatient substance abuse treatment: 1995–2000. *Journal of Behavioral Health Services and Research, 33*(1), 1–19.

Carey, B. (2007, May 3). Drug makers to widen suicide risk warning. *Boston Globe,* A1, A19.

Cargiulo, T. (2007, March 1). Understanding the health impact of alcohol dependence. *American Journal of Health-System Pharmacy, 64,* supplement 3, S1–S17.

Carlson, B. E. (1977). Battered women and their assailants. *Social Work, 22,* 455–460.

Carlson, K. A. (1994). The prevention of substance abuse and misuse among the elderly. Olympia: University of Washington, Alcohol and Drug Abuse Institute.

CASA (National Center on Addiction and Substance Abuse at Columbia University). (2008). *"You've got drugs!" V: Prescription drug pushers on the Internet.* CASA White Paper. New York: CASA.

Cashin, J., and Meilman, P. (1998). Alcohol use in the Greek system: Follow the leader. *Journal of Studies on Alcohol, 59,* 63–70.

Casriel, D. (1966). *So fair a house.* Englewood Cliffs, NJ: Prentice-Hall.

Castile, G. P. (1996). The commodification of Indian identity. *American Anthropologist, 98*(4), 743–749.

Caudill, B. D., Crosse, S. B., Campbell, B., Howard, J., Luckey, B., and Blane, H. T. (2006). High-risk drinking among college fraternity members: A national perspective. *Journal of American College Health, 55*(3), 141–155.

Caulkins, J. P., Pacula, R. L., Paddock, S., and Chiesa, J. (2004). What we can—and cannot—expect from school-based drug prevention. *Drug and Alcohol Review, 23*(1), 79–87.

Cavendish, J. (2000). Church-based community activism: A comparison of black and white Catholic congregations. *Journal for the Scientific Study of Religion, 39,* 64–77.

Center for Alcohol Marketing and Youth (CAMY) (2007). Youth exposure to alcohol advertising on television and in national magazine, 2001–2006. Retrieved on January 22, 2008, from http://camy.org/research/tvmag1207/.

Center for Applied Behavioral Health Policy (2004, Fall). Motivational Incentives 101: What is it and why should we do it? *Bridging the Gap.* Tempe: University of Arizona. Retrieved September 12, 2005, from http://abhp.Arizona.edu/Training/Bridging_the_Gap_Fall_2004.pdf.

Center for Substance Abuse Prevention (2008). *Prevention platform.* Retrieved on July 4, 2008, from http://www.prevention.samhsa.gov/.

Center for Substance Abuse Treatment (1994a). *Screening and assessment for alcohol and other drug abuse among adults in the criminal justice system.* Treatment Improvement Protocol (TIP) Series, no. 7, DHHS Publication No. SMA 94-2076. Rockville, MD: Substance Abuse and Mental Health Services Administration.

Center for Substance Abuse Treatment (1994b). *Simple screening instruments for outreach for alcohol and other drug abuse and infectious diseases.* Treatment Improvement Protocol (TIP) Series, no. 11, DHHS Publication No. SMA 94-2094. Rockville, MD: Substance Abuse and Mental Health Services Administration.

Center for Substance Abuse Treatment (1997). *A guide to substance abuse services for primary care physicians.* Treatment Improvement Protocol (TIP) Series, DHHS Publication No. SMA 02-3687. Rockville, MD: Substance Abuse and Mental Health Services Administration.

Center for Substance Abuse Treatment (1999a). *Screening and assessing adolescents for substance use disorders.* Treatment Improvement Protocol (TIP) Series, no. 31, DHHS Publication No. (SMA) 02-3646. Rockville, MD: Substance Abuse and Mental Health Services Administration.

Center for Substance Abuse Treatment (1999b). *Treatment of adolescents with substance use disorders.* Treatment Improvement Protocol Series, no. 32, DHHS Publication No. (SMA) 99-3345. Rockville, MD: Substance Abuse and Mental Health Services Administration.

Center for Substance Abuse Treatment (2000). Workforce issues. Retrieved on December 28, 2008, from http://www.ct.gov/dmhas/LIB/dmhas?HRDWorkforceDevelopment.

Center for Substance Abuse Treatment (2001). *A provider's introduction to substance abuse treatment for lesbian, gay, bisexual and transgender individuals.* DHHS Publication No. SMA 01-3498. Rockville, MD: Substance Abuse and Mental Health Services Administration.

Center for Substance Abuse Treatment (2004). *Substance abuse treatment and family therapy.* Treatment Improvement Protocol (TIP) Series, no. 39, DHHS Publication No. SMA 04-3957. Rockville, MD: Substance Abuse and Mental Health Services Administration.

Center for Substance Abuse Treatment (2005). *Buprenorphine.* Retrieved on February 18, 2005, from http://buprenorphine.samhas.gov/.

Center for Substance Abuse Treatment (2006). *Introduction to methadone.* Rockville, MD: Substance Abuse and Mental Health Services Administration.

Center for Youth Development and Policy Research. (2003, March). *Pathways to prevention: Guiding youth to wise decisions—A prevention guide for youth leaders in FAITH communities.* Minnesota Institute of Public Health: Fleishman-Hillard, United States.

Center for Youth Development and Policy Research (2008). *AED: Center for Youth Development and Policy Research.* Retrieved on July 21, 2008, from cydpr.aed.org/.

Centers for Disease Control (2005). *Hepatitis C fact sheet.* Retrieved on May 8, 2007, from http://www.cdc.gov/hepatitis.

Centers for Disease Control (2006a). *Fetal alcohol spectrum disorders.* Retrieved on January 22, 2008, from http://www.cdc.gov/NCBDDD/fas/fasask.htm#how.

Centers for Disease Control (2006b). *Impaired driving facts–NCIPC.* Retrieved on April 26, 2007, from http://www.cdc.gov/ncipc/factsheets/driving.htm.

Centers for Disease Control (2007). *A glance at the HIV/AIDS epidemic.* Retrieved on May 8, 2007, from http://www.cdc.gov/hiv/resources/factsheets/At-A-Glance.htm.

Cermak, T. L. (1986). *Diagnosing and treating co-dependence.* Minneapolis: Johnson Institute.

Chan, A.W., Pristach, E. A., Welte, J. W., and Russell, M. (1993). Use of the TWEAK test in screening for alcoholism/heavy drinking in three populations. *Alcoholism: Clinical and Experimental Research, 17*(6), 1188–1192.

Chang, G. (2002). Brief intervention for problem drinking and women. *Journal of Substance Abuse Treatment, 23*(1), 1–7.

Chang, G. (2004/2005). Screening and brief intervention in prenatal care settings. *Alcohol Research and Health, 28*(2). Retrieved on July 11, 2007, from http://pubs.niaaa.nih.gov/publications/arh28-2/80-84.htm.

Chan-Pensley, E. (1999). Alcohol Use Disorders Identification Test: A comparison between paper and pencil and computerized versions. *Alcohol and Alcoholism, 34*(6), 882–885.

Chavez, E. L., and Swain, R. C. (1992). Hispanic substance abuse: Problems in epidemiology. *Drugs and Society, 6*(3/4), 211–230; also in J. E. Trimble, C. S. Bolek, and S. J. Niemcryk (eds.), *Ethnic and multicultural drug abuse.* New York: Haworth.

Cheng, D. M., Nunes, D., Libman, H., Vidaver, J., Alperen, J. K., Saitz, R., and Samet, J. H. (2007). Impact of hepatitis C on HIV progression in adults with alcohol problems. *Alcoholism: Clinical and Experimental Research, 31*(5), 829–836.

Cherpitel, C. J. (1997). Brief screening instruments for alcoholism. *Alcohol Health and Research World, 21*(4), 348–351.

Cherpitel, C. J. (1999). Screening for alcohol problems in the US general population: A comparison of the CAGE and TWEAK by gender, ethnicity, and services utilization. *Journal of Studies on Alcohol, 60*(5), 705–711.

Cherpitel, C. J. (2000). Brief screening instrument for problem drinking in the emergency room: The RAPS4. *Journal of Studies on Alcohol, 613*, 447–449.

Cherpitel, C. J., and Bazargan, S. (2003). Screening for alcohol problems: Comparison of the audit, RAPS4 and RAPS4-QF among African American and Hispanic patients in an inner city emergency department. *Drug and Alcohol Dependence, 71*, 275–280.

Cherpitel, C. J., and Borges, G. (2000). Screening instruments for alcohol problems: A comparison of cut points between Mexican American and Mexican patients in the emergency room. *Substance Use and Misuse, 35*(10), 1419–1430.

Chezem, L. (2004/2005). Legal barriers to alcohol screening in emergency department and trauma centers. *Alcohol Research and Health, 28*(2), 73–77.

Chinman, M. P., Imm, P., and Wandersman, A. (2004). *Getting to outcomes 2004: Promoting accountability through methods and tools for planning, implementation, and evaluation.* TR-101-CDC. Santa Monica, CA: Rand.

Cho, H., Hallfors, D., and Sanchez, V. (2005). Evaluation of a high school peer group intervention for at-risk youth. *Journal of Abnormal Child Psychology, 33*(3), 363–374.

Cho, Y. (2004). Composition of occupation and industry and women's alcohol consumption. *Journal of Studies on Alcohol, 65*, 345–352.

Chopra, R. N., Chopra, G. S., and Chopra, I. C. (1942). Alcoholic beverages in India. *Indian Medical Gazette, 77*, 225–230.

Clark, W. (1991). Conception of alcohol problems. In W. Clark and M. Hilton (eds.), *Alcohol in America* (165–172). Albany: State University of New York.

Clark, W., and Hilton, M. (eds.) (1991). *Alcohol in America.* Albany: State University of New York.

Clatts, M. C., Goldsamt, L., Yi, H., and Gwadz, M. V. (2005). Homelessness and drug abuse among young men who have sex with men in New York City: A preliminary epidemiological trajectory. *Journal of Adolescence, 28*(2), 201–214.

Cloninger, C. R. (1987). Neurogenetic adaptive mechanisms in alcoholism. *Science, 236*, 410–416.

Cloninger, C. R., Sigvardsson, S., Reich, T., and Bohman, M. (1986). Inheritance of risk to develop alcoholism. In M. C. Braude and H. M. Chao (eds.), *Genetic and biological markers in drug abuse and alcoholism* (86–96). NIDA Research Monograph, 66.

Coccaro, E. F., and Miles, A. M. (1984). The attitudinal impact of training gerontology/geriatrics in medical school: A review of the literature and perspective. *Journal of the American Geriatrics Society, 32*, 762–768.

Cochran, B. N., and Cauce, A. M. (2006). Characteristics of lesbian, gay, bisexual, and transgendered individuals entering substance abuse treatment. *Journal of Substance Abuse Treatment, 30*(2), 135–146.

Cochran, B. N., Peavy, K. M., and Robohm J. S. (2007). Do specialized services exist for LGBT individuals seeking treatment for substance misuse? A study of available treatment programs. *Substance Use and Misuse, 42*, 161–176.

Cochran, B. N., Stewart, A. J., Ginzler, J. A., and Cauce, A. M. (2002). Challenges faced by homeless sexual minorities: Comparisons of gay, lesbian, bisexual, and transgender homeless adolescents with their heterosexual counterparts. *American Journal of Public Health, 92*(5), 773–777.

Cochran, S. D., Ackerman, D., Mays, V. M., and Ross, M. W. (2004). Prevalence of non-medical drug use and dependence among homosexually active men and women in the U.S. population. *Addiction, 99*(8), 989–998.

Cohn, E. S., and White, S. O. (1990). *Legal socialization: A study in norms and rules.* New York: Springer-Verlag.

Colfax, G., Vittinghoff, E., Husnik, M. J., McKiman, D., Buchbinder, S., Koblin, B., Celum, C., Chesney, M., Huang, Y., Mayer, K., Bozeman, S., Judson, F. N., Bryant, K. J., and Coates, T. J. (2004). Substance use and sexual risk: A participant- and episode-level analysis among a cohort of men who have sex with men. *American Journal of Epidemiology, 159*(10), 1002–1012.

"College Drinking—Changing the Culture." (2005). Retrieved on April 1, 2007, from http://www.collegedrinkingprevention.gov/StatsSummaries.

Collins, B. G. (1993). Reconstruing codependency using self-in-relation theory: A feminist perspective. *Social Work, 38*(4), 361–504.

Collins, R. L. (1992). Methodological issues in conducting substance abuse research on ethnic minority populations. *Drugs and Society 6*, 211–230; also in J. E. Trimble, C. S. Bolek, and S. J. Niemcryk (eds.), *Ethnic and multicultural drug abuse.* New York: Haworth.

Collins, R., Ellickson, P., and Bell, R. (1999). Simultaneous polydrug use among teens: Prevalence and predictors. *Journal of Substance Abuse, 10*(3), 233–253.

Collins, R. L., and McNair, L. D. (2002). Minority women and alcohol use. *Alcohol Research and Health, 26*(4), 251–256.

Collins, R., Schell, T., Ellickson, P., and McCaffrey, D. (2003). Predictors of beer advertising awareness among eighth graders. *Addictions, 98*(9), 1297–1306.

Compton, W. M., Cottler, L. B., Abdallah, A. B., Phelps, D. L., Spitznagal, E. L., and Horton, J. C. (2000). Substance dependence and other psychiatric disorders among drug dependent subjects: Race and gender correlates. *American Journal of Addictions, 9*(2), 113–125.

Conlon, E. (2004). *Blue blood.* New York: Riverhead.

Connors, N. A., Bradley, R. H., Whiteside-Mansell, L., and Crone, C. C. (2001). A comprehensive substance abuse treatment program for women and their children: An initial evaluation. *Journal of Substance Abuse Treatment, 21*(2), 67–75.

Coogle, C. L., Osgood, N. J., and Parham, I. A. (2001). Addictions services: Follow-up to the statewide model detection and prevention program for geriatric alcoholism and alcohol abuse. *Community Mental Health Journal, 37*(5), 381–391.

Cope, N. (2006). Drug use in prison: The experience of young offenders. In R. Tewksbury, *Behind bars: Readings on prison culture.* Upper Saddle River, NJ: Pearson Prentice Hall, 285–297. (Reprinted from *Drugs: Education, Prevention and Policy, 7*[4], 2000, 355–366.)

CORE Institute (2006a). *Alcohol and Drug Survey 2005.* Carbondale: Southern Illinois University. Retrieved on April 1, 2007, from http://www.sie/edu/departments/coreinst/.

CORE Institute (2006b, June). *Benchmarks for success: Gauging the performance of college prevention efforts.* Carbondale: Southern Illinois University.

Corliss, H. L., Grella, C., and Mays, V. (2006). Drug use, drug severity, and help-seeking behaviors of lesbian and bisexual women. *Journal of Women's Health, 15*(5), 556–568.

Cornelius, M. D., Day, N. L., Cornelius, J. R., Geva, D., Taylor, P. M., and Richardson, G. A. (1993). Drinking patterns and correlates of drinking among pregnant teenagers. *Alcoholism: Clinical and Experimental Research, 17*(2), 290–294.

Courtwright, T. D., Joseph, H., and Des Jarlais, D. C. (1981). Memories from the street: Oral histories of elderly methadone patients. *The Oral History Review,* 947–964.

Covington, S. S. (2002). Helping women recover: Creating gender-responsive treatment. In S. L. A. Straussner and S. Brown (eds.), *The handbook of addiction treatment for women* (52–72). San Francisco: Jossey-Bass.

Coyle, M. (2003). *Race and class penalties in crack cocaine sentencing.* The Sentencing Project. Retrieved on December 20, 2005, from http://www.sentencingproject.org.

Crothers, M., and Warren, L. W. (1996). Parental antecedents of adult codependency. *Journal of Clinical Psychology, 52*(2), 231–239.

Cruz, J. M., and Peralta, R. L. (2001). Family violence and substance use: The perceived effects of substance use within gay male relationships. *Violence and Victims, 16*(2), 161–172.

Curtis, O. (1999). *Chemical dependency: A family affair.* Pacific Grove, CA: Brooks/Cole.

Davies, D. (1962). Normal drinking in recovered alcohol addicts. *Quarterly Journal of Studies on Alcohol, 23,* 94–104.

Dawson, D., Grant, B., Chou, S., and Stinson, F. (2007). The impact of partner alcohol problems on women's physical and mental health. *Journal of Studies on Alcohol, 68,* 66–75.

Dawson, D., Grant, B., Stinson, F., and Chou, S. (2006). Maturing out of alcohol dependence: The impact of transitional life events. *Journal of Studies on Alcohol, 67,* 195–203.

Dawson, D. A., Li, T. K., and Grant, B. F. (2007). A prospective study of risk drinking: At risk for what? *Journal of Clinical Psychiatry, 68*(12), 1913–1920.

Day, N. L. (1995). Editorial: Research on the effects of prenatal alcohol exposure—A new direction. *The American Journal of Public Health, 85*(12), 1614–1615.

Dayton, T. (2004, Sept.–Oct.) When natural disasters happen. *NACoA Network.* Retrieved on January 26, 2007, from www.nacoa.org.

Dear, G. E. (2004). Test-retest reliability of the Holyoake Codependency Index with Australian students. *Psychological Reports, 94*(2), 482–484.

Dear, G. E., and Roberts, C. M. (2005). Validation of the Holyoake Codependency Index. *The Journal of Psychology, 139*(4), 293–313.

DeBellis, R., Smith, B. S., Choi, S., and Malloy, M. (2005). Management of delirium tremens. *Journal of Intensive Care Medicine, 20*(3), 164–173.

Degenhardt, L. (2005). Drug use and risk behaviour among regular Ecstasy users: Does sexuality make a difference? *Culture, Health and Sexuality, 7*(6), 599–614.

DeJong, W., Schneider, S., Towvim, L., Murphy, M., Doerr, E., Simonsen, N., Mason, K., and Scribner, R. (2006). A multisite randomized trial of social norms marketing campaigns to reduce college student drinking. *Journal of Studies on Alcohol, 67,* 868–879.

De Leon, G. (1997). *Community as method: Therapeutic communities for special populations and special settings.* Westport, CT: Praeger.

de Miranda, J. (2004). Disability policy matters in addiction education. *Journal of Teaching in the Addictions, 3*(1), 65–69.

Dew, B. J., and Chaney, M. (2004). Sexual addiction and the Internet: Implications for the gay male. *Journal of Addictions and Offender Counseling 24,* 101–114.

DiBari, M., Silvestrini, G., Chiarlone, M., De Alfieri, W., Patussi, V., Timpanelli, M., Pini, R., Masotti, G., and Marchionni, A. (2002). Features of excessive alcohol drinking in older adults distinctively captured by behavioral and biological screening instruments: An epidemiological study. *Journal of Clinical Epidemiology, 55*(1), 41–47.

Dolcini, M. M., Catania, J., Stall, R. D., and Pollack, L. (2003). The HIV epidemic among older men who have sex with men. *Journal of Acquired Immune Deficiency Syndromes, 33,* S115–S121.

Dolin, B. (2001). National drug policy: United States of America. (Prepared for the Senate Special Committee on Illegal Drugs.) Retrieved on October 10, 2005, from http://www.parl.gc.ca/37/1/parlbus/commbus/senate/com-e/ille-e/library-e/dolin2-e.htm.

D'Onofrio, G., and Degutis, L. C. (2004/2005). Screening and brief intervention in the emergency department. *Alcohol Research and Health, 28*(2), 63–72.

Dorris, M. (1989). *The broken cord.* New York: Harper & Row.

Douglass, F. (1892). *Life and times of Fredrick Douglass.* New York: Collier.

Downs, M. F. (2006, March 14). Reports raise questions about sleeping pill side effect. Is Ambien sleepwalking understood? *Washington Post,* HE01.

Drabble, L., and Trocki, K. (2005). Alcohol consumption, alcohol-related problems, and other substance use among lesbian and bisexual women. *Journal of Lesbian Studies, 9*(3), 19–30.

Drake, R. E., O'Neal, E. L., and Wallach, M. A. (2008). A systematic review of psychosocial research on psychosocial interventions for people with co-occurring severe mental and substance use disorders. *Journal of Substance Abuse Treatment, 34,* 123–138.

Drapkin, M. L., McCrady, B. S., Swingle, J. M., and Epstein, E. E. (2005). Exploring bidirectional couple violence in a clinical sample of female alcoholics. *Journal of Studies on Alcohol, 66,* 213–219.

Drevenstedt, G. (1998). Race and ethnic differences in the effects of religious attendance on subjective health. *Review of Religious Research, 39*(3), 245–263.

Drug Abuse Warning Network (2005). *National estimates of drug-related emergency department visits.* Rockville, MD: Substance Abuse and Mental Health Services Administration, Office of Applied Studies.

Drug Enforcement Administration Congressional Testimony (2001, March 27). Laura M. Nagel, deputy assistant administrator, Office of Diversion Control, before the House Committee on Government Reform. Retrieved on February 9, 2009, from http://www.usdoj.gov/dea/pubs/angrtest/ct032701.htm.

Drug Enforcement Administration (2005). *Drugs of abuse.* Retrieved on May 3, 2007, from http://www.usdoj.gov/dea/pubs/abuse/.

Drug Enforcement Administration (2008, April). *Lists of controlled substances.* Retrieved on July 8, 2008, from http://www.deadiversion.usdog.gov/schedules/schedules.htm.

Dube, S. R., Felitti, V. J., Dong, M., Chapman, D. P., Giles, W. H., and Anda, R. F. (2003). Childhood abuse, neglect, and household dysfunction and the risk of illicit drug use: The Adverse Childhood Experiences Study. *Pediatrics, 111*(3), 564–572.

Dunn, M., and Goldman, M. (1998). Age and drinking related differences in the memory organization of alcohol experiences in third, sixth, ninth, and twelfth grade children. *Journal of Consulting and Clinical Psychology, 66,* 579–585.

Easton, C. J. (2006, Jan. 1). The role of substance abuse in intimate partner violence. *Psychiatric Times, 25*(1), 1–2.

Ebberhart, N. C., Luzcak, S. E., Avanecy, N., and Wall, T. L. (2003). Family history of alcohol dependence in Asian Americans. *Journal of Psychoactive Drugs, 35*(3), 375–377.

Ebell, M. H. (2004). Routine screening for depression, alcohol problems, and domestic violence. *American Family Physician, 69*(10), 2421–2422.

Eberle, P. A. (1982). Alcohol abusers and non-abusers: A discriminant analysis of differences between two subgroups of batterers. *Journal of Health and Social Behavior, 23,* 260–271.

Edenberg, H. J., and Foroud, T. (2006). The genetics of alcoholism: Identifying specific genes through family studies. *Addiction Biology, 11*(3–4), 386–396.

Eisenberg, M., and Wechsler, H. (2003). Social influences on substance-use behaviors of gay, lesbian and bisexual college students: Findings from a national study. *Social Science and Medicine, 57*(10), 913–923.

El-Bassel, N., Gilbert, L., Wu, E., Go, H., and Hill, J. (2005). Relationship between drug abuse and intimate partner violence: A longitudinal study among women receiving methadone. *American Journal of Public Health, 95*(3), 465–470.

El-Guebaly, N. (1995). Alcohol and polysubstance abuse among women. *The Canadian Journal of Psychiatry, 40*(2), 73–79.

Eliason, M. J., and Hughes, T. (2004). Treatment counselors' attitudes about lesbian, gay, bisexual, and transgendered clients: Urban vs. rural settings. *Substance Use and Misuse, 39*(4), 625–644.

Ellickson, P., Martino, S., and Collins, R. (2004). Marijuana use from adolescence to young adulthood: Multiple developmental trajectories and their associated outcomes. *Health Psychology, 23*(3), 299–307.

Ellickson, P., Tucker, J., and Klein, D. (2003). Ten year prospective study of public health problems associated with early drinking. *Pediatrics, 111*(5), 949–955.

Ellis, A., McInerney, J. F., DiGiuseppe, R., and Yeager, R. J. (1988). *Rational-emotive therapy with alcoholics and substance abusers.* Boston: Allyn and Bacon.

Emery, T. (2000, Sept. 16). MIT agrees to pay $4.75 million. Associated Press. Retrieved on December 24, 2008, from http://www.greekchat.com/gcforums/archive/index.php/t-526.html.

Enoch, M. A., and Goldman, D. (2002). Problem drinking and alcoholism: Diagnosis and treatment. *American Family Physician, 65*(3), 441–448.

Ettner, S. L., Huang, D., Evans, E., Ash, D. R., Jourabechi, M., and Hser, Y. I. (2006). Benefit-cost in the California Treatment Outcome Project: Does substance abuse treatment "pay for itself"? *Health Sciences Research, 41*(1), 192–213.

Ewing, J. A. (1984). Detecting alcoholism: The CAGE questionnaire. *Journal of the American Medical Association, 252*, 1905–1907.

Facts on Drug Courts (2008). Retrieved March 4, 2008, from http://www.nadcp.org/whatis/.

Fagan, J. (1990). Editor's introduction: Myths and realities about crack. *Contemporary Drug Problems, 17*(1), 1–7.

Faiia, M. (1991). Community perceptions of a social problem: The case of pre-teen drinking. Doctoral diss. (unpublished), Northeastern University, Boston.

Fancher, R. (1995). *Cultures of healing: Correcting the image of American mental health care.* New York: W. H. Freeman.

Faupel, C. E., Horowitz, A. M., and Weaver, G. S. (2004). *The sociology of American drug use.* New York: McGraw-Hill.

Fendrich, M., Hubell, A., and Lurigio, A. J. (2006). Providers' perceptions of gender-specific drug treatment. *Journal of Drug Issues, 36*(3), 667–687.

Ferraro, K. F., and Albrecht-Jensen, C. M. (1991). Does religion influence adult health? *Journal for the Scientific Study of Religion, 30*, 193–202.

Ferraro, K. F., and Koch, J. R. (1994). Religion and health among black and white adults: Examining social support and consolation. *Journal for the Scientific Study of Religion, 33*(4), 362–375.

Field, P. (1962). A new cross-cultural study of drunkenness. In D. J. Pittman and C. R. Snyder (eds.), *Society, culture and drinking patterns* (48–74). New York: Wiley.

Figdor, E., and Kaeser, L. (2005). Concerns mount over punitive approaches to substance abuse among pregnant women. *The Guttmacher Report on Public Policy, 1*(5), 3–5.

Finlayson, R. E. (1995). Comorbidity in elderly alcoholics. In T. Beresford and E. Gomberg (eds.), *Alcohol and aging* (56–69). New York: Oxford University Press.

Fischer, J. L., Spann, L., and Crawford, D. (1991). Measuring codependency. *Alcoholism Treatment Quarterly, 8*(1), 352–363.

Fishbein, D. H., and Perez, D. M. (2000). A regional study of risk factors for drug abuse and delinquency: Sex and racial differences. *Journal of Child and Family Studies, 9*(4), 461–479.

Fisher, B. (2005, Feb. 27). Drinking: An adolescent story. *Boston Sunday Globe*, D7.

Flanzer, J. D. (1982). *The many faces of family violence.* Springfield, IL: Charles C. Thomas.

Fleming, M. F. (1997). Strategies to increase alcohol screening in health care settings. *Alcohol Health and Research World, 21*(4), 340–347.

Fleming, M. F. (2004/2005). Screening and brief intervention in primary care settings. *Alcohol Research and Health, 28*(2). Retrieved on July 11, 2007, from http://pubs.niaaa.nih/gov/publications/arh28-2/57-62.htm.

Fleming, M. F., and Manwell, L. B. (1999). Brief intervention in primary care settings: A primary treatment method for at-risk, problem, and dependent drinkers. *Alcohol Health and Research World, 23*(2), 128–133.

Floyd, R. L., Sobell, M., Velasquez, M. M., Ingersoll, K., Nettleman, M., Sobell, L., Dolan Mullen, P., Ceperich, S., von Sternberg, K., Bolton, B., Skarpness, B., and Nagaraja, J. (2007). Preventing alcohol-exposed pregnancies: A randomized controlled trial. *American Journal of Preventive Medicine, 32*(1), 1–10.

Fong, T. W., and Tsuang, J. (2007, Nov.). Asian-Americans, addictions, and barriers to treatment. *Psychiatry, MMC*. Retrieved on December 19, 2008, from www.psychiarymmc.com/asian-americans-addiction-and-barriers-to-treatment/.

Ford, C. V., and Sbordone, R. J. (1980). Attitudes of psychiatrists toward elderly patients. *American Journal of Psychiatry, 137*, 571–575.

Ford, J., and Kadushin, C. (2002). Between sacral belief and moral community: A multidimensional approach to the relationship between religion and alcohol among whites and blacks. *Sociological Forum, 17*(2), 255–279.

Forsberg, L., Ekman, S., Halldin, J., and Ronnberg, S. (2000). Brief intervention for risk consumption of alcohol at an emergency surgical ward. *Addictive Behaviors, 25*(3), 471–475.

Franken, I. H. A., and Hendricks, V. M. (2001). Screening and diagnosis of anxiety and mood disorders in substance abuse patients. *The American Journal of Addictions, 10*, 30–39.

French, L. A. (2004). Alcohol and other drug addictions among Native Americans: The movement toward tribal-centric treatment programs. *Alcoholism Treatment Quarterly, 22*(1), 81–91.

Frone, M. (2006). Prevalence and distribution of alcohol use and impairment in the workplace: US national survey. *Journal of Studies on Alcohol, 67*, 147–156.

Gallon, S. L., Gabriel, R. M., and Knudsen, J. R. W. (2003). The toughest job you'll ever love: A Pacific Northwest treatment workforce survey. *Journal of Substance Abuse Treatment, 24*, 183–196. Retrieved on September 20, 2005, from http://www.annapoliscoalition.org/pdfs/Advancing%20the%20Current%20State%202003%20FINAL.pdf.

Gambert, S. R., Newton, M., and Duthie, E. H., Jr. (1984). Medical issues in alcoholism in the elderly. In J. T. Hartford and T. Samorajski (eds.), *Alcoholism in the elderly: Social and biomedical issues* (175–191). New York: Raven.

Gans, S. E., and Shook, K. L. (eds.) (1994). *Policy compendium on tobacco, alcohol, and other substances affecting adolescents: Alcohol and other harmful substances* (Report Order Department OPO 18694). Chicago: American Medical Association.

Garbarino, M. (1971). Life in the city: Chicago. In J. O. Waddell and O. M. Watson (eds.), *The American Indian in urban society* (168–205). Boston: Little, Brown.

Garcia, V., and Gondolf, E. (2004). Transnational Mexican farmworkers and problem drinking: A review of the literature. *Contemporary Drug Problems, 31*(1), 129–164.

Garrett, G. R., and Anderson, W. (2003). Italy report. In S. Nemes and S. V. Libretto (eds.), *Promising practices in drug treatment: Findings from Europe* (vol. 1), *Latin America* (vol. 2), *and Southeast Asia* (vol. 3) (79–90). Washington, DC: US Department of State, Bureau of International Narcotics and Law Enforcement Affairs.

Garrett, G. R., Gallon, S., and Earp, B. (2003). Malaysia report. In S. Nemes and S. V. Libretto (eds.), *Promising practices in drug treatment: Findings from Europe* (vol. 1), *Latin America* (vol. 2), *and Southeast Asia* (vol. 3) (17–34). Washington, DC: US Department of State, Bureau of International Narcotics and Law Enforcement Affairs.

Garrity, T., Leukefeld, C., Falck, R., Wang, J., and Booth, B. (2007). Physical health, illicit drug use, and demographic characteristics in rural stimulant users. *Rural Health, 23*, 99–107.

Gary, I. E., and Gary, R. B. (1985). Treatment needs of black alcoholic women. *Alcoholism Treatment Quarterly, 2*, 97–113.

George, W. H., La Marr, J., Barrett, K., and McKinnon, T. (1999). Alcoholic parentage, self-labeling, and endorsement of ACOA-codependent traits. *Psychology of Addictive Behaviors, 13*(1), 39–48.

Gerstein, D. R., Johnson, R. A., Harwood, H., Fountain, D., Suter, N., and Malloy, K. (1994). Evaluating recovery services: The California Drug and Alcohol Treatment Assessment (CALDATA), Executive summary. Retrieved on December 27, 2008, from http://www.ncjrs.gov/App/Publications/abstract.aspx?ID_188556.

Gfellner, B. M., and Hundleby, J. D. (1994). Developmental and gender differences in drug use and problem behaviour during adolescence. *Journal of Child and Adolescent Substance Misuse, 3*(3), 59–74.

Gilbert, L., El-Bassel, N., Manuel, J., Wu, E., Go, H., Golder, S., Seewald, R., and Sanders, G. (2006). An integrated relapse prevention and relationship safety intervention for women on methadone: Testing short-term effects on intimate partner violence and substance use. *Violence and Victims, 21*(5), 657–672.

Gil-Rivas, V., Fiorentine, R., Anglin, M. D., and Taylor, E. (1997). Sexual and physical abuse: Do they compromise drug treatment outcomes? *Journal of Substance Abuse Treatment, 14*(4), 351–358.

Girls and substance abuse: Special risks, predictors, and needs. (2006, March). *Child Protection Law Report, 32*(3), 24.

Glover, N. M., Janikowski, T. P., and Benshoff, J. J. (1996). Substance abuse and past incest contact: A national perspective. *Journal of Substance Abuse Treatment, 13*(3), 185–193.

Goetz, B., and Mitchell, R. E. (2006). Pre-arrest/booking drug control strategies: Diversion to treatment, harm reduction and police involvement. *Contemporary Drug Problems, 33*(3), 473–520.

Goldbloom, D. S., Naranjo, C. A., Bremner, K. E., and Hicks, L. K. (1992). Eating disorders and alcohol abuse in women. *British Journal of Addictions, 87*(6), 913–920.

Goldstein, P. (1985). The drugs/violence nexus: A tripartite conceptual framework. *Journal of Drug Issues, 15,* 493–506.

Goldstein, S. (2006, Summer). The marketing of ADHD. *Annals of the American Psychotherapy Association, 32–33.

Golub, A., Johnson, B. D., and Dunlap, E. (2005). The growth in marijuana use among American youths during the 1990s and the extent of blunt smoking. *Journal of Ethnicity in Substance Abuse, 4*(3–4), 1–21.

Gomberg, E. S. L. (1995). Older alcoholics: Entry into treatment. In T. Beresford and E. Gomberg (eds.), *Alcohol and aging* (169–185). New York: Oxford University Press.

Gonnerman, J. (2004). *Life on the outside: The prison odyssey of Elaine Bartlett.* New York: Farrar, Straus, and Giroux.

Gordon, A. J. (1978). Hispanic drinking after migration: The case of Dominicans. *Medical Anthropology, 2*(4), 61–83.

Gordon, A. J. (1981). The cultural context of drinking and indigenous therapy for alcohol problems in three migrant Hispanic cultures. *Journal of Studies on Alcohol,* supplement no. 9, 217–240.

Gordon, S. M. (2007, Aug.). Barriers to treatment for women. *Counselor Magazine.* Retrieved on December 17, 2008, from http://www.counselormagazine.com/content/view/593/63/.

Gorman, D. M., Speer, P. W., Gruenewald, P. J., and Labouvie, E. W. (2001). Spatial dynamics of alcohol availability, neighborhood structure and violent crime. *Journal of Studies on Alcohol, 62*(5), 628–636.

Gorney, B. (1989). Domestic violence and chemical dependency: Dual problems, dual interventions. *Journal of Psychoactive Drugs, 21,* 229–238.

Gorsline, D., Holl, A., Pearson, J. C., and Child, J. T. (2006). It's more than drinking, drugs, and sex: College student perceptions of family problems. *College Student Journal, 40*(4), 802–807.

Gossop, M., Marsden, J., Stewart, D., and Rolfe, A. (2000). Reduction in acquisitive crime and drug use after treatment of addiction problems: 1-year follow-up outcomes. *Drug and Alcohol Dependence, 58*(1–2), 165–172.

Graham, K. (1986). Identifying and measuring alcohol abuse among the elderly: Serious problems with instrumentation. *Journal of Studies on Alcohol, 47*(4), 322–326.

Graham, K., and Braun, K. (1999). Concordance of use of alcohol and other substances among older adult couples. *Addictive Behaviors, 24*, 839–856.

Graham, K., Osgood, D., Wells, S., and Stockwell, T. (2006). To what extent is intoxication associated with aggression in bars? A multilevel analysis. *Journal of Studies on Alcohol, 67*, 382–390.

Graham, K., Saunders, S. J., Flower, M. C., Timney, C. B., White-Campbell, M., and Pietropaolo, A. Z. (1995). *Addictions treatment for older adults: Evaluation of an innovative client-centered approach.* New York: Haworth.

Graham, K., Yetman, R., Ross, R., and Guistra, E. (1980). Aggression and barroom environments. *Journal of Studies on Alcohol, 14*, 277–292.

Graham, N. (1997). A test of magnitude: Does the strength of predictors explain the differences in drug use among adolescents? *Journal of Drug Education, 27*(1), 83–104.

Granfield, R., and Cloud, W. (1996). The elephant in the room that no one sees: Natural recovery among middle-class addicts. *Journal of Drug Issues, 26*(1), 45–61.

Grant, T., Ernst, C., Streissguth, A., and Stark, K. (2005). Preventing alcohol and drug exposed births in Washington state: Intervention findings from three parent-child assistance program sites. *American Journal of Drug and Alcohol Abuse, 31*(3), 471–490.

Green, A. (2003). "Chem friendly": The institutional basis of "club-drug" use in a sample of urban gay men. *Deviant Behavior, 24*(5), 427–447.

Green, A. I., and Halkitis, P. N. (2006). Crystal methamphetamine and sexual sociality in an urban gay subculture: An elective affinity. *Culture, Health and Sexuality, 8*, 317–333.

Green, B. L., Rockhill, A., and Furrer, C. (2006). Understanding patterns of substance abuse treatment for women involved with child welfare: The influence of the Adoption and Safe Families Act (ASFA). *The American Journal of Drug and Alcohol Abuse, 32*, 149–176.

Greene, M., Hoffman, S., Charon, R., and Adelman, R. (1987). Psychosocial concerns in the medical encounter: A comparison of the interactions of doctors with their old and young patients. *The Gerontologist, 27*, 164–168.

Greenfield, S. F., Keliher, A., Sugarman, D., Kozloff, R., Reizes, J. M., Kopans, B., and Jacobs, D. (2003). Who comes to voluntary, community-based alcohol screening? Results of the first annual National Alcohol Screening Day, 1999. *American Journal of Psychiatry, 160*(9), 1677–1683.

Greenstein, R. A., Fudula, P. J., and O'Brien, C. P. (1997). Alternative pharmacotherapies for opiate addiction. In J. H. Lowinson, P. Ruiz, R. B. Millman, and J. G. Langrod (eds.), *Substance Abuse: A Comprehensive Textbook,* 3rd ed. (415–429). Baltimore: Williams and Wilkins.

Greenwood, G. L., White, E. W., Page-Shafer, K., Bein, E., Osmond, D. H., Paul, J., and Stall, R. D. (2000). Correlates of heavy substance use among young gay and bisexual men: The San Francisco Young Men's Health Study. *Drug and Alcohol Dependence, 61*(2), 105.

Griffin, K. W., Botvin, G. J., Nichols, T. R., and Doyle, M. M. (2003). Effectiveness of a universal drug abuse prevention approach for youth at high risk for substance use initiation. *Preventive Medicine, 36*, 1–7.

Grinspoon, L., and Bakalar, J. B. (1990). What is phencyclidine? *The Harvard Medical School Mental Health Letter, 6*(7), 8.

Grinspoon, L., and Bakalar, J. B. (1997). Marihuana. In J. H. Lowinson, P. Ruiz, R. B. Millman, and J. G. Langrod. *Substance abuse: A comprehensive textbook.* (199–206). Baltimore, MD: Williams and Wilkins.

Gross, S. (2004). *Pathways to lasting self-esteem.* Bloomington, IN: Author House.

Gruber, K. J., and Taylor, M. F. (2006). A family perspective for substance abuse: Implications from the literature. In S. L. A. Straussner and C. H. Fewell (eds.), *Impact of substance abuse on children and families: Research and practice implications* (1–29). New York: Haworth.

Gruskin, E., Byrne, K., Kools, S., and Altschuler, A. (2006). Consequences of frequenting the lesbian bar. *Women and Health, 44*(2), 103–120.

Gullotta, T., Adams, G., and Montemayer, R. (eds.) (1995). *Advances in adolescent development.* Thousand Oaks, CA: Sage.

Gunderson, A., Tomkowiak, J., Menachemi, N., and Brooks, A. (2005). Rural physicians' attitudes toward the elderly: Evidence of ageism? *Quality Management in Health Care, 14*(3), 167–176.

Gunter, T. D., and Arndt, S. (2004). Maximizing treatment of substance abuse in the elderly. *Behavioral Health Management, 24*(2), 38–43.

Guo, J., Collins, L., and Hawkins, J. (2000). Developmental pathways to alcohol abuse and dependence in young adulthood. *Journal of Studies on Alcohol, 61*, 796–808.

Gurnack, A. M., and Hoffman, N. G. (1992). Elderly alcohol misuse. *The International Journal of the Addictions, 27*, 869–878.

Gurnack, A. M., and Thomas, J. L. (1989). Behavioral factors related to elderly alcohol abuse: Research and policy issues. *The International Journal of the Addictions, 24*, 641–654.

Guttman, D. (1978). Patterns of legal drug use by older Americans. *Addictive Diseases: An International Journal, 3*, 337–356.

Hahm, H. C., Wong, F. Y., Ozonoff, A., and Lee, J. (2008). Asian American Pacific Islanders (AAPI) sexual minority adolescents' longitudinal patterns of substance use and abuse: Findings from the National Longitudinal Study of Adolescent Health. *Journal of Adolescent Health, 42*, 275–283.

Hahn, D., Payne, W., and Mauer, E. (2005). *Focus on health,* 7th ed. Boston: McGraw-Hill.

Halkitis, P. N., and Palamar, J. J. (2006). GHB use among gay and bisexual men. *Addictive Behaviors, 31*(11), 2135–2139.

Halkitis, P. N., Palamar, J. J., and Mukherjee, P. P. (2007). Poly-club-drug use among gay and bisexual men: A longitudinal analysis. *Drug and Alcohol Dependence, 89*(2–3), 153–160.

Halkitis, P. N., and Shrem, M. T. (2006). Psychological differences between binge and chronic methamphetamine using gay and bisexual men. *Addictive Behaviors, 31*(3), 549–552.

Halkitis, P. N., Shrem, M. T., and Martin, F. W. (2005). Sexual behavior patterns of methamphetamine-using gay and bisexual men. *Substance Use and Misuse, 40*, 703–719.

Halpern, J. H., and Pope, H. G. (2001). Hallucinogens on the Internet: A vast new source of "underground" drug information. *American Journal of Psychiatry, 158*(3), 481–483.

Hamid, A. (1992). The developmental cycle of a drug epidemic. *Journal of Psychoactive Drugs, 24*, 337–348.

Hamilton, R. M. (2007). *The police notebook.* University of Oklahoma Police Department. Retrieved on April 25, 2007, from http://www.edu/oupd/frombac.htm.

Hanna, J. M. (1974). Coca leaf use in southern Peru: Some biosocial aspects. *American Anthropologist 76*(2), 281–296.

Hanson, B., Beschner, G., Waters, J., and Bovelle, E. (1985). *Life with heroin.* Lanham, MD: Lexington.

Hanson, M., and Gutheil, I. (2004). Motivational strategies with alcohol involved older adults: Implications for social work practice. *Social Work, 49*(3), 364–372.

Hardy-Fanta, C., and Mignon, S. (2000). *Alternatives to incarceration for substance abusing female defendants/offenders in Massachusetts, 1996–1998.* Boston: University of Massachusetts.

Harford, T., and Gaines, L. (1981). *Social drinking contexts.* Research monograph no. 7. Rockville, MD: National Institute on Alcohol Abuse and Alcoholism.

Harford, T., Wechsler, H., and Muthen, B. (2003). Alcohol-related aggression and drinking at off-campus parties: A national survey of current drinkers in college. *Journal of Studies on Alcohol, 64,* 705–711.

Harford, T., Wechsler, H., and Seibring, M. (2002). Attendance and alcohol use at parties and bars in college: A national survey of current drinkers. *Journal of Studies on Alcohol, 63,* 726–733.

Harford, T., Yi, H.-Y., and Hilton, M. (2006). Alcohol abuse and dependence in college and noncollege samples: A ten-year prospective follow-up in a national survey. *Journal of Studies on Alcohol, 67,* 803–809.

Harkness, D., and Cotrell, G. (1997). The social construction of co-dependency in the treatment of substance abuse. *Journal of Substance Abuse Treatment, 41*(5), 473–479.

Harner, M. J. (ed.) (1973). *Hallucinogens and shamanism.* London: Oxford University Press.

Harrell, A. (2003). Judging drug courts: Balancing the evidence. *Criminology and Public Policy, 2*(2), 207–212.

Harris, K. M., and Edlund, M. J. (2005). Use of mental health care and substance abuse treatment among adults with co-occurring disorders. *Psychiatric Services, 56*(8), 954–959.

Harrison, L. D., and Martin, S. S. (2001, March). *Residual substance abuse treatment (RSAT) for state prisoners formula grant: Compendium of program implementation and accomplishments, final report.* Document no. 187099. Washington, DC: US Department of Justice.

Harrison, P. M., and Beck, A. J. (2005). *Prison and jail inmates at midyear 2004.* Rockville, MD: US Department of Justice, Bureau of Justice Statistics.

Hartwell, S., Mignon, S., and Lempecki, L. (1998). *Reducing alcohol misuse among college students: Results from a model brief intervention feasibility study.* Boston: University of Massachusetts.

Hays, R. D., and Revetto, J. P. (1992). Old and new MMPI-derived scales and the Short-MAST as screening tools for alcohol disorder. *Alcohol and Alcoholism, 27*(6), 685–695.

Hazelden Corporation (1996). *Alcoholism and drug abuse: A growing problem among the elderly.* Retrieved on July 23, 2004, from http://www.hazelden.org.

Hendrickson, J. C., and Gerstein, D. R. (2005). Criminal involvement among young male ecstasy users. *Substance Use and Misuse, 40,* 1557–1575.

Herper, M. J. (1999, Nov.). Binge and purge: Scolding students won't make them safer. *Reason Online.* Retrieved March 5, 2005, from http://www.reason.com9911/fe.mh.binge.shtml.

Herzog, D. B., Franko, D. L., Dorer, D. J., Keel, P., Jackson, S., and Manzo, M. P. (2006). Drug abuse in women with eating disorders. *International Journal of Eating Disorders, 30*(5), 364–368.

Hettinger, M. E. (2000). Substance abuse and the elderly. *Counselor: The Magazine for Addiction Professionals, 2,* 14–20.

Heuser, S. (2006, April 14). Alkermes alcoholism drug wins tentative OK. *Boston Globe,* C1, C8.

Higgins-Biddle, J. C., Babor, T. F., Mullahy, J., Daniels, J., and McRee, B. (1997). Alcohol screening and brief intervention: Where research meets practice. *Connecticut Medicine, 61*(9), 565–575.

Hilberman, E., and Munson, K. (1978). Sixty battered women. *Victimology, 2,* 460–471.

Hingson, R., Heeren, T., Winter, M., and Wechsler, H. (2005). Magnitude of alcohol-related mortality and morbidity among US college students ages 18–24: Changes from 1998–2001. *Annual Review of Public Health, 26,* 259–279.

Hinkin, C. H., Castellon, S. A., Dickson-Fuhrman, E., Daum, G., Jaffee, J., and Jarvik, L. (2001). Screening for drug and alcohol abuse among older adults using a modified version of the CAGE. *American Journal on Addictions, 10*(4), 319–326.

Hirschi, T. (1969). *Causes of delinquency.* Berkeley: University of California Press.

Hirshfield, S., Chiasson, M., and Remien, R. (2006). Crystal methamphetamine use among men who have sex with men: Results from two national online studies. *Journal of Gay and Lesbian Psychotherapy, 10*(3), 85–93.

Hogan, T. M. S., Myers, B. J., and Elswick, R. K., Jr. (2006). Child abuse potential among mothers of substance-exposed and nonexposed infants and toddlers. *Child Abuse and Neglect, 30*(2), 145–156.

Holdcraft, L. C., and Iacono, W. G. (2002). Cohort effects on gender differences in alcohol dependence. *Addiction, 97,* 1025–1036.

Holder, H. (1998). Cost benefits of substance abuse treatment: An overview of results from alcohol and drug abuse. *The Journal of Mental Health Policy and Economics, 1,* 23–29.

Holder, H. D. (1999). Prevention aimed at the environment. In B. S. McCrady and E. E. Epstein (eds.), *Addictions: A comprehensive guidebook* (573–594). New York: Oxford University Press.

Holmes, K. A., and Hodge, R. H. (1995). Gay and lesbian persons. In J. Philleo, F. L. Brisbane, and L. G. Epstein (eds.), *Cultural competence for social workers: Guide for alcohol and other drug abuse prevention professionals working with ethnic/racial communities* (3–39). Rockville, MD: US Department of Health and Human Services, Center for Substance Abuse Prevention.

Homish, G., and Leonard, K. (2007). The drinking partnership and marital satisfaction: The longitudinal influence of discrepant drinking. *Journal of Consulting and Clinical Psychology, 75,* 43–51.

Horney, K. (1950). *Neurosis and human growth.* New York: Norton.

Horton, D. (1943). The functions of alcohol in primitive societies: A cross-cultural study. *Quarterly Journal of Studies on Alcohol, 4,* 199–320.

Hubbard, R. L., Craddock, S. G., and Anderson, J. (2003). Overview of 5-year follow-up outcomes in the Drug Abuse Treatment Outcomes Studies (DATOS). *Journal of Substance Abuse Treatment, 25*(3), 125–134.

Hudson, S. A., and Boyter, A. C. (1997). Pharmaceutical care of the elderly. *The Pharmaceutical Journal, 259,* 686–688.

Hughes-Hammer, C., Martsolf, D. S., and Zeller, R. A. (1998). Development and testing of the codependency assessment tool. *Archives of Psychiatric Nursing, 12*(5), 264–272.

Hurcom, C., Copello, A., and Orford, J. (2000). Family and alcohol: Effects of excessive drinking and conceptualizations of spouses over recent decades. *Substance Use and Misuse, 35*(4), 473–502.

Hutchison, I. W. (1999). Alcohol, fear and woman abuse. *Sex Roles, 40*(11–12), 893–920.

Imm, P., Chinman, M., Wandersman, A., Rosenbloom, D., Guckenburg, S., and Leis, R. (2007). *Preventing underage drinking: Using Getting to Outcomes with the SAMHSA Strategic Prevention Framework to achieve results.* RAND Technical Report. Santa Monica, CA: RAND Corporation.

Inciardi, J. A. (1996, July). The drug policy debate: Prohibition versus legalization. *Drugs and Society, Global Issues USIA Electronic Journals, 1*(7). Retrieved on May 1, 2007, from http://www.tc.columbia.edu/centers/cifas/drugsandsociety/resources/inc/.

Inciardi, J., and Surratt, H. L. (1998). African-Americans, crack, and crime. In J. A. Inciardi and K. McElrath (eds.), *The American drug scene: An anthology,* 2nd ed. (170–180). Los Angeles: Roxbury.

Inglehart, A. P., and Becerra, R. M. (1995). *Social services and the ethnic community.* Long Grove, IL: Waveland Press.

Institute of Medicine (1990). *Broadening the base of treatment for alcohol problems.* Washington, DC: National Academies.

Institute of Medicine (2001). *Crossing the quality chasm: A new health system for the 21st century.* Washington, DC: National Academies.

International Certification and Reciprocity Consortium (ICRC). (2008). Retrieved on July 20, 2008, from http://www.icrcoda.org/abouticrc.cfm.

Irwin, T. W. (2006). Strategies for the treatment of methamphetamine use disorders among gay and bisexual men. *Journal of Gay and Lesbian Psychotherapy, 10*(3–4), 131–141.

Ivis, F. J., Adlaf, E. M., and Rehm, J. (2000). Incorporating the AUDIT into a general population telephone survey: A methodological experiment. *Drug and Alcohol Dependence, 60,* 97–104.

Jackim, L. W. (2003, May/June). The role of antabuse (disulfiram) in the treatment of alcohol use problems. Roundtable proceedings. *Addiction Professional,* Supplement, 2–4.

Jackson, J. K. (1954). The adjustment of the family to the crisis of alcoholism. *Quarterly Journal of Studies on Alcohol, 15,* 562–586.

Jacob, T., Buckholz, K. K., Sartor, C. E., Howell, D. N., and Wood, P. K. (2005). Drinking trajectories from adolescence to the mid-forties among alcohol dependent males. *Journal of Studies on Alcohol, 66,* 745–755.

Jacobs, K., and Gill, K. (2002). Substance abuse in an urban aboriginal population: Social, legal, and psychosocial consequences. *Journal of Ethnicity in Substance Abuse 1*(1), 7–25.

Jacobson, J. L., and Jacobson, S. W. (1999). Drinking moderately and pregnancy: Effects on child development. *Alcohol Health Research World, 23,* 25–30.

Jaffe, C., Clance, P. R., Nichols, M., and Emshoff, J. G. (2000). The prevalence of alcoholism and feelings of alienation in lesbian and heterosexual women. *Journal of Gay and Lesbian Psychotherapy, 3*(3–4), 25–35.

James, W. (1961). *The varieties of religious experience.* New York: Collier.

Janik, S. W., and Dunham, R. G. (1983). A nationwide examination of the need for specific alcoholism treatment programs for the elderly. *Journal of Studies on Alcohol, 44*(2), 307–317.

Jeffery, R. (1979). Normal rubbish: Deviant patients in casualty departments. *Sociology of Health and Illness, 1,* 90–107.

Jellinek, E. M. (1952). Phases of alcohol addiction. *Quarterly Journal of Studies on Alcohol, 13,* 673–684.

Jellinek, E. M. (1960). *The disease concept of alcoholism.* New Haven, CT: College and University Press.

Jentsch, J. D., Redmond, D. E., Elsworth, J. D., Taylor, J. R., Youngren, K. D., and Roth, R. H. (1997). Enduring cognitive deficits and cortical dopamine dysfunction in monkeys after long-term administration of phencyclidine. *Science, 277*, 953–955.

Jessor, R., Costa, F., Krueger, P., and Turbin, M. (2006). A developmental study of heavy episodic drinking among college students: The role of psychosocial and behavioral protective and risk factors. *Journal of Studies on Alcohol, 67*, 86–94.

Jochelson, W. (1906). Kumiss festivals of the Yakut and the decoration of kumiss vessels. In B. Laufer (ed.), *Boas anniversary volume: Papers written in honor of Franz Boas* (259–271). New York: G. E. Stechert.

Johnsen, L. W., and Harlow, L. L. (1996). Childhood sexual abuse linked with adult substance use, victimization, and AIDS-risk. *AIDS Education and Prevention 8*(1), 44–57.

Johnson, J. C. (2002). Letter to the Department of Health and Human Services from Director of the American Geriatrics Society. Retrieved on March 12, 2008, from http://www.americangeriatrics.org/news/dhhsresp.stml.

Johnson, J. L., and Leff, M. (1999). Children of substance abusers: Overview of research findings. *Pediatrics, 103*(5), 1085–1099.

Johnson, P. C. (1995). Shamanism from Ecuador to Chicago: A case study in ritual appropriation. *Religion, 25*, 163–178.

Johnson, R., Richter, L., Kleber, H., McLellan, A., and Carise, D. (2005). Telescoping of drinking-related behaviors: Gender, racial/ethnic and age comparisons. *Substance Use and Misuse, 40*, 1139–1151.

Johnson, R. C. (2008, Jan. 5). Probe targets cops over missing drugs. *Boston Herald.* Retrieved on July 17, 2008, from http://www.freerepublic.com/focus/f-news/1948662/posts.

Johnson, V. (1980). *I'll quit tomorrow.* New York: Harper & Row.

Johnson, V. (1986). *Intervention: How to help someone who doesn't want help.* Minneapolis: Johnson Institute.

Johnston, L. D., O'Malley, P. M., Bachman, J. G., and Schulenberg, J. E. (2007, Dec. 11). *Overall, illicit drug use by American teens continues gradual decline in 2007.* Ann Arbor: University of Michigan News Service. Retrieved on January 22, 2008, from http://www.monitoringthefuture.org.

Jones, H. E. (2006). Drug addiction during pregnancy: Advances in maternal treatment and understanding child outcomes. *Current Direction in Psychological Science, 15*(3), 126–130.

Jones, M. (1953). *The therapeutic community.* New York: Basic Books.

Jones-Webb, R., McKee, P., Hannan, P., Wall, M., Pham, L., Erickson, D. J., and Wagenaar, A. C. (2008). Alcohol and malt liquor availability and promotion and homicide in inner cities. *Substance Use and Misuse, 43*, 159–177.

Jordan, K. (2000). Substance abuse among gay, lesbian, bisexual, transgender and questioning adolescents. *School Psychology Review, 29*(2), 201–206.

Jordan, L. J. (2008, May 3). Data dispel image of cocaine user: Hispanic offender rate is on the rise. *Boston Globe*, A9.

Jorgensen, T., Johansson, S., Kennerfalk, A., Wallander, M. A., and Svardsudd, K. (2001). Prescription drug use, diagnoses, and healthcare utilization among the elderly. *The Annals of Psychotherapy, 35*(9), 1004–1009.

Joy, J. E., Watson, S. J., and Benson, J. A. (eds.) (1999). *Marijuana and medicine: Assessing the science base.* Washington, DC: National Academies/Institute of Medicine.

Jung, J. (1994). *Under the influence: Alcohol and human behavior.* Pacific Grove: Brooks/Cole.

Jung, J. (2001). *Psychology of alcohol and other drugs: A research perspective.* Thousand Oaks, CA: Sage.

Karberg, J. C., and James, D. J. (2005, July). *Substance dependence, abuse, and treatment of jail inmates 2002*. Washington, DC: US Department of Justice, Bureau of Justice Statistics.

Kashner, T. M., Rodell, D. E., Ogne, S. R., Guggenheim, F. G. L., and Karson, C. N. (1992). Outcomes and costs of two VA inpatient treatment programs for older alcoholic patients. *Hospital and Community Psychiatry, 43*, 985–989.

Katz, R. S. (2002). Older women and addictions. In S. L. A. Straussner and S. Brown (eds.), *The handbook of addiction treatment for women* (272–297). San Francisco: Jossey-Bass.

Kautt, P. M. (2002). Location, location, location: Interdistrict and intercircuit variation in sentencing outcomes for federal drug trafficking offenses. *Justice Quarterly, 19*(4), 633–671.

Kautt, P., and Spohn, C. (2002). *Crack*-ing down on black drug offenders?: Testing for interaction between offender race, drug type, and sentencing strategy in federal drug sentences. *Justice Quarterly, 18*, 651–688.

Kelly, T. M., and Donovan, J. E. (2001). Confirmatory factor analyses of the Alcohol Use Disorder Identification Test (AUDIT) among adolescents treated in emergency departments. *Journal of Studies on Alcohol, 62*, 838–842.

Kenkel, D. S. (1996). New estimates of the optimal tax on alcohol. *Economic Inquiry, 34*, 296–319.

Kessler, R. C., Chiu, W. T., Demler, O., and Walters, E. E. (2005). Prevalence, severity, and comorbidity of 12-month DSM-IV disorders in the National Comorbidity Survey replication. *Archives of General Psychiatry, 62*(6), 617–627.

Kick, S. D. (1999, April 15). Evaluation and management of chronic alcohol abuse. *Hospital Practice,* 95–98, 104–106.

Kilts, C. D., Gross, R. E., Ely, T. B., and Karen, P. G. (2004). The neural correlates of cue-induced craving in cocaine-dependent women. *American Journal of Psychiatry, 161*, 233–241.

Kinder, D. C. (1992). Shutting out the evil: Nativism and narcotics control in the United States. In W. O. Walker (ed.), *Drug control policy* (117–142). University Park: Pennsylvania State University Press.

Kinsey, A. C., Pomeroy, W. B., and Martin, C. E. (1998). *Sexual behavior in the human female,* reprint ed. Bloomington: Indiana University Press.

Kleiman, M. A. R. (2004). Toward (more nearly) optimal sentencing for drug offenders. *Criminology and Public Policy, 3*(3), 435–440.

Klein, W. C., and Jess, C. (2002). One last pleasure? Alcohol use among elderly people in nursing homes. *Health and Social Work, 27*(3), 193–203.

Klitzman, R. (2006). From "male bonding rituals" to "suicide Tuesday": A qualitative study of issues faced by gay male ecstasy (MDMA) users. *Journal of Homosexuality, 51*(3), 7–32.

Klitzner, M., Fisher, D., Stewart, K., and Gilbert, S. (1992). *Substance abuse: Early intervention for adolescents*. Princeton, NJ: Robert Wood Johnson Foundation.

Knight, D. K., and Wallace, G. (2003). Where are the children? An examination of children's living arrangements when mothers enter residential drug treatment. *Journal of Drug Issues, 33*(2), 305–324.

Knight, J., Harris, S., Sherrit, L., Kelley, K., Van Hook, S., and Wechsler, H. (2003). Heavy drinking and alcohol policy enforcement in a statewide public college system. *Journal of Studies on Alcohol, 64*, 696–703.

Knight, J., Wechsler, H., and Seibring, M. (2002). Alcohol abuse and dependence among college students. *Journal of Studies on Alcohol, 63*, 263–270.

Knight, K., Hiller, M. L., and Simpson, D. D. (1999). Evaluating corrections-based treatment for the drug-abusing criminal offender. *Journal of Psychoactive Drugs, 31*(33), 299–304.

Knudsen, H. K., Ducharme, L. T., and Roman, P. M. (2006). Early adoption of buprenorphine in substance abuse treatment centers: Data from the private and public sectors. *Journal of Substance Abuse Treatment, 30,* 363–373.

Knudsen, J. R. W., and Gabriel, R. M. (2003). *Advancing the current state of addiction treatment: A regional needs assessment of substance abuse treatment professionals in the Pacific Northwest.* Portland, OR: RMC Research.

Kofoed, L. L., Tolson, R. L., Atkinson, R. M., Toth, R. L., and Turner, J. A. (1987). Treatment compliance of older alcoholics: An elder-specific approach is superior to "mainstreaming." *Journal of Studies on Alcohol, 48*(1), 47–51.

Kokin, M. (with Walker, I.) (1989). *Women married to alcoholics: Help and hope for nonalcoholic partners.* Toronto: Macmillan.

Kueffler, J., Lim, J., and Choi, J. (2005, Winter). Alcohol use among intercollegiate student-athletes. *The Sport Journal, 8*(1). Retrieved on April 9, 2007, from http://www.thesportjournal.org/2005Journal/Vol18-No1.

Kulaga, V. (2006). Cognitive processing speed among children exposed to fetal alcohol. *Journal of FAS International, 4*(3), 1–4.

Kunitz, S. J., Woodall, W. G., Zhao, H., Wheeler, D. R., Lillis, R., and Rogers, E. (2002). Rearrest rates after incarceration for DWI: A comparative study in a southwestern US county. *American Journal of Public Health, 92*(11), 1826–1831.

Kurtz, E. (1988). *AA—The story.* San Francisco: Harper & Row.

Kurtz, S. P. (2005). Post-circuit blues: Motivations and consequences of crystal meth use among gay men in Miami. *AIDS and Behavior, 9*(1), 63–72.

Kuure, T. (2002). Literature review—Finland. In A. Stevens and B. Gladstone (eds.), *Learning, not offending: Effective interventions to tackle youth transitions to crime in Europe* (9–20). Brasted, UK: RPS Rainer.

La Barre, W. (1938). *The peyote cult.* Yale University Publications in Anthropology, no. 19. New Haven, CT: Yale University Press.

Labrie, J. W., Pedersen, E. R., and Tawalbeh, S. (2007). Classifying risky-drinking college students: Another look at the two-week drinker-type categorization. *Journal of Studies on Alcohol, 68,* 86–90.

Lammers, S. M. M., Schippers, G. M., and VanderStaak, C. P. F. (1995). Submission and rebellion: Excessive drinking of women in problematic heterosexual partner relationships. *The International Journal of Addiction, 30*(7), 901–917.

Lang, S. (1998). Teen alcohol use is a prime-time TV staple. *Journal of Studies on Alcohol, 59*(3), 305–310.

Lankenau, S. E., and Clatts, M. C. (2004). Drug injection practices among high risk youths: The first shot of ketamine. *Journal of Urban Health, 81*(2), 232–248.

Lanternari, V. (1963). *The religions of the oppressed.* New York: Alfred A. Knopf.

Lapham, S. (2004/2005). Screening and brief intervention in the criminal justice system. *Alcohol Research and Health, 28*(2), 85–93.

Larkins, S., Reback, C. J., and Shoptaw, S. (2006). HIV risk behaviors among gay male methamphetamine users: Before and after treatment. *Journal of Gay and Lesbian Psychotherapy, 10*(3–4), 123–129.

Lauderback, D., and Waldorf, D. (1993). Whatever happened to ice?: The latest drug scare. *Journal of Drug Issues, 23,* 597–613.

Leason, K. (2003, July 17–23). Mental health tsar admits services suffer from institutional racism. *Community Care Magazine, 18–19.*

Lee, S. J., Galanter, M., Dermatis, H., and McDowell, D. (2003). Circuit parties and patterns of drug use in a subset of gay men. *Journal of Addictive Diseases 22*(4), 47–60.

Leeder, E. (2004). *The family in global perspective: A gendered journey.* London: Sage.

Lehman, L. B., Pilich, A., and Andrews, N. (1993). Neurological disorders resulting from alcoholism. *Alcohol Health and Research World, 17*(4), 305–309.

Leichliter, J., Meilman, P., Presley, C., and Cashin, J. (1998). Alcohol use and related consequences among athletes with varying levels of involvement with athletics. *Journal of American College Health, 46,* 357–362.

Lemert, E. M. (1954). *Alcohol and the Northwest Coast Indians.* University of California Publications in Culture and Society, *2,* 303–406. Berkeley: University of California Press.

Lemert, E. M. (1956). Alcoholism: Theory, problem, and challenge, III: Alcoholism and the sociocultural situation. *Quarterly Journal of Studies on Alcohol, 17,* 307–317.

Lemke, S., and Moos, R. H. (2003). Treatment and outcomes of older patients with alcohol use disorders in community residential programs. *Journal of Studies on Alcohol, 64*(2), 219–226.

Lender, M., and Martin, J. (1982). *Drinking in America.* New York: Free Press.

Leonard, C. (2005, Dec. 14). Crime takes hold in land of fiction: Drugs, economy bring real trouble. *Boston Globe,* A2.

Leonard, K. E., and Jacob, T. (1988). Alcohol, alcoholism, and family violence. In V. B. Van Hasselt, R. L. Morrison, A. S. Bellack, and M. Hersen (eds.), *Handbook of family violence* (383–406). New York: Plenum.

Leonard, K. E., and Rothbard, L. (1999). Alcohol and the marriage effect. *Journal of Studies on Alcohol, 60,* 139–146.

Leppel, K. (2006). College binge drinking: Deviant versus mainstream behavior. *The American Journal of Drug and Alcohol Abuse, 32,* 519–525.

Levin, J., Taylor, R., and Chatters, L. (1994). Race and gender differences in religiosity among older adults. *Journal of Gerontology: Social Sciences, 49,* 137–145.

Levitt, S. D. (2004). Understanding why crime fell in the 1990s: Four factors that explain the decline and six that do not. *Journal of Economic Perspectives, 18*(1), 163–190.

Lex, B. W. (1994). Alcohol and other drug use among women. *Alcohol Health and Research World, 18*(3), 212–219.

Liberto, J. G., and Oslin, D. W. (1997). Early versus late onset of alcoholism in the elderly. In A. M. Gurnack (ed.), *Older adults' misuse of alcohol and medicines, and other drugs: Research and practice issues* (54–93). New York: Springer.

Liberto, J. G., Oslin, D. W., and Ruskin, P. E. (1992). Alcoholism in older persons: A review of the literature. *Hospital and Community Psychiatry, 43*(10), 975–984.

Lindesmith, A. (1965). *The addict and the law.* Chicago: University of Chicago Press.

Lindley, N. R., Giordano, P. J., and Hammer, E. D. (1999). Codependency: Predictors and psychometric issues. *Journal of Clinical Psychology, 55*(1), 59–64.

Linn, B. S., and Zeppa, R. (1987). Predicting third year medical students' attitudes toward the elderly and treating the old. *Addictive Diseases: An International Journal, 7,* 167–175.

Lo, C. C., and Stephens, R. C. (2000). Drugs and prisoners: Treatment needs on entering prison. *The American Journal of Drug and Alcohol Abuse, 26*(2), 229–245.

Lock, C. (2004, June 12). Setting a stage for cancer. *Science News, 165*(24), 372.

Logan, T. K., Walker, R., Cole, J., and Leukefeld, C. (2002). Victimization and substance use among women: Contributing factors, interventions, and implications. *Review of General Psychology, 6*(4), 325–397.

Lonczak, H., Huang, B., Catalano, R., Hawkins, J., Hill, K., Abbot, R., and Kosterman, R. (2001). The social predictors of adolescent alcohol misuse: A test of the social development model. *Journal of Studies on Alcohol, 62*, 166–178.

Longclaws, L., Barnes, G., Grieve, L., and Dumoff, R. (1980). Alcohol and other drug use among the Brokenhead Ojibwa. *Journal of Studies on Alcohol, 41*(1), 21–36.

Low, N., Cui, L., and Merikangas, K. R. (2007, Jan. 2). Spousal concordance for substance use and anxiety disorders. *Journal of Psychiatric Research, 41,* 942–951. Retrieved on January 31, 2008, from www.elesevier.com/locate/jpsychires.

Lucas, B. D. (1998, Dec. 15). Recognizing and treating patients with drinking problems. *Patient Care*, 113–122.

Lundgren, L. M., Schilling, R. F., and Peloquin, S. D. (2005). Evidence-based drug treatment practice and the child welfare system: The example of methadone. *Social Work, 50*(1), 53–63.

Lupton, C., Burd, L., and Harwood, R. (2004). Cost of fetal alcohol spectrum disorders. *American Journal of Medical Genetics, 27C*, 42–50.

Machlan, B., Brostrand, H. L., and Benshoff, J. (2004). Vocational rehabilitation in substance abuse treatment programs. *Journal of Teaching in the Addictions, 3*(1), 71–80.

MacMurray, V. D. (1979). The effect and nature of alcohol abuse in cases of child neglect. *Victimology, 4*, 29–45.

Madsen, W. (1967). *The Mexican-Americans of South Texas,* 2nd ed. New York: Holt, Rinehart & Winston.

Maiden, R. P. (1997). Alcohol dependence and domestic violence: Incidence and treatment implications. *Alcoholism Treatment Quarterly, 15*(2), 31–50.

Maier, S. E., and West, J. R. (2001). Drinking patterns and alcohol-related birth defects. *Alcohol Research and Health, 25*(3), 168–174.

Maisto, S. A., Carey, M. P., Carey, K. B., Gordon, C. M., and Gleason, J. R. (2000). Use of the AUDIT and the DAST-10 to identify alcohol and drug use disorders among adults with a severe and persistent mental illness. *Psychological Assessment, 12,* 186–192.

Maisto, S. A., and Saitz, R. (2003). Alcohol use disorders: Screening and diagnosis. *The American Journal on Addictions, 12*, S12–S25.

Makela, K. (2004). Studies of the reliability and validity of the Addiction Severity Index. *Addiction, 99*(4), 398–410.

Makimoto, K. (1998). Drinking patterns and drinking problems among Asian-Americans and Pacific Islanders. *Alcohol Health and Research World, 22*(4), 270–275.

Males, M. A. (1996). *The scapegoat generation: America's war on adolescents.* Monroe, ME: Common Courage.

Manninen, L., Poikolainen, K., Vartianen, E., and Laatikainen, T. (2006). Heavy drinking occasions and depression. *Alcohol and Alcoholism, 41*(3), 293–299.

Manning, V., Wanigaratne, S., Best, D., Strathdee, G., Schrover, I., and Gossop, M. (2007). Screening for cognitive functioning in psychiatric outpatients with schizophrenia, alcohol dependence, and dual diagnosis. *Schizophrenia Research, 91*(1–3), 151–158.

Manning, W., Keeler, E., Newhouse, J. P., Sloss, E., and Wasserman, J. (1991). *The costs of poor health habits: A RAND study.* London: Harvard University Press.

Mansergh, G., Colfax, G. N., Marks, G., Rader, M., Guzman, R., and Buchbinder, S. (2001). Circuit party men's health survey: Findings and implications for gay and bisexual men. *American Journal of Public Health, 91*(6), 953–958.

Mansergh, G., Shouse, R. L., Marks, G., Guzman, R., Rader, M., Buchbinder, S., and Colfax, G. N. (2006). Methamphetamine and sildenafil (Viagra) use are linked to unprotected receptive and insertive anal sex, respectively, in a sample of men who have sex with men. *Sexually Transmitted Infections, 82,* 131–134.

Manzardo, A. M., and Penick, E. C. (2006). A theoretical argument for inherited insensitivity as one possible biological cause of familial alcoholism. *Alcoholism: Clinical and Experimental Research, 30*(9), 1545–1550.

Marcell, A. V., and Millstein, S. G. (2000). Prevalence and quality of adolescent alcohol screening and education among primary care physicians. *Pediatric Research, 47*(4), 8A.

Marks, A. (2002). Illicit drug use grows among the elderly. *Christian Science Monitor, 94*(85), 3.

Marlatt, G. A., and Gordon, J. R. (1985). *Relapse prevention.* New York: Guilford.

Marsch, L. A. (1998). The efficacy of methadone maintenance treatment interventions in reducing illicit opiate use, HIV risk behavior and criminality: A meta-analysis. *Addiction, 93*(4), 515–532.

Marsh, J. C., D'Aunno, T. A., and Smith, B. D. (2000). Increasing access and providing social services to improve drug abuse treatment for women with children. *Addiction, 95,* 1237–1247.

Marshall, M. (1979a). *Weekend warriors: Alcohol in a Micronesian culture.* Palo Alto, CA: Mayfield.

Marshall, M. (1979b). *Beliefs, behavior, and alcoholic beverages: A cross-cultural survey.* Ann Arbor: University of Michigan Press.

Martens, M. P., Ferrier, A. G., and Cimini, M. D. (2007). Do protective behavioral strategies mediate the relationship between drinking motives and alcohol use in college students? *Journal of Studies on Alcohol and Drugs, 68,* 106–114.

Martin, C. S., and Winters, K. C. (1998). Diagnosis and assessment of alcohol use disorders among adolescents. *Alcohol Health and Research World, 22*(2), 95–105.

Martin, P., and Hummer, R. (1989). Fraternities and rape on campus. *Gender and Society, 3,* 457–473.

Martin, S. E., Maxwell, C. D., White, R. R., and Zhang, Y. (2004). Trends in alcohol use, cocaine use, and crime: 1989–1998. *The Journal of Drug Issues, 4*(2), 333–360.

Martino, S. (2007). Contemplating the use of motivational interviewing with patients who have schizophrenia and substance use disorders. *Clinical Psychology: Science and Practice, 14*(1), 58–63.

Martino, S. C., Collins, R. L., and Ellickson, P. L. (2005). Cross-lagged relationships between substance use and intimate partner violence among a sample of young adult women. *Journal of Studies on Alcohol, 66*(1), 139–148.

Martino, S. C., Collins, R. L., Ellickson, P. L., and Klein, D. J. (2006). Explaining the link between substance use and abortion: The roles of unconventionality and unplanned pregnancy. *Perspectives on Sexual and Reproductive Health, 38*(2), 66–75.

Martinotti, G., DiNicola, M., Romanelli, R., Andreoli, S., Pozzi, G., Moroni, N., and Janiri, L. (2007). High and low dosage oxcarbazepine versus naltrexone for the prevention of relapse in alcohol-dependent patients. *Human Psychopharmacology: Clinical and Experimental, 22*(3), 149–156.

Martsolf, D. S., Hughes-Hammer, C., Estok, P., and Zeller, R. A. (1999). Codependency in male and female helping professionals. *Archives of Psychiatric Nursing, 13*(2), 97–103.

Mason, M. (2006, Dec. 12). The energy-drink buzz is unmistakable: The health impact is unknown. *New York Times,* F5.

Matherlee, K. (2003). *The U.S. health workforce: Definitions, dollars and dilemmas.* Washington, DC: George Washington University.

Mathias, R. (1996). Marijuana impairs driving-related skills and workplace performance. *NIDA Notes, 11*(1). Retrieved on June 29, 2008, from http://www.drugabuse.gov/NIDA_Notes/NNVol11N1/Marijuana.html.

Matthews, C. R., Lorah, P., and Fenton, J. (2006). Treatment experiences of gays and lesbians in recovery from addiction: A qualitative inquiry. *Journal of Mental Health Counseling, 28*(2), 111–132.

Matthews, C. R., Selvidge, M. M. D., and Fisher, K. (2005). Addictions counselors' attitudes and behaviors toward gay, lesbian, and bisexual clients. *Journal of Counseling and Development, 83*(1), 57–65.

Mauer, M., Potler, C., and Wolf, R. (1999, Nov.). *Gender and justice: Women, drugs, and sentencing policy.* Washington, DC: Sentencing Project.

Mayer, M. J. (1979). Alcohol and the elderly: A review. *Health and Social Work, 4*(4), 129–143.

Mayfield, D., McLeod, G., and Hall, P. (1974). The CAGE questionnaire: Validation of a new alcoholism screening instrument. *American Journal of Psychiatry, 131*, 1121–1123.

McAndrew, C., and Edgerton, R. (1969). *Drunken comportment: A social explanation.* Chicago: Aldine.

McBride, D. C., VanderWaal, C. J., and Terry-McElrath, Y. M. (2001, Nov.). *The drugs-crime wars: Past, present and future direction in theory, policy and program interventions.* Research Paper Series, no. 14. Chicago: ImpacTeen.

McCabe, S. E., Boyd, C. J., Cranford, J. A., Morales, M., and Slayden, J. (2006). A modified version of the Drug Abuse Screening Test among undergraduate students. *Journal of Substance Abuse Treatment, 31*(3), 297–303.

McColl, W., and Opio, S. (2003). Treatment instead of incarceration. *Behavioral Health Management, 23*(2), 21–24.

McCormick, A. (2003, Nov. 6). Hit by the bottle. *Community Care,* 38–40.

McDowell, D. (2000). Gay men, lesbians, and substances of abuse and the "club and circuit party scene": What clinicians should know. *Journal of Gay and Lesbian Psychotherapy, 3*(3–4), 37–57.

McGovern, M. P., Xie, H., Segal, S. R., Siembab, L., and Drake, R. E. (2006). Addiction treatment services and co-occurring disorders: Prevalence estimates, treatment practices, and barriers. *Journal of Substance Abuse Treatment, 31*, 267–275.

McHugh, D. (2007, Feb. 15). US, Britain ranked last on child welfare: UNICEF survey of 21 rich nations weighs social ills. *Boston Globe,* A4.

McHugo, G. J., Caspi, Y., Kammerer, N., Mazelis, R., Jackson, E. W., Russell, L., Clark, C., Liebschutz, J., and Kimerling, R. (2005). The assessment of trauma history in women with co-occurring substance abuse and mental disorders and a history of interpersonal violence. *Journal of Behavioral Health Services and Research, 32*(2), 113–127.

McKetin, R., McLaren, J., Riddell, S., and Robins, L. (2006, Aug.). The relationship between methamphetamine use and violent behaviour. *Crime and Justice Bulletin, 97,* 1–15.

McKirnan, D. J., and Peterson, P. L. (1992). Gay and lesbian alcohol use: Epidemiological and psycho-social perspectives. *Research on Alcohol and Other Drug Problem Prevention Among Lesbians and Gay Men.* Los Angeles: California Department of Alcohol and Drug Programs.

McLellan, A. T. (2002). Have we evaluated addiction treatment correctly? Implications from a chronic care perspective. *Addiction, 97*(3), 249–252.

McLellan, A. T., Cacciola, J., Alterman, A., Rikoon, S., and Carise, D. (2006). The Addiction Severity Index at 25: Origins, contributions and transitions. *American Journal of Addiction, 15*(2), 113–124.

McLellan, A. T., Carise, D., and Kleber, H. D. (2003). Can the national addiction treatment infrastructure support the public's demand for quality care? *Journal of Substance Abuse Treatment, 25,* 117–121.

McPhee, M. (2006, Nov. 15). Mom, DSS stand ground. *Boston Herald,* 5.

Medication + counseling: The "new paradigm" in alcoholism treatment (2005, July 25). *Alcoholism and Drug Abuse Weekly, 17*(28), 1, 6.

Medrano, M. A., Zule, W. A., Hatch, J., and Desmond, D. P. (1999). Prevalence of childhood trauma in a community sample of substance abusing women. *American Journal of Drug and Alcohol Abuse, 25*(3), 449–462.

Mehegan, D. (2005, Feb. 8). Coming clean. *Boston Globe,* E1, E6.

Meier-Tackmann, D., Leonhardt, R. A., Agarwal, D. P., and Goedde, H. W. (1990). Effect of acute ethanol drinking on alcohol metabolism in subjects with different ADH and ALDH genotypes. *Alcohol, 7*(5), 413–418.

Melnick, G., and De Leon, G. (1999). Clarifying the nature of therapeutic community treatment: The Survey of Essential Elements Questionnaire (SEEQ). *Journal of Substance Abuse Treatment, 16*(4), 307–313.

Mennella, J. A. (2001). Regulation of milk intake after exposure to alcohol in mother's milk. *Alcoholism: Clinical and Experimental Research, 25,* 590–593.

Merrick, E., Horgan, C. M., Hodgkin, D., Garnick, D. W., Houghton, S. F., Panas, L., Saitz, R., and Blow, F. C. (2008). Unhealthy drinking patterns in older adults: Prevalence and associated characteristics. *Journal of the American Geriatrics Society, 56*(2), 214–223.

Meyers, R., and Wolfe, B. (2004). *Get your loved one sober: Alternatives to nagging, pleading and threatening.* Center City, MN: Hazelden.

Michael, K. D., Curtin, L., Kirkley, D. E., Harris, R., and Jones, D. L. (2006). Group-based motivational interviewing for alcohol use among college students: An exploratory study. *Professional Psychology, Research and Practice, 37*(6), 629–634.

Mignon, S. I. (1993/1994). Physicians' treatment of elderly alcoholics. *Sociological Practice, 11,* 197–211.

Mignon, S. I. (1995). The discovery of patients' alcoholism by physicians. *Research in the Sociology of Health Care, 21,* 175–187.

Mignon, S. I. (1996). Physicians' perceptions of alcoholics: The disease concept reconsidered. *Alcoholism Treatment Quarterly, 41*(4), 33–45.

Mignon, S. I. (1998). Husband battering: A review of the debate over a controversial social phenomenon. In N. A. Jackson and G. C. Oates (eds.), *Violence in intimate relationships: Examining sociological and psychological issues* (137–159). Boston: Butterworth-Heinemann.

Mignon, S. I., and Holmes, W. M. (1995). Police response to mandatory arrest laws. *Crime and Delinquency, 41*(4), 430–442.

Mignon, S. I., Larson, C. J., and Holmes, W. M. (2002). *Family abuse: Consequences, theories and responses.* Boston: Allyn and Bacon.

Miller, B. A., Nochajski, T. H., Leonard, K. E., Blane, H. T., Gondoli, D. M., and Bowers, P. M. (1990). Spousal violence and alcohol/drug problems among parolees and their spouses. *Women and Criminal Justice, 1*(2), 55–71.

Miller, J. Q., Naimi, T. S., Brewer, R. D., and Jones, S. E. (2007). Binge drinking and associated health risk behaviors among high school students. *Pediatrics, 119*(1), 76–85.

Miller, K. E., Hoffman, J. H., Barnes, G. M., Sabo, D., Melnick, M. J., and Farrell, M. P. (2005). Adolescent anabolic steroid use, gender, physical activity, and other problem behaviors. *Substance Use and Misuse, 40,* 1637–1657.

Miller, W. R., and Rollnick, S. (1991). *Motivational interviewing: Preparing people to change addictive behavior.* New York: Guilford.

Miller, W. R., and Rollnick, S. (2002). *Motivational interviewing: Preparing people for change,* 2nd ed. New York: Guilford.

Miller, W. R., Walters, S. T., and Bennett, M. E. (2001). How effective is alcoholism treatment in the United States? *Journal of Studies on Alcohol, 62,* 211–220.

Moffatt, M. (1989). *Coming of age in New Jersey: College and American culture.* New Brunswick, NJ: Rutgers University Press.

Mohler-Kuo, M., Dowdall, G. W., Koss, M. P., and Wechsler, H. (2004). Correlates of rape while intoxicated in a national sample of college women. *Journal of Studies on Alcohol, 65,* 37–45.

Mojtabai, R., and Olfson, M. (2003). Medications costs, adherence, and health outcomes among Medicare beneficiaries. *Health Affairs, 22*(4), 220–229.

Moncrieff, J., and Farmer, R. (1998). Sexual abuse and the subsequent development of alcohol problems, *Alcohol and Alcoholism, 33*(6), 592–601.

Moog, C. (1991). Selling of addiction to women. *Media and Values,* 20–22.

Moore, A. A., Beck, J. C., Babor, T. F., Hays, R. D., and Reuben, D. B. (2002). Beyond alcoholism: Identifying older, at-risk drinkers in primary care. *Journal of Studies on Alcohol, 64*(3), 316–324.

Moos, R. H. (2003). Addictive disorders in context: Principles and puzzles of effective treatment and recovery. *Psychology of Addictive Behavior, 17*(1), 3–12.

Moos, R. H., Mertens, J. R., and Brennan, P. L. (1993). Patterns of diagnosis and treatment among late-middle-aged and older substance abuse patients. *Journal of Studies on Alcohol, 54,* 479–487.

Moriyama, Y., Mimura, M., Kato, M., and Kashima, H. (2006). Primary alcoholic dementia and alcohol-related dementia. *Psychogeriatrics, 6*(3), 114–118.

Morral, A., McCaffrey, D., and Paddock, S. (2002). Re-assessing the marijuana gateway effect. *Addiction, 97*(12), 1493–1504.

Morral, A. R., McCaffrey, D. F., Ridgeway, G., Mukherji, A., and Beighley, C. (2006). *The relative effectiveness of 10 adolescent substance abuse treatment programs in the United States.* Technical report (TR-346-CSAT). Rockville, MD: Center for Substance Abuse Treatment.

Morrow, D. (2004). Social work practice with gay, lesbian, bisexual and transgendered adolescents. *Families in Society, 85*(1), 91–99.

Mosher-Ashley, P., and Rabon, C. E. (2001). A comparison of older and younger adults attending Alcoholics Anonymous. *Clinical Gerontologist, 24,* 27–37.

MOST of Us (2008). *Social norms marketing.* Retrieved on July 23, 2008, from http://www.mostofus.org/about_us.php.

Moxey, E. D., O'Connor, J. P., Novielli, K. D., Teutsch, S., and Nash, D. B. (2003). Prescription drug use in the elderly: A descriptive analysis. *Health Care Financing Review, 24*(4), 127–141.

Mulligan, J. E. (2008, Oct. 5). Mental-health parity bill's long road to becoming law. *Providence Journal.* Retrieved on December 30, 2008, from www.facesandvoices ofrecovery.org/resources/in_the_news/2008/2008-10-06_becoming_law.

Mumola, C. J., and Karberg, J. C. (2007). *Drug use and dependence, state and federal prisoners.* Washington, DC: US Department of Justice, Bureau of Justice Statistics. Retrieved on December 27, 2008, from http://www.ojp.usdoj.gov/bjs/pub/pdf/dudsfp04.pdf.

Murphy, S., and Waldorf, D. (1998). Kickin' down to the street doc: Shooting galleries in the San Francisco Bay Area. In J. A. Inciardi and K. McElrath (eds.), *The American drug scene: An anthology,* 2nd ed. (122–131). Los Angeles: Roxbury.

Murray, M. D., and Callahan, C. M. (2003). Improving medication use for older adults: An integrated research agenda. *Annals of Internal Medicine, 139*(5) (part 2), 425–429.

Musick, M. A. (1996). Religion and subjective health among black and white elders. *Journal of Health and Social Behavior, 37*(3), 221–237.

Musto, D. (1987). *The American disease: Origins of narcotic control.* New Haven, CT: Yale University Press.

Myers, P. L. (2001). Editorial: Killing of the Innu. *Journal of Ethnicity in Substance Abuse, 1*(2), 1–7.

Myers, P. L. (2002a). Review of the book *Chemical dependency: A family affair. Journal of Teaching in the Addictions, 1*(1), 91–94.

Myers, P. L. (2002b). Beware the man of one book: Processing ideology in addictions education. *Journal of Teaching in the Addictions, 1*(1), 69–90.

Myers, P. L. (2002c). Pain, poverty, and hope: The charter issue. *Journal of Ethnicity in Substance Abuse, 1* (1), 1–5.

Myers, P. L., and Salt, N. (2007). *Becoming an addictions counselor: A comprehensive text,* 2nd ed. Sudbury, MA: Jones and Bartlett.

Najavits, L. M., Weiss, R. D., and Shaw, S. R. (1997). The link between substance abuse and posttraumatic stress disorder in women: A research review. *American Journal on Addictions, 6*(40), 273–283.

National Alliance of Methadone Advocates (2008). Retrieved on March 13, 2008, from http://www.methadone.org.

National Association of African Americans for Positive Imagery (2007). *Zipper Intelligence Briefing.* Retrieved on February 12, 2007, from http://www.naaapi.org/documents/zipper_briefing.asp.

National Association of Alcohol and Drug Abuse Counselors (2008). Retrieved on March 13, 2008, from http://www.naadac.org/documents/index.php.

National Center on Addiction and Substance Abuse at Columbia University (1999). *No safe haven: Children of substance-abusing parents.* New York: National Center on Addiction and Substance Abuse.

National Center on Addiction and Substance Abuse at Columbia University (2003, Dec.). *Food for thought: Substance abuse and eating disorders.* New York: National Center on Addiction and Substance Abuse.

National Center on Addiction and Substance Abuse at Columbia University (2005, March). *Family matters: Substance abuse and the American family.* CASA white paper. New York: National Center on Addiction and Substance Abuse.

National Center on Addiction and Substance Abuse at Columbia University (2006a). *Women under the influence.* Baltimore: Johns Hopkins University Press.

National Center on Addiction and Substance Abuse at Columbia University (2006b). *"You've got drugs": Prescription drug pushers on the Internet, 2006 update.* New York: National Center on Addiction and Substance Abuse.

National Center on Birth Defects and Developmental Disabilities (2004, July). *Fetal alcohol syndrome: Guidelines for referral and diagnosis.* Washington, DC: Centers for Disease Control and Prevention, US Department of Health and Human Services.

National Institute of Health (2004). *Inhalant Abuse.* NIH Publication No. 00-3818. Washington, DC: US Government Printing Office.

National Institute of Justice (2006, June). *Drug courts: The second decade.* Washington, DC: Office of Justice Programs.

National Institute on Alcohol Abuse and Alcoholism (1995, Oct.). Diagnostic criteria for alcohol abuse and dependence. *Alcohol Alert, no. 30.* Retrieved on December 29, 2008, from http://pubs.niaaa.nih.gov/publications/aa30.htm.

National Institute on Alcohol Abuse and Alcoholism (2000a). *10th special report to the US Congress on alcohol and health: Highlights from current research.* Rockville, MD: US Department of Health and Human Services.

National Institute on Alcohol Abuse and Alcoholism (2000b). Fetal alcohol exposure and the brain. *Alcohol Alert, no. 50.* Washington, DC: US Department of Health and Human Services.

National Institute on Alcohol Abuse and Alcoholism (2002, April). Screening for alcohol problems—An update. *Alcohol Alert, 56.* Retrieved on May 1, 2003, from http://www.niaaa.nih.gov/publications/aa56.htm.

National Institute on Alcohol Abuse and Alcoholism (2004). *Research on the prevention of alcohol abuse in the older population.* Retrieved on July 23, 2004, from http://www.niaaa.nih.gov/extramural/adults-text.htm.

National Institute on Alcohol Abuse and Alcoholism (2006, Dec. 13). *Apparent ethanol consumption for the United States, 1850–2003.* Retrieved on April 12, 2007, from http://www.niaa.gov.ResourcesDatabaseResources/QuickFacts/AlcoholSales.

National Institute on Alcohol Abuse and Alcoholism (2007). *Resources: State laws and drinking.* Retrieved on June 11, 2008, from http://www.niaaa.nih.gov/Resources/DatabaseResources/QuickFacts/Other/default.htm.

National Institute on Alcohol Abuse and Alcoholism (2008). *Alcohol Policy Classification System.* Retrieved on December 30, 2008, from http://www.alcoholpolicy.niaaa.nih.gov/.

National Institute on Drug Abuse (2001, Jan.). Facts about inhalant abuse. *NIDA Notes, 15*(6). Retrieved on December 31, 2008, from http://www.drugabuse.gov/NIDA_Notes/NNVol115N6/tearoff.html.

National Institute on Drug Abuse (2004). *Cocaine abuse and addiction.* NIH Publication no. 99-4342, printed May 1999, revised November 2004.

National Institute on Drug Abuse (2006, June). *Epidemiologic trends in drug abuse: Advance report.* Community Epidemiology Work Group. Washington, DC: US Government Printing Office.

National Institute on Drug Abuse (2008). *Research report series—Prescription drugs: Abuse and addiction.* Retrieved on December 21, 2008, from http://www.nida.nih.gov/ResearchReports/Prescription/prescription5.html.

Nawyn, S. J., Richman, J. A., Rospenda, K. M., and Hughes, T. L. (2000). Sexual identity and alcohol-related outcomes: Contributions of workplace harassment. *Journal of Substance Abuse, 11*(3), 289–304.

Nelson, T. F., and Wechsler, H. (2001). Alcohol and college athletes. *Medicine and Science in Sports and Exercise, 33*(1), 43–47.

Nelson-Zlupko, L., Kauffman, E., and Dore, M. M. (1995). Gender differences in drug addiction and treatment: Implications for social work intervention with substance-abusing women. *Social Work, 40*(10), 45–64.

Nemoto, T., Aoki, B., Huang, K., Morris, A., Nguyen, H., and Wong, W. (1999). Drug use behaviors among Asian drug users in San Francisco. *Journal of Addictive Behaviors, 24*(6), 823–838.

Nemoto, T., Operario, D., Nguyen, H. M., and Sugano, E. (2005). Promoting health for transgendered women: Transgender Resources and Neighborhood Space (TRANS) program in San Francisco. *American Journal of Public Health, 95*(3), 382–384.

Newman, P. A., Rhodes, F., and Weiss, R. E. (2004). Correlates of sex trading among drug-using men who have sex with men. *American Journal of Public Health, 94*(11), 1998–2003.

Nimmer, R. (1971). *Two million unnecessary arrests.* Chicago: American Bar Foundation.

Niv, N., and Hser, Y.-I. (2006). Drug treatment and outcomes for Hispanic and white methamphetamine users. *Health Services Research, 41*(4.1), 1242–1257.

Norris, J. (1994). Alcohol and female sexuality: A look at expectancies and risks. *Alcohol Health and Research World, 18*, 197–201.

Northeast Addiction Technology Transfer Center (NeATTC) (2004, Jan. 27). *Workforce development summit: Take action to build a stronger addiction workforce.* Pittsburgh, PA: Institute for Research, Education, and Training in Addictions.

Nuwer, H. (2002). *Wrongs of passage: Fraternities, sororities, hazing, binge drinking.* Bloomington: Indiana University Press.

Nuwer, H. (2004). *The hazing reader.* Bloomington: Indiana University Press.

Obst, P., Davey, J., and Sheehan, M. (2001). Does joining the police service drive you to drink? A longitudinal study of the drinking habits of police recruits. *Drugs: Education, Prevention and Policy, 8,* 347–357.

O'Connor, M. J., and Whaley, S. E. (2003). Alcohol use in pregnant low-income women. *Journal of Studies on Alcohol, 64*(6), 773–783.

Odgers, P., Houghton, S., and Douglas, G. (1996). Reputation enhancement theory and adolescent substance use. *Journal of Child Psychology, 37,* 1015–1022.

O'Farrell, T. J., and Fals-Stewart, W. (2006). *Behavioral couples therapy for alcoholism and drug abuse.* New York: Guilford.

Office of National Drug Control Policy (2006). *Marijuana—drug facts.* Retrieved on May 1, 2007, from http://www.whitehousedrugpolicy.gov/DrugFact/Marijuana/marijuana_ff.html.

Office of National Drug Control Policy (2007). *Cocaine facts and figures.* Washington, DC: US Government Printing Office. Retrieved on July 8, 2008, from http://www.whitehousedrugpolicy.gov/drugfact/cocaine/cocaine/cocaine_ff.html.

Office of National Drug Control Policy (2008, April 7). Federal health insurers add new substance abuse services. Press release. Retrieved on July 21, 2008, from http://www.whitehousedrugpolicy.gov/news/press08/040708.html.

O'Gorman, P. (1993). Codependency explored: A social movement in search of definition and treatment. *Psychiatric Quarterly, 64*(2), 199–212.

O'Hare, T. (1990). Drinking in college: Consumption patterns, sex differences, and legal drinking. *Journal of Studies on Alcohol, 51,* 536–541.

O'Hare, T., and Sherrer, M. V. (1999). Validating the Alcohol Use Disorder Identification Test with college first-offenders. *Journal of Substance Abuse Treatment, 17*(1–2), 113–119.

Older problem drinkers: Their special needs, and a nursing home geared toward those needs (1975, Spring). *Alcohol Health and Research World,* 12–17.

O'Neill, J. V. (2003). Educators focus on aging: Social work education in aging moves out of the shadows. *NASW News, 48*(4), 10.

Oostveen, T., Knibbe, R., and de Vries, H. (1996). Social influences on young adults' alcohol consumption: Norms, modeling, pressure, socializing, and conformity. *Addictive Behaviors, 21*(2), 187–197.

Opler, M. E. (1938). The use of peyote by the Carrizo and Lipan Apache tribes. *American Anthropologist, 40,* 271–285.

Ornes, S. (2006, Nov. 29). What ever happened to crack babies? *Discover Magazine.* Retrieved on February 11, 2008, from http://discovermagazine.com/2006/dec/crack-baby-unfounded-stigma.

Oslin, D. W. (2006, Nov. 1). The changing face of substance misuse in older adults. *Psychiatric Times, 23*(13), 33–41.

Oslin, D. W., Slaymaker, V. J., Blow, F. C., Owen, P. L., and Colleran, C. (2005). Treatment outcomes for alcohol dependence among middle-aged and older adults. *Addictive Behaviors, 30*(7), 1431–1436.

Paltrow, L. M. (1992). *Criminal prosecutions against pregnant women* (Reproductive Freedom Project of the American Civil Liberties Union). New York: American Civil Liberties Union.

Pandina, R. (1982). Effects of alcohol on psychological processes. In E. Gomberg, H. White, and J. Carpenter (eds.), *Alcohol, science and society revisited* (38–62). Ann Arbor: University of Michigan Press.

Patterson, T. L., and Jeste, D. V. (1999). The potential impact of the baby-boom generation on substance abuse among elderly persons. *Psychiatric Services, 50*(9), 1184–1188.

Pattilo-McCoy, M. (1998). Black church culture as a community strategy of action in the black community. *American Sociological Review, 63*(6), 767–784.

Paul, P., Stall, R., and Bloomfield, K. (1991). Gay and alcoholic: Epidemiological and clinical issues. *Alcohol Health and Research World, 15*, 151–160.

Peake, M. (1994). The culture of binge drinking: Alcohol initiation in adolescent males. *Health Promotion Journal of Australia, 4*(1), 62–63.

Peele, S. (1989). *Diseasing of America: Addiction treatment out of control.* Boston: Houghton Mifflin.

Peleg-Oren, N., and Teichman, M. (2006). Young children of parents with substance use disorders (SUD): A review of the literature and implications for social work practice. *Journal of Social Work Practice in the Addictions, 6*(1–2), 49–61.

Peralta, R. L. (2007). College alcohol use and the embodiment of hegemonic masculinity among European American men. *Sex Roles, 56*(11–12), 741–756.

Perkins, H. (2002). Social norms and the prevention of alcohol misuse in collegiate contexts. *Journal of Studies on Alcohol,* Supplement No. 14, 164–172.

Peters, R., Copeland, J., and Dillon, P. (1999). Anabolic-androgenic steroids: User characteristics, motivations, and deterrents. *Psychology of Addictive Behavior, 13*(3), 232–242.

Peterson, L. E. (2007, Winter). Hazelden adds anti-addiction medications as a treatment tool. *Voice, 12*(1), 1, 6.

Pettiway, L. E. (1993). Identifying, gaining access to, and collecting data on African-American drug addicts. In M. R. De La Rosa and J.-L. R. Andrados (eds.), *Drug use among minority youth: Advances in research and methodology.* NIDA Research Monograph 130 (258–279). Rockville, MD: National Institute on Drug Abuse.

Peveler, R., and Fairburn, C. (1990). Eating disorders in women who abuse alcohol. *British Journal of Addictions, 85*(12), 1633–1638.

Physicians' Desk Reference (2008). 62nd ed. Montville, NJ: Thomson Health Care.

Picard, F. L. (1991). *Family intervention: Ending the cycle of addiction and codependence.* New York: Prentice-Hall.

Pilat, J. M., and Jones, J. W. (1984/1985, Winter). Identification of alcoholics: Two empirical studies. *Alcohol Health and Research World,* 27–36.

Pincus, A. H. (2003). The future of behavioral health and primary care: Drowning in the mainstream or left on the bank? *Psychosomatics, 44*(1), 1–11.

Plasse, B. R. (1995). Parenting groups for recovering addicts in a day treatment center. *Social Work, 40*(1), 65–74.

Polsky, N. (1969). *Hustlers, beats and others.* Garden City, NY: Doubleday/Anchor.

Preboth, M. (2001, Feb. 15). AAP statement on prenatal exposure to alcohol. *American Family Physician, 63*(4), 793.

Presley, C., Meilman, P., and Leichliter, J. (2002). College factors that influence drinking. *Journal of Studies on Alcohol,* Supplement no. 14, 82–90.

Preusser, D. F., Williams, A. F., and Weinstein, H. B. (1994). Policing underage alcohol sales. *Journal of Safety Research, 25*, 127–133.

Prochaska, J. O., and DiClemente, C. C. (1982). Stages and process of self-change in smoking: Towards an integrative model of change. *Psychotherapy, 20*, 161–173.

Prochaska, J. O., Norcross, J. C., and DiClemente, C. C. (1994). *Changing for good.* New York: William Morrow.

Quigley, B. M., and Leonard, K. E. (2005). Alcohol use and violence among young adults. *Alcohol Research and Health, 28*(4), 191–194.

Radin, P. (1970). *The Winnebago tribe.* Lincoln: University of Nebraska Press. (Originally *Thirty-seventh annual report of the Bureau of American Ethnography* [1923]. Washington, DC: Smithsonian Institution.)

Rasch, R. F., Weisen, C. A., MacDonald, B., Wechsberg, W. M., Perritt, R., and Dennis, M. L. (2000). Patterns of HIV risk and alcohol use among African-American crack abusers. *Drug and Alcohol Dependence, 58*(3), 259–266.

Rathbone-McCuan, E., and Triegaardt, J. (1979, Summer). The older alcoholic and the family. *Alcohol Health and Research World,* 7–12.

Ratner, M. (ed.) (1993). *Crack pipe as pimp: An ethnographic investigation of sex-for-crack exchanges.* New York: Lexington Books.

Ray, H. (2000, Sept. 14). MIT, Krueger family settle freshman's alcohol-related death for $6M. *Daily Free Press Online Edition.* Retrieved on January 12, 2005, from http://www.dailyfreepress.com/news/1.948038-1.948038.

Rebach, H. (1992). Alcohol and drug use among American minorities. In J. E. Trimble, C. S. Bolek, and S. J. Niemcryk (eds.), *Ethnic and multicultural drug abuse: Perspectives on current research* (23–57). New York: Haworth.

Reid, M. C., Tinetti, M. E., O'Connor, P. G., Kosten, T. R., and Concato, J. (2003). Measuring alcohol consumption among older adults: A comparison of available methods. *The American Journal on Addictions, 12*(3), 211–219.

Reinarman, C., and Levine, H. G. (eds.) (1997). *Crack in America: Demon drugs and social justice.* Berkeley: University of California Press.

Reinert, D. F. (1999). Group intervention for children of recovering alcoholic parents. *Alcoholism Treatment Quarterly, 17*(4), 15–27.

Resnicow, K. Soler, R., Braithwaite, R. L., Ahluwalia, J. S., and Butler, J. (2000). Cultural sensitivity in substance abuse prevention. *Journal of Community Psychology, 28*(3), 271–290.

Ridgely, M. S., and Iguchi, M. Y. (2004). Coercive use of vaccines against drug addiction: Is it permissible and is it good public policy? *Virginia Journal of Social Policy and the Law, 12*(2), 260–261.

Rienzi, B. M., McMillin, J. D., Dickson, C. L., Crauthers, D., McNeill, K. F., Pesina, M. D., and Mann, E. (1996). Gender differences regarding peer influence and attitude towards substance abuse. *Journal of Drug Education, 26*(4), 339–347.

Riggs, L. (1970). College administration of alcoholic beverage regulation. In G. L. Maddox (ed.), *The domesticated drug: Drinking among collegians* (408–436). New Haven, CT: College and University Press.

Rigler, S. K. (2000, March 15). Alcoholism in the elderly. *American Family Physician, 61*(6), 1710–1716.

Ritner, B., and Dozier, C. D. (2000). Effects of court-ordered substance abuse treatment in child protection services cases. *Social Work, 45*(2), 131–140.

Rivara, F. P., Mueller, B. A., Somes, G., Mendoza, C. T., Rushforth, N. B., and Kellermann, A. L. (1997). Alcohol and illicit drug abuse and the risk of violent death in the home. *Journal of the American Medical Association, 278*(7), 569–575.

Rivers, P. (1994). *Alcohol and human behavior.* Englewood Cliffs, NJ: Prentice Hall.

Roberts, A. R. (1987). Psychosocial characteristics of batterers: A study of 234 men charged with domestic violence offenses. *Journal of Family Violence, 2*(1), 81–93.

Roberts, D. E. (1991). Punishing drug addicts who have babies: Women of color, equality, and the right of privacy. *Harvard Law Review, 104*, 124–155.

Roberts, S. J., Grindel, C. G., Patsdaughter, C. A., and Demarco, R. (2005). Lesbian use and abuse of alcohol: Results of the Boston Lesbian Health Project II. *Substance Abuse, 25*(4), 1–9.

Rogan, M. (2001, March 4). Please take our children away. *New York Times*, final ed., section 6, 40.

Roland, E. J., and Kaskutas, L. A. (2002). Alcoholics Anonymous and church involvement as predictors of sobriety among three ethnic treatment populations. *Journal of Child and Adolescent Substance Abuse, 20*(1), 61–77.

Room, R. (1984). Alcohol and ethnography: A case of problem deflation? *Current Anthropology, 25*, 169–191.

Rosinski, J. (2004, Dec. 22). Hookers, crack and gramps. *Boston Herald*, 8.

Ross, M. W., Mattison, A. M., and Franklin, D. R. (2003). Club drugs and sex on drugs are associated with different motivations for gay circuit party attendance in men. *Substance Use and Misuse, 38*(8), 1173–1183.

Rotunda, R. J., and Doman, K. (2001). Partner enabling of substance use disorders: Critical review and future directions. *The American Journal of Family Therapy, 29*(4), 257–262.

Royal Commission on Aboriginal Peoples (1996). *Report of the Royal Commission on Aboriginal Peoples*. Ottawa, Canada: Royal Commission on Aboriginal Peoples.

Royce, J. E., and Scratchley, D. (1996). *Alcoholism and other drug problems*, revised ed. New York: Free Press.

Ruben, D. H. (1999). Diagnosing alcoholism and its addictive patterns using self-report rating scales. *Alcoholism Treatment Quarterly, 17*(3), 37–46.

Rubington, E. (1997). Prohibition and freshman residence halls: A study of university alcohol policy. In P. Rivers and E. Shore (eds.), *Substance abuse on campus* (141–161). Westport, CT: Greenwood Press.

Sacks, S., Chandler, R., and Gonzales, J. (2008). Responding to the challenge of co-occurring disorders: Suggestions for future research. *Journal of Substance Abuse Treatment, 34*(1), 139–146.

Salinger, S. S. (2002). *Taverns and drinking in early America*. Baltimore: Johns Hopkins University Press.

Saltzman, J. (2008a, July 18). Inequity's end means new start for 31: Crack offenders see US sentences trimmed. *Boston Globe*, A1, A19.

Saltzman, J. (2008b, Dec. 25). Drug law puzzles police. *Boston Globe*, A1, A14.

Samet, J. J., Rollnick, S., and Barnes, H. (1996). Beyond CAGE: A brief clinical approach after detection of substance abuse. *Archives of Internal Medicine, 156*, 2287–2293.

Samson, C., Wilson, J., and Mazower, J. (1999). *Canada's Tibet: The killing of the Innu*. London: Survival International.

Sanday, P. R. (2007). *Fraternity gang rape: Sex, brotherhood, and privilege on campus*, 2nd ed. New York: New York University Press.

Santisteban, D. A., Tejeda, M., Dominicis, C., and Szpocznik, J. (1999). An efficient tool for screening for maladaptive family functioning in adolescent drug abusers: The problem oriented screening instrument for teenagers. *American Journal of Drug and Alcohol Abuse, 25*(2), 197–206.

SASSI Institute (2008). *SASSI promotional materials*. Retrieved on July 17, 2008, from http://www.sassi.com.

Schliebner, C. T., and Peregoy, J. J. (1998). Alcohol and other drug prevention and intervention: Characteristics and issues of selected populations. In P. Stevens and R. Smith (eds.), *Substance abuse prevention and intervention: Theory and practice* (193–219). New York: Macmillan.

Schlit, R., Lie, G. Y., and Montagne, M. (1990). Substance use as a correlate of violence in intimate lesbian relationships. *Journal of Homosexuality, 19*(3), 51–65.

Schmid, J. (2002). Women in self-help programs. In S. L. A. Straussner and S. Brown (eds.), *The handbook of addiction treatment for women* (539–557). San Francisco: Jossey-Bass.

Schneider Institute for Health (2001). *Substance abuse: The nation's number one health problem: Key indicators for policy.* Waltham, MA: Brandeis University.

Schonfeld, L., and Dupree, L. W. (1996). Treatment alternatives for older alcohol abusers. In A. Gurnack (ed.), *Older adults' misuse of alcohol, medicines, and other drugs: Research and practice issues* (113–131). New York: Springer.

Schuckit, M. A., Tsuang, J. W., Anthenelli, R. M., Tipp, J. E., and Nurnberger, J. I., Jr. (1996). Alcohol challenges in young men from alcoholic pedigrees and control families: A report from the COGA project. *Journal of Studies on Alcohol, 57,* 368–377.

Schuh J. H., and Shore, E. R. (1997). Policy development: An essential element in addressing campus substance abuses. In P. Rivers and E. Shore (eds.), *Substance abuse on campus* (101–117). Westport, CT: Greenwood.

Schulenberg, J., and Maggs, J. (2002). A developmental perspective on alcohol use and heavy drinking in young adulthood. *Journal of Studies on Alcohol,* Supplement no. 14, 54–70.

Schultz, S. K., Arndt, S., and Liesveld, J. (2003). Locations of facilities with special programs for older substance abuse clients in the U.S. *International Journal of Geriatric Psychiatry, 18*(9), 839–843.

Schutte, K., Byrne, E., Brennan, P., and Moos, R. (2001). Successful remission of late-life drinking problems: A 10-year follow-up. *Journal of Studies on Alcohol, 62,* 322–330.

Selzer, M. L. (1971). The Michigan Alcohol Screening Test: The quest for a new diagnostic instrument. *American Journal of Psychiatry, 127,* 1653–1658.

Selzer, M. L., Vinokur, A., and Van Rooijan, L. (1975). A self-administered Short Michigan Alcoholism Screening Test (SMAST). *Journal of Studies on Alcohol, 3*(6), 117–126.

Shafer Commission Report (1972). *Marihuana: A signal of misunderstanding.* Washington, DC: National Commission on Marihuana and Drug Abuse.

Shedlin, M. G., and Deren, S. (2002). Cultural factors influencing HIV risk behavior among Dominicans in New York City. *Journal of Ethnicity in Substance Abuse, 1*(1), 71–95.

Sherman, S. G. (2006). Critical condition facing needle exchange programs: The politics of science. *Substance Use and Misuse, 41*(6–7), 827–829.

Shipley, A. (2007, Oct. 5). Jones admits steroid use in letter. *Boston Globe,* E1.

Shoptaw, S., and Reback, C. (2007, April). Methamphetamine use and infectious disease–related behaviors in men who have sex with men: Implications for interventions. *Addiction, 102,* 130–135.

Shore, E. R., and Pieri, S. (1992). Drinking behavior of women in four occupational groups. *Women's Health, 19,* 55–64.

Silkworth, W. (1976). The doctor's opinion. In *The big book,* 3rd ed. (xxiii–xxx). New York: AA World Services.

Skinner, H. A. (1982). Drug Abuse Screening Test. *Addictive Behavior, 7*(4), 363–371.

Small, W., Kain, S., Laliberte, N., Schechter, M. T., O'Shaughnessy, M. V., and Spittal, P. M. (2005). Incarceration, addiction and harm reduction: Inmates experience injecting drugs in prison. *Substance Use and Misuse, 40*(6), 831–843.

Smith, D. A., Johnson, A. B., Pears, K. C., Fisher, P. A., and DeGarmo, D. S. (2007). Child maltreatment and foster care: Unpacking the effects of prenatal and postnatal parental substance abuse. *Child Maltreatment, 12*(2), 150–160.

Smith, D. M., and Atkinson, R. M. (1997). Alcoholism and dementia. In A. M. Gurnack (ed.), *Older adults' misuse of alcohol, medicines, and other drugs: Research and practice issues* (132–157). New York: Springer.

Smyth, N. J., and Miller, B. A. (1998). Parenting issues for substance abusing women. In S. L. A. Straussner and E. Zelvin (eds.), *Gender issues in addiction: Men and women in treatment* (125–150). New York: Jason Aronson.

Spindler, G., and Spindler, L. (1971). *Dreamers without power: The Menomini Indians.* New York: Holt, Rinehart & Winston.

Spohn, C., and Holleran, D. (2002). The effect of imprisonment on recidivism rates of felony offenders: A focus on drug offenders. *Criminology, 40*(2), 329–358.

Stall, R., Paul, J., Greenwood, G., Pollack, L., Bein, E., Crosby, G. M., Mills, T., Binson, D., Coates, T., and Catania, J. (2001). Alcohol use, drug use, and alcohol-related problems among men who have sex with men: The Urban Men's Health Study. *Addiction, 96*(11), 1589–1602.

Starks, M. (1982). *Cocaine fiends and reefer madness: An illustrated history of drugs in the movies.* New York: Cornwall.

Stein, R. (2005, Jan. 20). Study of women finds moderate drinking protects mental ability. *Boston Globe*, A3.

Sterk-Elifson, C. (1996). Just for fun? Cocaine use among middle-class women. *Journal of Drug Issues, 26*(1), 63–66.

Stewart, D., Gossop, M., and Trakada, K. (2007). Drug dependent parents: Childcare responsibilities, involvement with treatment services, and treatment outcomes. *Addictive Behaviors, 32*(8), 1657–1668.

Stewart, O. C. (1987). *Peyote religion.* Norman: University of Oklahoma Press.

Stoesen, L. (2008, March 6). Courts hear cases on pregnancy in prison. *NASW News*, 6.

Storm, T., and Cutler, R. (1981). Observation of drinking in natural settings: Vancouver beer parlors and cocktail lounges. *Journal of Studies on Alcohol, 42*, 972–997.

Straus, R. (1976). Problem drinking in the perspective of social change, 1940–1973. In W. J. Filstead, J. J. Rossi, and M. Keller (eds.), *Alcohol and alcohol problems: New thinking and new directions* (29–56). Cambridge, MA: Ballinger.

Stuart, G. L. (2005). Improving violence intervention outcomes by integrating alcohol treatment. *Journal of Interpersonal Violence, 20*(4), 388–393.

Substance Abuse and Mental Health Services Administration (1997). *National household survey on drug use: Office of applied studies.* Rockville, MD: SAMHSA.

Substance Abuse and Mental Health Services Administration (1998). *Prevalence of substance use among racial and ethnic subgroups in the United States 1991–1993.* DHHS Publication No. SMA 983202. Rockville, MD: SAMHSA.

Substance Abuse and Mental Health Services Administration (2002). *Promoting older adult health: Aging network partnerships to address medications, alcohol, and mental health.* Rockville, MD: SAMHSA.

Substance Abuse and Mental Health Services Administration, Center for Mental Health Services Administration (2003). *Co-occurring mental and substance abuse disorders: A guide for mental health planning and advisory councils.* Rockville, MD: SAMHSA. Retrieved August 30, 2005, from http://media.shs.net/ken/pdf/NMH03-0146/NMH03-0146.pdf.

Substance Abuse and Mental Health Services Administration (2004). *Mandatory guidelines for federal workplace drug testing programs.* Retrieved on December 11, 2005, from http://dwp.samhsa.gov/index.aspx.

Substance Abuse and Mental Health Services Administration, Office of Applied Studies (2005a). *The DASIS Report: National survey of substance abuse treatment services: 2003.* Retrieved on August 30, 2005, from http://www.drugabuse statistics.samhsa.gov/2k5/NSSATS/NSSATS.pdf.

Substance Abuse and Mental Health Services Administration, Office of Applied Statistics (2005b). *Overview of the findings of the 2004 National Survey on Drug Use and Health,* NSDUH Series H-27, DHHS Publication No. SM 5-4061. Rockville, MD: SAMHSA.

Substance Abuse and Mental Health Services Administration (2006a). Emergency department visits involving ADHD stimulant medications. *The New DAWN Report, 29.* Rockville, MD: SAMHSA.

Substance Abuse and Mental Health Services Administration (2006b). *Characteristics of recent adolescent inhalant initiates national survey of drug use and health: NSDUH report.* Rockville, MD: SAMHSA.

Substance Abuse and Mental Health Services Administration (2006c). *Results from the 2005 National Survey on Drug Use and Health: National Findings.* Office of Applied Statistics, NSDUH Series H-30, DHHS Publication No. SMA 6-4194. Rockville, MD: SAMHSA.

Substance Abuse and Mental Health Services Administration (2007a). *Results from the 2006 National Survey on Drug Use and Health: National findings.* Office of Applied Studies NSDUH Series H-32, DHHS Publication No. SMA 07-4293. Rockville, MD: SAMHSA.

Substance Abuse and Mental Health Services Administration (2007b, March 30). Sexually transmitted diseases and substance use. *The NSDUH report.* Rockville, MD: SAMHSA.

Substance Abuse and Mental Health Services Administration (2008). *Results from the 2007 National Survey on Drug Use and Health: National findings.* Office of Applied Studies, NSDUH Series H-34, DHHS Publication No. SMA 08-4343. Rockville, MD: SAMHSA.

Sun, A. P. (2006). Program factors related to women's substance abuse treatment retention and other outcomes: A review and critique. *Journal of Substance Abuse Treatment, 30*(1), 1–20.

Surratt, H. L., and Inciardi, J. A. (1998). Cocaine, crack, and the criminalization of pregnancy. In J. A. Inciardi and K. McElrath (eds.), *The American drug scene: An anthology,* 2nd ed. (181–190). Los Angeles: Roxbury.

Sutherland, E. (1970*). Criminology.* Philadelphia: J. B. Lippincott.

Sweet, R. I., and Saules, K. K. (2003). Validity of the Substance Abuse Subtle Screening Inventory–Adolescent Version (SASSI-A). *Journal of Substance Abuse Treatment, 24*(4), 331–340.

Taleff, M. J. (1997). *A handbook to assess and treat resistance in chemical dependency.* Dubuque, IA: Kendall/Hunt.

Teitelbaum, L., and Mullen, B. (2000). The validity of the MAST in psychiatric settings: A meta-analytic integration. *Journal of Studies on Alcohol, 61*(2), 254–261.

Teplin, L. A. (2001, Jan.). Assessing alcohol, drug, and mental disorders in juvenile detainees. *OJJDP fact sheet.* Washington, DC: US Department of Justice, Office of Juvenile Justice and Delinquency Prevention.

Terry, C. E., and Pellens, M. (1928). *The opium problem.* New York: Committee on Drug Addictions, Bureau of Social Hygiene, Inc.

Thio, A. (2001). *Deviant behavior.* Boston: Allyn and Bacon.

Thomas, B. S. (1995). The effectiveness of selected risk factors in mediating gender differences in drinking and its problems. *Journal of Adolescent Health, 17*(2), 91–98.

Thomas, D. (1993). *Manual for developing a substance abuse screening protocol for the juvenile court and implementing the Client Substance Index–Short Form (CSI-SF)*. Pittsburgh: National Center for Juvenile Justice.

Thompson, M. P., and Kingree, J. B. (2006). The roles of victim and perpetrator alcohol use in intimate partner violence outcomes. *Journal of Interpersonal Violence, 21*(2), 163–177.

Thornton, M. (2007, Winter). Prohibition versus legalization: Do economists reach a conclusion on drug policy? *The Independent Review, 11*(3), 417–433.

Tiet, Q. Q., and Mausbach, B. (2007). Treatments for patients with dual diagnosis: A review. *Alcoholism: Clinical and Experimental Research, 31*(4), 513–536.

Tjaden, P., and Thoennes, N. (2006, Jan.). Extent, nature, and consequences of rape victimization: Findings from the National Violence Against Women Survey. NCJ210346. Washington, DC: US Department of Justice, Office of Justice Programs.

Toomey, T., and Wagenaar, A. (2002). Environmental policies to reduce college drinking: Options and research findings. *Journal of Studies on Alcohol*, Supplement no. 14, 193–205.

Trice, H., and Wahl, J. (1958). A rank order analysis of the symptoms of alcoholism. *Quarterly Journal of Studies on Alcohol, 19*, 636–648.

Trocki, K. F., Drabble, L., and Midanik, L. (2005). Use of heavier drinking contexts among heterosexuals, homosexuals and bisexuals: Results from a national household probability survey. *Journal of Studies on Alcohol, 66*(1), 105–111.

Tuchfield, B. (1981). Spontaneous remission in alcoholics: Empirical observations and theoretical implications. *Journal of Studies on Alcohol, 42*, 626–641.

Tucker, J. S., Orlando, M., and Ellickson, P. (2003). Patterns and correlates of binge drinking trajectories from early adolescence to young adulthood. *Health Psychology, 2*(1), 79–87.

Turner, E. H., Matthews, A. M., Linardatos, E., and Rosenthal, R. (2008, Jan. 17). Selective publication of antidepressant trials and its influence on apparent efficacy. *New England Journal of Medicine, 358*(3), 252–260.

Ullman, A. (1953). The first drinking experience of addictive and "normal" drinkers. *Quarterly Journal of Studies on Alcohol, 14*, 181–191.

Underwood, M. (2008, April 15). One legged 76-year-old busted in drug sting. *Boston Herald*, 19.

United Nations Office on Drugs and Crime (2004). *Substance abuse treatment and care for women: Case studies and lessons learned; Drug Abuse Treatment Toolkit*. New York: United Nations.

United Nations Office on Drugs and Crime (2006). *World drug report*. Retrieved on July 8, 2007, from http://www.unodc.org/unodc/en/worlddrugreport.html.

US Census Bureau (2007). *2006 American Community Survey*. Retrieved on July 5, 2007, from http://www.census.gov/acs/www/.

US Department of Justice, Federal Bureau of Investigation (2006, Sept.). *Crime in the United States 2005*. Retrieved on December 27, 2008, from http://www.fbi.gov/ucr/05cius/offenses/violent_crime/murder_homicide.html.

Vaccaro, D., and Wills, T. A. (1998). Stress-coping factors in adolescent substance use: Test of ethnic and gender differences in a sample of urban adolescents. *Journal of Drug Education, 28*, 257–282.

VanDeMark, N. R., Russell, L. A., O'Keefe, M., Finkelstein, N., Noether, C. D., and Gampel, J. C. (2005). Children of mothers with histories of substance abuse, mental illness, and trauma. *Journal of Community Psychology, 33*(4), 445–459.

Van Den Berg, C. (2007). Full participation in harm reduction programmes is associated with decreased risk for human immunodeficiency virus and hepatitis C virus: Evidence from the Amsterdam Cohort Studies among drug users. *Addiction, 102*(9), 1454–1462.

Vander Bilt, J., Hall, M. N., Shaffer, H. J., and Higgins-Biddle, J. C. (1997). Assessing substance abuse treatment provider training needs: Screening skills. *Journal of Substance Abuse Treatment, 14*(2), 163–171.

Vanderbilt Addiction Center (2001). *Drug Abuse Screening Test (DAST)*. Retrieved on July 17, 2008, from http://kc.vanderbilt.edu/addiction/dast.html.

Vanicelli, M. (1989). *Group psychotherapy with adult children of alcoholics*. New York: Guilford Press.

van Wormer, K., and McKinney, R. (2003). What schools can do to help gay/lesbian/ bisexual youth: A harm reduction approach. *Adolescence, 38*(151), 409–420.

Vaznis, J. (2007, March 21). Promgoer drinking spurs some schools to take the wheel. *Boston Globe*, A1, A18.

von Zielbauer, P. (2007). For US troops at war, liquor is spur to crime. *New York Times,* 4, A10.

Waern, M., Runeson, B. S., Allebeck, P., Beskow, J., Rubenowitz, E., Skoof, I., and Wilhelmsson, K. (2002). Mental disorder in elderly suicides: A case-control study. *American Journal of Psychiatry, 159*(3), 450–455.

Walsh, C., MacMillan, H. L., and Jamieson, E. (2003). The relationship between parental substance abuse and child maltreatment: Findings from the Ontario Health Supplement. *Child Abuse and Neglect, 27*(12), 1409–1425.

Walter, H., Gutierrez, K., Ramskogler, K., Hertling, I., Dvorak, A., and Lesch, O. M., et al. (2003). Gender-specific differences in alcoholism: Implications for treatment. *Archives of Women's Mental Health, 6, 253–258.*

Warner, H. (1970). Alcohol trends in college life: Historical perspective. In C. Maddox (ed.), *The domesticated drug: Drinking among collegians* (45–80). New Haven, CT: College and University Press.

Warner, L., White, H., and Johnson, V. (2007). Alcohol initiation experiences and family history of alcoholism as predictors of problem-drinking trajectories. *Journal of Studies on Alcohol, 68*, 56–65.

Weatherburn, D., and Lind, B. (2001). Street-level drug law enforcement and entry into methadone maintenance treatment. *Addiction, 94*(4), 577–587.

Wechsberg, W. M., Zule, W. A., Riehman, K. S., Luseno, W. K., and Lam, W. K. K. (2007). African-American crack abusers and drug treatment initiation: Barriers and effects of a pretreatment intervention. *Substance Abuse Treatment, Prevention, and Policy, 2*(10), 1–18.

Wechsler, H., Davenport, A., Dowdall, G. W., Moeykens, B., and Castillo, S. (1994a). Health and behavioral consequences of binge drinking in college: A national survey of students at 140 campuses. *Journal of the American Medical Association, 272*, 1672–1677.

Wechsler, H., and Isaac, N. (1992). "Binge" drinkers at Massachusetts colleges. *Journal of the American Medical Association, 267*(21), 2929–2931.

Wechsler, H., Isaac, N., Grodstein, F., and Sellers, S. (1994b). Continuation and initiation of alcohol use from the first to the second year of college. *Journal of Studies on Alcohol, 55*, 41–45.

Wechsler, H., Kelley, K., Weitzman, E., Sangiovanni, J., and Sebring, M. (2000). What colleges are doing about binge drinking: A survey of college administrations. *Journal of American College Health, 48*, 219–226.

Wechsler, H., Lee, J., Gledhill, J., and Nelson, T. (2001a). Alcohol use and problems at colleges banning alcohol: A national survey. *Journal of Studies on Alcohol, 62,* 133–141.

Wechsler, H., Lee, J. E., Kuo, M., Seibring, M., Nelson, T. F., and Lee, H. (2002). Trends in college binge drinking during a period of increased prevention efforts: Findings from 4 Harvard School of Public Health College Alcohol Study surveys: 1993–2001. *Journal of American College Health, 50*(5), 203–217.

Wechsler, H., Lee, J., Nelson, T., and Lee, H. (2001b). Drinking levels, alcohol problems, and secondhand effects in substance-free college residences: A national study. *Journal of Studies on Alcohol, 62*, 23–31.

Wechsler, H., Moeykens, K., Davenport, A., Castillo, S., and Hansen, J. (1995). The adverse effect of heavy episodic drinkers on other college students. *Journal of Studies on Alcohol, 56*, 628–634.

Wechsler, H., Nelson, T., Lee, J., Sebring, M., Lewis, C., and Keeling, R. (2003). Perception and reality: A national evaluation of social norms marketing interventions to reduce college students' heavy alcohol use. *Journal of Studies on Alcohol, 64*, 484–494.

Wegscheider-Cruse, S. (1985). *Choice-making: For co-dependents, adult children, and spirituality seekers.* Pompano Beach, FL: Health Communications.

Weinberg, L., and Wyatt, J. P. (2006). Children presenting to hospital with acute alcohol intoxication. *Emergency Medicine Journal, 23*, 774–776. Retrieved on January 27, 2007, from http://emj.bmj.com/cgi/content/abstract/23/10/774.

Weitzman, E. R., and Nelson, T. F. (2004). College student binge drinking and the "prevention paradox": Implications for prevention and harm reduction. *Journal of Drug Education, 34*(3), 247–266.

Wells, K., Klap, R., Koike, A., and Sherbourne, C. (2001). Ethnic disparities in unmet need for alcoholism, drug abuse, and mental health care. *American Journal of Psychiatry, 158*, 2027–2032.

Wells, M., Glickauf-Hughes, C., and Jones, R. (1999). Codependency: A grass roots construct's relationship to shame-proneness, low self-esteem, and childhood parentification. *The American Journal of Family Therapy, 27*(1), 63–71.

Wesson, D., and Smith, D. E. (1977). *Barbiturates.* New York: Human Sciences.

Westermeyer, J., Wahmanholm, K., and Thuras, P. (2001). Effects of childhood physical abuse on course and severity of substance abuse. *American Journal on Addictions, 5*(2), 101–110.

Westermeyer, J., Yargic, I., and Thuras, P. (2004). Michigan Assessment Screening Test for Alcohol and Drugs (MAST/AD): Evaluation in a clinical sample. *American Journal on Addictions, 13*(2), 151–162.

Westmaas, J., Moeller, S., and Woicik, P. B. (2007). Validation of a measure of college students' intoxicated behaviors: Association with alcohol outcome expectancies, drinking motives, and personality. *Journal of American College Health, 55*(4), 227–237.

Whitaker, J. O. (1982). Alcohol and the Standing Rock Sioux Tribe: A twenty-year follow-up study. *Journal of Studies on Alcohol, 43*, 191–200.

White, W. (1996). *Pathways from the culture of addiction to the culture of recovery.* Center City, MN: Hazelden.

White, W. (2005, May). Recovery management: What if we really believed that addiction was a chronic disorder. *GLATTC Bulletin.* Retrieved on December 13, 2006, from http://www.nattc.org/recoveryresourc/rec_resources.htm.

White, W. L. (1998). *Slaying the dragon: The history of addiction treatment and recovery in America.* Bloomington, IL: Chestnut Health Systems/Lighthouse Institute.

White Bison (2002). *The red road to wellbriety in the Native American way.* Colorado Springs, CO: White Bison.

Whiting, J. W., and Child, I. L. (1953). *Child training and personality: A cross-cultural study.* New Haven, CT: Yale University Press.

Whitten, L. (2006, March). Treatment curbs methamphetamine abuse among gay and bisexual men. *NIDA Notes, 20*(4), 4–5.

Widom, C. S., and Hiller-Sturmhofel, S. (2001). Alcohol abuse as a risk factor for and consequence of child abuse. *Alcohol Research and Health, 25*(1), 52–57.

Widom, C. S., Ireland, T., and Glynn, P. J. (1995). Alcohol abuse in abused and neglected children followed up: Are they at risk? *Journal of Studies on Alcohol, 56*(2), 207–217.

Wieczorek, W. F., Welte, J. W., and Abel, E. L. (1990). Alcohol, drugs, and murder: A study of convicted homicide offenders. *Journal of Criminal Justice, 18*(3), 217–227.

Wilens, T. E., Biederman, J., Bredin, E., Hahesy, A. L., Abrantes, A., Neft, D., Millstein, R., and Spencer, T. J. (2002). A family study of the high-risk children of opioid- and alcohol-dependent parents. *The American Journal on Addictions, 11*, 41–51.

Wilke, D. J., Kamata, A., and Cash, S. J. (2005). Modeling treatment motivation in substance-abusing women with children. *Child Abuse and Neglect, 29*(11), 1313–1323.

Williams, F., and Knox, R. (1997). Alcohol abuse intervention in a university setting. *Journal of American College Health, 36*, 97–102.

Williams, J. M., Ballard, M. B., and Alessi, H. (2005). Aging and alcohol abuse: Increasing counselor awareness. *ADULTSPAN Journal, 4*(1), 7–18.

Williams, R., and Vinson, D. C. (2001). Validation of a single screening question for problem drinking. *Journal of Family Practice, 50*, 307–312.

Williams, T. (1990). *The cocaine kids: The inside story of a teenage drug ring.* New York: Addison-Wesley.

Williams, T. (1992). *Crack house: Notes from the end of the line.* Reading, MA: Addison-Wesley.

Willson, P., Malecha, J. M. A., Watson, K., Lemmey, D., Schultz, P., and Fredland, J. G. N. (2000). Severity of violence against women by intimate partners and associated use of alcohol and/or illicit drugs by the perpetrator. *Journal of Interpersonal Violence, 15*(9), 996–1008.

Wilsnack, S. C., Vogeltanz, N. D., Klassen, A. D., and Harris, T. R. (1997). Childhood sexual abuse and women's substance abuse: National survey findings. *Journal of Studies on Alcohol, 58*(3), 264–271.

Wilsnack, S., and Wilsnack, R. (2002). International gender and alcohol research findings and future directions. *Substance Abuse, 22*, 39–53.

Wilsnack, S. C., Wilsnack, R. W., and Hiller-Sturmhofel, S. (1994). How women drink: Epidemiology of women's drinking and problem drinking. *Alcohol Health and Research World, 18*(3), 173–181.

Windle, M. (1996). Effect of parental drinking on adolescents. *Alcohol Health and Research World, 20*, 181–184.

Windle, M. (1997). Concepts and issues in COA research. *Alcohol Health and Research World, 21*(3), 185–191.

Wines, J. D., Gruber, A. J., Pope, H. G., and Lukas, S. (1999), Nalbuphine hydrochloride dependence in anabolic steroid abusers. *American Journal of Addictions 8*, 161–164.

Winker, M. A. (2004). Measuring race and ethnicity: Why and how? *Journal of the American Medical Association, 292*, 1612–1614.

Wisconsin Department of Transportation. (2006). *Blood/breath alcohol concentration (BAC) calculator.* Retrieved on December 31, 2008, from www.dot.wisconsin.gov/safety/motorist/drunkdriving/calculator.htm.

Woititz, J. G. (1983). *Adult children of alcoholics.* Pompano Beach, FL: Health Communications.

Wojnar, M., Wasilewski, D., Zmigrodzka, I., and Grobel, I. (2001). Age-related differences in the course of alcohol withdrawal in hospitalized patients. *Alcohol and Alcoholism, 36*(6), 577–583.

Wolfgang, M. (1958). *Patterns of criminal homicide*. Philadelphia: University of Pennsylvania Press.

Woman's Health Weekly Staff (2003, Oct. 9). Doctors need to know alcohol, pregnancy don't mix. *Women's Health Weekly*, 77–79.

Womble, M. (1990). Black women. In R. C. Engs (ed.), *Women: Alcohol and other drugs* (127–135). Dubuque, IA: Kendall/Hunt.

Wong, J. Y. (2006). Social support: A key to positive parenting outcomes for mothers in residential drug treatment with their children. In S. L. A. Straussner and C. H. Fewell (eds.), *Impact of substance abuse on children and families: Research and practice implications* (113–137). New York: Haworth.

Woody, R. H. (2006). Family interventions with law enforcement officers. *The American Journal of Family Therapy, 34*(2), 95–104.

World Health Organization (2004). *Global status report on alcohol 2004*. Geneva: WHO.

Wright, E. M. (2001). Substance abuse in African American communities. In S. L. A. Straussner (ed.), *Ethnocultural factors in substance abuse treatment* (31–51). New York: Guilford.

Wu, N. S., Lu, Y., Sterling, S., and Weisner, C. (2004). Family environment factors and substance abuse severity in an HMO adolescent treatment population. *Clinical Pediatrics, 43*(4), 323–333.

Young, N. K., and Gardner, S. L. (2002). Navigating the pathways: Lessons and promising practices in linking alcohol and drug services with child welfare. Technical Assistance Publication (TAP) Series 27. SAMHSA Publication No. SMA 04-3920. Rockville, MD: Substance Abuse and Mental Health Services Administration.

Young, R. M., Friedman, S. R., Case, P., Asencio, M. W., and Clatts, M. (2000). Women injection drug users who have sex with women exhibit increased HIV infection and risk behaviors. *Journal of Drug Issues, 30*(3), 499–524.

Young, T. J. (1991). Native American drinking: A neglected subject of study and research. *Journal of Drug Education, 21*(1), 65–72.

Zailckas, K. (2005). *Smashed: Story of a drunken girlhood*. Boston: Viking.

Zhankun, C. (2003). Issues and standards in counseling lesbians and gay men with substance abuse concerns. *Journal of Mental Health Counseling, 25*(4), 323–336.

Zickler, P. (2000, Aug.). NIDA initiative targets increasing teen use of anabolic steroids. *NIDA Notes, 15*(3). Retrieved on March 22, 2007, from http://www.nidanih.gov/NIDA_notes.NNvol15N3/Initiative.html.

Zimberg, S. (1978). Treatment of the elderly alcoholic in the community and an institutional setting. *Addictive Diseases: An International Journal, 3*(3), 417–427.

Zucker, R. (1994). Pathways to alcohol problems and alcoholism: A developmental account of the evidence for multiple alcoholisms and for contextual contributions to risk. In R. A. Zucker, J. Howard, and G. M. Boyd (eds.), *The development of alcohol problems: Exploring the biopsychosocial matrix of risk* (255–289). NIAAA Research Monograph No. 26, NIH Publication No. 94-3495. Bethesda, MD: National Institute on Alcohol Abuse and Alcoholism.

Zucker, R., and Gomberg, E. (1986). Etiology of alcoholism reconsidered: The case for a biopsychosocial process. *American Psychologist, 41*, 783–795.

Index

About the Book

In this comprehensive introduction to the study of substance use and abuse, the authors explore both the personal and the societal consequences of alcohol and drug problems. A series of provocative chapters also helps students to navigate the unique problems facing women, adolescents, college students, the elderly, racial minorities, and the GLBT (gay, lesbian, bisexual, transgender) community. Trends in diagnosis, treatment, prevention, and policy are all thoroughly covered.

Among its many outstanding features, the book

- Puts a human face on the problems of alcohol and drug addiction.
- Highlights the implications of theory and research for policy and practice.
- Includes thematic discussion questions and a glossary of key terms.
- Emphasizes readability for a challenging but not overly technical approach.

Sylvia I. Mignon is director of the Master of Science in Human Services Program and associate professor of human services and criminal justice at the University of Massachusetts at Boston. **Marjorie Marcoux Faiia** is professor of sociology and women's studies at Rivier College. **Peter L. Myers** is retired director of the Addictions Counselor Training Program at Essex County College. **Earl Rubington** is professor emeritus of sociology at Northeastern University.